ents

Dreamin'
Sun

6

volume
six

Dreamin'
Sun

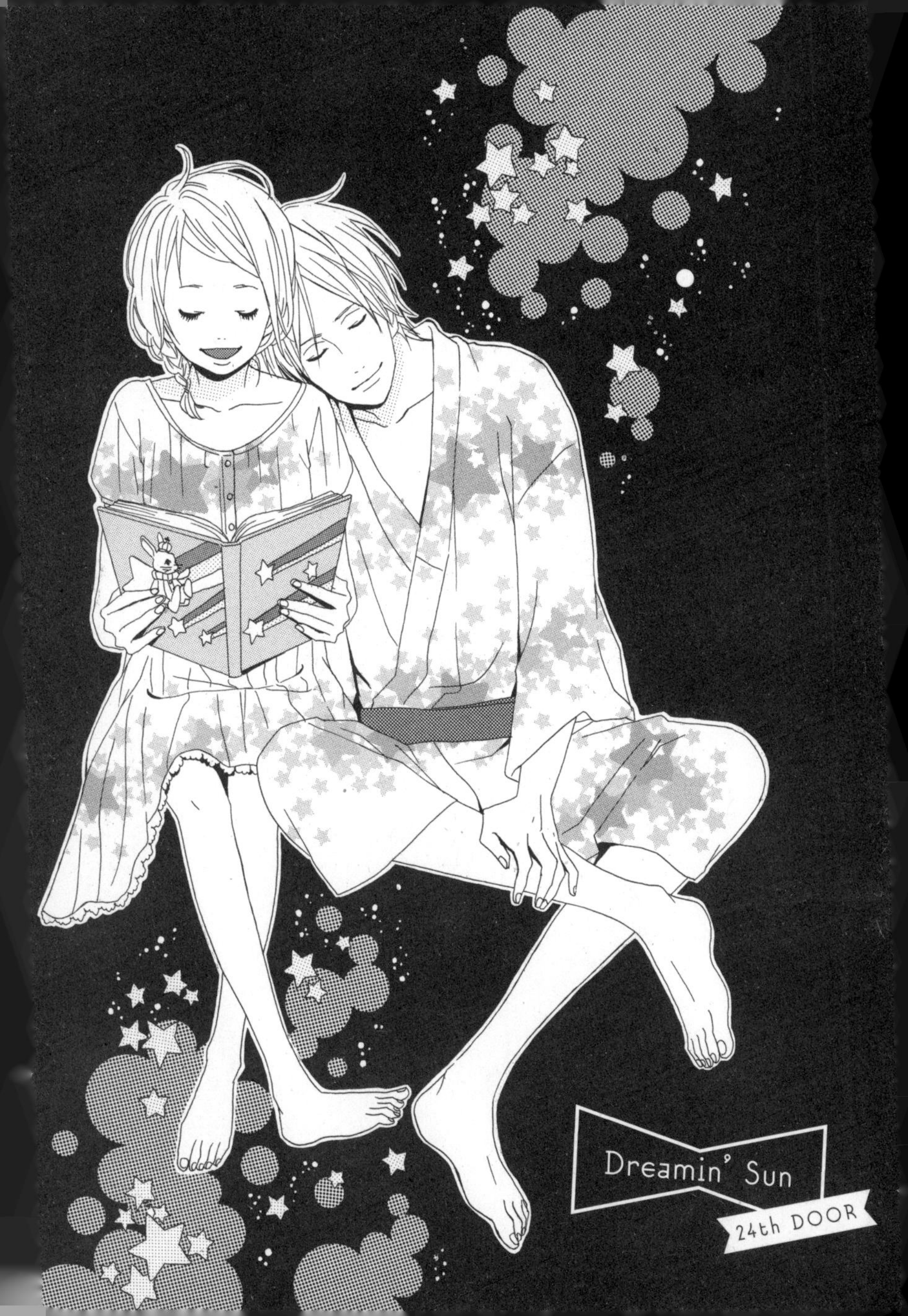
Dreamin' Sun
24th DOOR

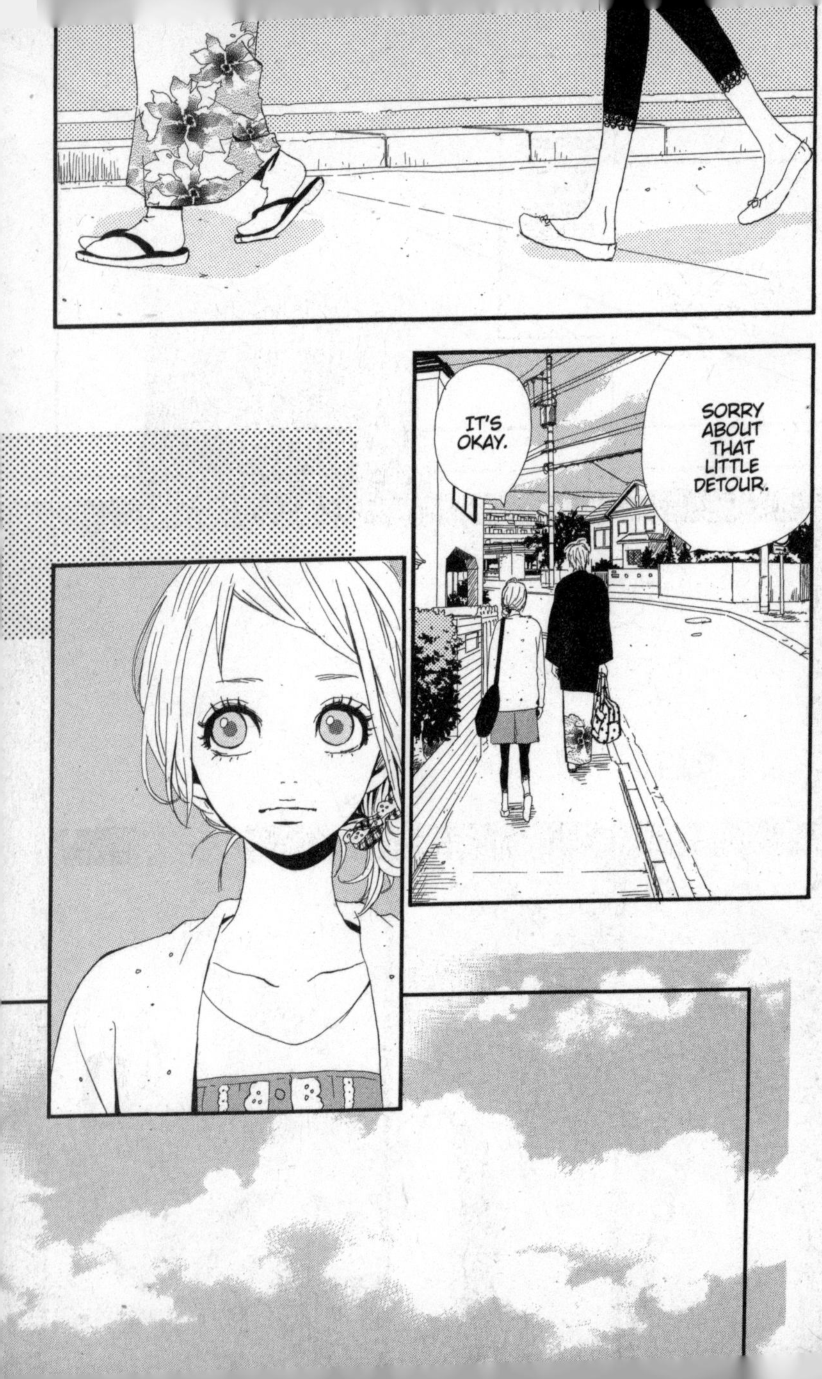
SORRY ABOUT THAT LITTLE DETOUR.
IT'S OKAY.

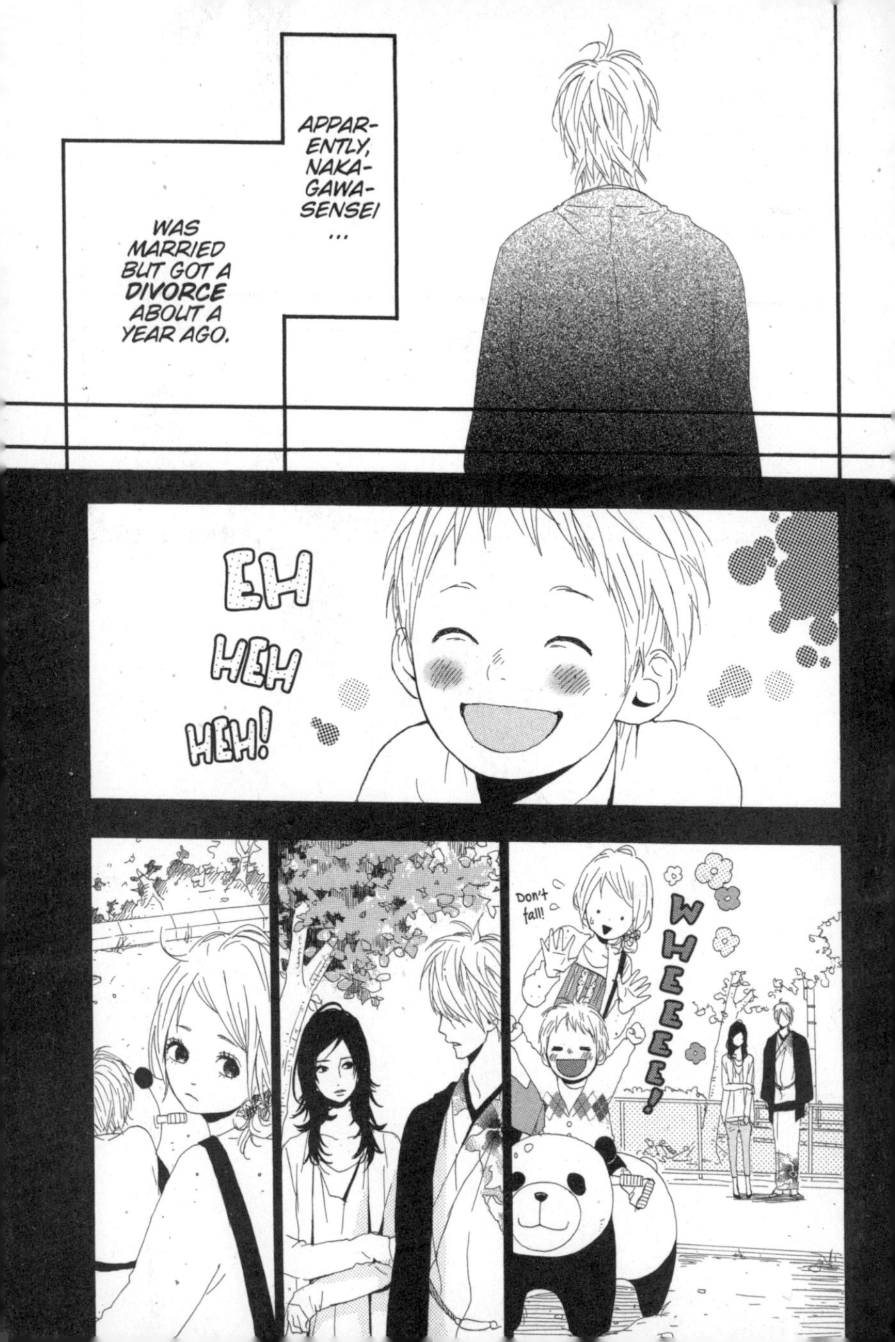
APPARENTLY, NAKAGAWA-SENSEI...
WAS MARRIED BUT GOT A DIVORCE ABOUT A YEAR AGO.
EH HEH HEH!
WHEEEE!
Don't fall!

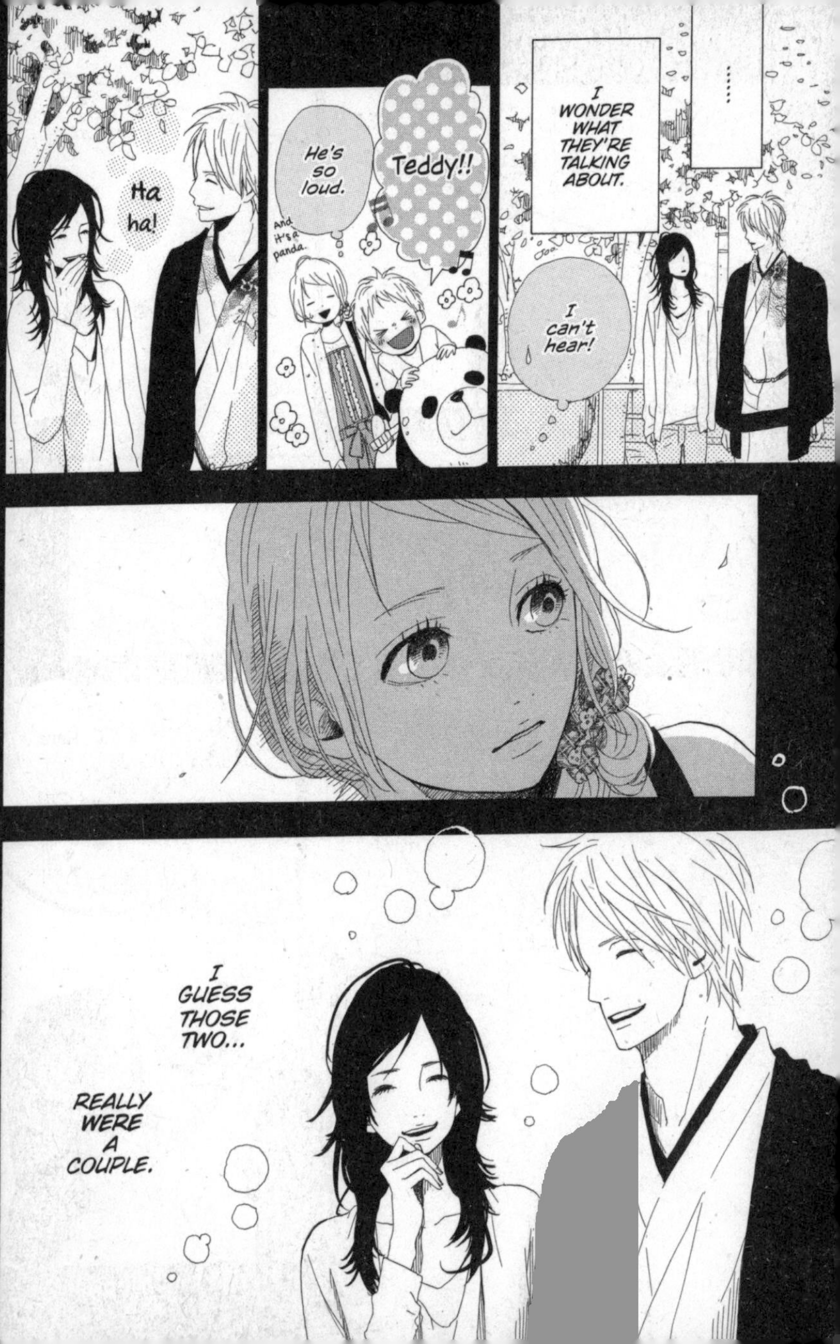
......
I WONDER WHAT THEY'RE TALKING ABOUT.
I can't hear!
Teddy!!
He's so loud.
And it's a panda.
Ha ha!
I GUESS THOSE TWO...
REALLY WERE A COUPLE.

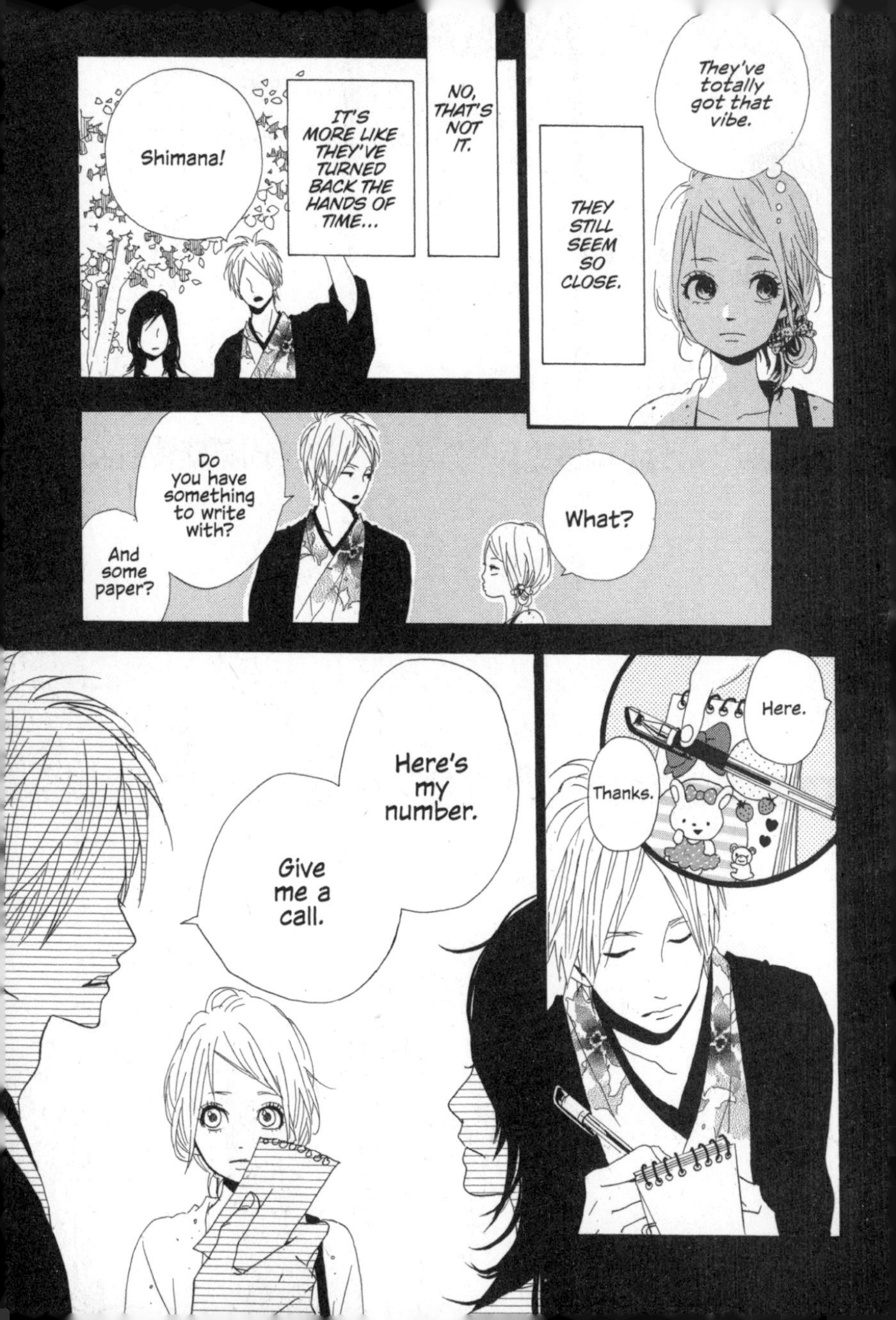
They've totally got that vibe.
THEY STILL SEEM SO CLOSE.
NO, THAT'S NOT IT.
IT'S MORE LIKE THEY'VE TURNED BACK THE HANDS OF TIME...
Shimana!
What?
Do you have something to write with?
And some paper?
Here.
Thanks.
Here's my number.
Give me a call.

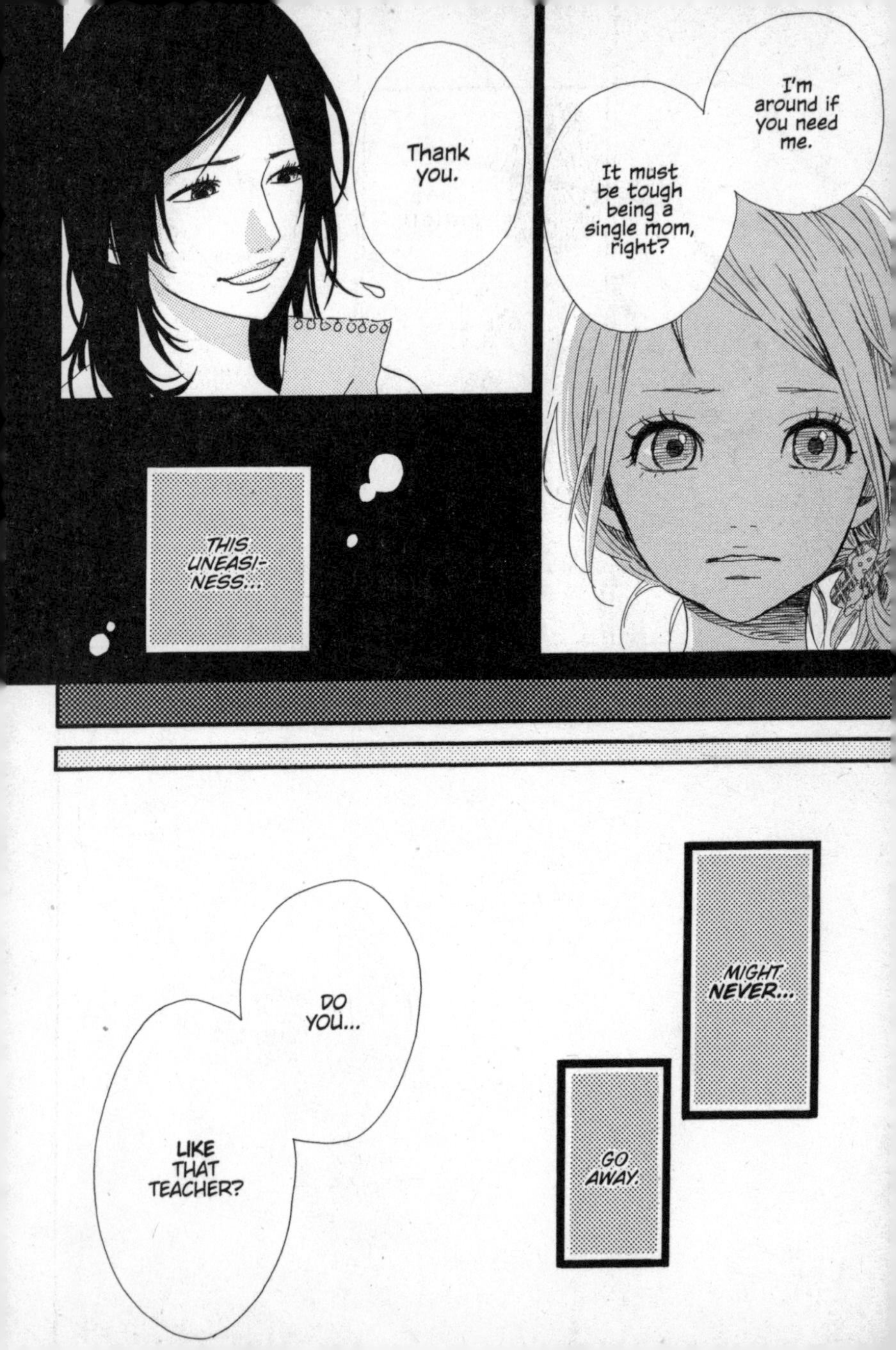
I'm around if you need me.
It must be tough being a single mom, right?
Thank you.
THIS UNEASINESS...
MIGHT NEVER...
GO AWAY.
DO YOU...
LIKE THAT TEACHER?

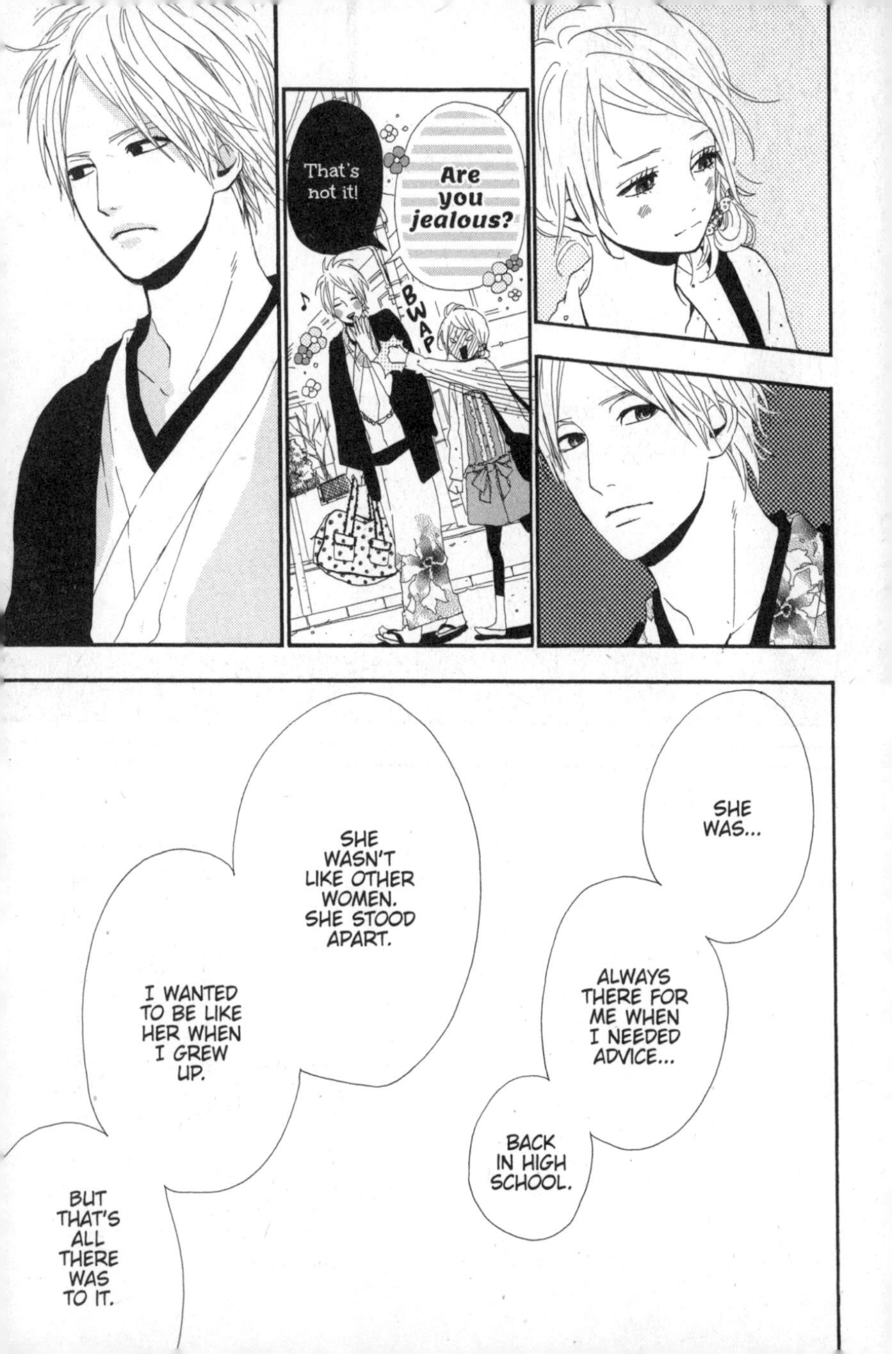

Are you jealous?
That's not it!
BWAP
SHE WAS...
ALWAYS THERE FOR ME WHEN I NEEDED ADVICE...
BACK IN HIGH SCHOOL.
SHE WASN'T LIKE OTHER WOMEN. SHE STOOD APART.
I WANTED TO BE LIKE HER WHEN I GREW UP.
BUT THAT'S ALL THERE WAS TO IT.

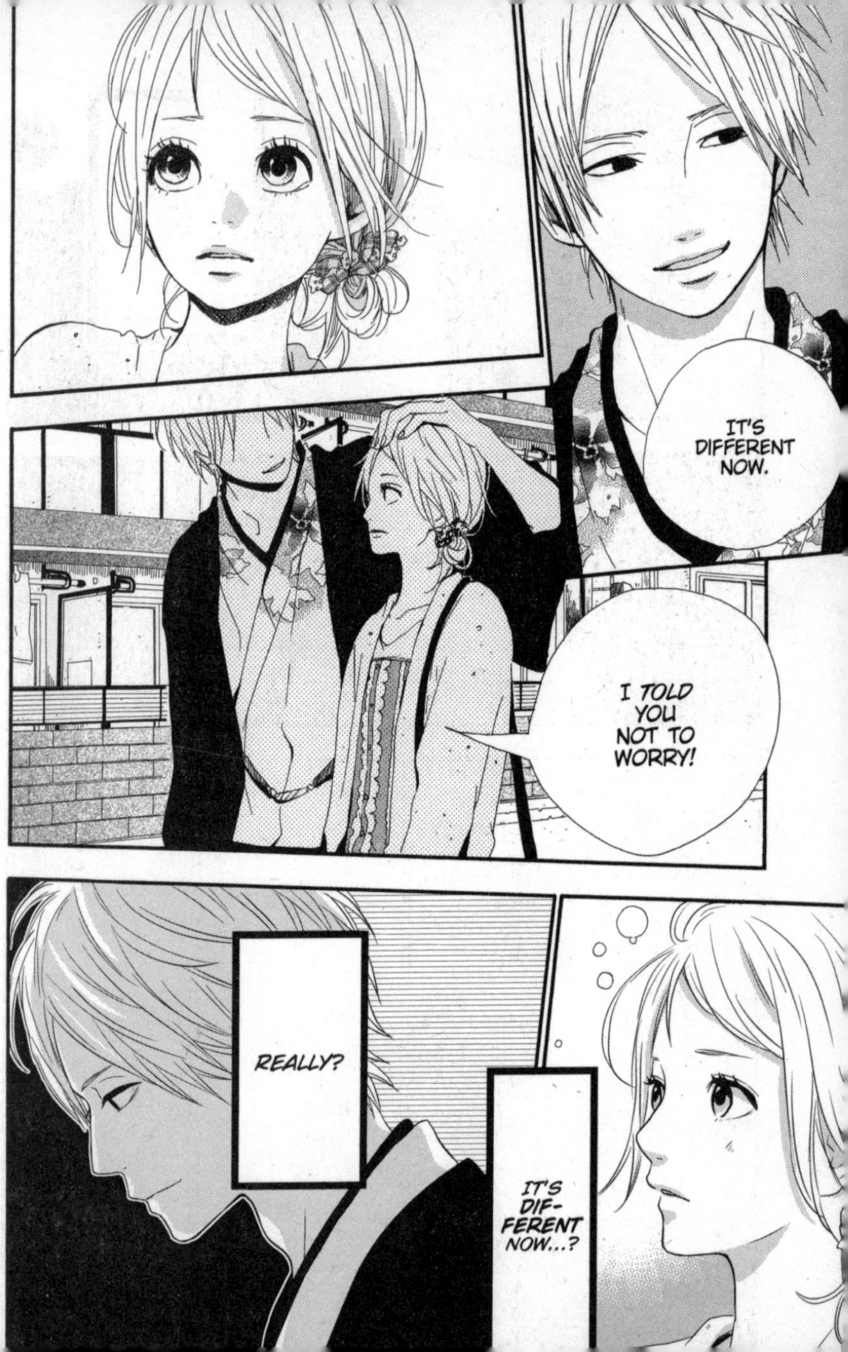
IT'S DIFFERENT NOW.
I *TOLD* YOU NOT TO WORRY!
IT'S DIF-FERENT NOW...?
REALLY?

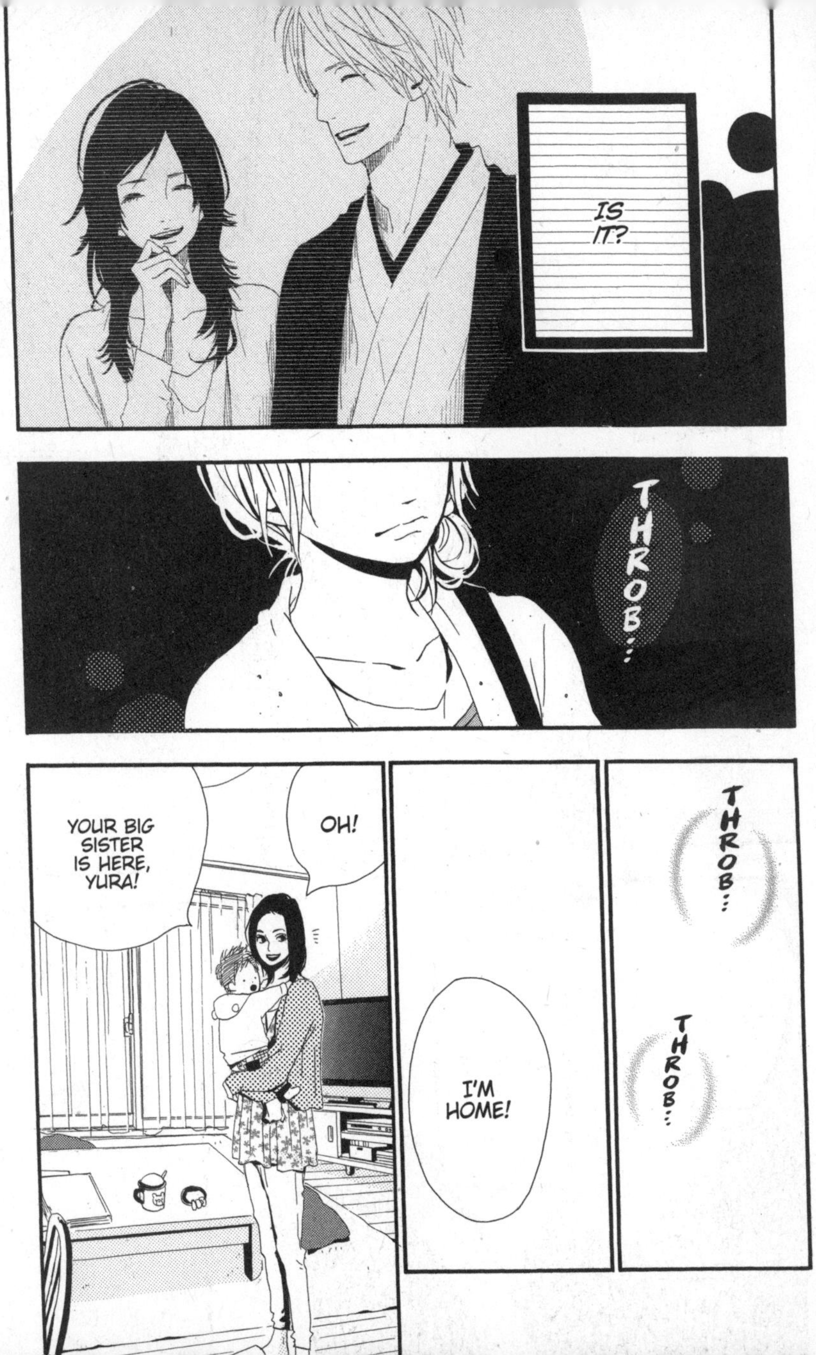
IS IT?
THROB...
THROB...
THROB...
I'M HOME!
OH!
YOUR BIG SISTER IS HERE, YURA!

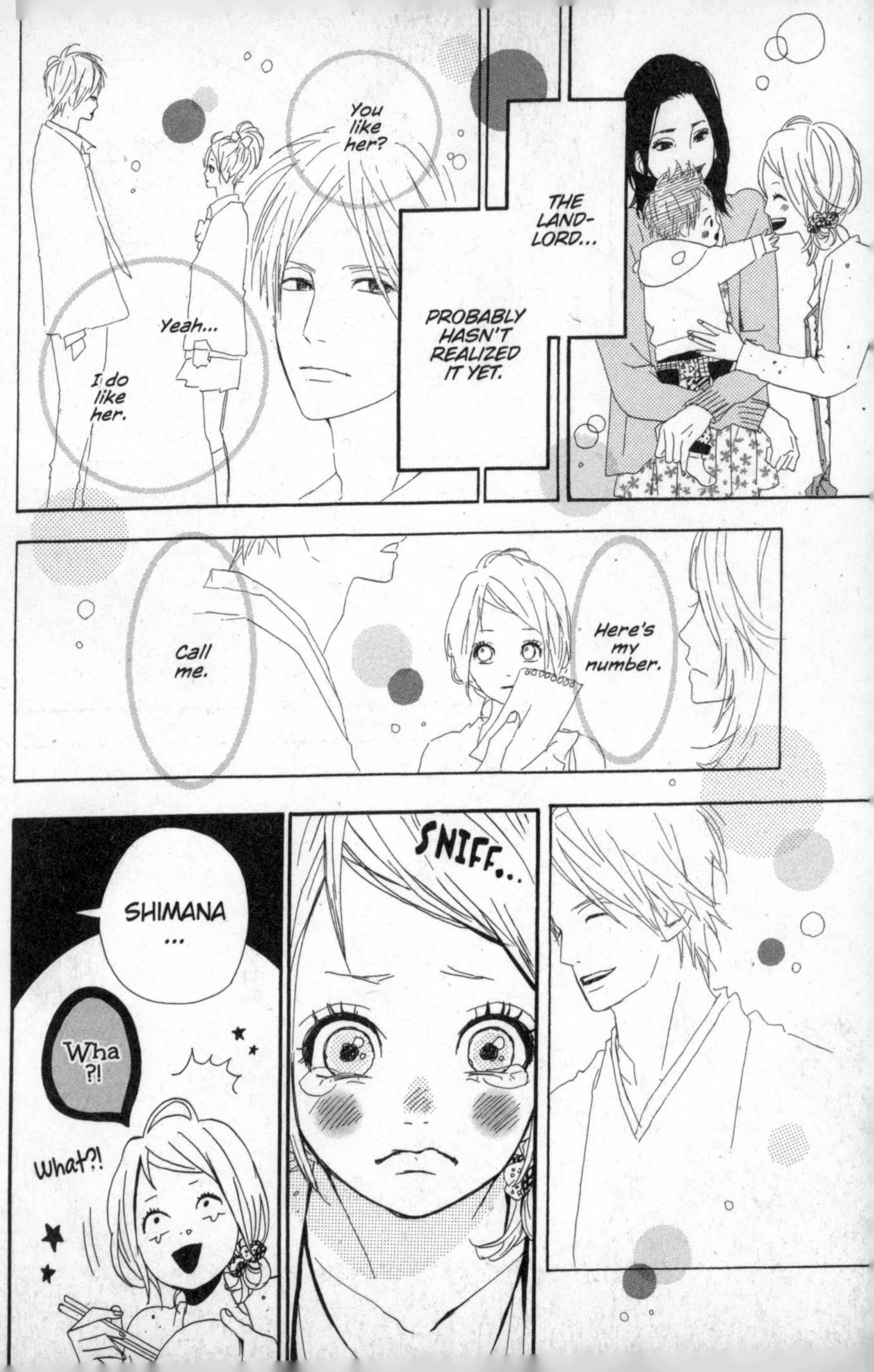
THE LANDLORD...
PROBABLY HASN'T REALIZED IT YET.
You like her?
Yeah...
I do like her.
Here's my number.
Call me.
SNIFF...
SHIMANA ...
Wha ?!
What?!

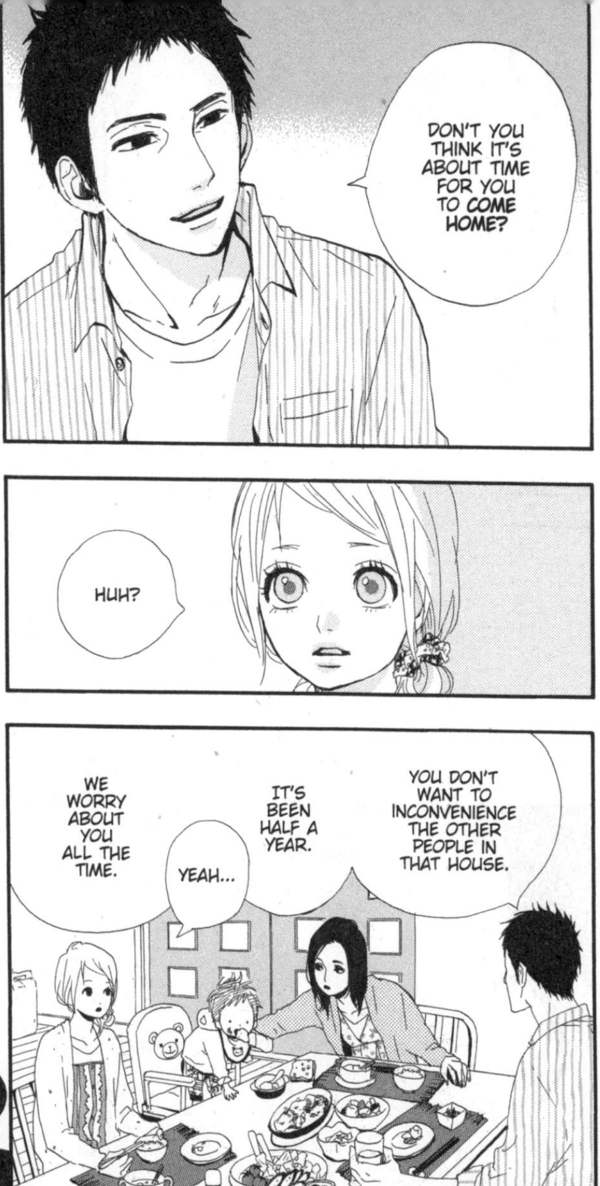
DON'T YOU THINK IT'S ABOUT TIME FOR YOU TO COME HOME?
HUH?
YOU DON'T WANT TO INCONVENIENCE THE OTHER PEOPLE IN THAT HOUSE.
IT'S BEEN HALF A YEAR.
WE WORRY ABOUT YOU ALL THE TIME.
YEAH...

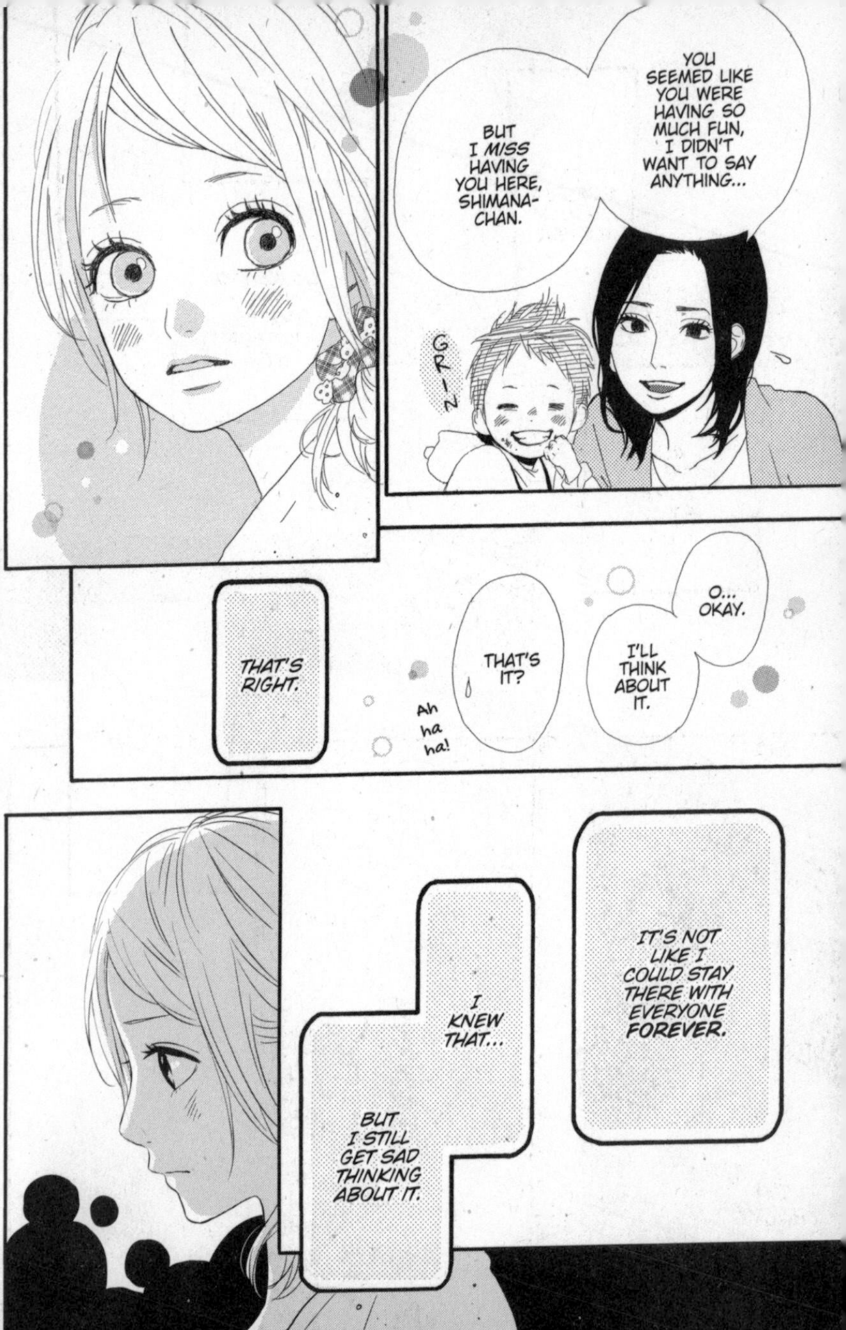
YOU SEEMED LIKE YOU WERE HAVING SO MUCH FUN, I DIDN'T WANT TO SAY ANYTHING...
BUT I *MISS* HAVING YOU HERE, SHIMANA-CHAN.
GRIN
O... OKAY.
I'LL THINK ABOUT IT.
THAT'S IT?
Ah ha ha!
THAT'S RIGHT.
IT'S NOT LIKE I COULD STAY THERE WITH EVERYONE **FOREVER**.
I KNEW THAT...
BUT I STILL GET SAD THINKING ABOUT IT.

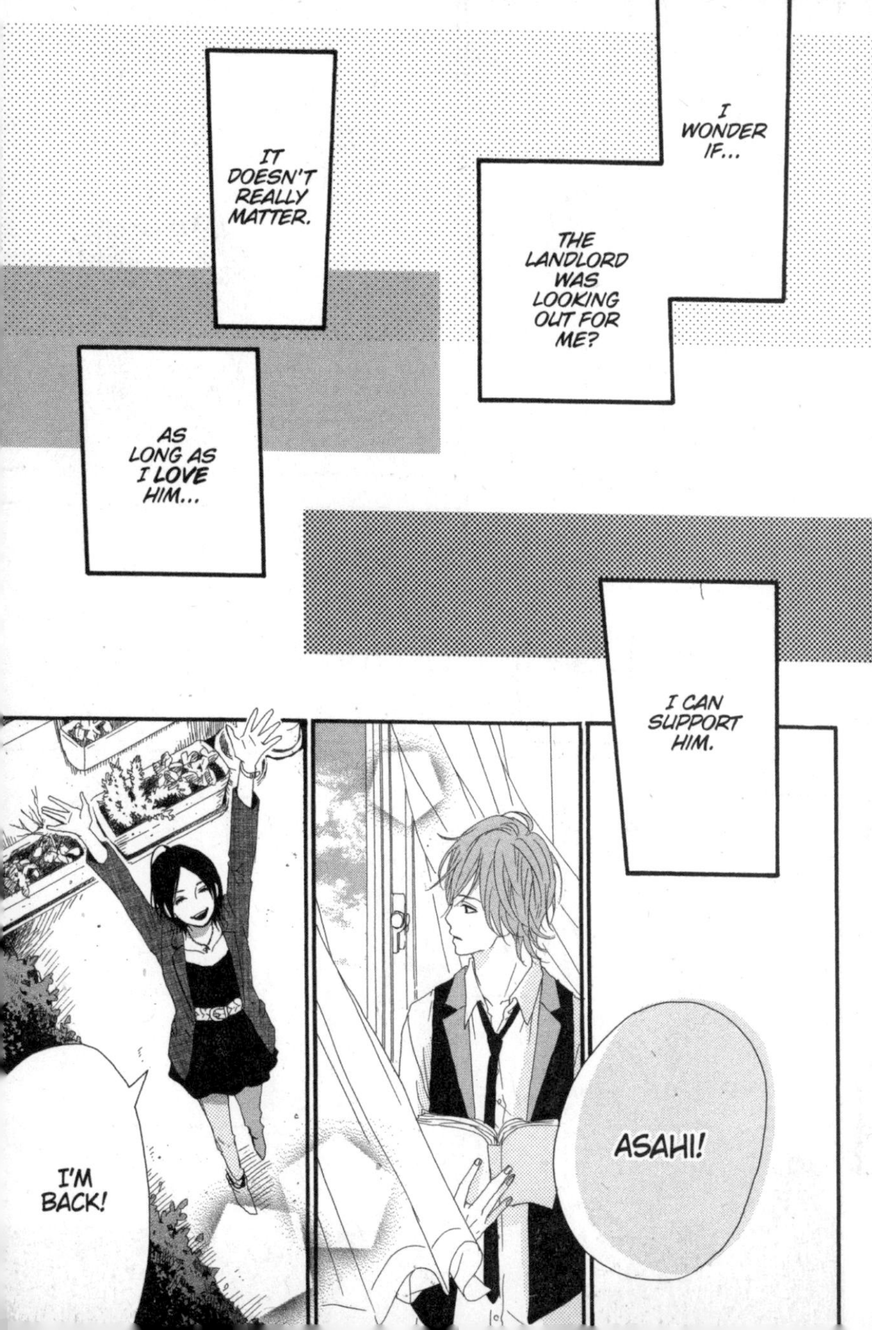
I WONDER IF...
THE LANDLORD WAS LOOKING OUT FOR ME?
IT DOESN'T REALLY MATTER.
AS LONG AS I **LOVE** HIM...
I CAN SUPPORT HIM.
ASAHI!
I'M BACK!

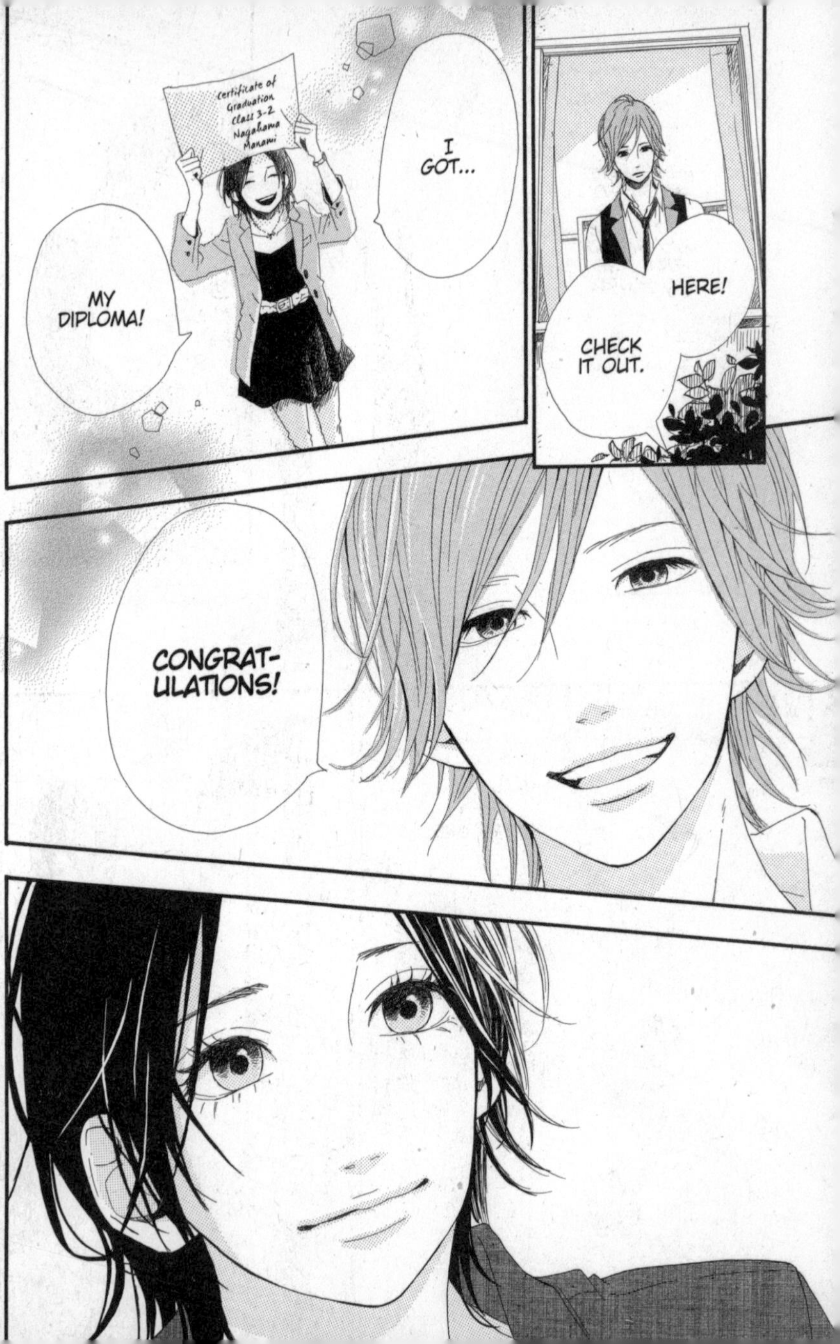
HERE!
CHECK IT OUT.
Certificate of Graduation Class 3-2 Nagahama Manami
I GOT...
MY DIPLOMA!
CONGRAT-ULATIONS!

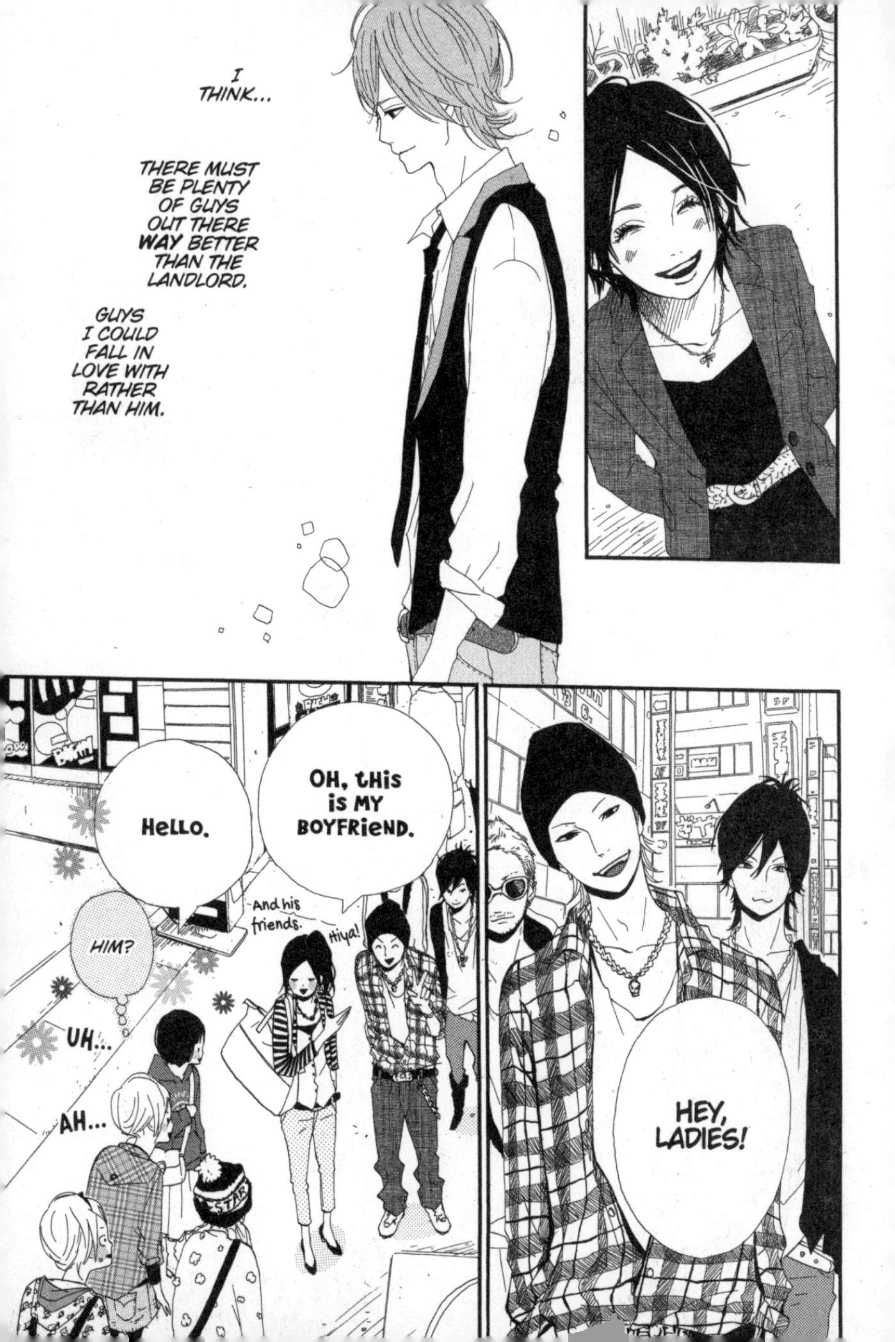
I THINK...
THERE MUST BE PLENTY OF GUYS OUT THERE WAY BETTER THAN THE LANDLORD.
GUYS I COULD FALL IN LOVE WITH RATHER THAN HIM.
HEY, LADIES!
OH, tHis is MY BOYFRiend.
Hello.
And his friends.
Hiya!
HIM?
UH...
AH...

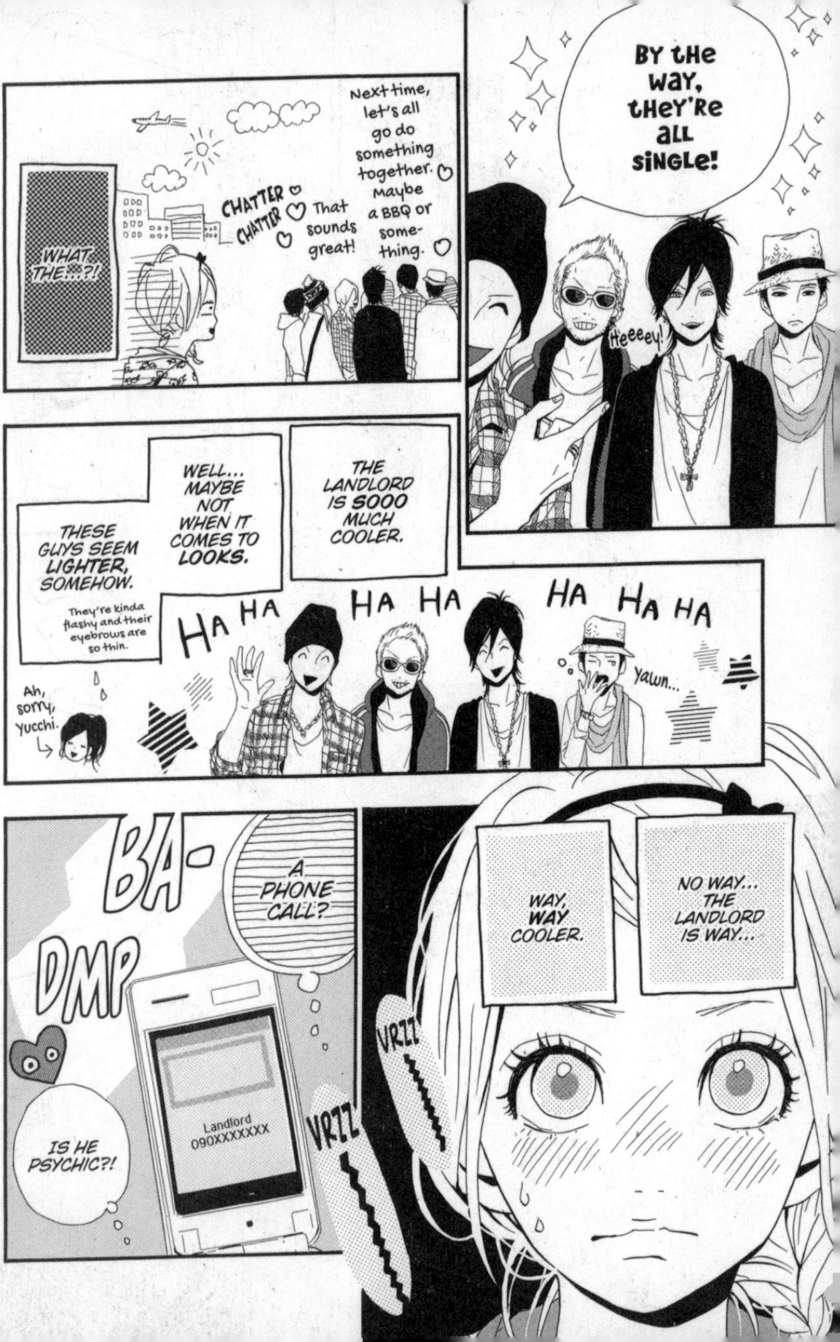
BY THE WAY, THEY'RE ALL SINGLE!
Heeeey!
Next time, let's all go do something together. Maybe a BBQ or something.
That sounds great!
CHATTER CHATTER
WHAT THE...?!
THE LANDLORD IS SOOO MUCH COOLER.
WELL... MAYBE NOT WHEN IT COMES TO LOOKS.
THESE GUYS SEEM LIGHTER, SOMEHOW.
They're kinda flashy and their eyebrows are so thin.
HA HA HA HA HA HA HA HA
Yawn...
Ah, sorry, Yucchi.
NO WAY... THE LANDLORD IS WAY...
WAY, WAY COOLER.
VRZZ
VRZZ
BA-DMP
A PHONE CALL?
Landlord
090XXXXXXX
IS HE PSYCHIC?!

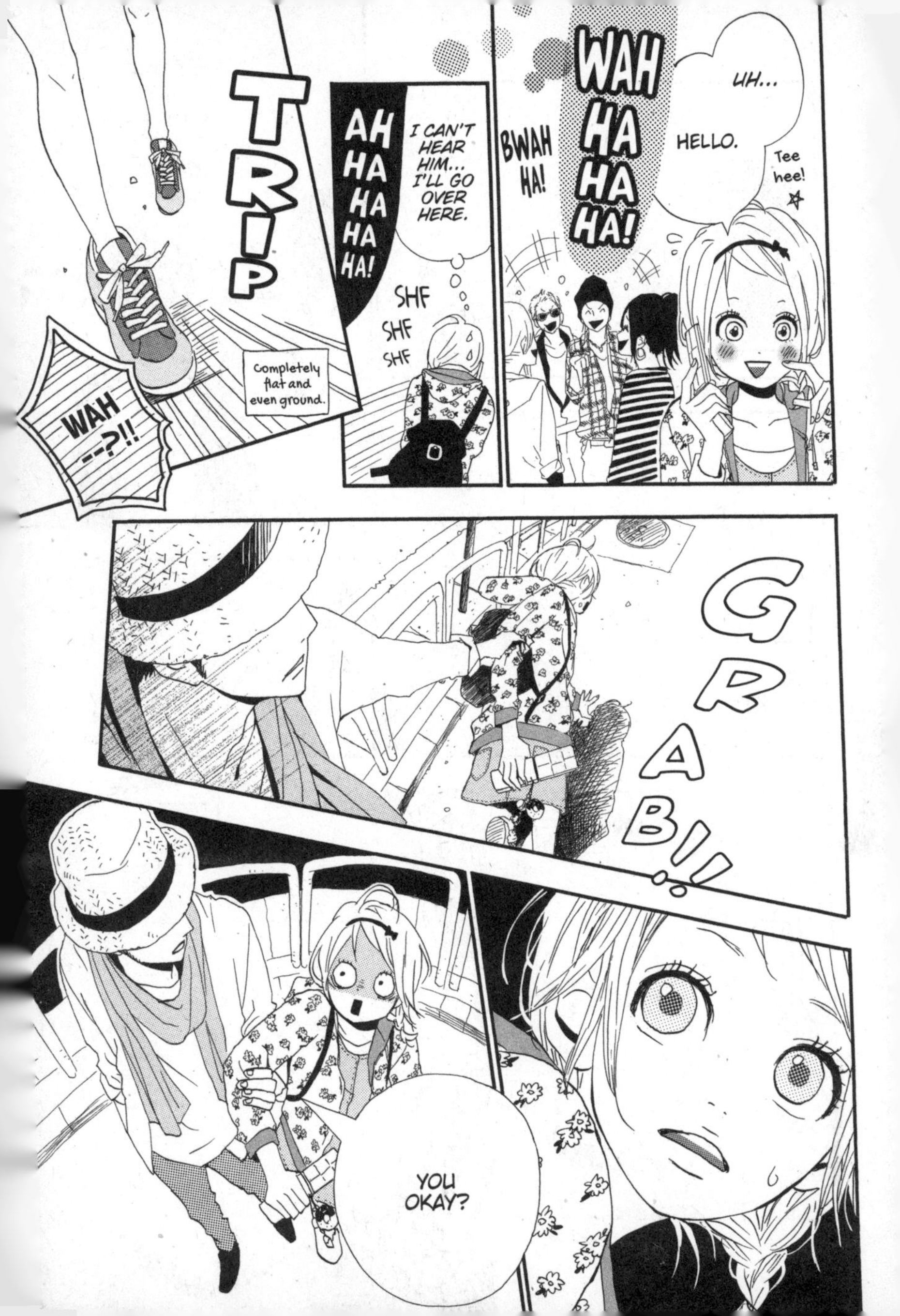
UH... HELLO.
Tee hee!
WAH HA HA HA HA!
BWAH HA!
I CAN'T HEAR HIM... I'LL GO OVER HERE.
AH HA HA HA HA HA!
SHF SHF SHF
TRIP
Completely flat and even ground.
WAH --?!!
GRAB!!
YOU OKAY?

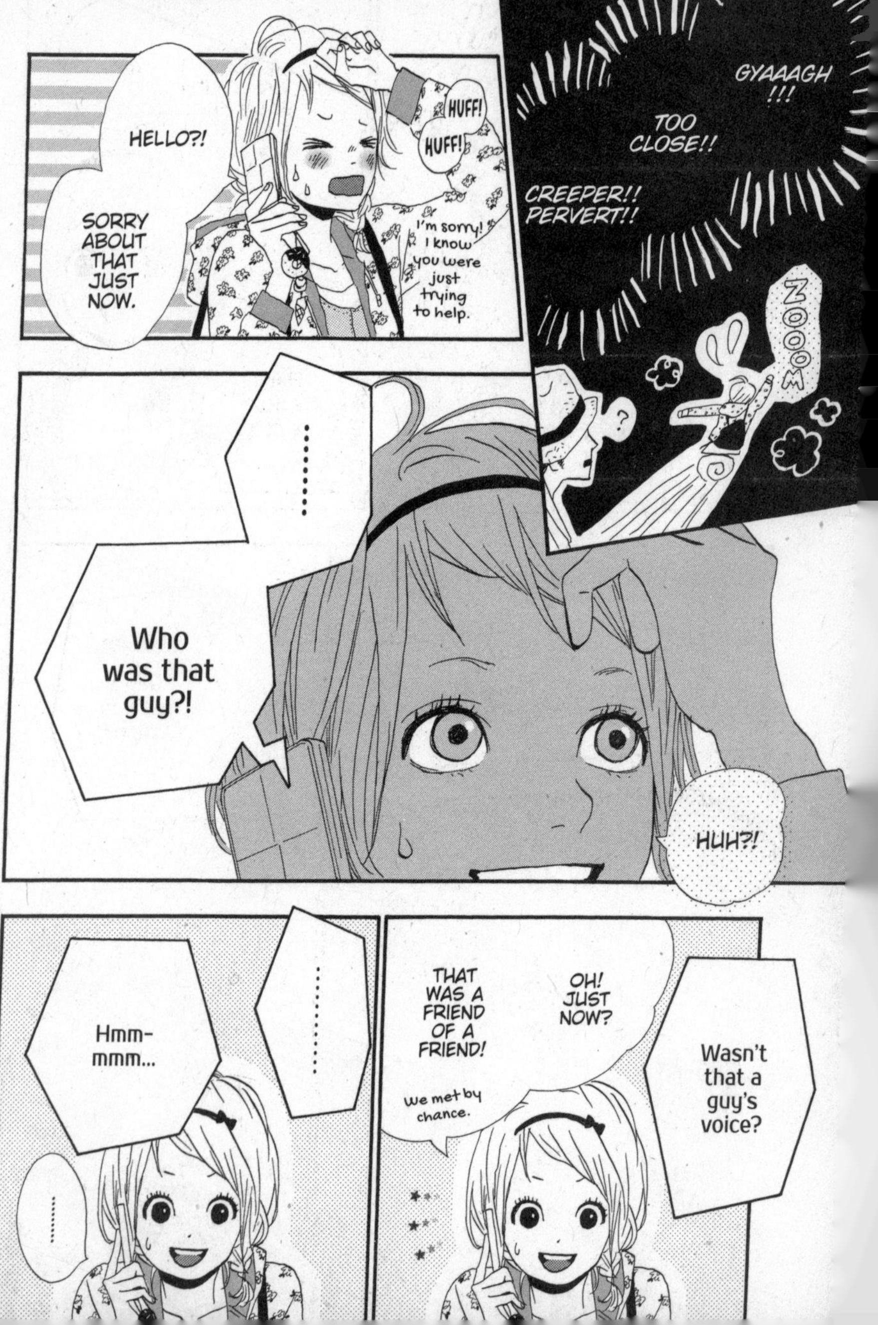
GYAAAGH!!!
TOO CLOSE!!
CREEPER!! PERVERT!!
ZOOOM
?
HUFF!
HUFF!
HELLO?!
I'm sorry! I know you were just trying to help.
SORRY ABOUT THAT JUST NOW.
HUH?!
......
Who was that guy?!
Wasn't that a guy's voice?
OH! JUST NOW?
THAT WAS A FRIEND OF A FRIEND!
We met by chance.
....
Hmm-mmm...
......

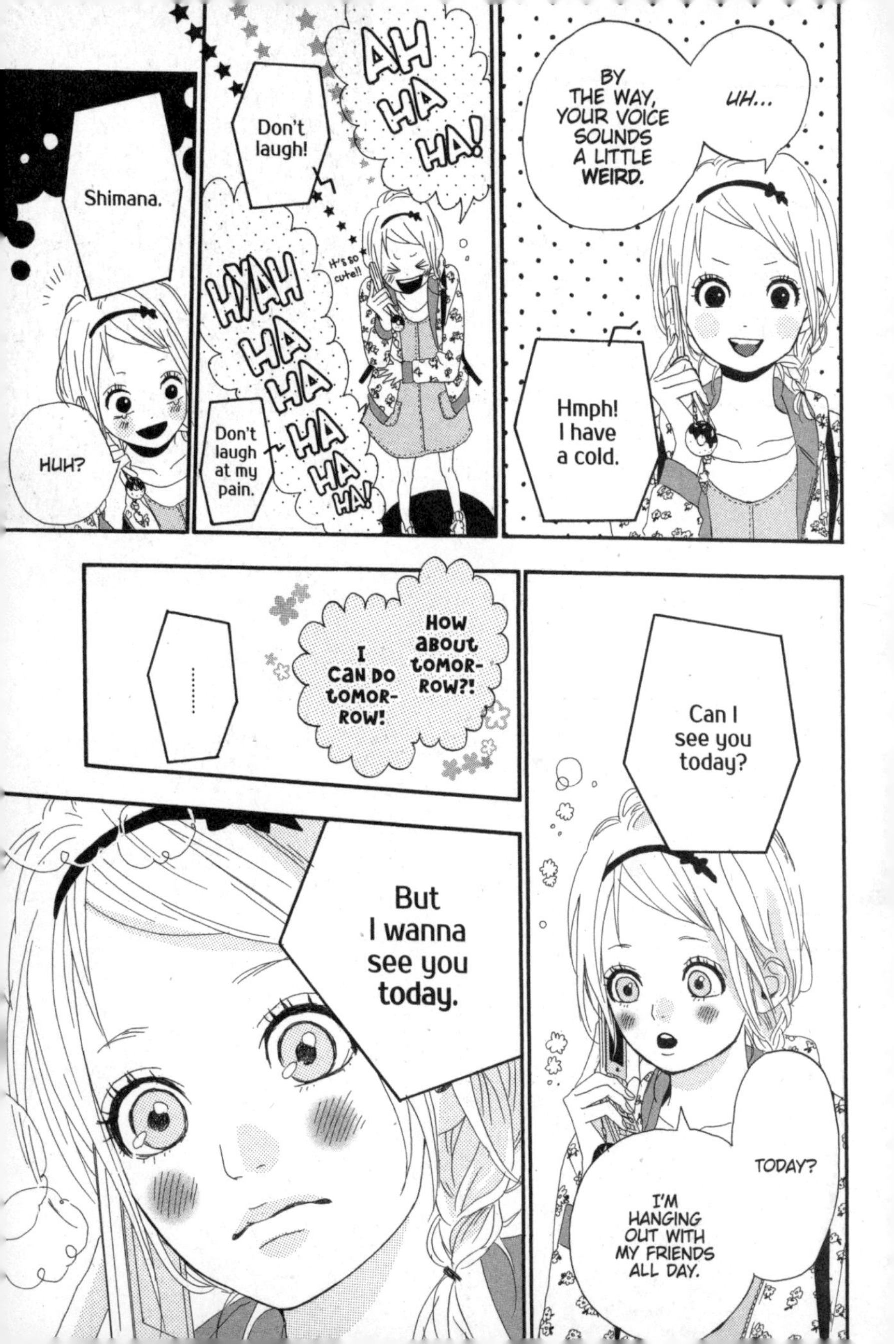
UH...
BY THE WAY, YOUR VOICE SOUNDS A LITTLE WEIRD.
Hmph! I have a cold.
AH HA HA!
Don't laugh!
It's so cute!!
HYAH HA HA HA HA HA!
Don't laugh at my pain.
Shimana.
HUH?
Can I see you today?
TODAY?
I'M HANGING OUT WITH MY FRIENDS ALL DAY.
HOW ABOUT TOMORROW?!
I CAN DO TOMORROW!
......
But I wanna see you today.

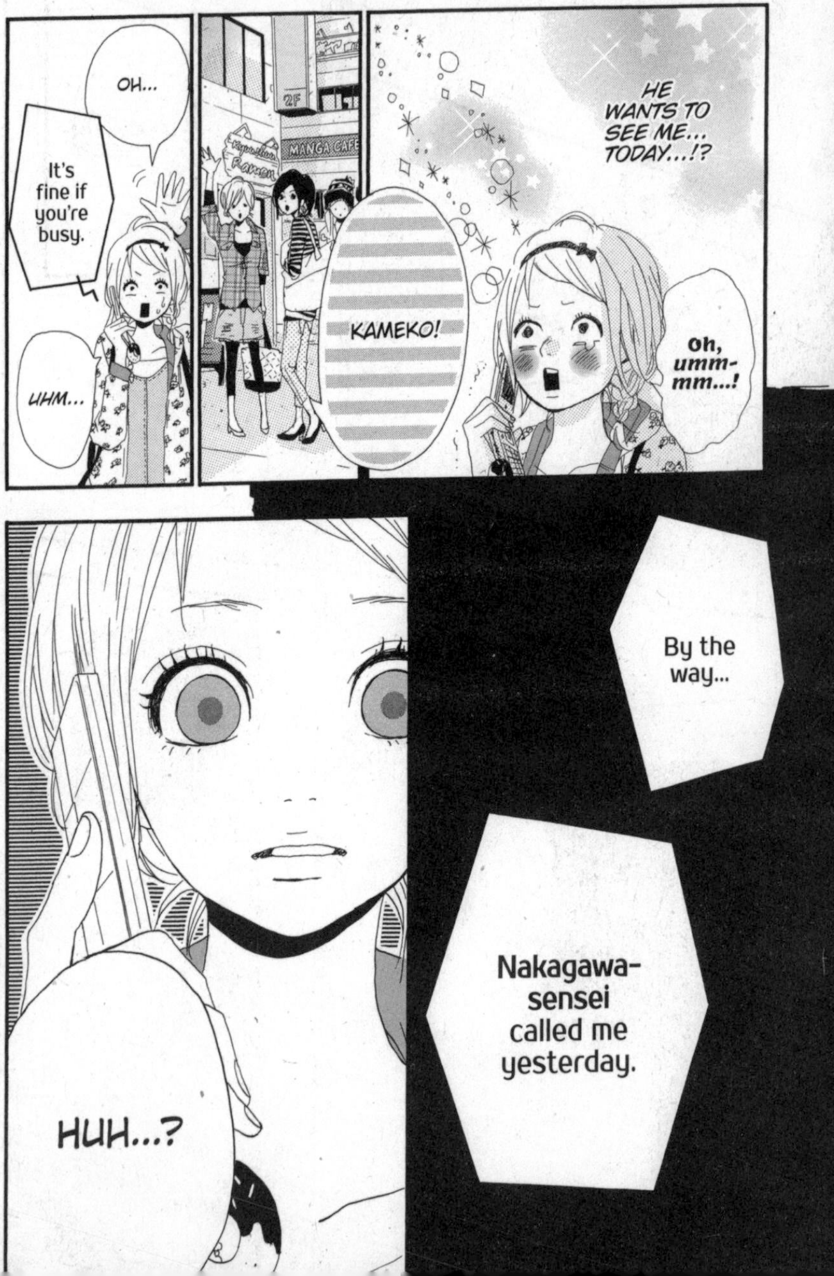
HE WANTS TO SEE ME... TODAY...!?
Oh, ummm-mm...!
KAMEKO!
2F
MANGA CAFE
OH...
It's fine if you're busy.
UHM...
By the way...
Nakagawa-sensei called me yesterday.
HUH...?

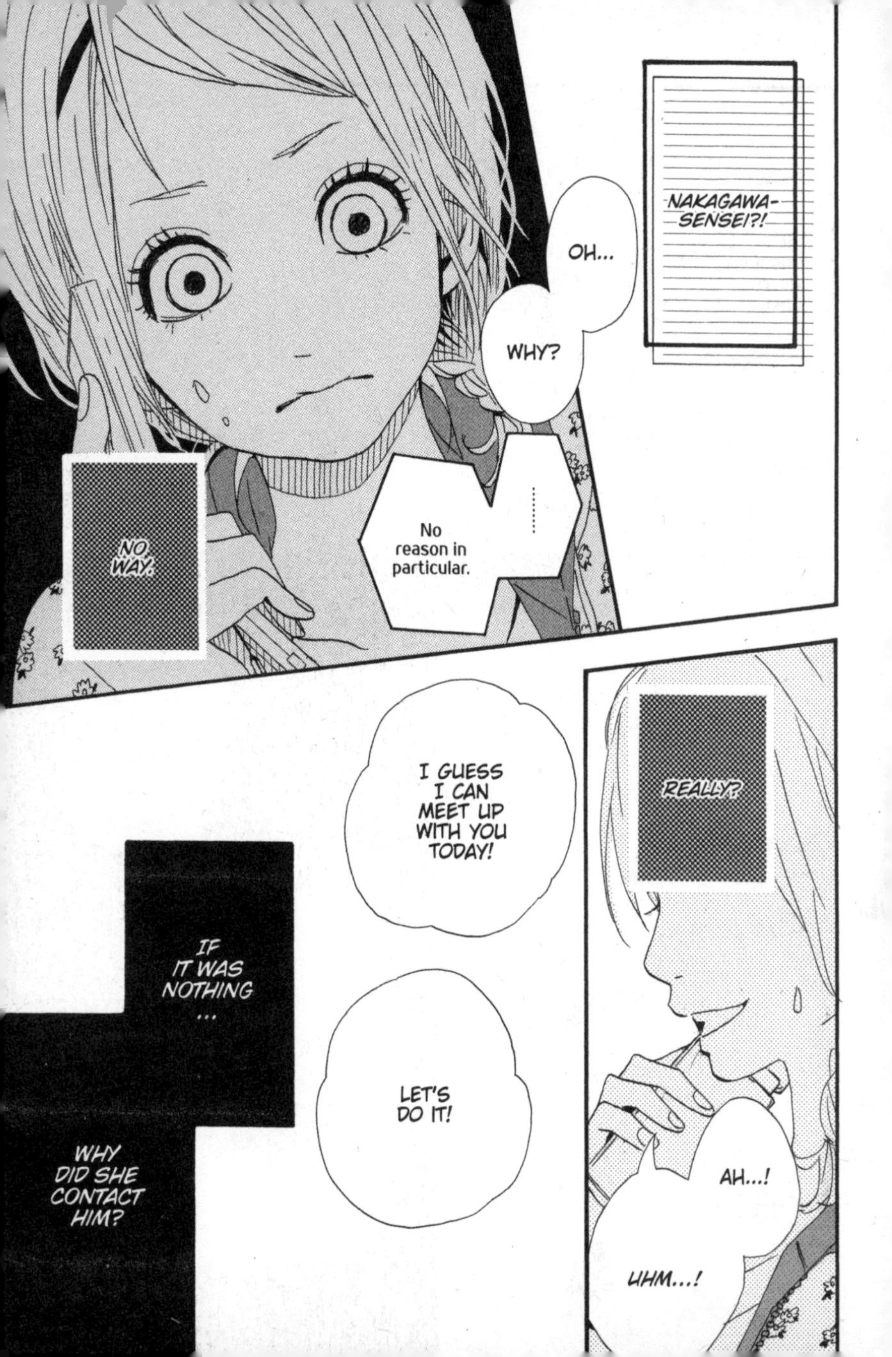
NAKAGAWA-SENSEI?!
OH...
WHY?
No reason in particular.
NO WAY.
REALLY?
AH...!
UHM...!
I GUESS I CAN MEET UP WITH YOU TODAY!
LET'S DO IT!
IF IT WAS NOTHING ...
WHY DID SHE CONTACT HIM?

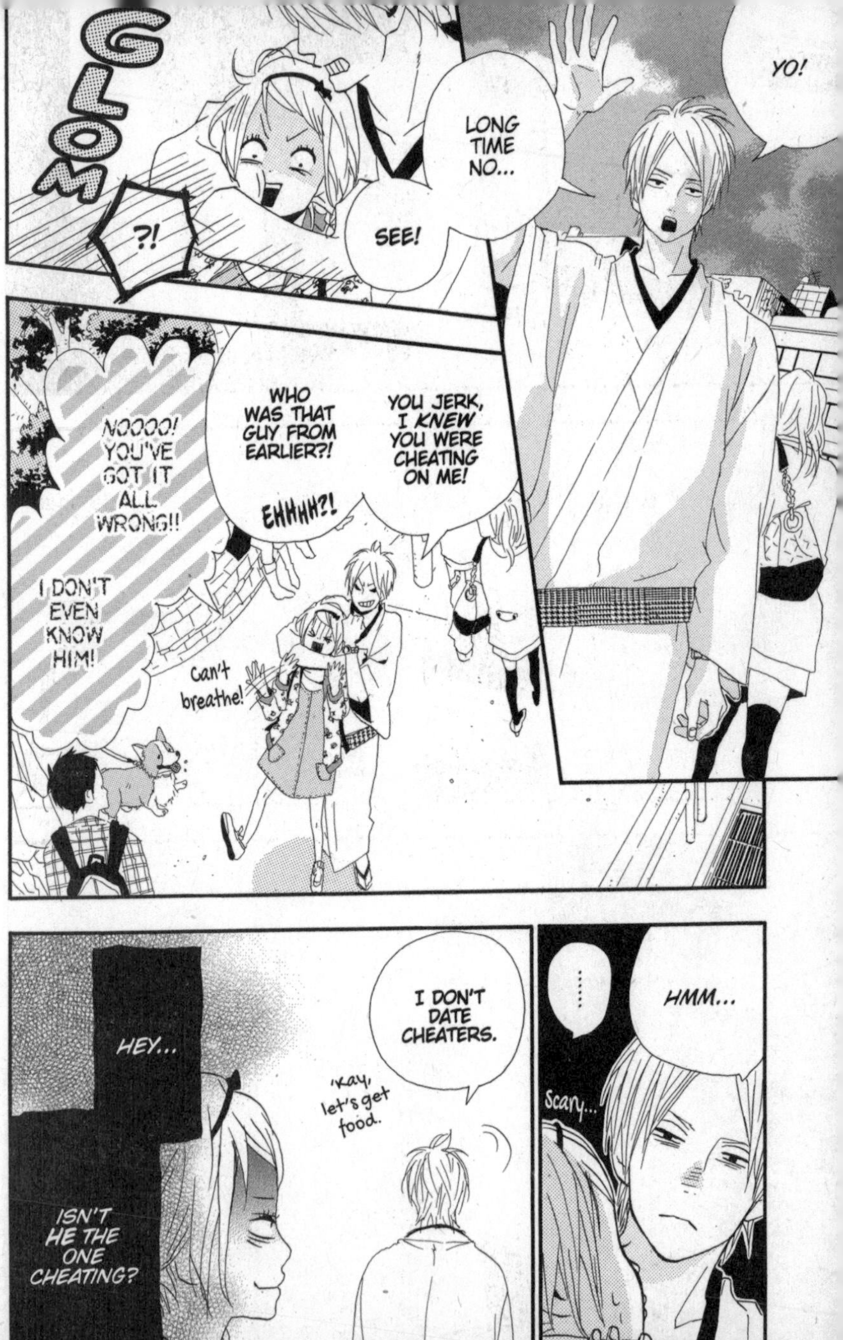
YO!
LONG TIME NO...
SEE!
GLOM
?!
YOU JERK, I *KNEW* YOU WERE CHEATING ON ME!
WHO WAS THAT GUY FROM EARLIER?!
EHHHH?!
NOOOO! YOU'VE GOT IT ALL WRONG!!
I DON'T EVEN KNOW HIM!
Can't breathe!
HMM...
......
Scary...
I DON'T DATE CHEATERS.
'Kay, let's get food.
HEY...
ISN'T HE THE ONE CHEATING?

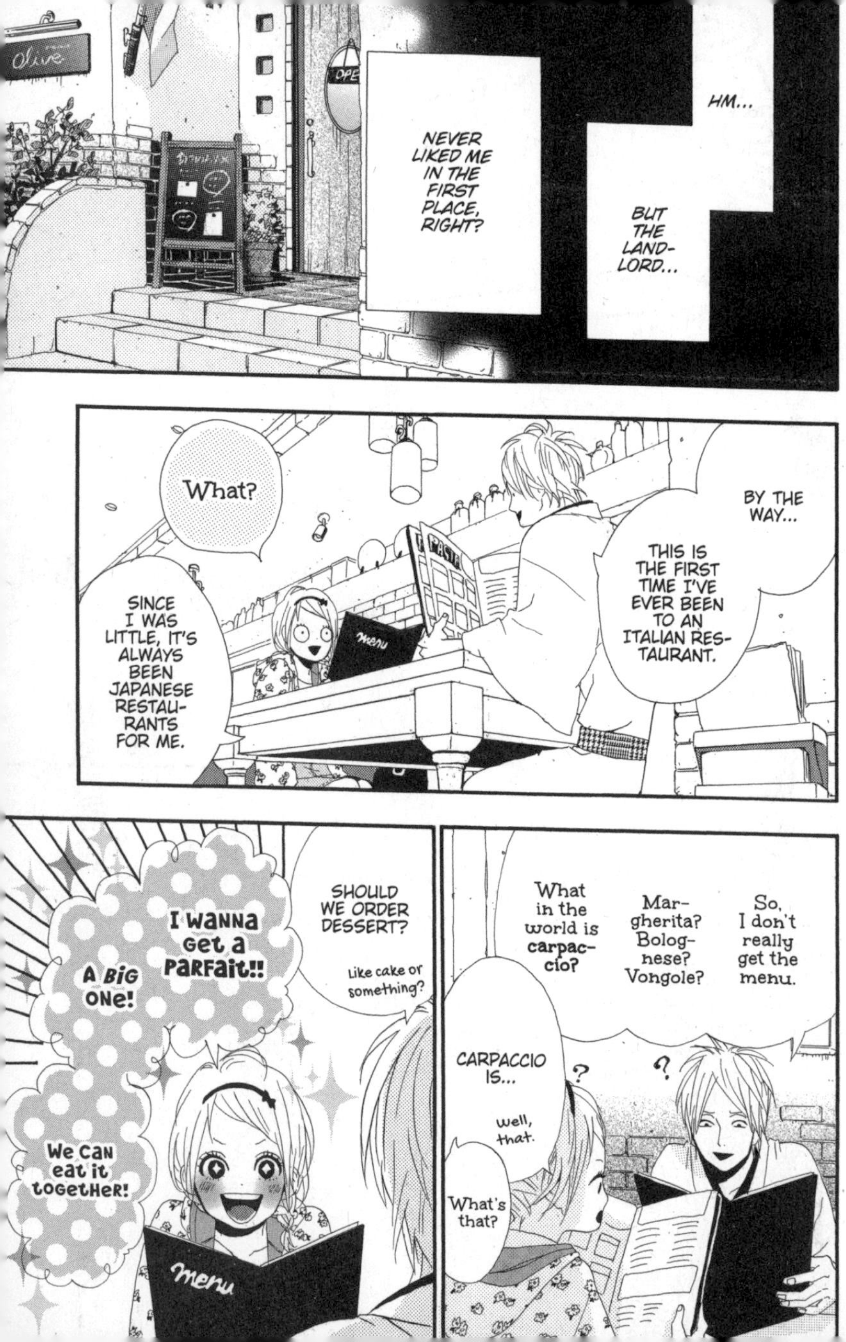
HM...
BUT THE LANDLORD...
NEVER LIKED ME IN THE FIRST PLACE, RIGHT?
BY THE WAY...
THIS IS THE FIRST TIME I'VE EVER BEEN TO AN ITALIAN RESTAURANT.
What?
SINCE I WAS LITTLE, IT'S ALWAYS BEEN JAPANESE RESTAURANTS FOR ME.
So, I don't really get the menu.
Margherita? Bolognese? Vongole?
What in the world is carpaccio?
CARPACCIO IS...
well, that.
What's that?
SHOULD WE ORDER DESSERT?
Like cake or something?
I WANNA GET A PARFAIT!!
A BIG ONE!
We can eat it together!

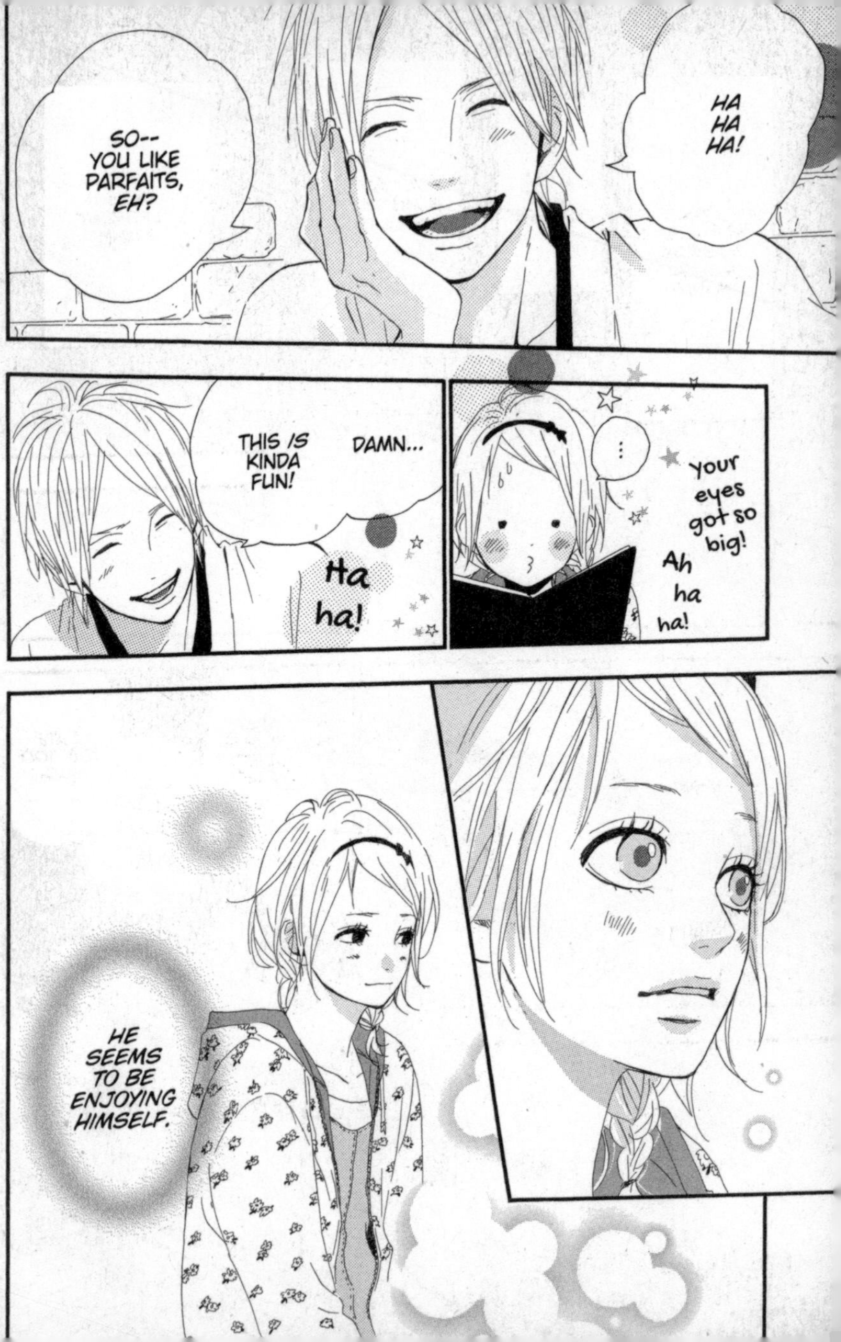
HA HA HA!
SO-- YOU LIKE PARFAITS, EH?
...
Your eyes got so big!
Ah ha ha!
DAMN...
THIS IS KINDA FUN!
Ha ha!
HE SEEMS TO BE ENJOYING HIMSELF.

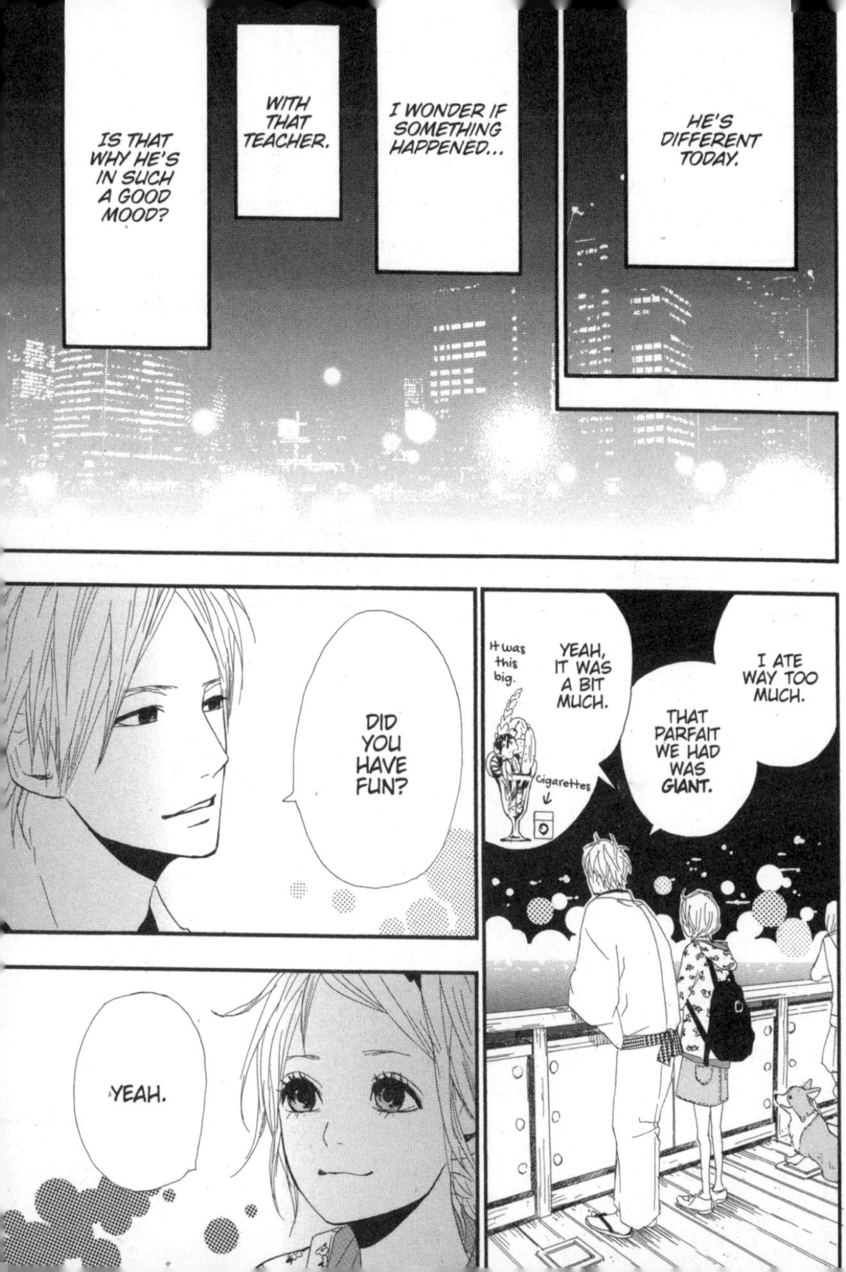
HE'S DIFFERENT TODAY.
I WONDER IF SOMETHING HAPPENED...
WITH THAT TEACHER.
IS THAT WHY HE'S IN SUCH A GOOD MOOD?
I ATE WAY TOO MUCH.
THAT PARFAIT WE HAD WAS GIANT.
YEAH, IT WAS A BIT MUCH.
It was this big.
Cigarettes
DID YOU HAVE FUN?
YEAH.

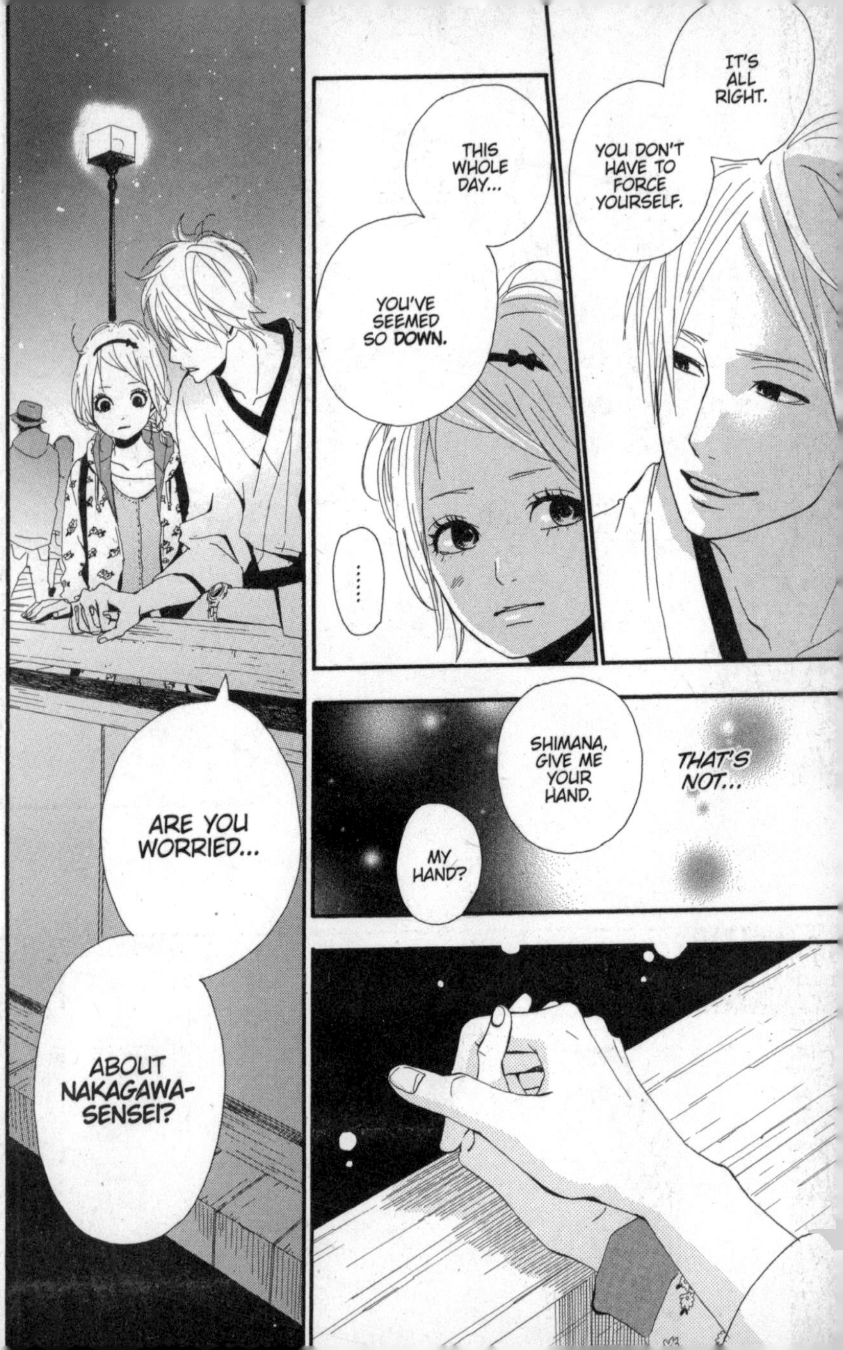
IT'S ALL RIGHT.
YOU DON'T HAVE TO FORCE YOURSELF.
THIS WHOLE DAY...
YOU'VE SEEMED SO DOWN.
......
THAT'S NOT...
SHIMANA, GIVE ME YOUR HAND.
MY HAND?
ARE YOU WORRIED...
ABOUT NAKAGAWA-SENSEI?

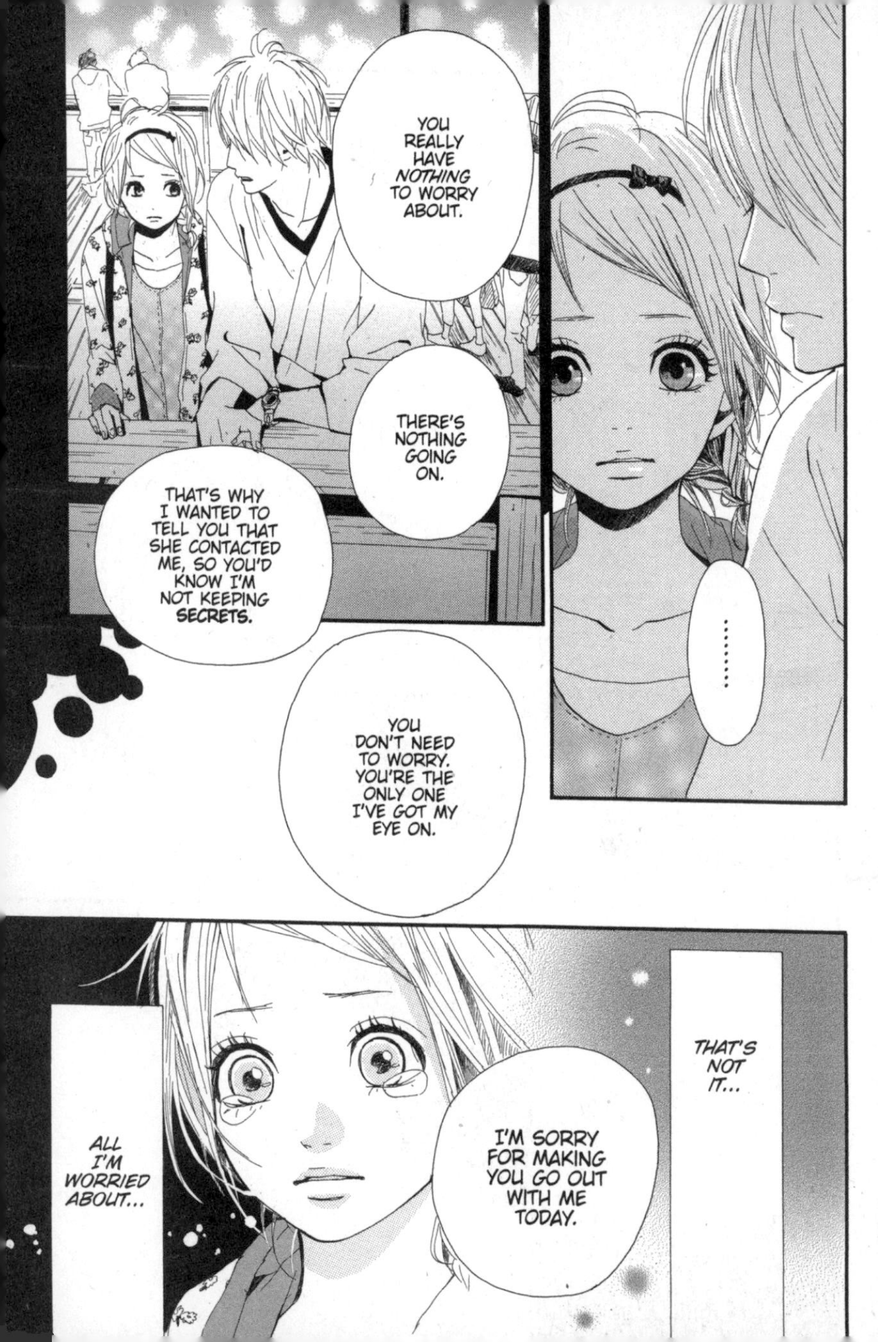

......
YOU REALLY HAVE NOTHING TO WORRY ABOUT.
THERE'S NOTHING GOING ON.
THAT'S WHY I WANTED TO TELL YOU THAT SHE CONTACTED ME, SO YOU'D KNOW I'M NOT KEEPING SECRETS.
YOU DON'T NEED TO WORRY. YOU'RE THE ONLY ONE I'VE GOT MY EYE ON.
THAT'S NOT IT...
I'M SORRY FOR MAKING YOU GO OUT WITH ME TODAY.
ALL I'M WORRIED ABOUT...

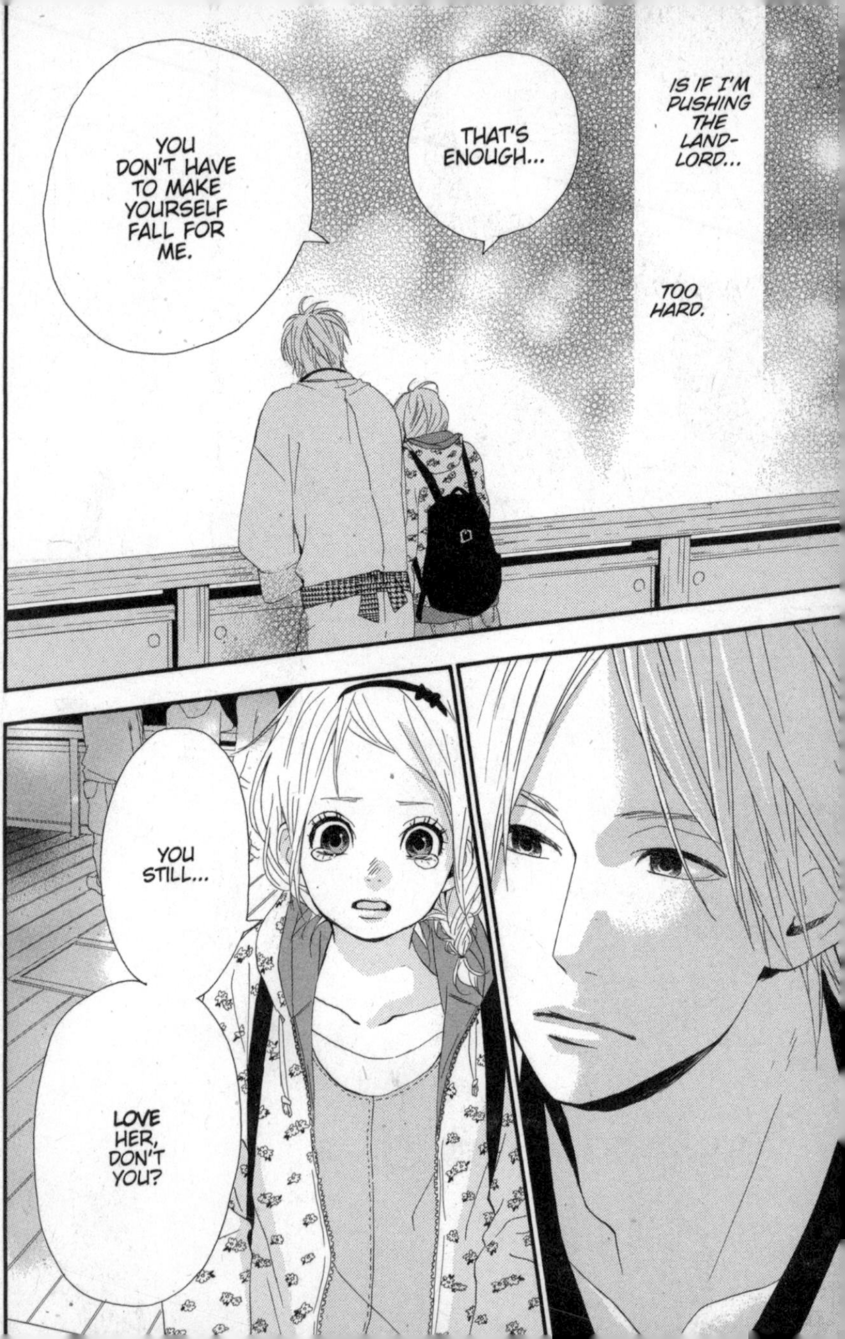
IS IF I'M PUSHING THE LAND-LORD...
TOO HARD.
THAT'S ENOUGH...
YOU DON'T HAVE TO MAKE YOURSELF FALL FOR ME.
YOU STILL...
LOVE HER, DON'T YOU?

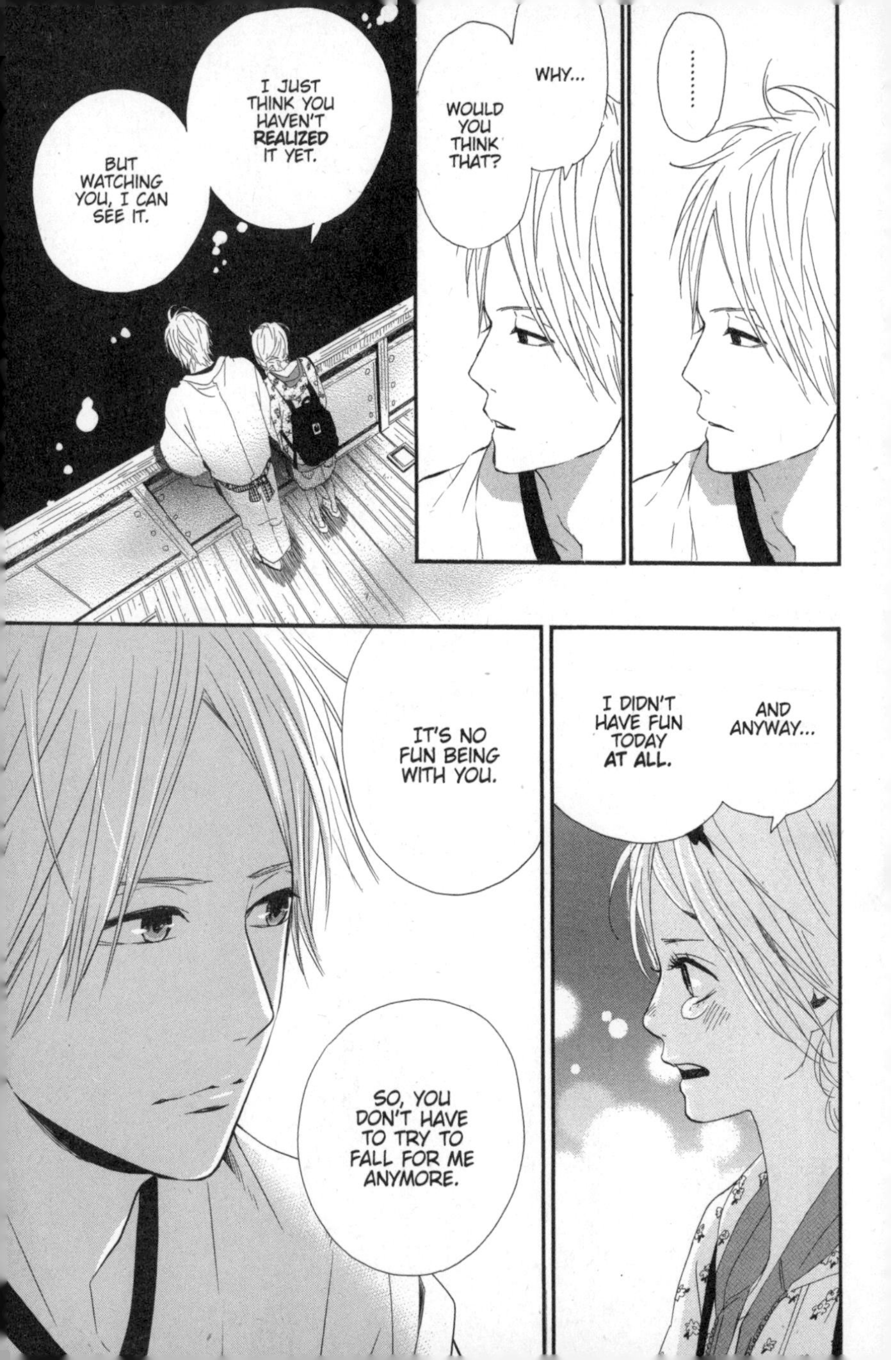
......
WHY...
WOULD YOU THINK THAT?
I JUST THINK YOU HAVEN'T REALIZED IT YET.
BUT WATCHING YOU, I CAN SEE IT.
AND ANYWAY...
I DIDN'T HAVE FUN TODAY AT ALL.
IT'S NO FUN BEING WITH YOU.
SO, YOU DON'T HAVE TO TRY TO FALL FOR ME ANYMORE.

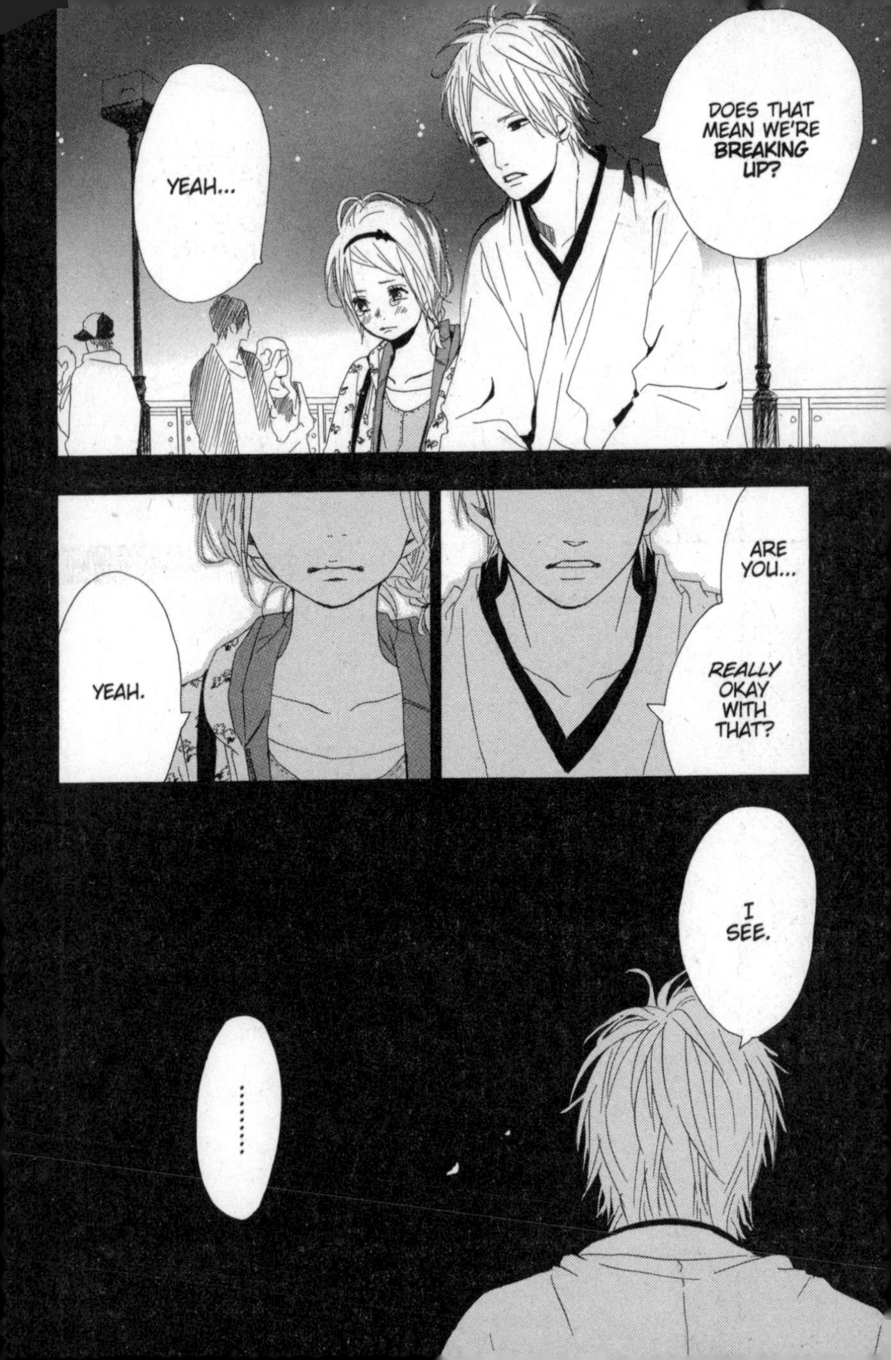
DOES THAT MEAN WE'RE BREAKING UP?
YEAH...
ARE YOU...
REALLY OKAY WITH THAT?
YEAH.
I SEE.
......

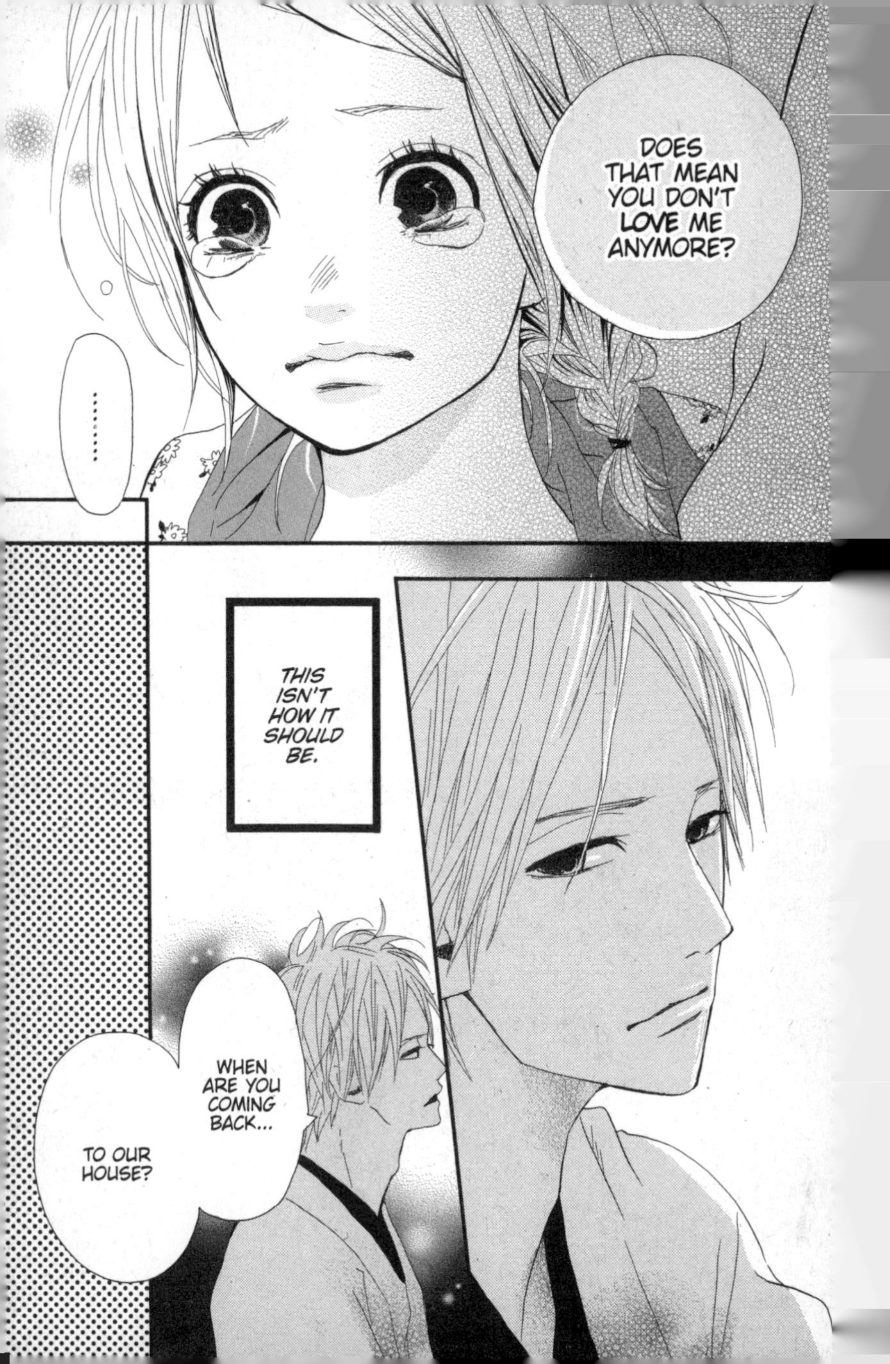
DOES THAT MEAN YOU DON'T LOVE ME ANYMORE?
......
THIS ISN'T HOW IT SHOULD BE.
WHEN ARE YOU COMING BACK...
TO OUR HOUSE?

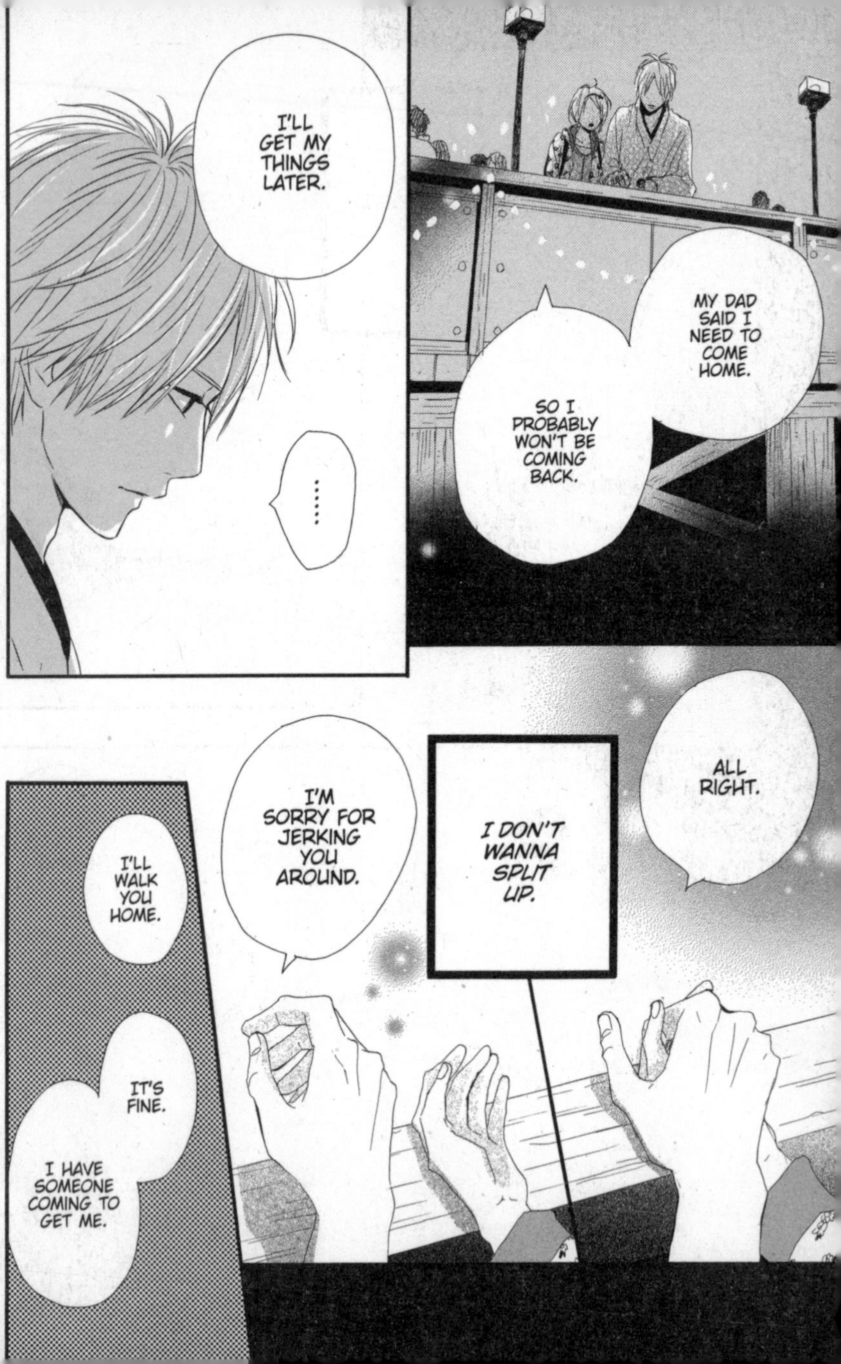
MY DAD SAID I NEED TO COME HOME.
SO I PROBABLY WON'T BE COMING BACK.
I'LL GET MY THINGS LATER.
......
ALL RIGHT.
I DON'T WANNA SPLIT UP.
I'M SORRY FOR JERKING YOU AROUND.
I'LL WALK YOU HOME.
IT'S FINE.
I HAVE SOMEONE COMING TO GET ME.

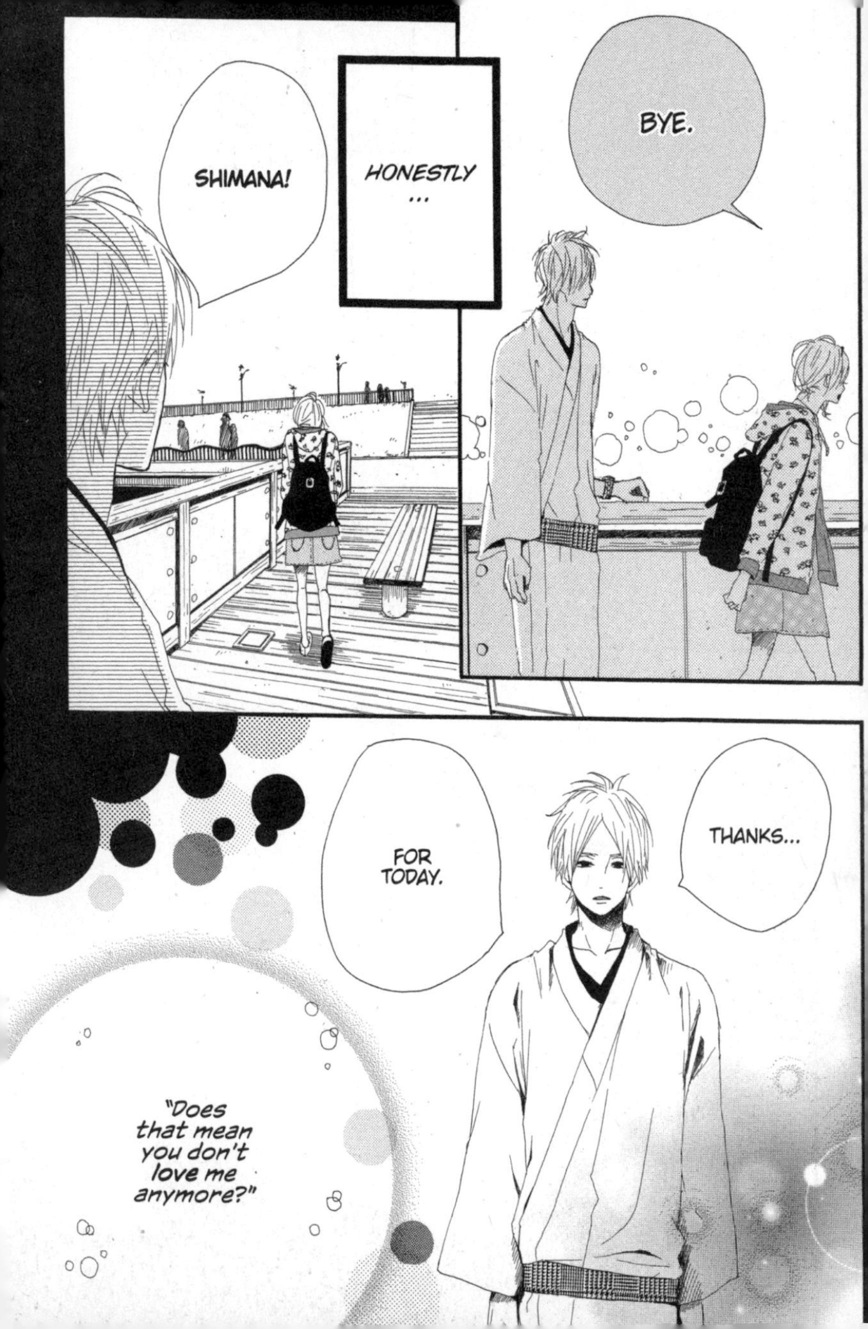
BYE.
HONESTLY ...
SHIMANA!
THANKS...
FOR TODAY.
"Does that mean you don't love me anymore?"

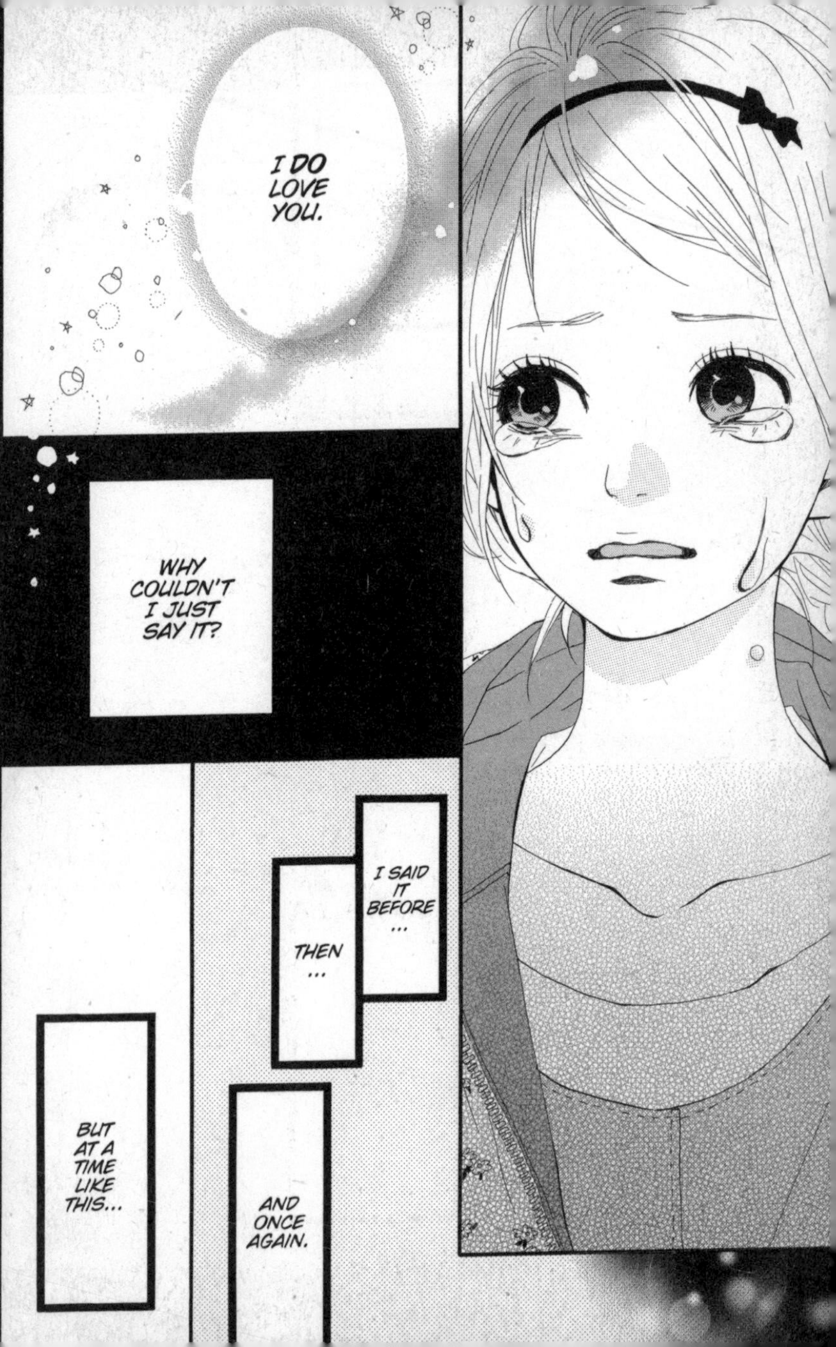
I DO LOVE YOU.
WHY COULDN'T I JUST SAY IT?
I SAID IT BEFORE ...
THEN ...
AND ONCE AGAIN.
BUT AT A TIME LIKE THIS...

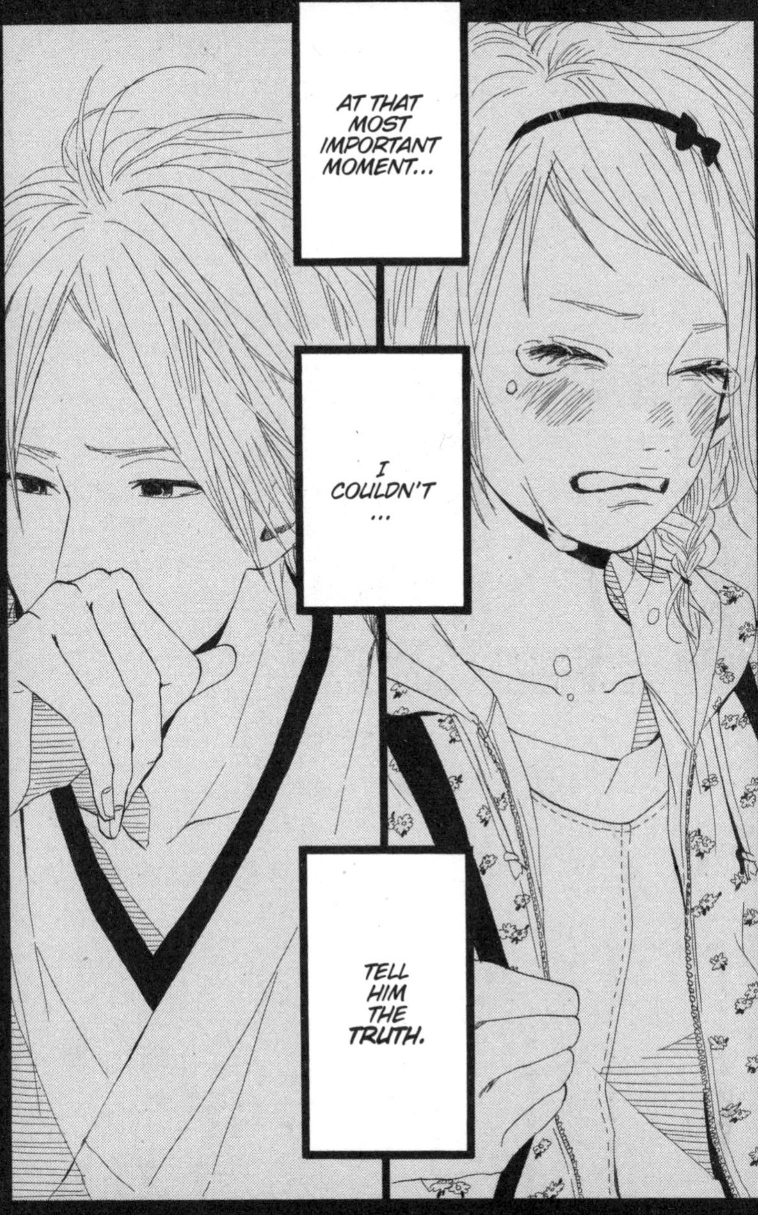
AT THAT MOST IMPORTANT MOMENT...
I COULDN'T ...
TELL HIM THE TRUTH.

Oho...

So, this is Volume 6...

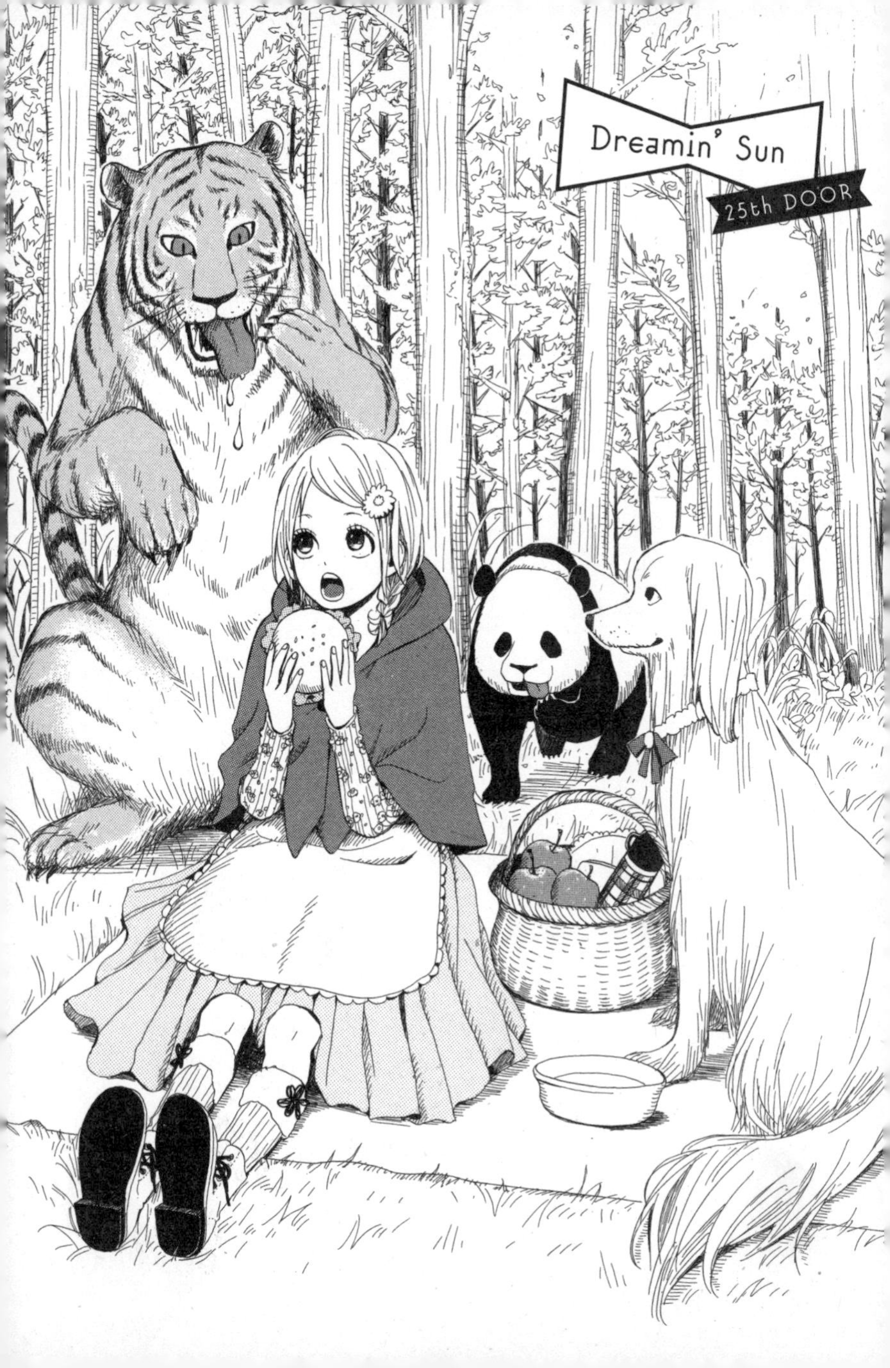
Dreamin' Sun
25th DOOR

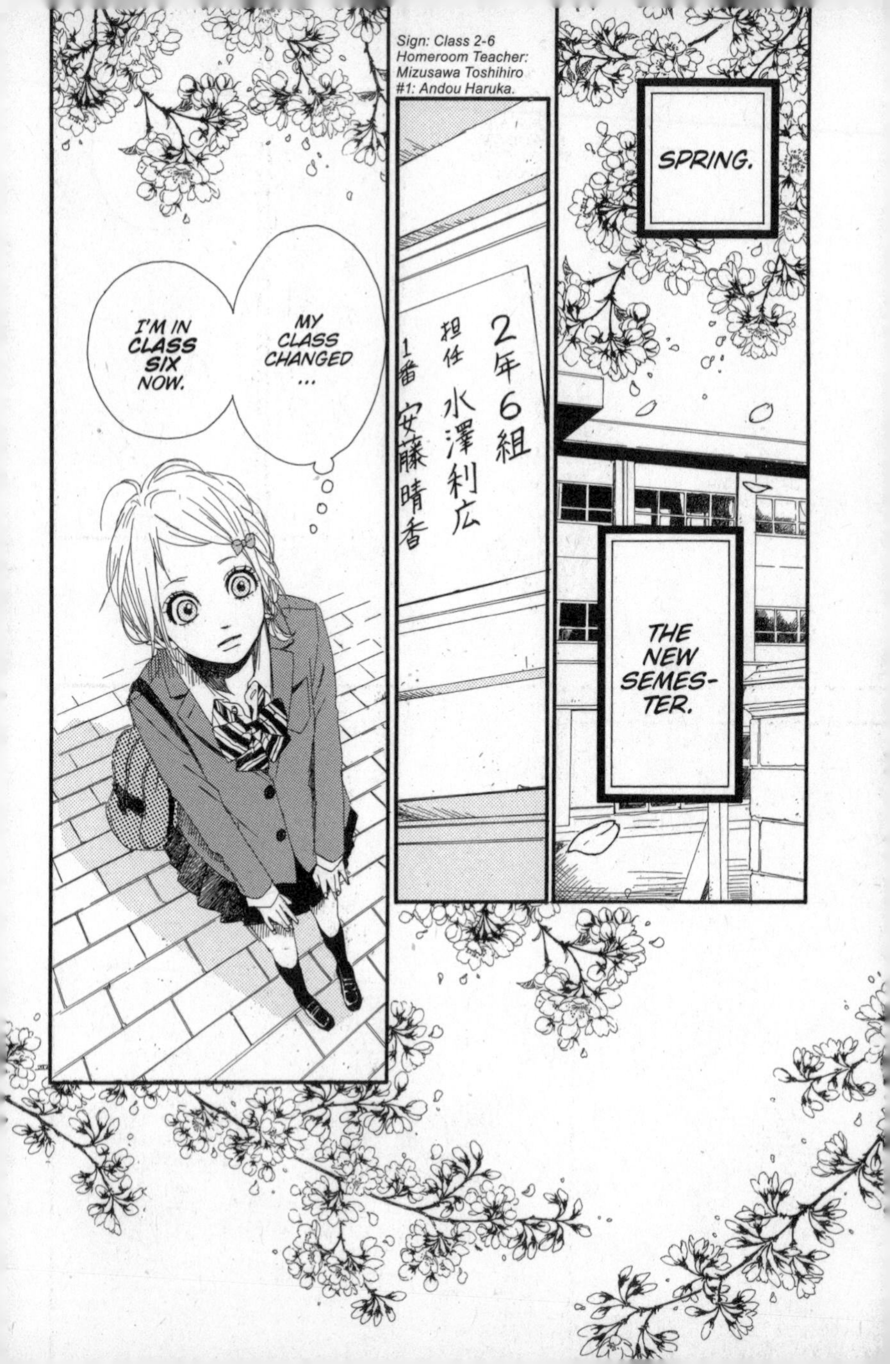
SPRING.
THE NEW SEMESTER.
2年6組
担任 水澤利広
1番 安藤晴香
Sign: Class 2-6 Homeroom Teacher: Mizusawa Toshihiro #1: Andou Haruka.
MY CLASS CHANGED...
I'M IN CLASS SIX NOW.

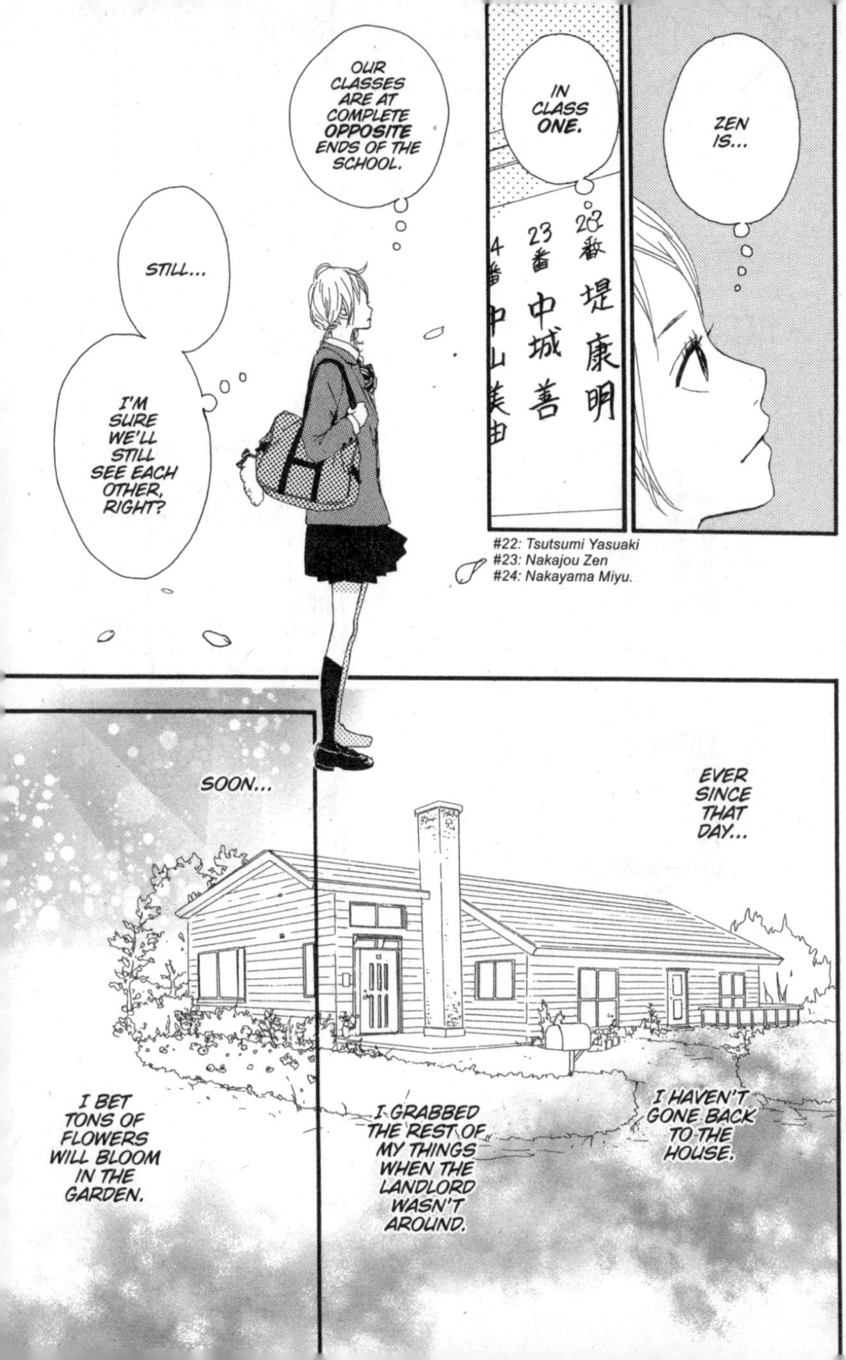
ZEN IS...
IN CLASS ONE.
22番 堤康明
23番 中城善
24番 中山美由
#22: Tsutsumi Yasuaki
#23: Nakajou Zen
#24: Nakayama Miyu.
OUR CLASSES ARE AT COMPLETE OPPOSITE ENDS OF THE SCHOOL.
STILL...
I'M SURE WE'LL STILL SEE EACH OTHER, RIGHT?
EVER SINCE THAT DAY...
I HAVEN'T GONE BACK TO THE HOUSE.
I GRABBED THE REST OF MY THINGS WHEN THE LANDLORD WASN'T AROUND.
SOON...
I BET TONS OF FLOWERS WILL BLOOM IN THE GARDEN.

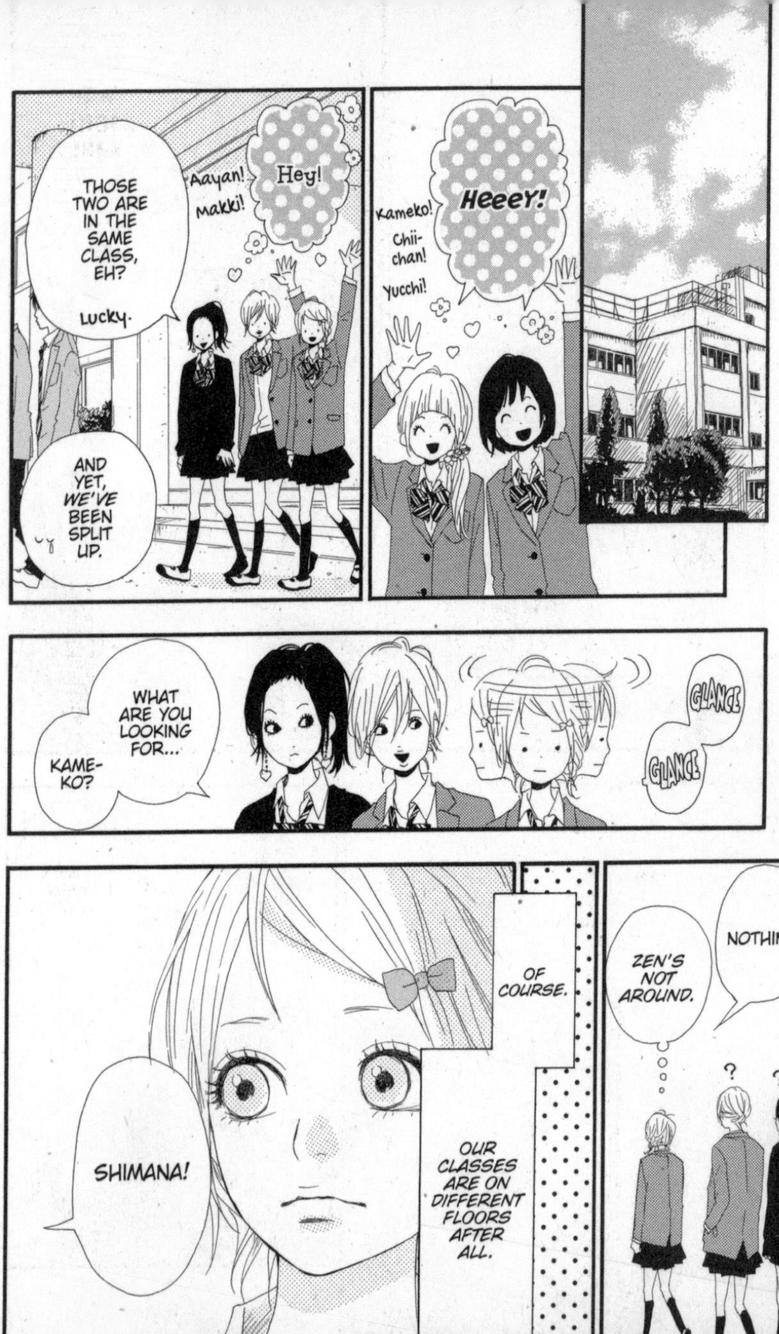
HEEEY!
Kameko!
Chii-chan!
Yucchi!
Hey!
Aayan!
Makki!
THOSE TWO ARE IN THE SAME CLASS, EH?
Lucky.
AND YET, WE'VE BEEN SPLIT UP.
GLANCE
GLANCE
WHAT ARE YOU LOOKING FOR...
KAME-KO?
NOTHING.
ZEN'S NOT AROUND.
OF COURSE.
OUR CLASSES ARE ON DIFFERENT FLOORS AFTER ALL.
SHIMANA!

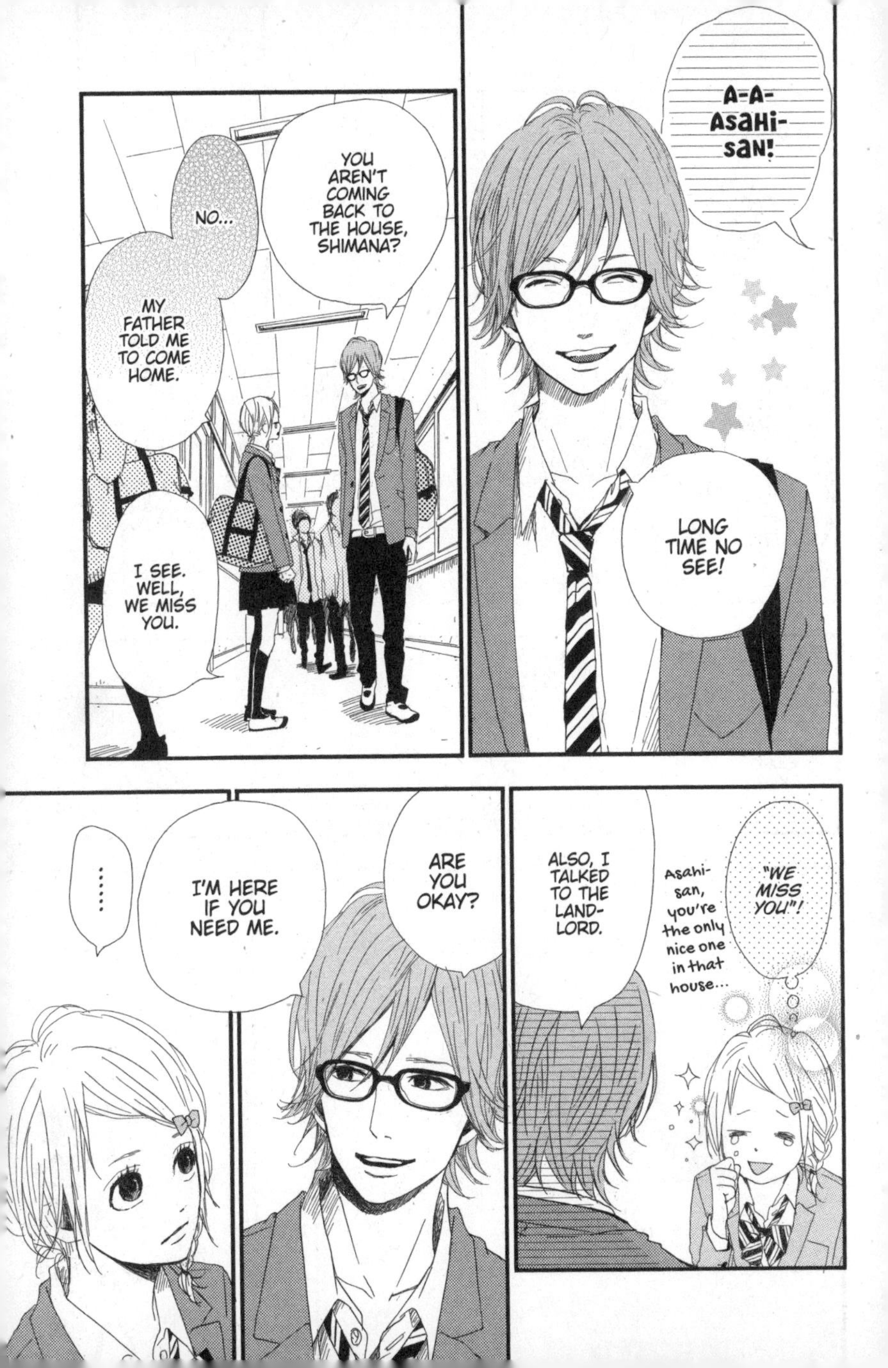

A-A-
Asahi-
san!
LONG TIME NO SEE!
YOU AREN'T COMING BACK TO THE HOUSE, SHIMANA?
NO...
MY FATHER TOLD ME TO COME HOME.
I SEE. WELL, WE MISS YOU.
"WE MISS YOU"!
Asahi-san, you're the only nice one in that house...
ALSO, I TALKED TO THE LAND-LORD.
ARE YOU OKAY?
I'M HERE IF YOU NEED ME.
......

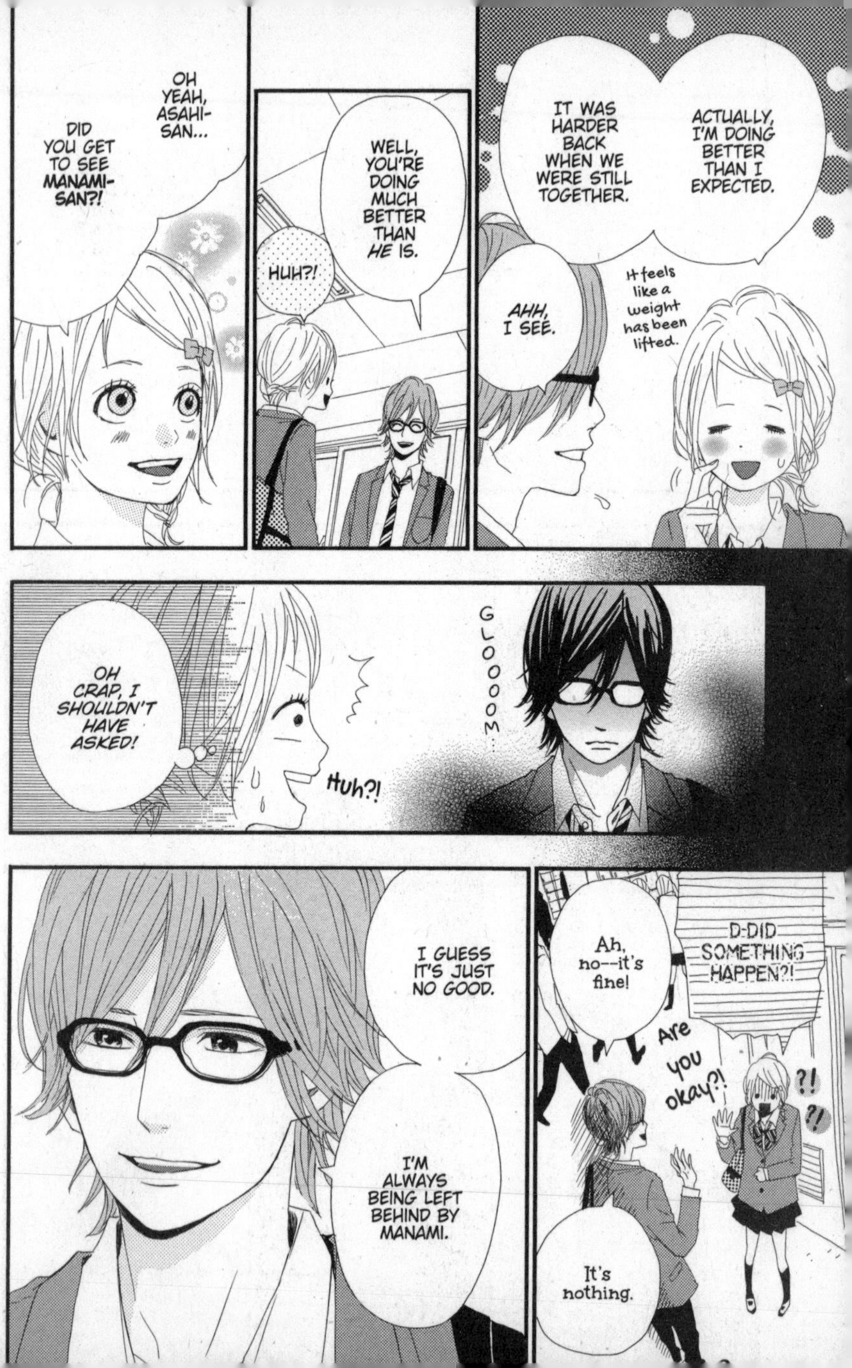
ACTUALLY, I'M DOING BETTER THAN I EXPECTED.
IT WAS HARDER BACK WHEN WE WERE STILL TOGETHER.
It feels like a weight has been lifted.
AHH, I SEE.
WELL, YOU'RE DOING MUCH BETTER THAN *HE* IS.
HUH?!
OH YEAH, ASAHI-SAN...
DID YOU GET TO SEE MANAMI-SAN?!
GLOOOOOM...
Huh?!
OH CRAP, I SHOULDN'T HAVE ASKED!
D-DID SOMETHING HAPPEN?!
?!
?!
Are you okay?!
Ah, no--it's fine!
It's nothing.
I GUESS IT'S JUST NO GOOD.
I'M ALWAYS BEING LEFT BEHIND BY MANAMI.

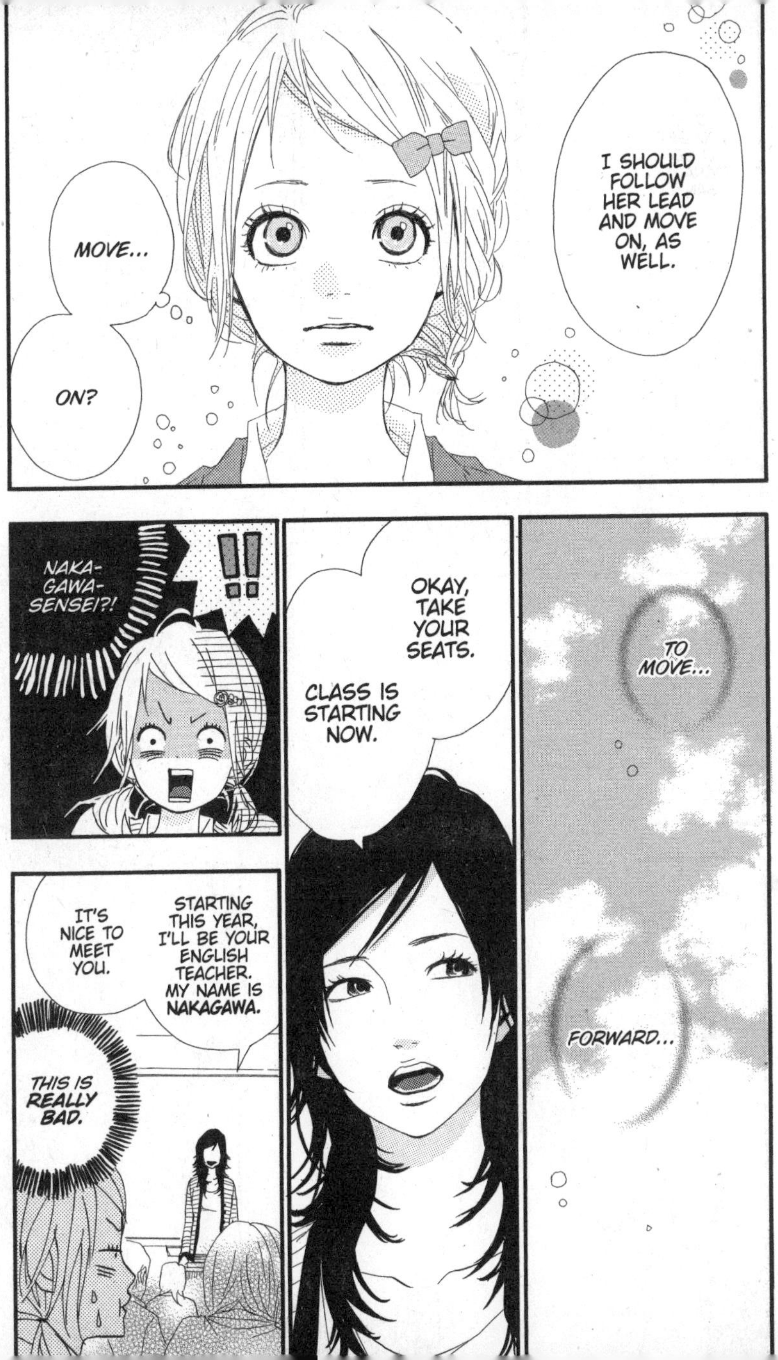
I SHOULD FOLLOW HER LEAD AND MOVE ON, AS WELL.
MOVE...
ON?
TO MOVE...
FORWARD...
OKAY, TAKE YOUR SEATS.
CLASS IS STARTING NOW.
!!
NAKA-GAWA-SENSEI?!
STARTING THIS YEAR, I'LL BE YOUR ENGLISH TEACHER. MY NAME IS NAKAGAWA.
IT'S NICE TO MEET YOU.
THIS IS REALLY BAD.

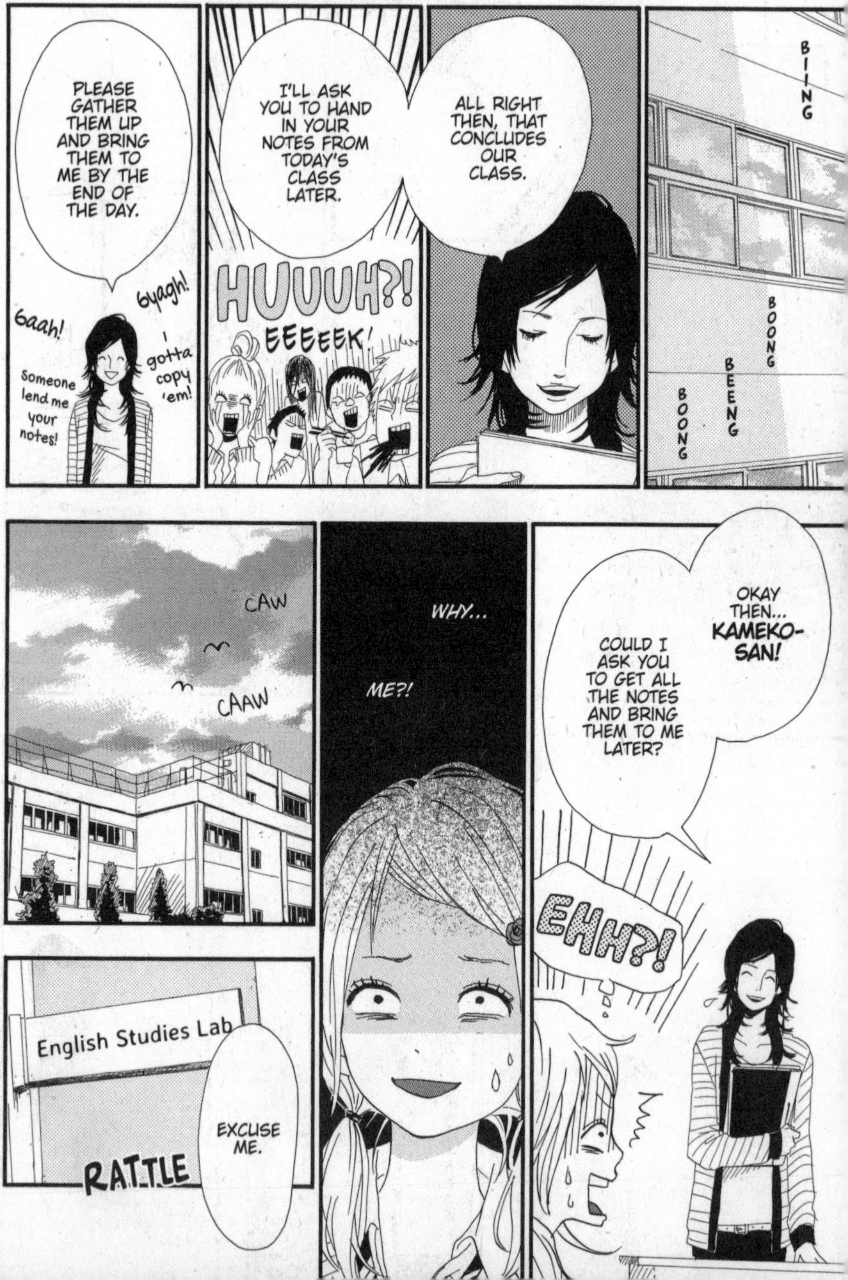
BIING
BOONG
BEENG
BOONG
ALL RIGHT THEN, THAT CONCLUDES OUR CLASS.
I'LL ASK YOU TO HAND IN YOUR NOTES FROM TODAY'S CLASS LATER.
HUUUH?!
EEEEEK!
PLEASE GATHER THEM UP AND BRING THEM TO ME BY THE END OF THE DAY.
6yagh!
I gotta copy 'em!
6aah!
Someone lend me your notes!
OKAY THEN... KAMEKO-SAN!
COULD I ASK YOU TO GET ALL THE NOTES AND BRING THEM TO ME LATER?
EHH?!
WHY...
ME?!
CAW
CAAW
English Studies Lab
EXCUSE ME.
RATTLE

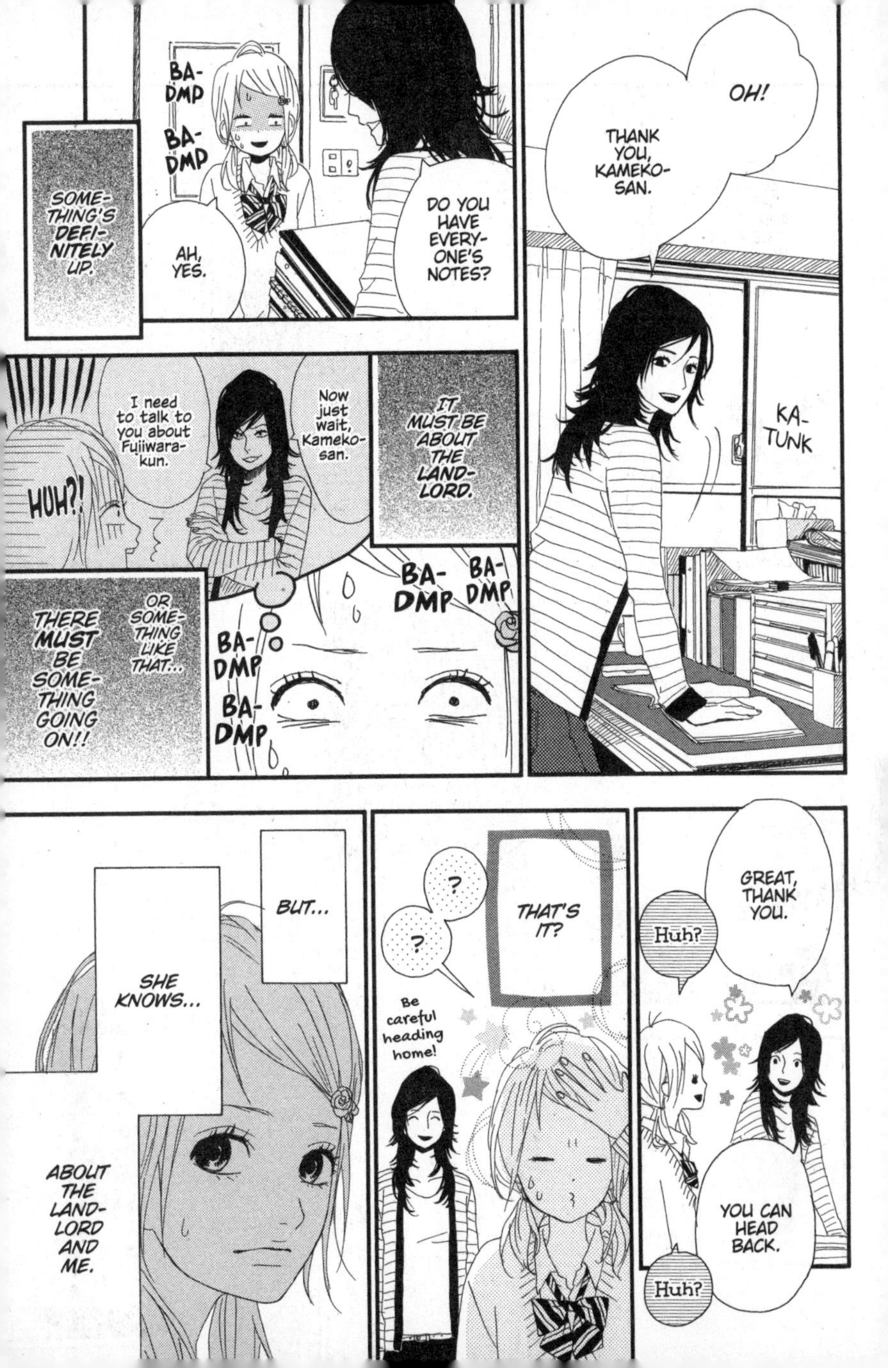
OH!
THANK YOU, KAMEKO-SAN.
KA-TUNK
DO YOU HAVE EVERYONE'S NOTES?
BA-DMP BA-DMP
AH, YES.
SOMETHING'S DEFINITELY UP.
IT MUST BE ABOUT THE LANDLORD.
Now just wait, Kameko-san.
I need to talk to you about Fujiwara-kun.
HUH?!
BA-DMP BA-DMP
BA-DMP BA-DMP
OR SOMETHING LIKE THAT...
THERE MUST BE SOMETHING GOING ON!!
GREAT, THANK YOU.
Huh?
YOU CAN HEAD BACK.
Huh?
THAT'S IT?
?
?
Be careful heading home!
BUT...
SHE KNOWS...
ABOUT THE LANDLORD AND ME.

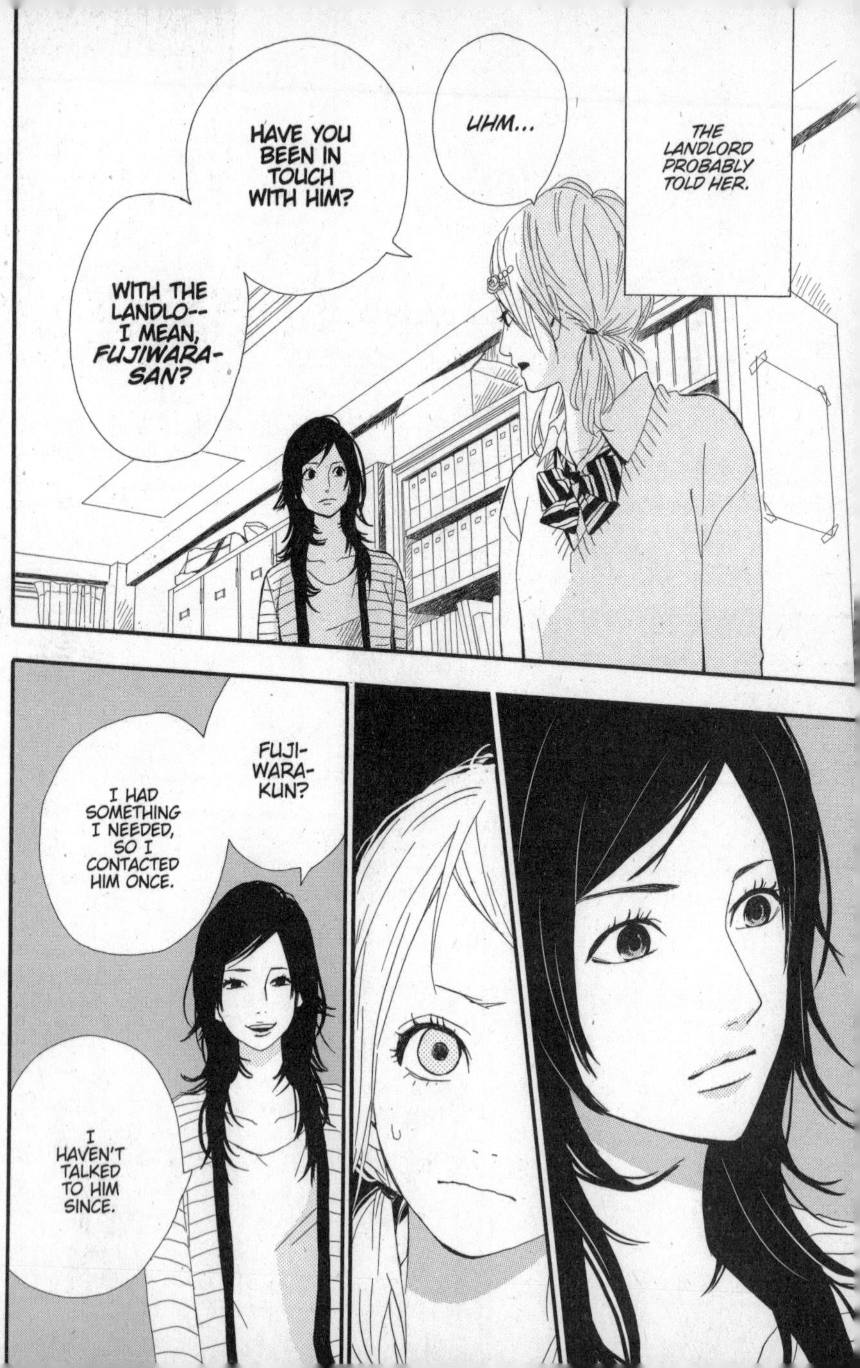
THE LANDLORD PROBABLY TOLD HER.
UHM...
HAVE YOU BEEN IN TOUCH WITH HIM?
WITH THE LANDLO-- I MEAN, *FUJIWARA-SAN?*
FUJI-WARA-KUN?
I HAD SOMETHING I NEEDED, SO I CONTACTED HIM ONCE.
I HAVEN'T TALKED TO HIM SINCE.

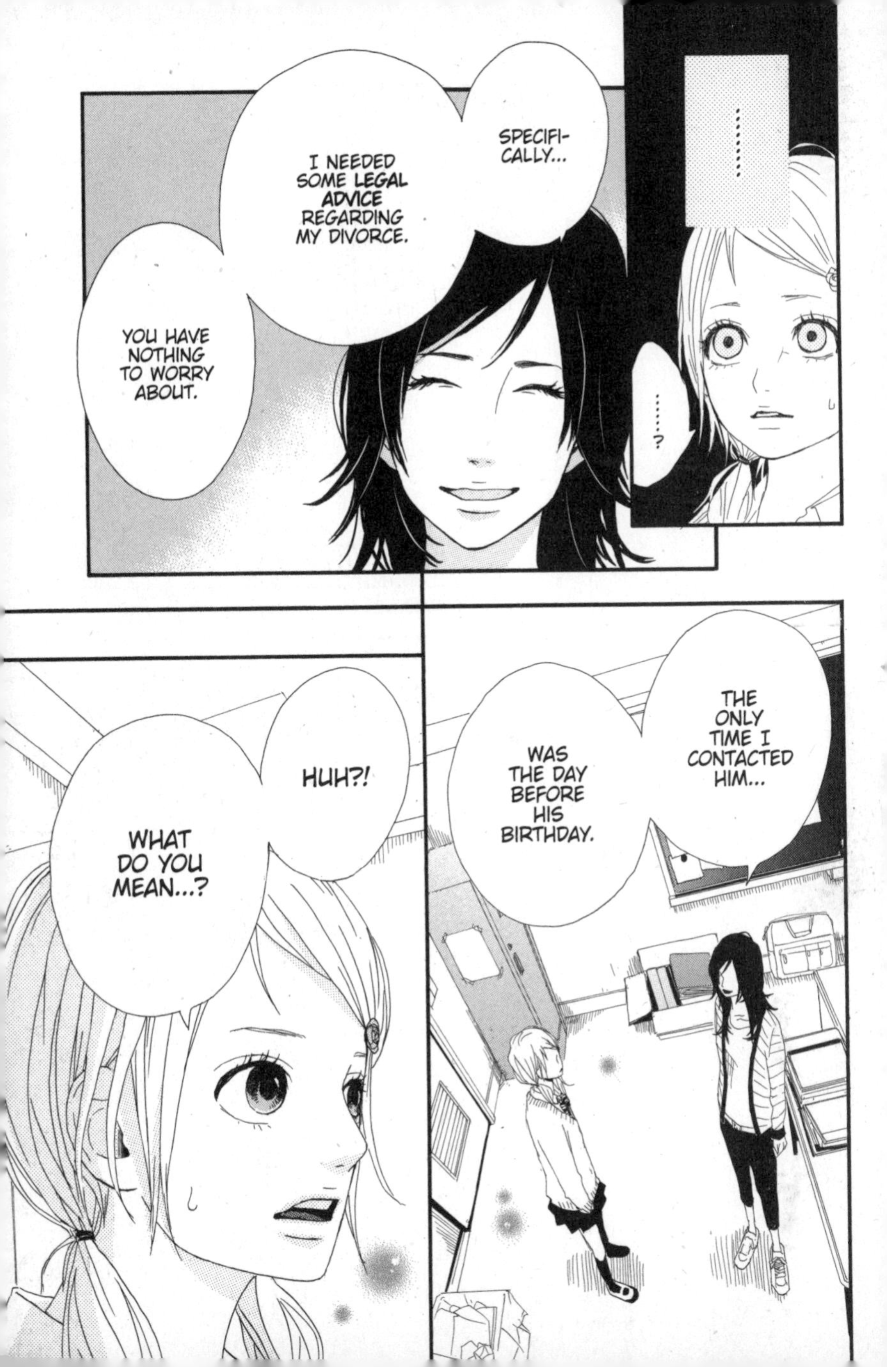
……
……?
SPECIFI-CALLY...
I NEEDED SOME LEGAL ADVICE REGARDING MY DIVORCE.
YOU HAVE NOTHING TO WORRY ABOUT.
THE ONLY TIME I CONTACTED HIM...
WAS THE DAY BEFORE HIS BIRTHDAY.
HUH?!
WHAT DO YOU MEAN...?

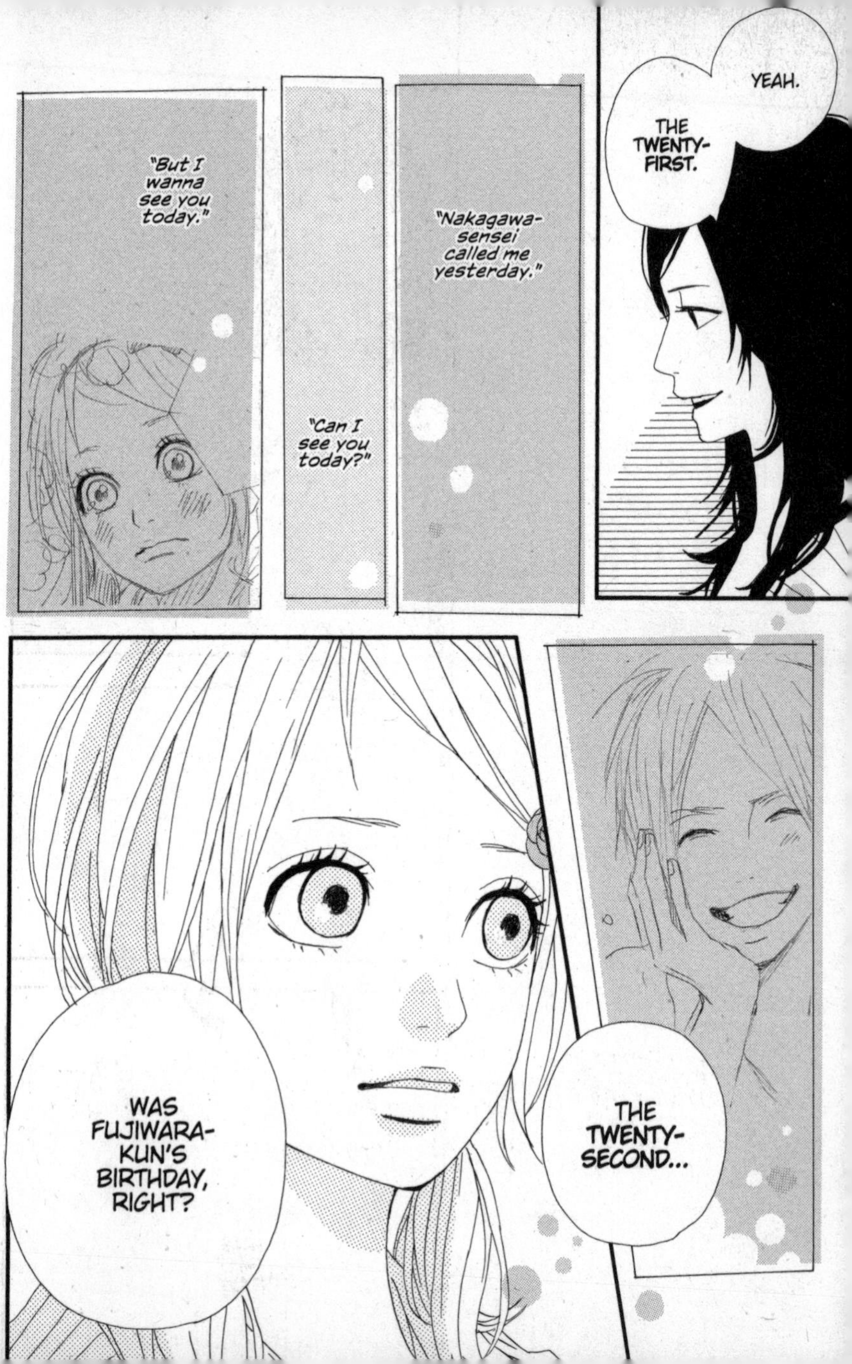
YEAH.
THE TWENTY-FIRST.
"Nakagawa-sensei called me yesterday."
"Can I see you today?"
"But I wanna see you today."
THE TWENTY-SECOND...
WAS FUJIWARA-KUN'S BIRTHDAY, RIGHT?

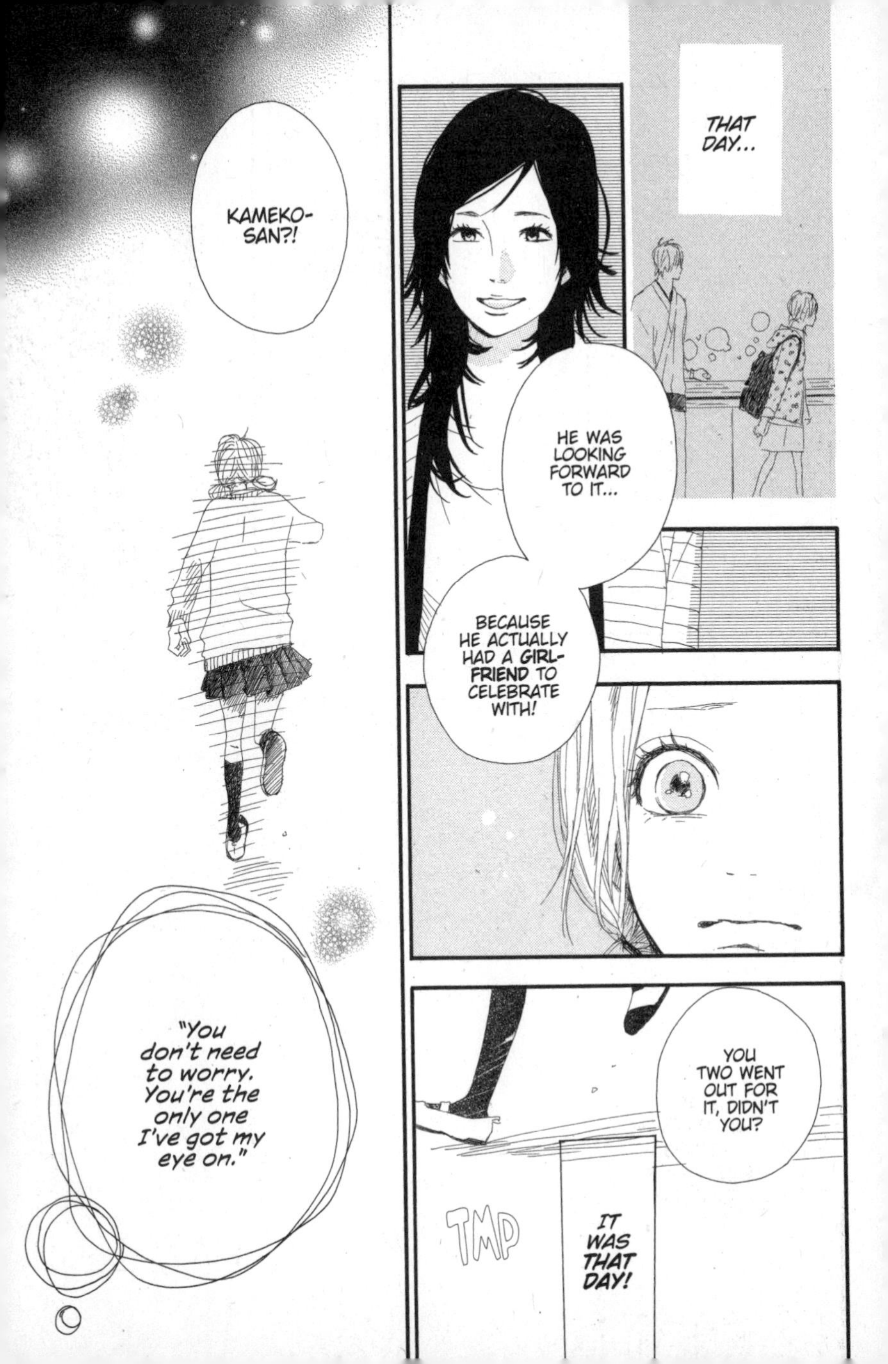
THAT DAY...
HE WAS LOOKING FORWARD TO IT...
BECAUSE HE ACTUALLY HAD A GIRL-FRIEND TO CELEBRATE WITH!
YOU TWO WENT OUT FOR IT, DIDN'T YOU?
TMP
IT WAS THAT DAY!
KAMEKO-SAN?!
"You don't need to worry. You're the only one I've got my eye on."

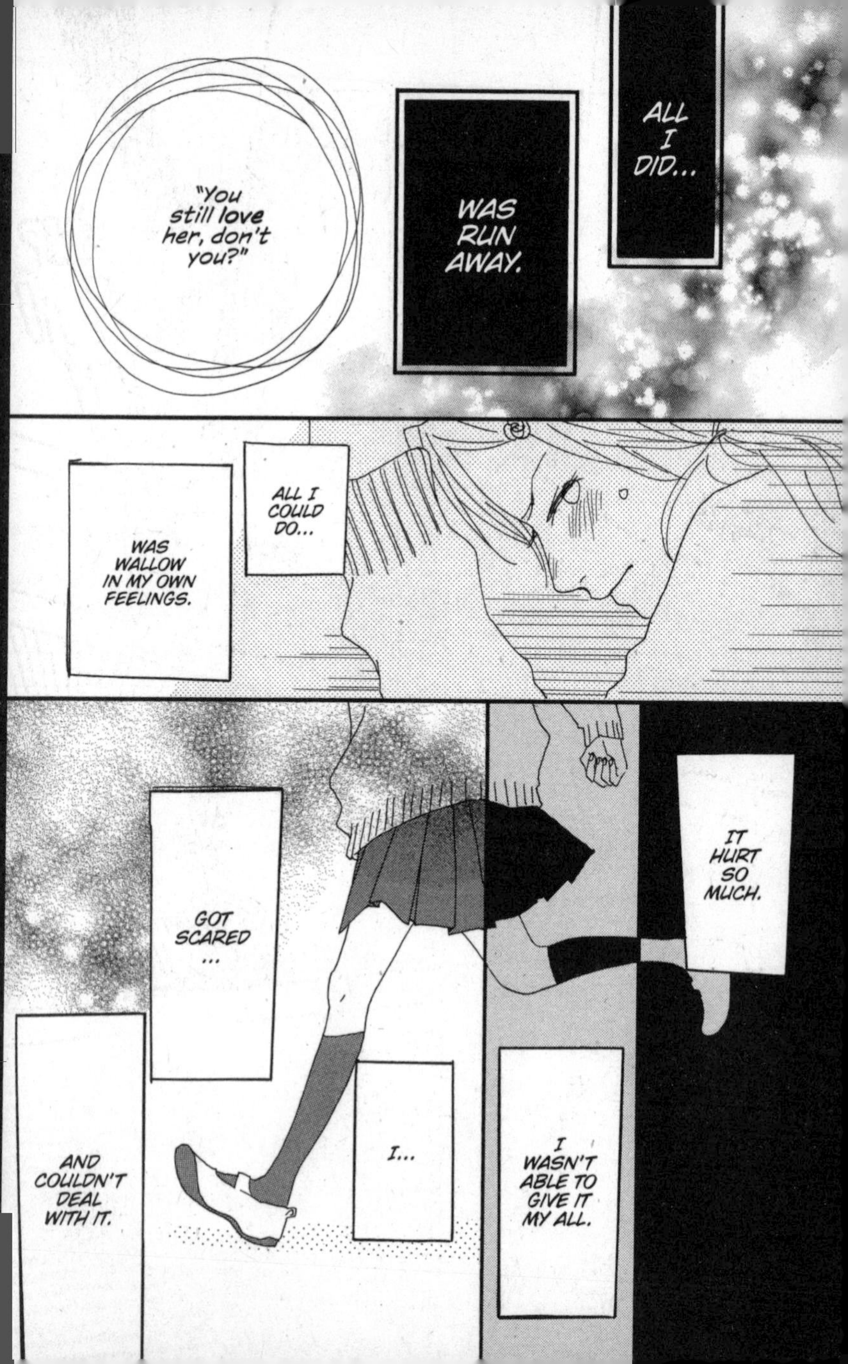
ALL I DID...
WAS RUN AWAY.
"You still love her, don't you?"
ALL I COULD DO...
WAS WALLOW IN MY OWN FEELINGS.
IT HURT SO MUCH.
I WASN'T ABLE TO GIVE IT MY ALL.
I...
GOT SCARED ...
AND COULDN'T DEAL WITH IT.

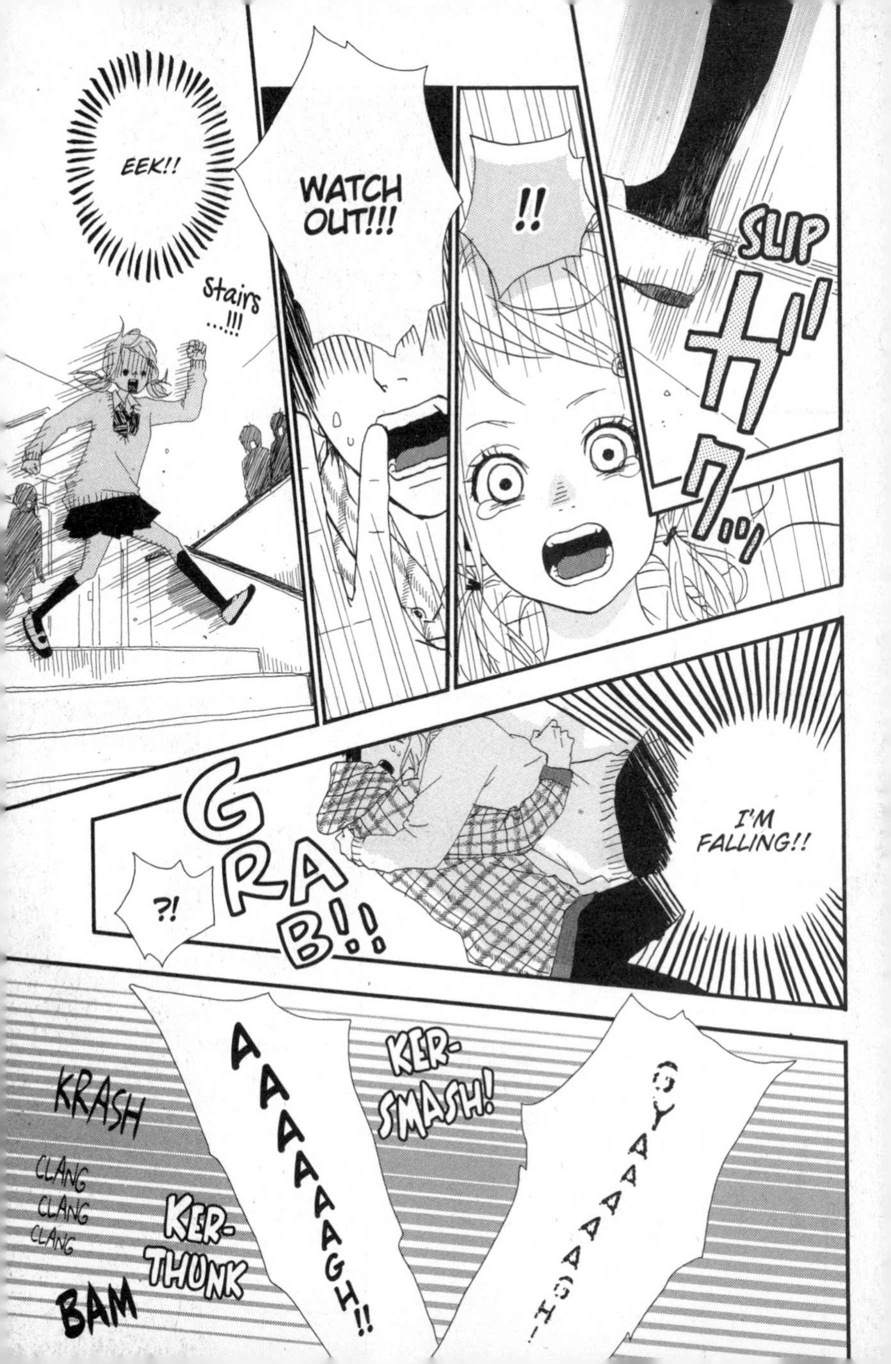

SLIP
!!
WATCH OUT!!!
EEK!!
Stairs ...!!!
I'M FALLING!!
GRAB!!
?!
GYAAAAAAGH—!
KER-SMASH!
AAAAAAAAGH!!
KRASH
CLANG CLANG CLANG
KER-THUNK
BAM

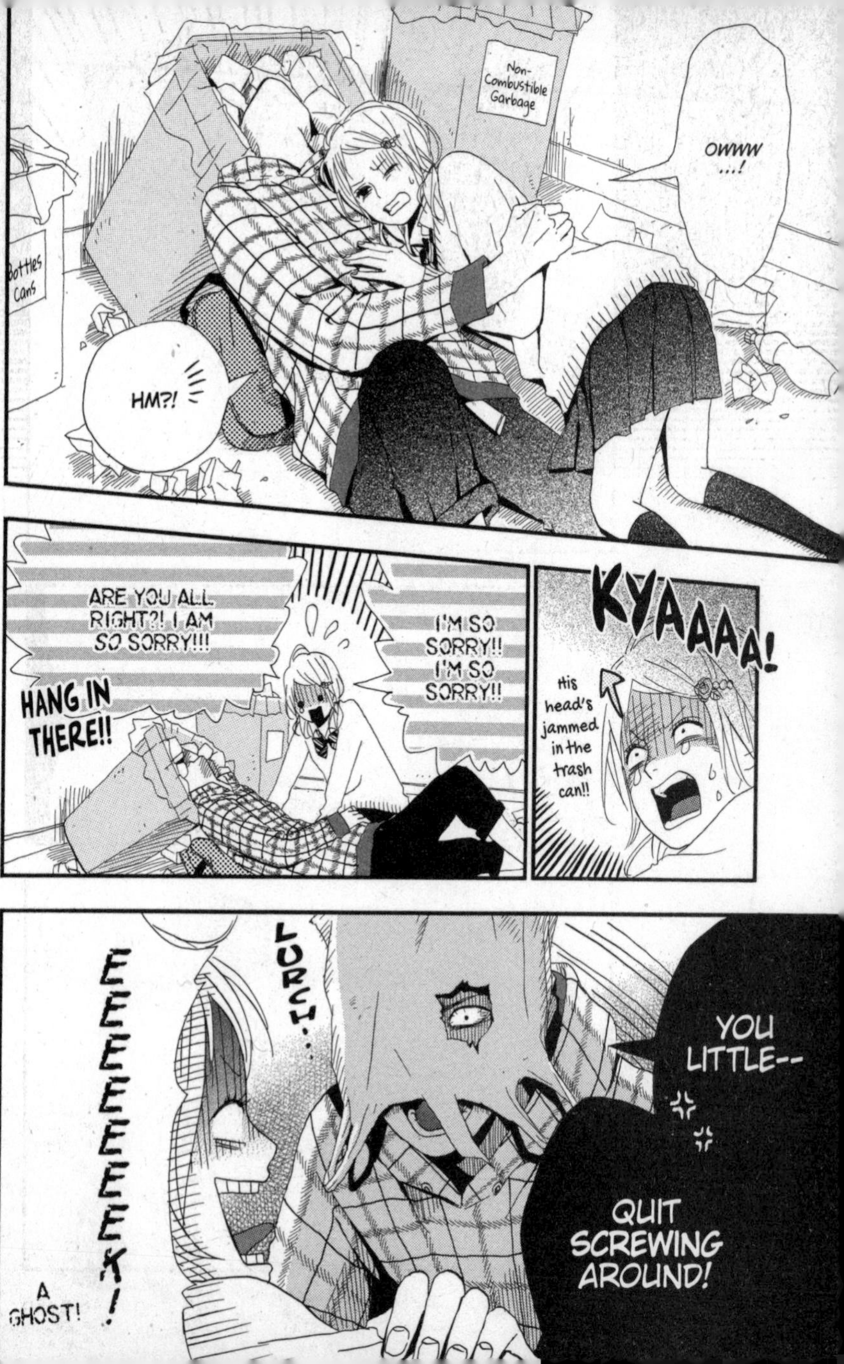
OWWW ...!
Non-Combustible Garbage
Bottles Cans
HM?!
KYAAAA!
His head's jammed in the trash can!!
I'M SO SORRY!! I'M SO SORRY!!
ARE YOU ALL RIGHT?! I AM SO SORRY!!!
HANG IN THERE!!
YOU LITTLE--
QUIT SCREWING AROUND!
LURCH...
EEEEEEEEEK!
A GHOST!

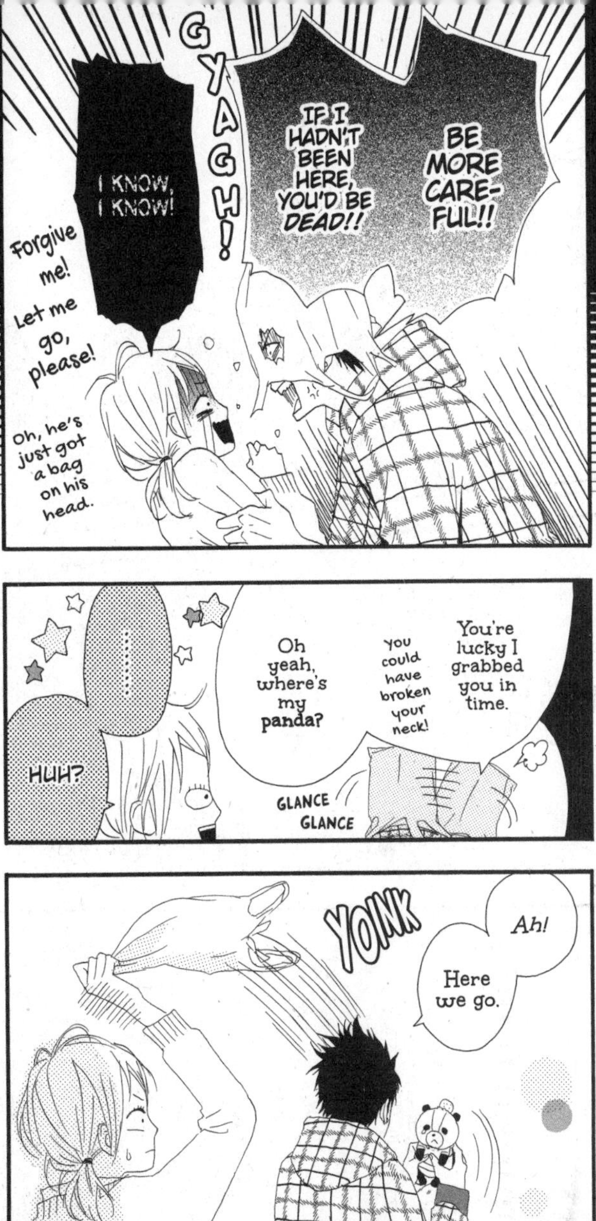
BE MORE CAREFUL!!
IF I HADN'T BEEN HERE, YOU'D BE DEAD!!
GYAGH!
I KNOW, I KNOW!
Forgive me! Let me go, please!
Oh, he's just got a bag on his head.
You're lucky I grabbed you in time.
You could have broken your neck!
Oh yeah, where's my panda?
GLANCE GLANCE
......
HUH?
Ah!
Here we go.
YOINK

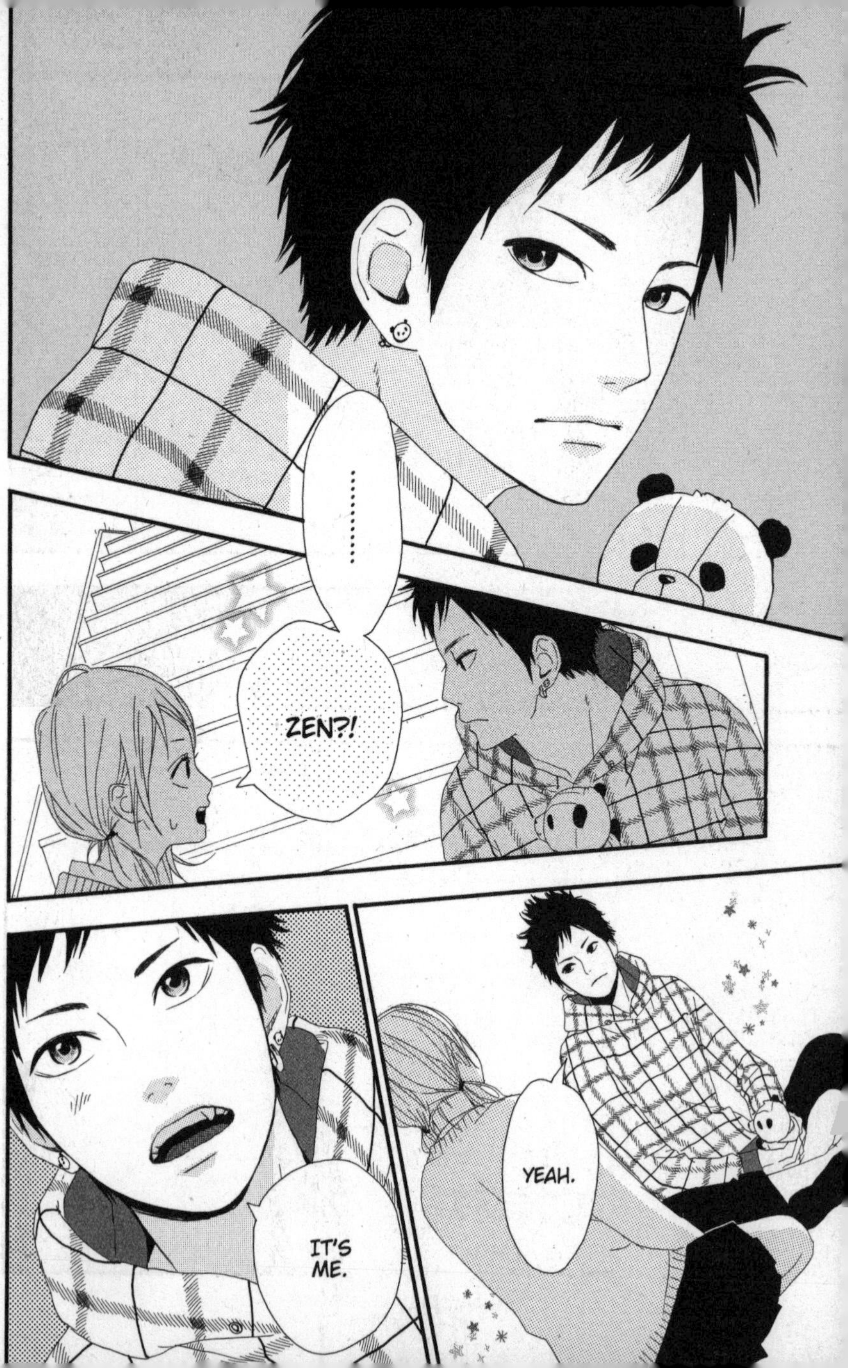
......
ZEN?!
YEAH.
IT'S ME.

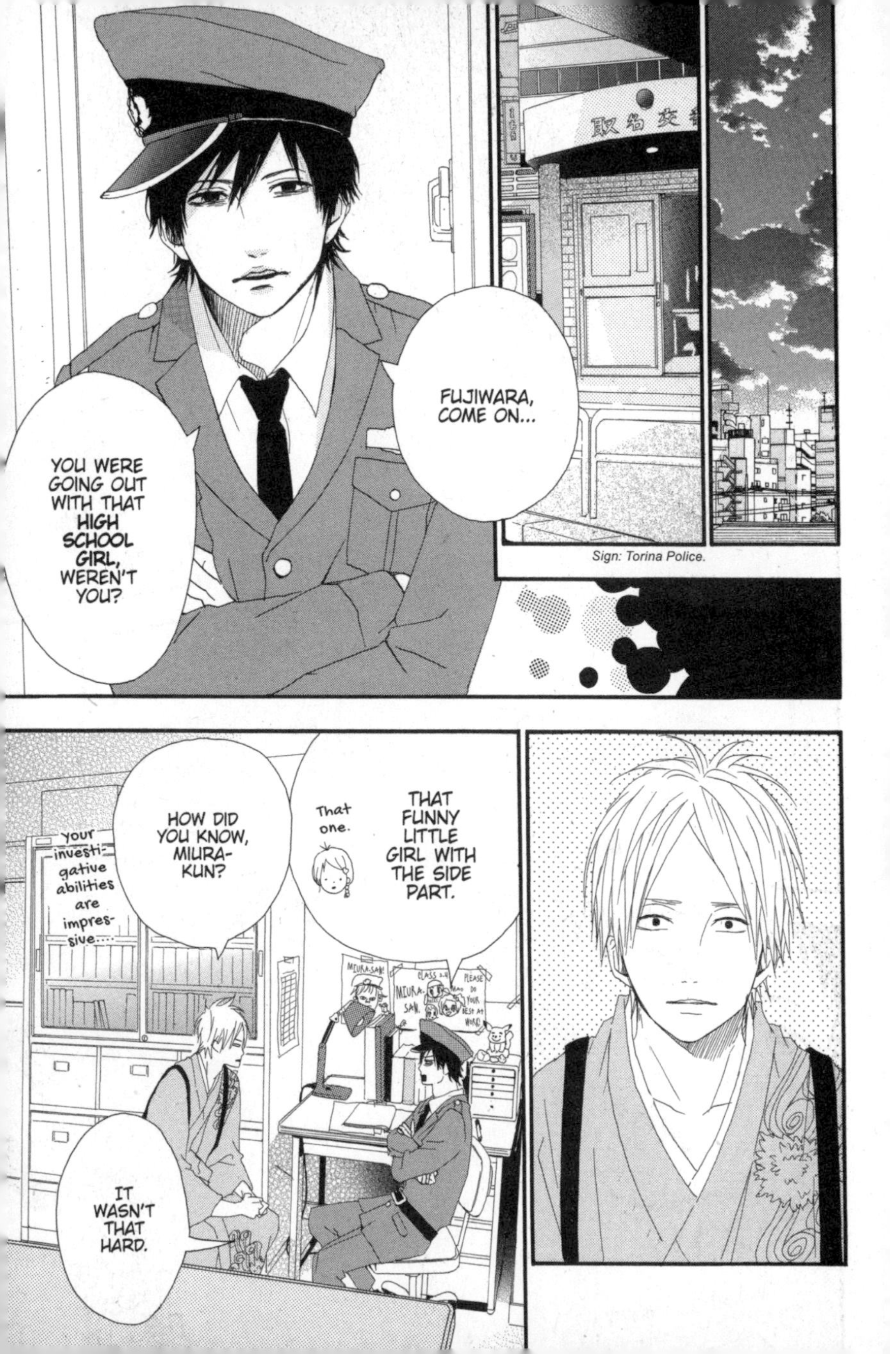
FUJIWARA, COME ON...
YOU WERE GOING OUT WITH THAT HIGH SCHOOL GIRL, WEREN'T YOU?
Sign: Torina Police.
THAT FUNNY LITTLE GIRL WITH THE SIDE PART.
That one.
HOW DID YOU KNOW, MIURA-KUN?
Your investi-gative abilities are impres-sive....
MIURA-SAN!
CLASS 2-4
MIURA-SAN.
PLEASE DO YOUR BEST AT WORK!
IT WASN'T THAT HARD.

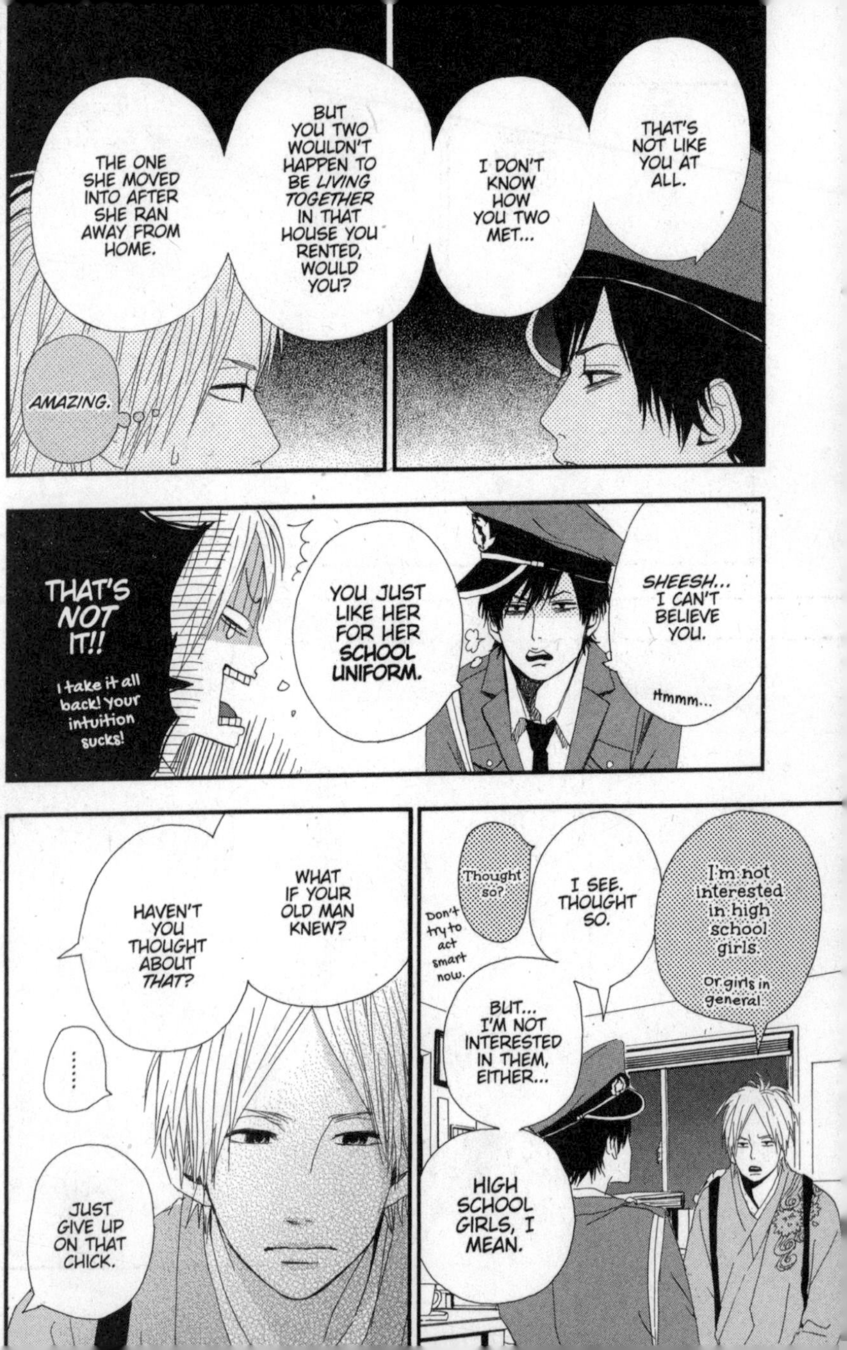
THAT'S NOT LIKE YOU AT ALL.
I DON'T KNOW HOW YOU TWO MET...
BUT YOU TWO WOULDN'T HAPPEN TO BE *LIVING TOGETHER* IN THAT HOUSE YOU RENTED, WOULD YOU?
THE ONE SHE MOVED INTO AFTER SHE RAN AWAY FROM HOME.
AMAZING.
SHEESH... I CAN'T BELIEVE YOU.
Hmmm...
YOU JUST LIKE HER FOR HER **SCHOOL UNIFORM.**
THAT'S *NOT* IT!!
I take it all back! Your intuition sucks!
I'm not interested in high school girls.
Or girls in general.
I SEE. THOUGHT SO.
Thought so?
Don't try to act smart now.
BUT... I'M NOT INTERESTED IN THEM, EITHER...
HIGH SCHOOL GIRLS, I MEAN.
WHAT IF YOUR OLD MAN KNEW?
HAVEN'T YOU THOUGHT ABOUT *THAT?*
......
JUST GIVE UP ON THAT CHICK.

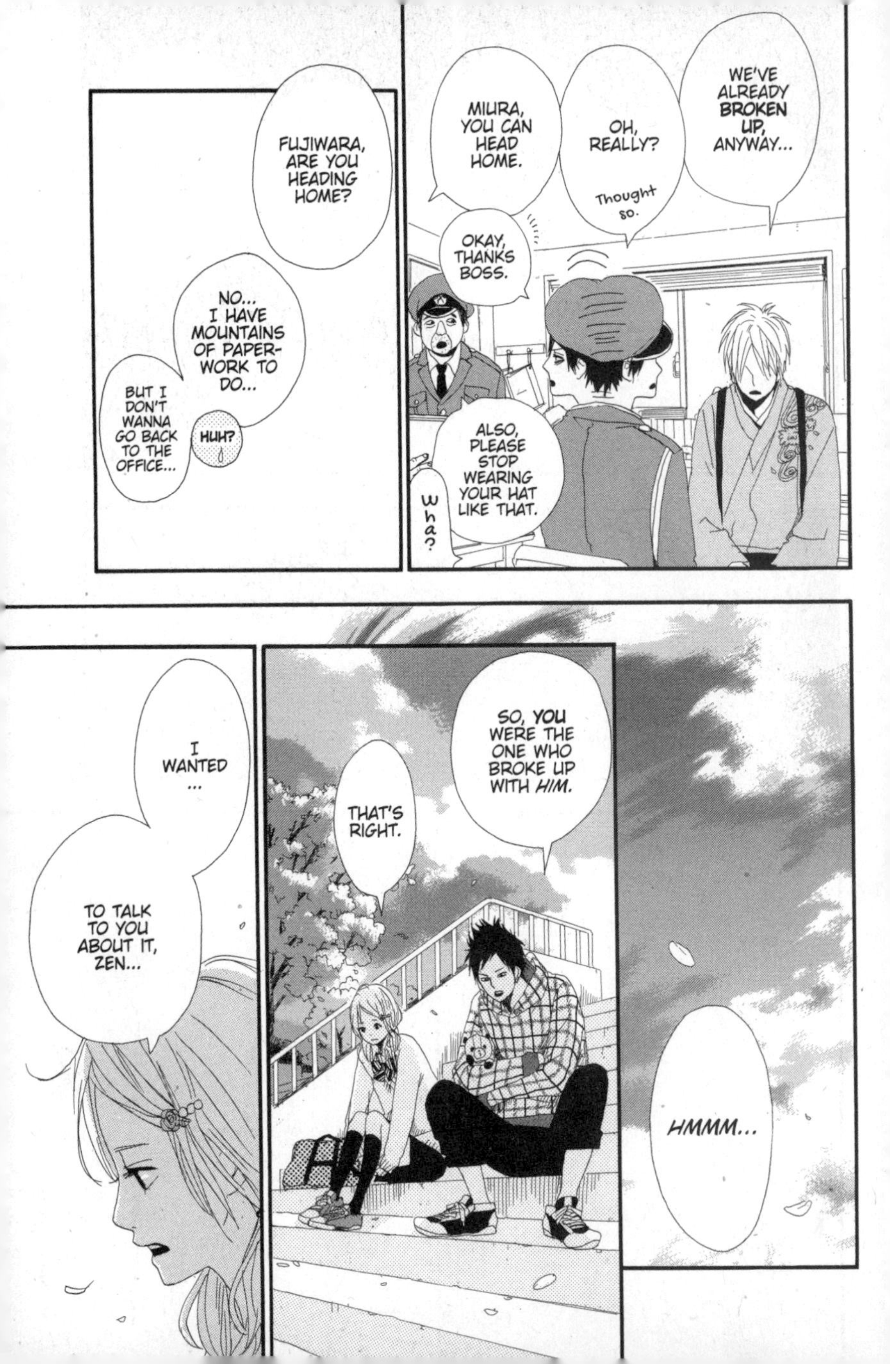
WE'VE ALREADY BROKEN UP, ANYWAY...
OH, REALLY?
Thought so.
MIURA, YOU CAN HEAD HOME.
OKAY, THANKS BOSS.
ALSO, PLEASE STOP WEARING YOUR HAT LIKE THAT.
Wha?
FUJIWARA, ARE YOU HEADING HOME?
NO... I HAVE MOUNTAINS OF PAPER-WORK TO DO...
HUH?
BUT I DON'T WANNA GO BACK TO THE OFFICE...
SO, YOU WERE THE ONE WHO BROKE UP WITH HIM.
THAT'S RIGHT.
HMMM...
I WANTED...
TO TALK TO YOU ABOUT IT, ZEN...

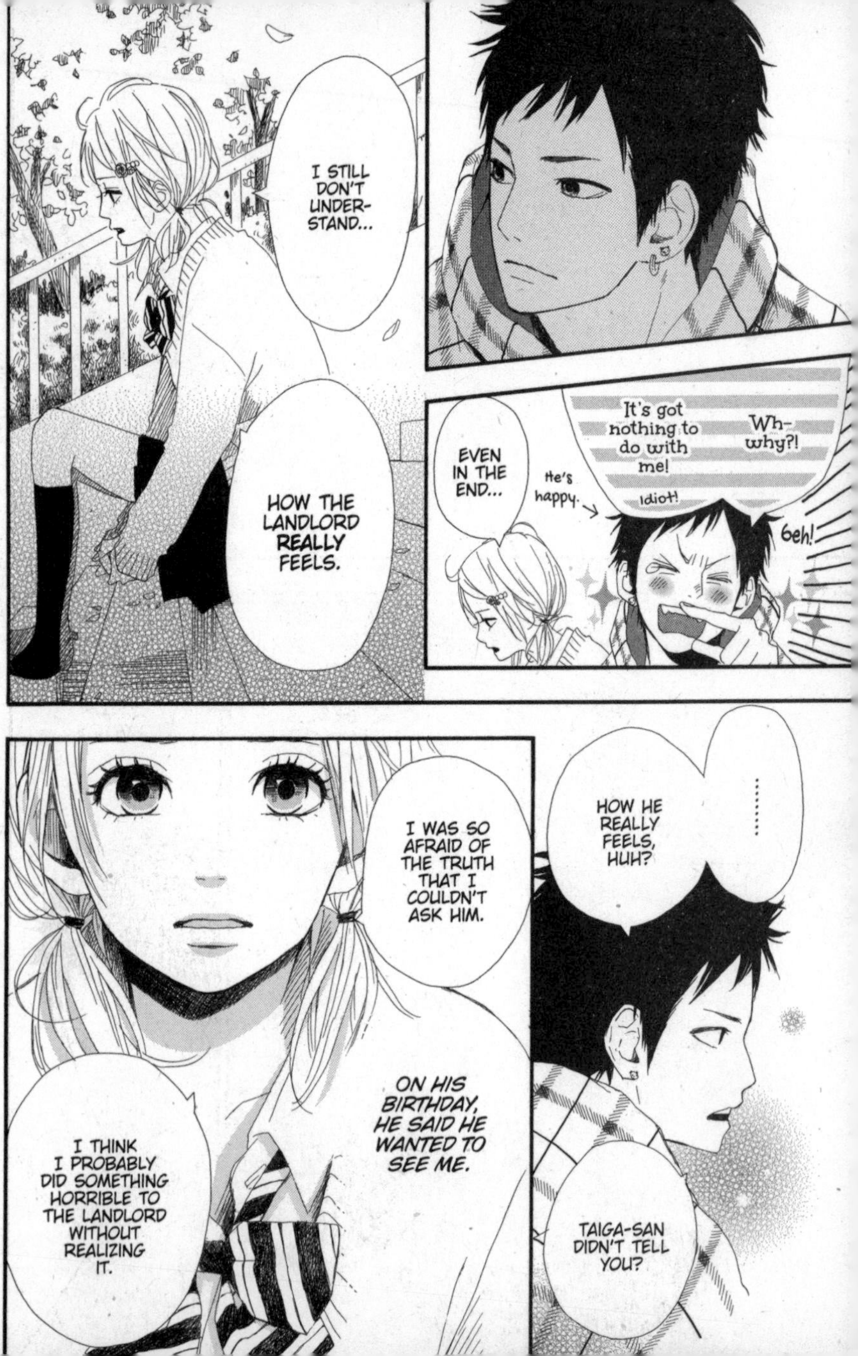
Wh-why?!
It's got nothing to do with me!
Idiot!
Geh!
He's happy.
EVEN IN THE END...
I STILL DON'T UNDER-STAND...
HOW THE LANDLORD REALLY FEELS.
......
HOW HE REALLY FEELS, HUH?
TAIGA-SAN DIDN'T TELL YOU?
I WAS SO AFRAID OF THE TRUTH THAT I COULDN'T ASK HIM.
ON HIS BIRTHDAY, HE SAID HE WANTED TO SEE ME.
I THINK I PROBABLY DID SOMETHING HORRIBLE TO THE LANDLORD WITHOUT REALIZING IT.

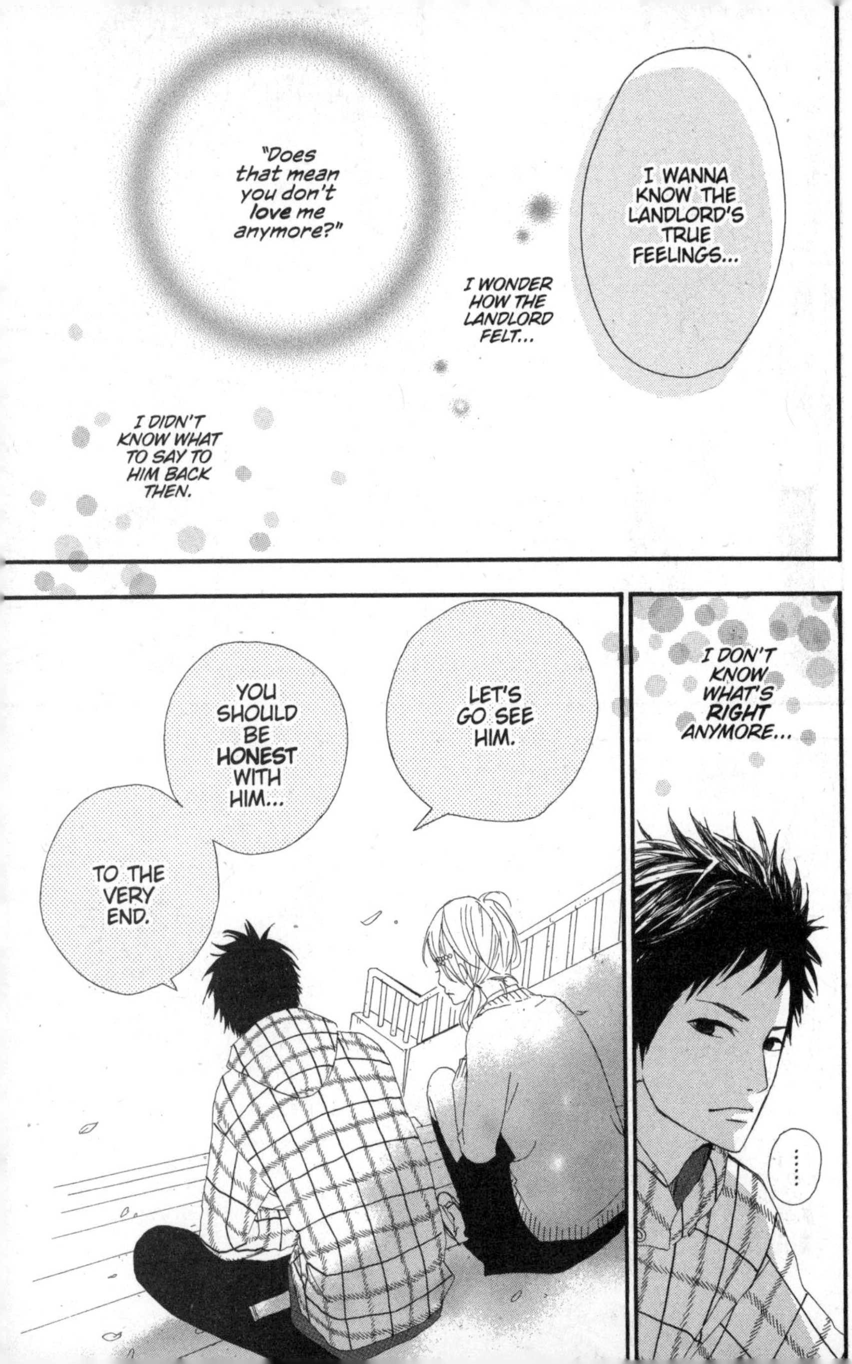
I WANNA KNOW THE LANDLORD'S TRUE FEELINGS...
I WONDER HOW THE LANDLORD FELT...
"Does that mean you don't love me anymore?"
I DIDN'T KNOW WHAT TO SAY TO HIM BACK THEN.
I DON'T KNOW WHAT'S RIGHT ANYMORE...
......
LET'S GO SEE HIM.
YOU SHOULD BE HONEST WITH HIM...
TO THE VERY END.

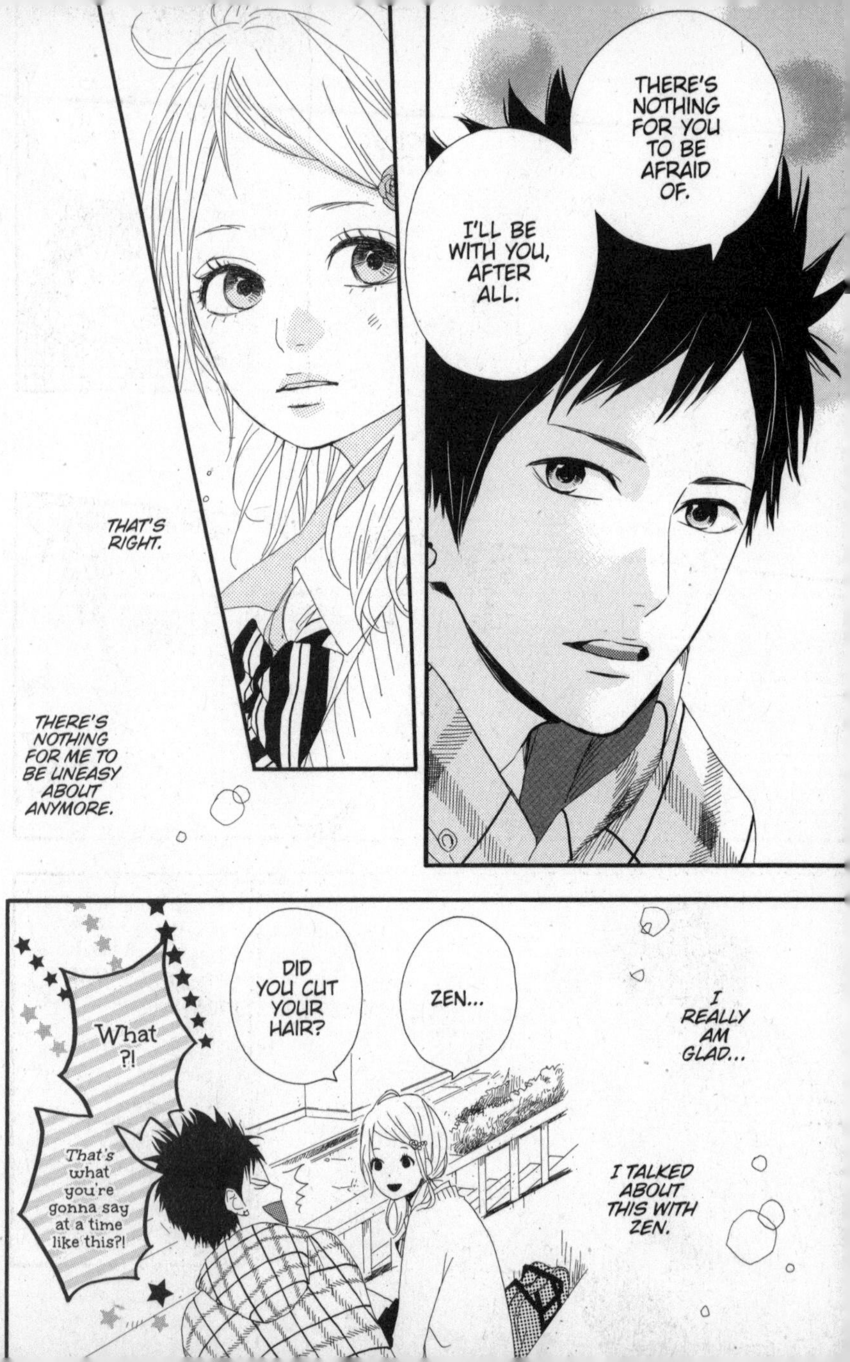
THERE'S NOTHING FOR YOU TO BE AFRAID OF.
I'LL BE WITH YOU, AFTER ALL.
THAT'S RIGHT.
THERE'S NOTHING FOR ME TO BE UNEASY ABOUT ANYMORE.
I REALLY AM GLAD...
I TALKED ABOUT THIS WITH ZEN.
ZEN...
DID YOU CUT YOUR HAIR?
What ?!
That's what you're gonna say at a time like this?!

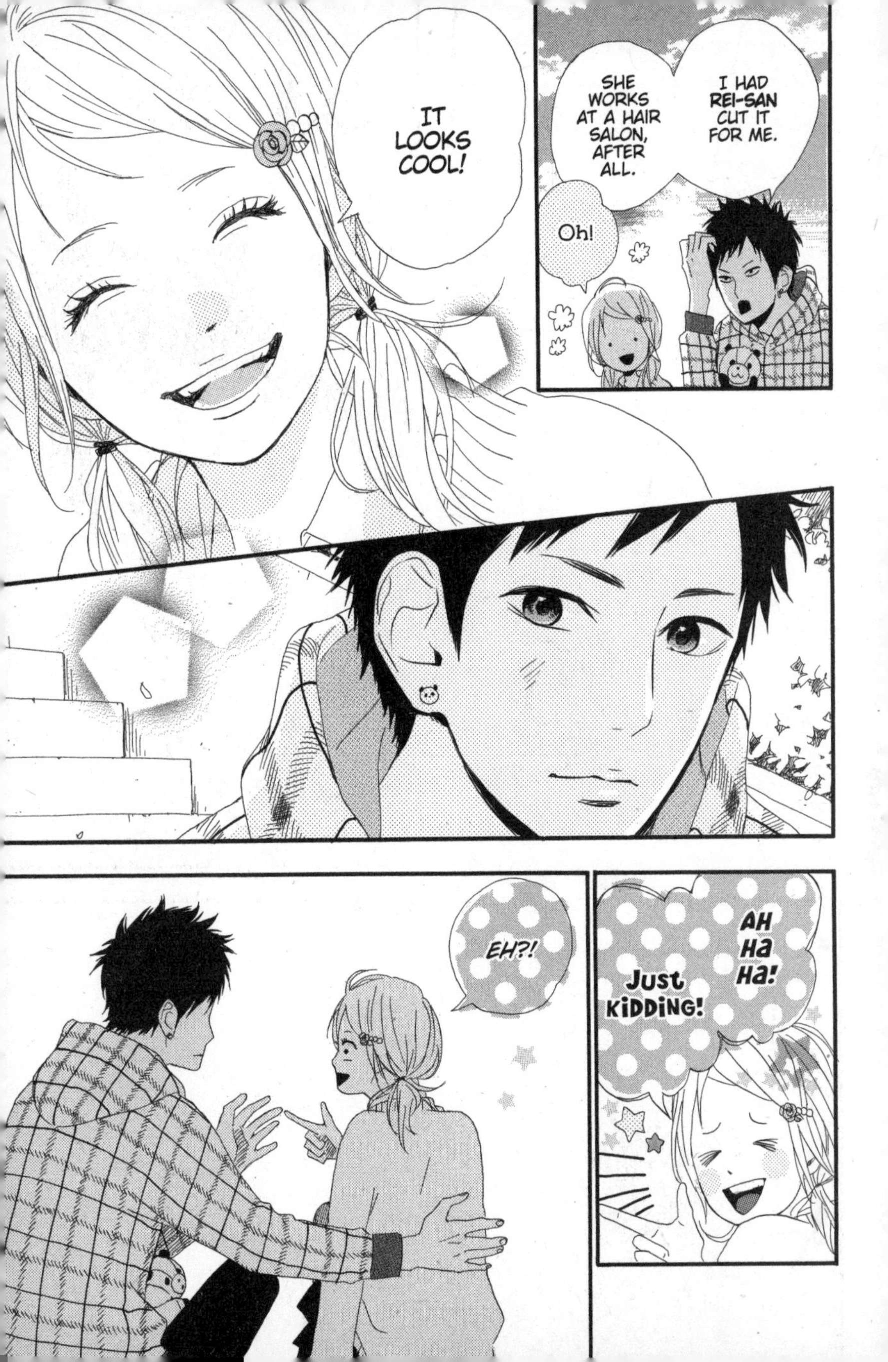
I HAD REI-SAN CUT IT FOR ME.
SHE WORKS AT A HAIR SALON, AFTER ALL.
Oh!
IT LOOKS COOL!
AH HA HA!
Just KIDDING!
EH?!

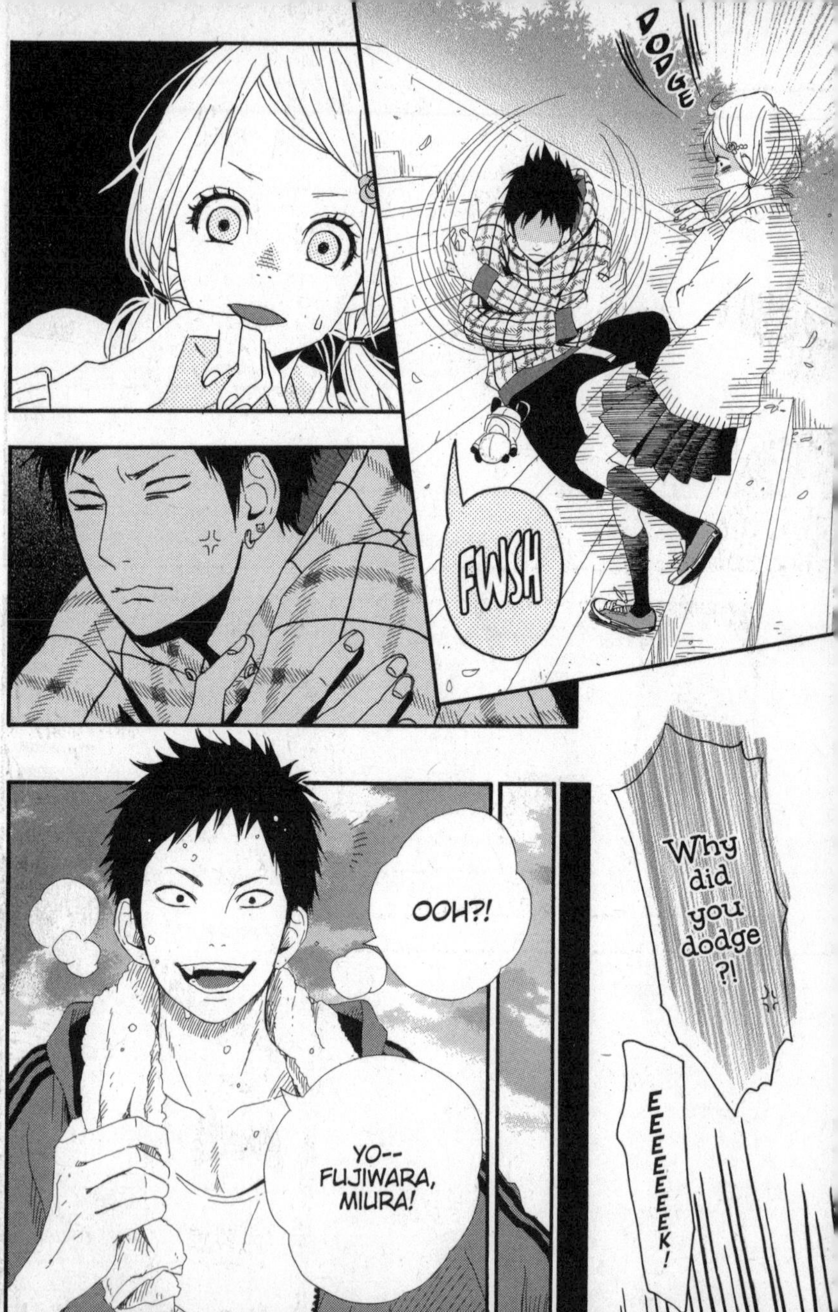
DODGE
FWSH
Why did you dodge?!
EEEEEEEK!
OOH?!
YO-- FUJIWARA, MIURA!

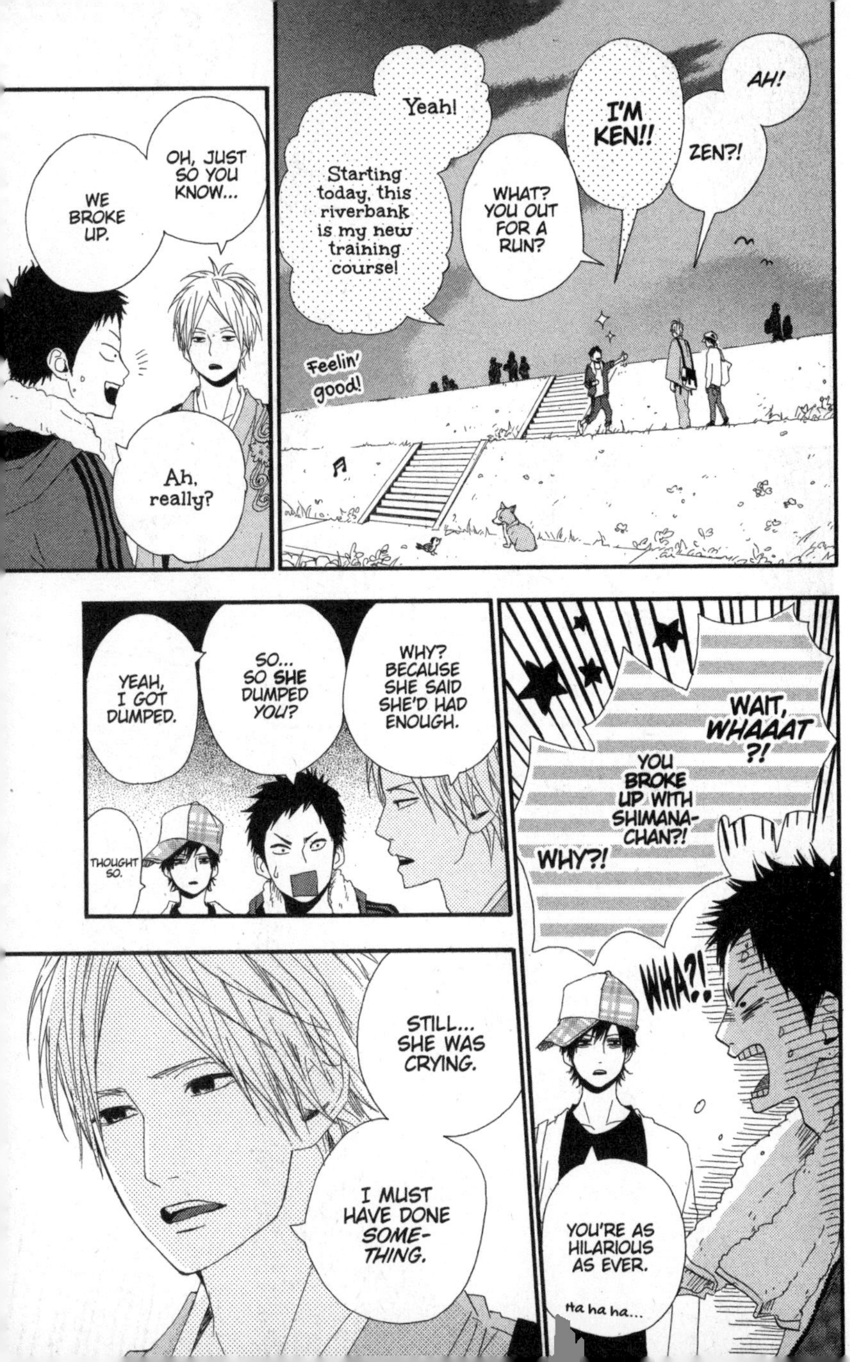
AH! ZEN?!
I'M KEN!!
WHAT? YOU OUT FOR A RUN?
Yeah!
Starting today, this riverbank is my new training course!
Feelin' good!
OH, JUST SO YOU KNOW...
WE BROKE UP.
Ah, really?
WAIT, WHAAAT?!
YOU BROKE UP WITH SHIMANA-CHAN?!
WHY?!
WHA?!
YOU'RE AS HILARIOUS AS EVER.
Ha ha ha...
WHY? BECAUSE SHE SAID SHE'D HAD ENOUGH.
SO... SO SHE DUMPED YOU?
YEAH, I GOT DUMPED.
THOUGHT SO.
STILL... SHE WAS CRYING.
I MUST HAVE DONE SOMETHING.

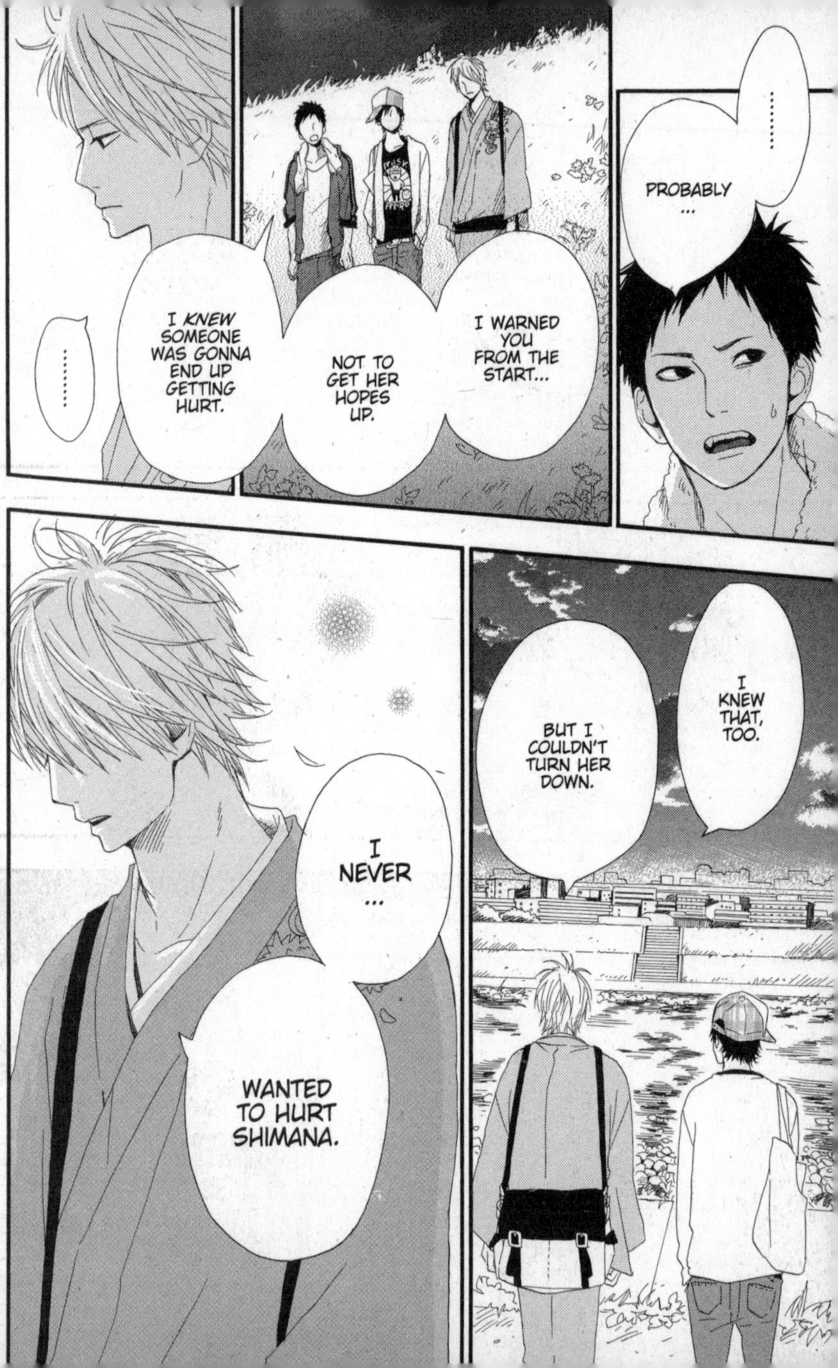
......
PROBABLY ...
I WARNED YOU FROM THE START...
NOT TO GET HER HOPES UP.
I *KNEW* SOMEONE WAS GONNA END UP GETTING HURT.
......
I KNEW THAT, TOO.
BUT I COULDN'T TURN HER DOWN.
I NEVER ...
WANTED TO HURT SHIMANA.

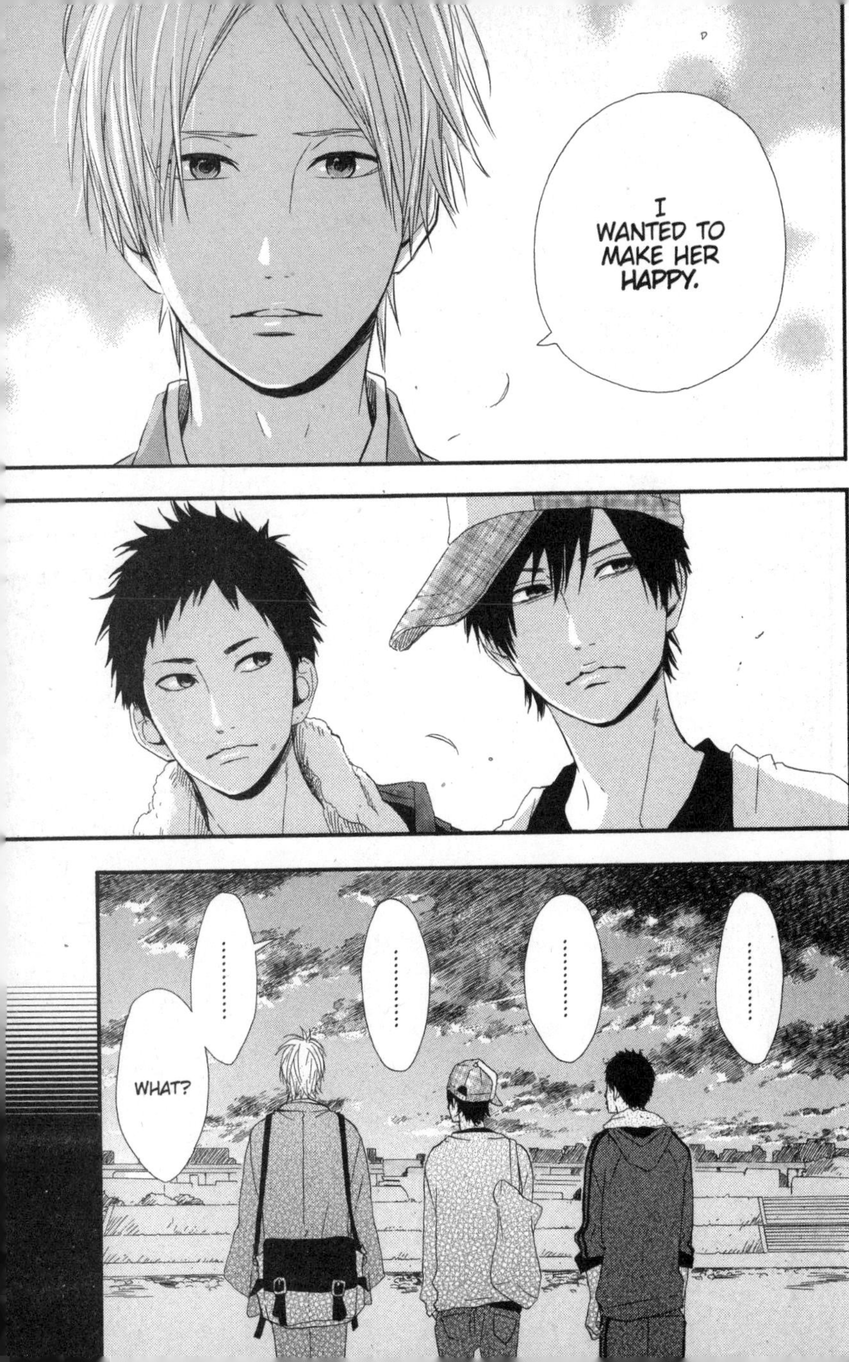
I WANTED TO MAKE HER HAPPY.
......
......
......
......
WHAT?

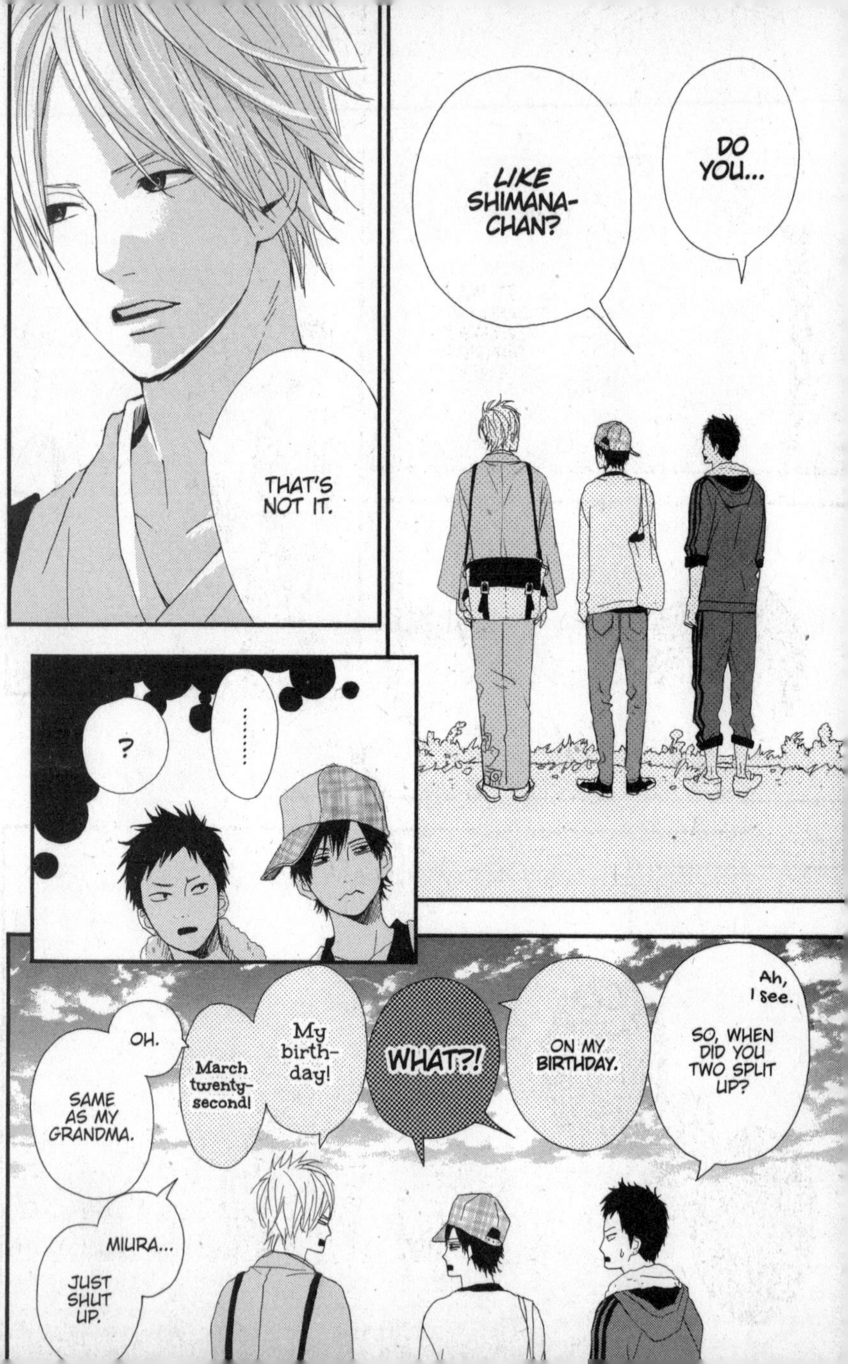
DO YOU...
LIKE SHIMANA-CHAN?
THAT'S NOT IT.
......
?
Ah, I see.
SO, WHEN DID YOU TWO SPLIT UP?
ON MY BIRTHDAY.
WHAT?!
My birth-day!
March twenty-second!
OH.
SAME AS MY GRANDMA.
MIURA...
JUST SHUT UP.

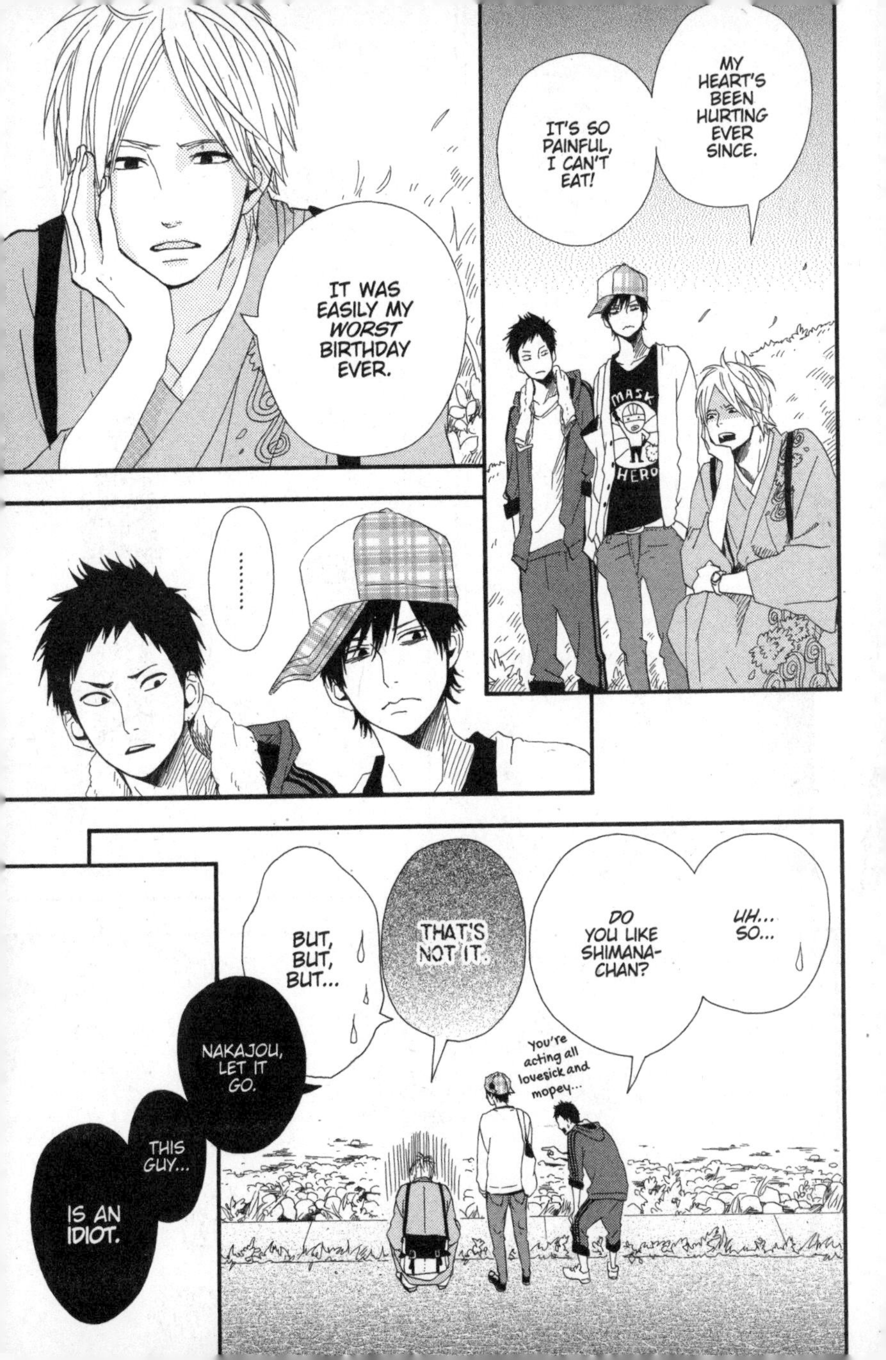
MY HEART'S BEEN HURTING EVER SINCE.
IT'S SO PAINFUL, I CAN'T EAT!
IT WAS EASILY MY *WORST* BIRTHDAY EVER.
......
UH... SO...
DO YOU LIKE SHIMANA-CHAN?
You're acting all lovesick and mopey...
THAT'S NOT IT.
BUT, BUT, BUT...
NAKAJOU, LET IT GO.
THIS GUY...
IS AN IDIOT.

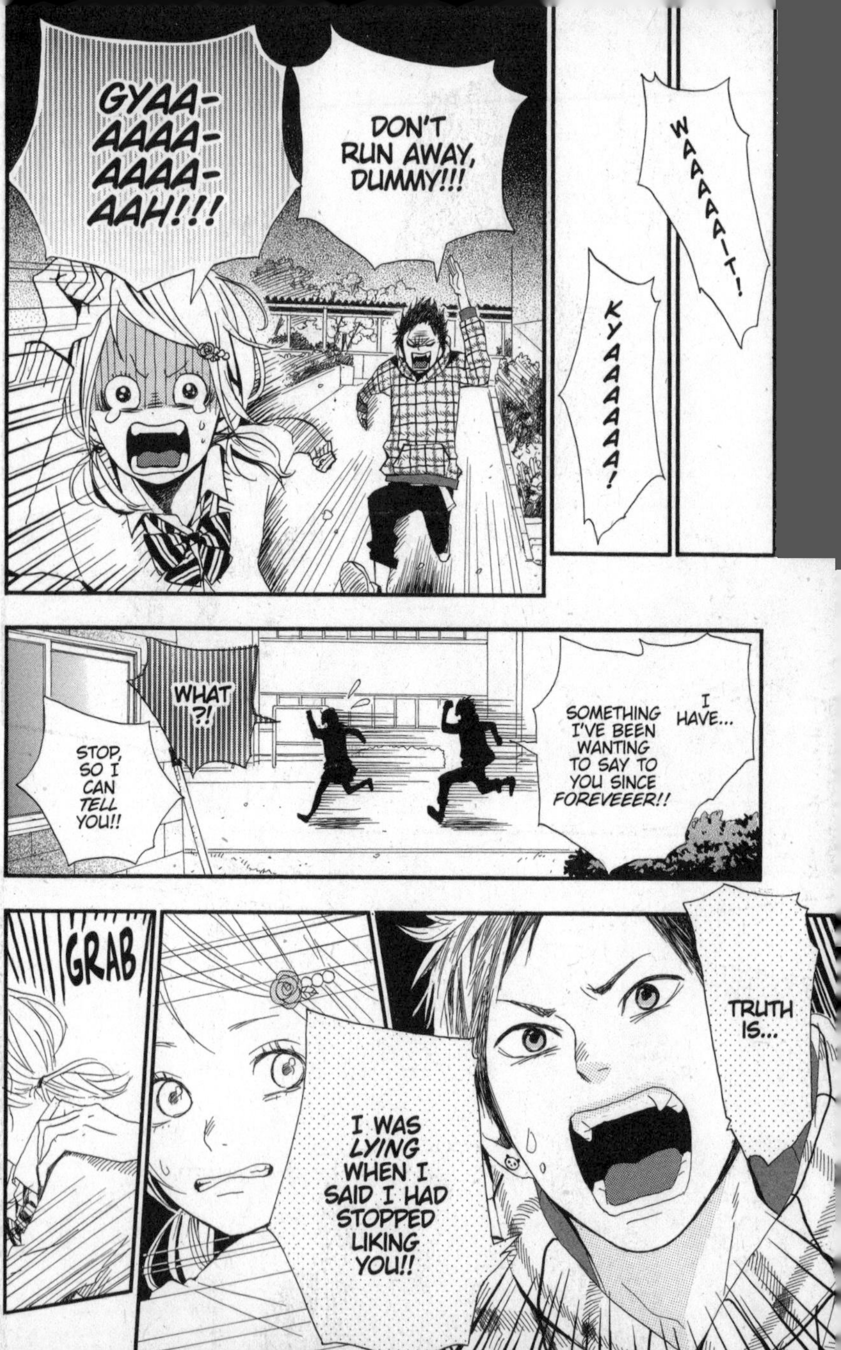
WAAAAAIT!
KYAAAAAAA!
DON'T RUN AWAY, DUMMY!!!
GYAA-AAAA-AAAA-AAH!!!
I HAVE... SOMETHING I'VE BEEN WANTING TO SAY TO YOU SINCE FOREVEEER!!
WHAT?!
STOP, SO I CAN TELL YOU!!
TRUTH IS...
I WAS LYING WHEN I SAID I HAD STOPPED LIKING YOU!!
GRAB

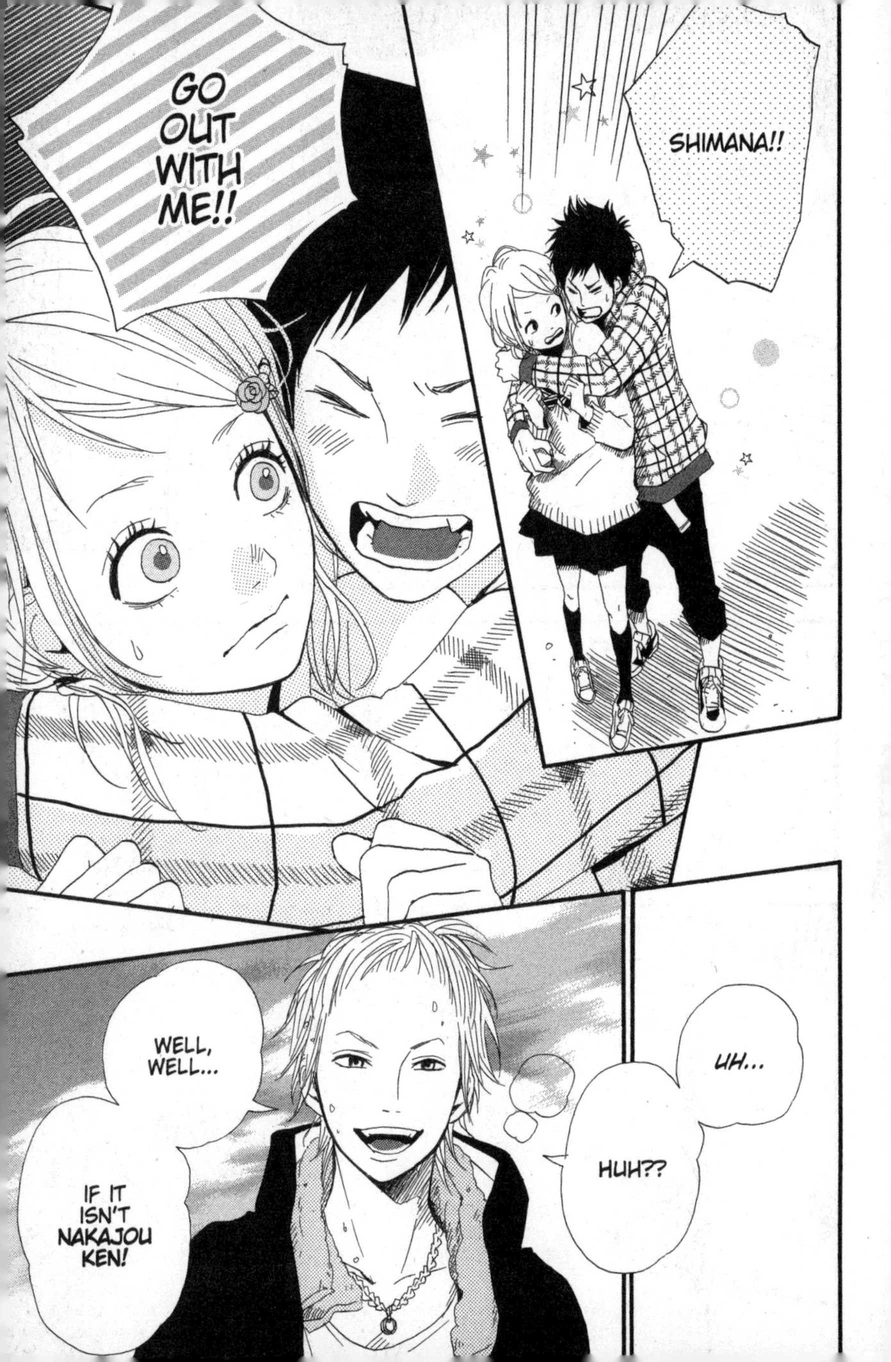
SHIMANA!!
GO OUT WITH ME!!
UH...
HUH??
WELL, WELL...
IF IT ISN'T NAKAJOU KEN!

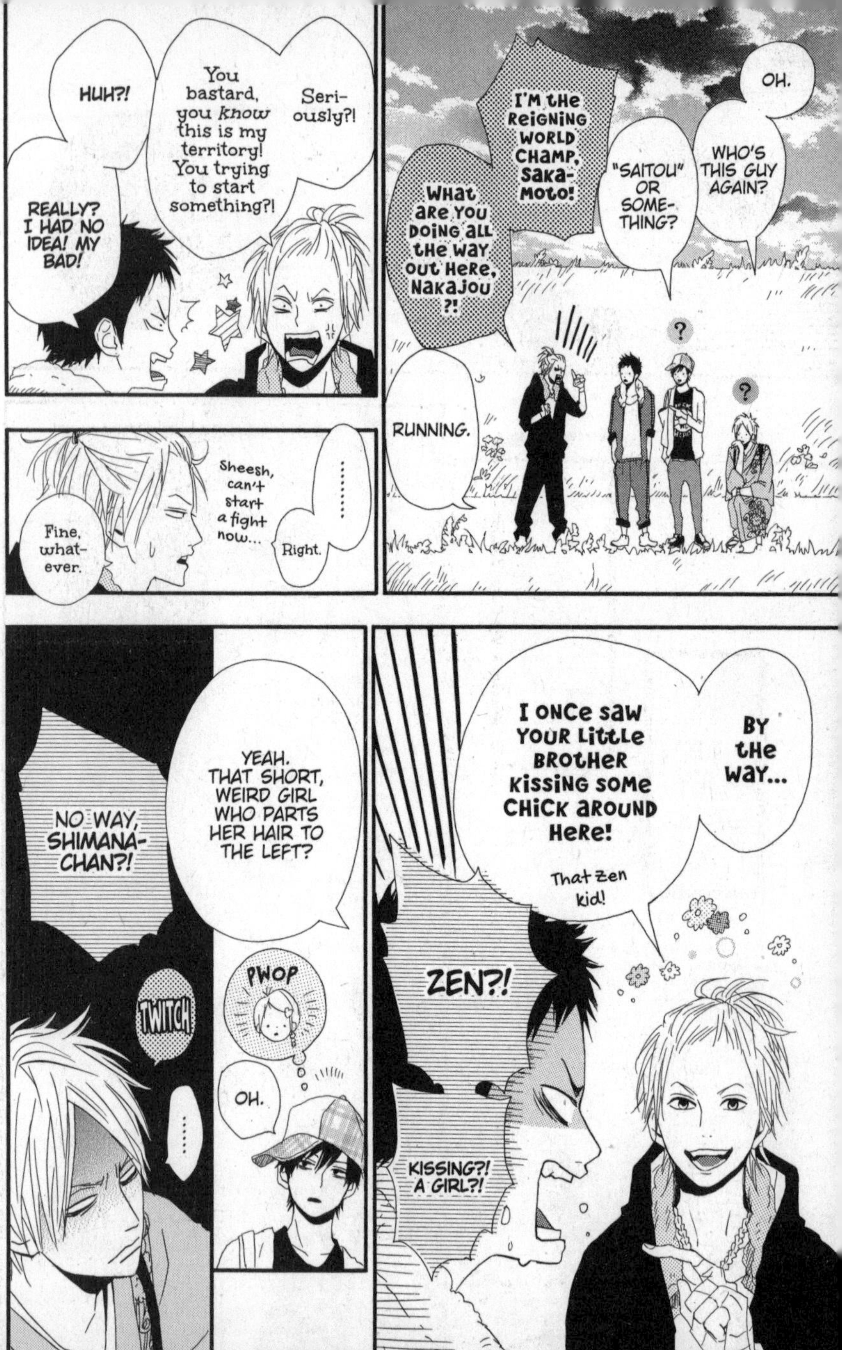
OH.
WHO'S THIS GUY AGAIN?
"SAITOU" OR SOMETHING?
I'M THE REIGNING WORLD CHAMP, SAKAMOTO!
What are you doing all the way out here, Nakajou?!
RUNNING.
Seriously?!
You bastard, you *know* this is my territory! You trying to start something?!
HUH?!
REALLY? I HAD NO IDEA! MY BAD!
......
Right.
Sheesh, can't start a fight now...
Fine, whatever.
By the way...
I once saw your little brother kissing some chick around here!
That Zen kid!
ZEN?!
KISSING?! A GIRL?!
YEAH. THAT SHORT, WEIRD GIRL WHO PARTS HER HAIR TO THE LEFT?
NO WAY, SHIMANA-CHAN?!
PWOP
TWITCH
OH.
......

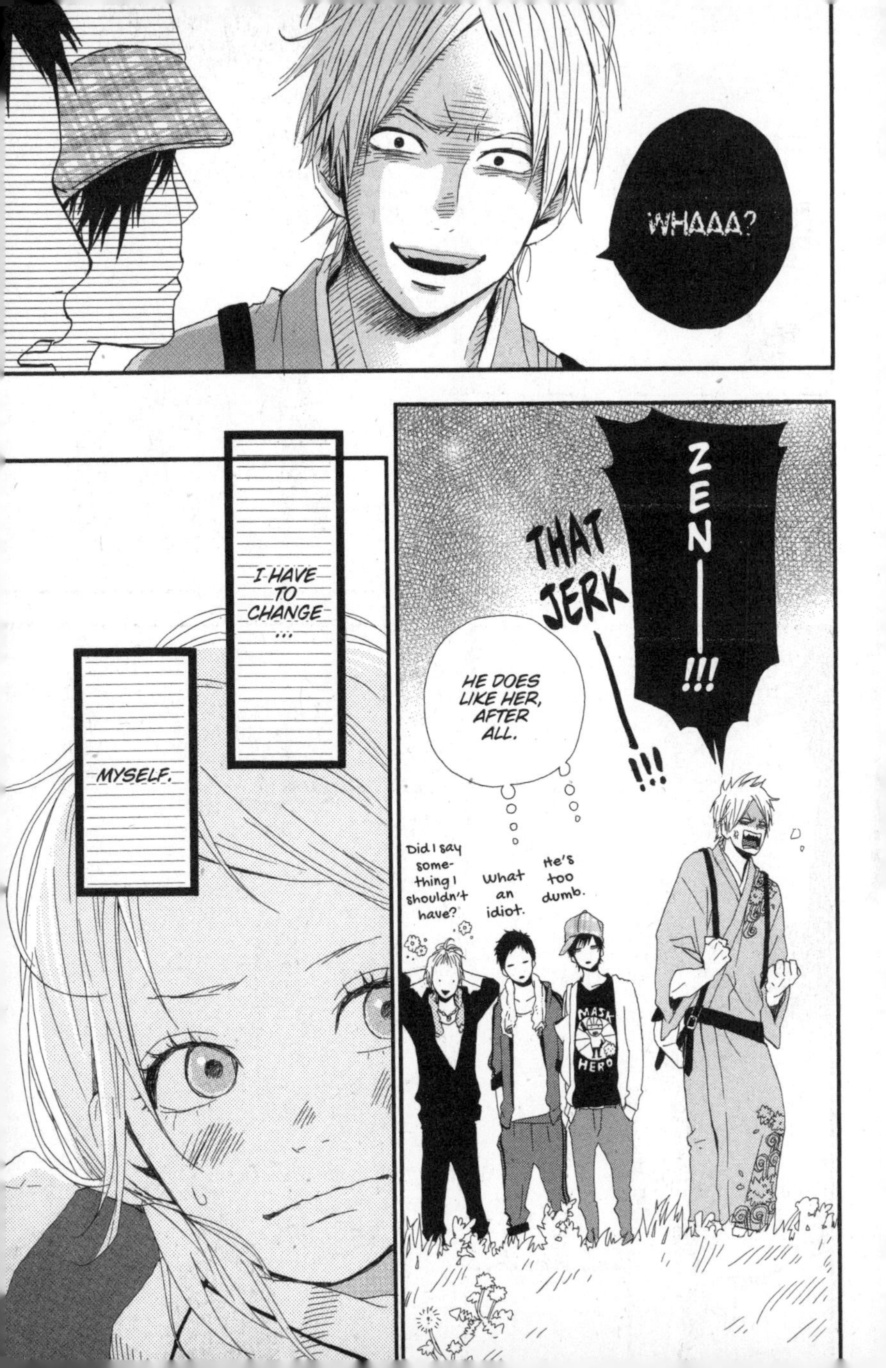
WHAAA?
ZEN—!!!
THAT JERK!!!
HE DOES LIKE HER, AFTER ALL.
He's too dumb.
What an idiot.
Did I say something I shouldn't have?
I HAVE TO CHANGE...
MYSELF.

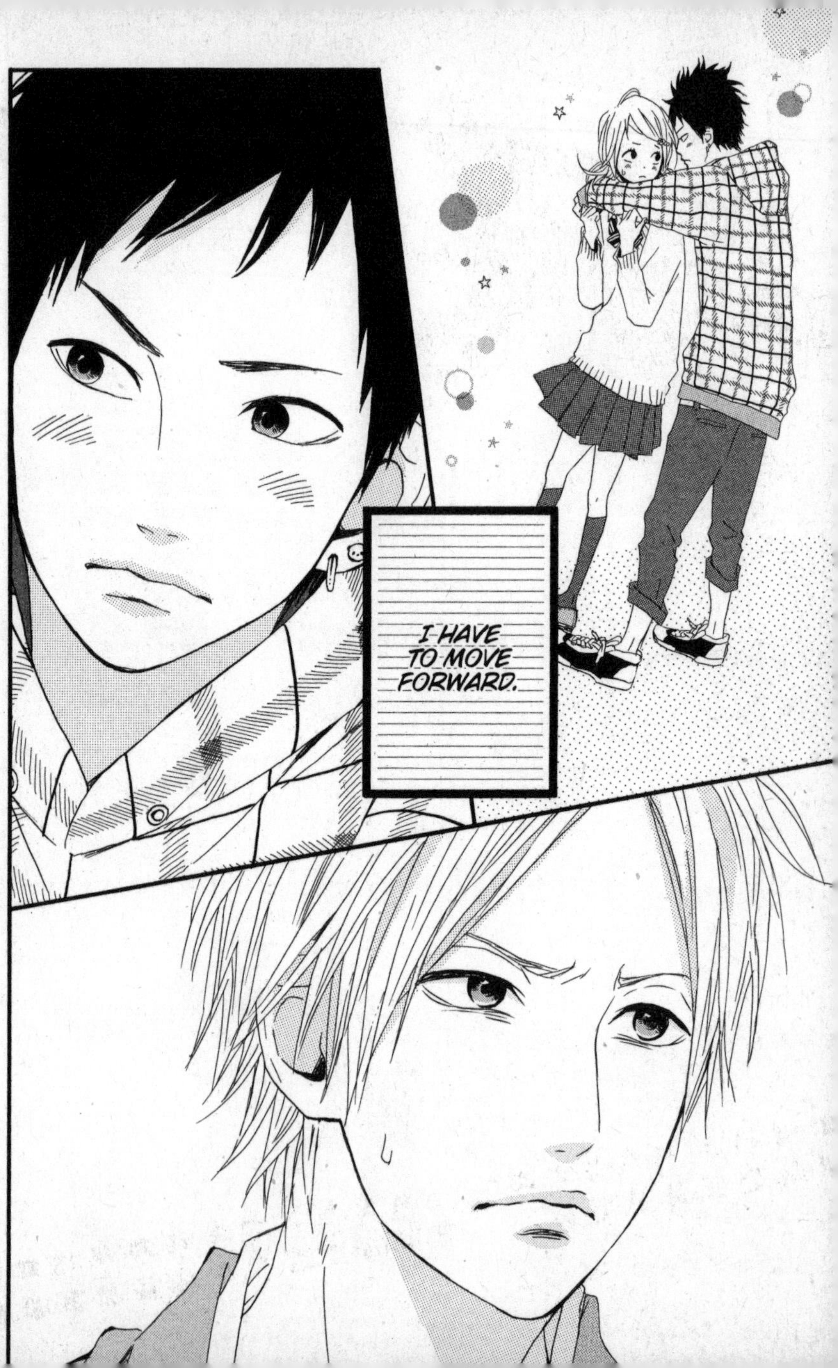
I HAVE TO MOVE FORWARD.

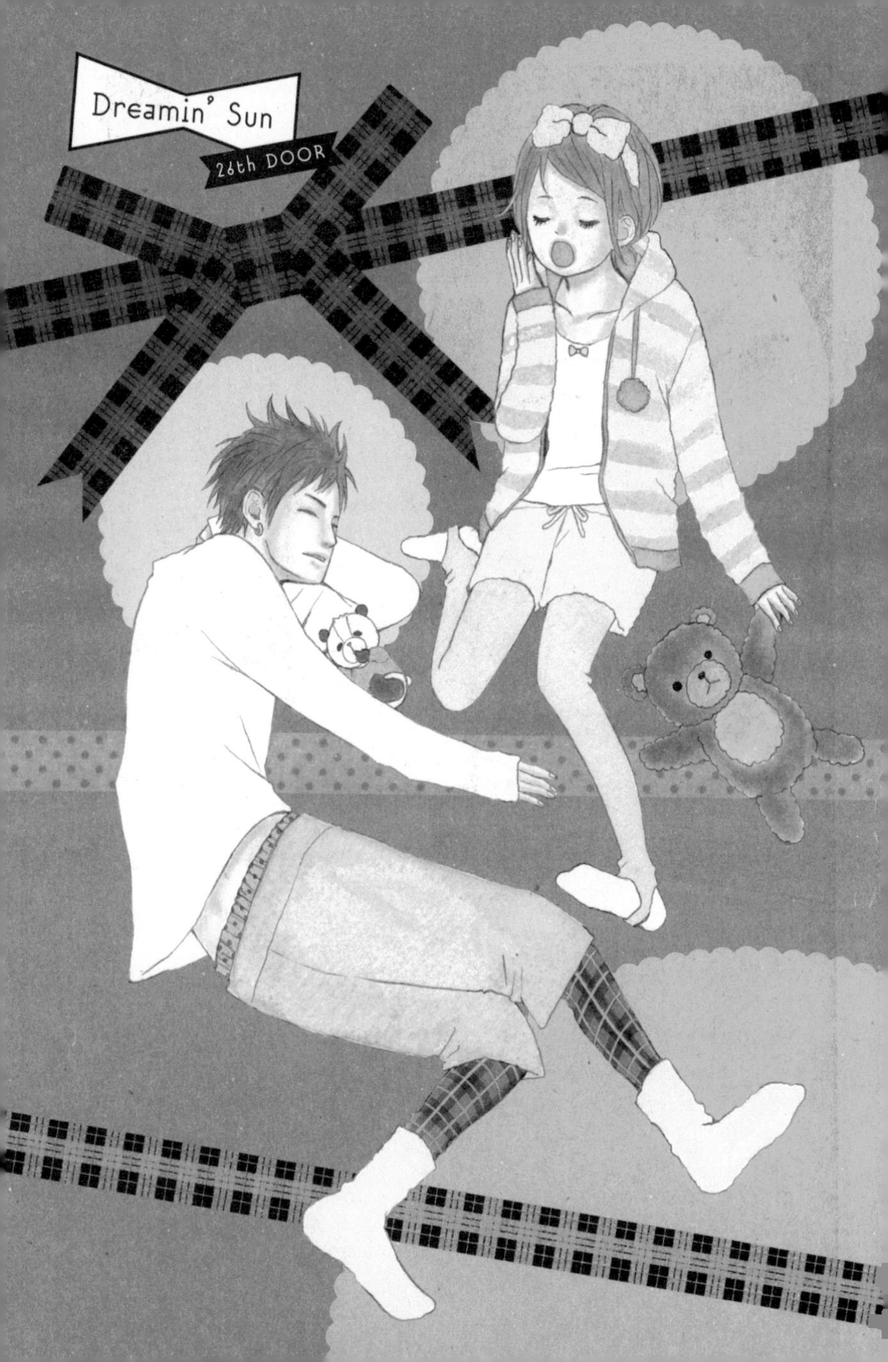
Dreamin' Sun
26th DOOR

Dreamin'
Sun

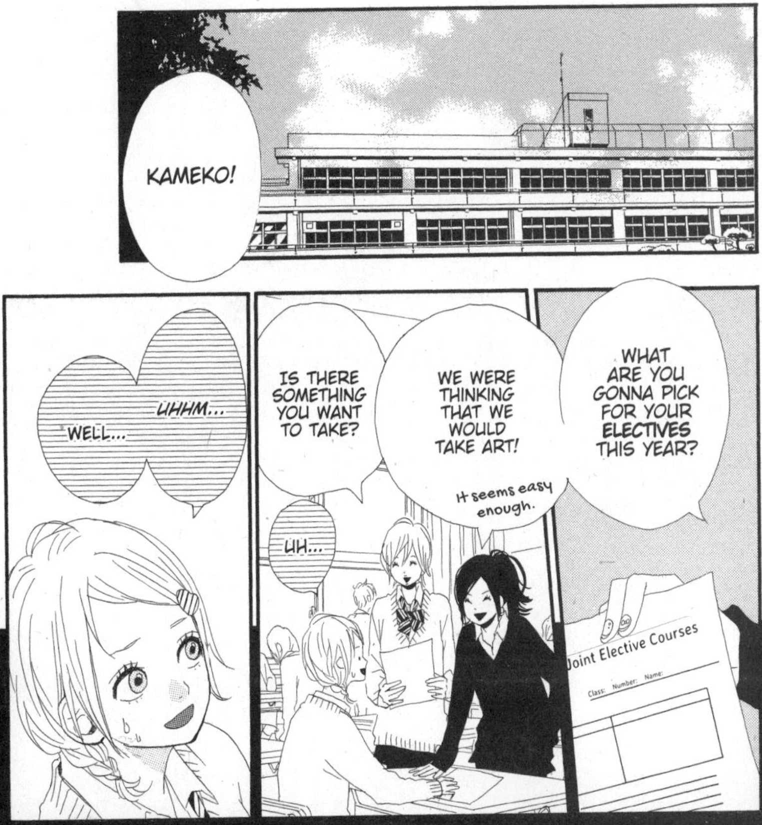
KAMEKO!
WHAT ARE YOU GONNA PICK FOR YOUR ELECTIVES THIS YEAR?
Joint Elective Courses
Class: Number: Name:
WE WERE THINKING THAT WE WOULD TAKE ART!
It seems easy enough.
IS THERE SOMETHING YOU WANT TO TAKE?
UH...
UHHM...
WELL...

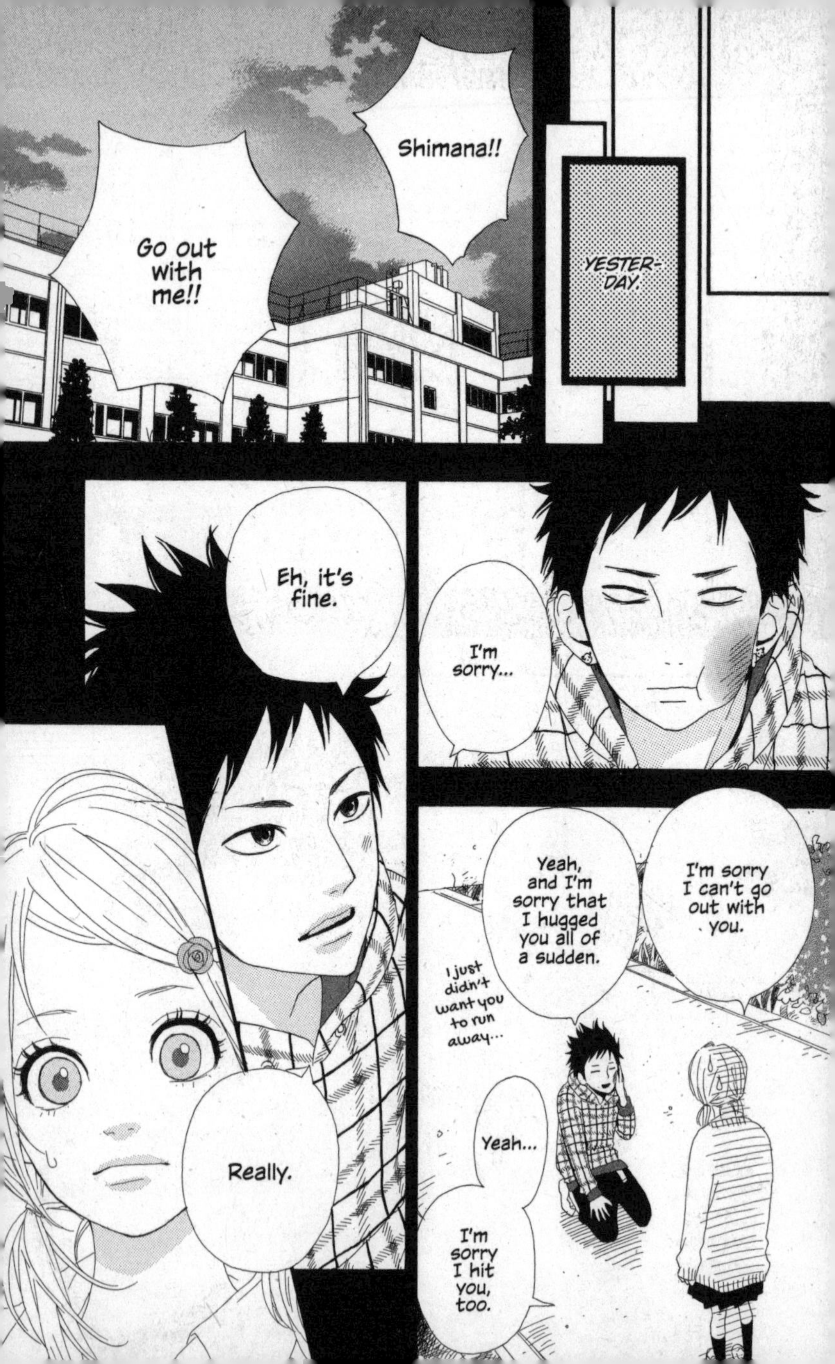
YESTER-DAY.
Shimana!!
Go out with me!!
I'm sorry...
I'm sorry I can't go out with you.
Yeah, and I'm sorry that I hugged you all of a sudden.
I just didn't want you to run away...
Yeah...
I'm sorry I hit you, too.
Eh, it's fine.
Really.

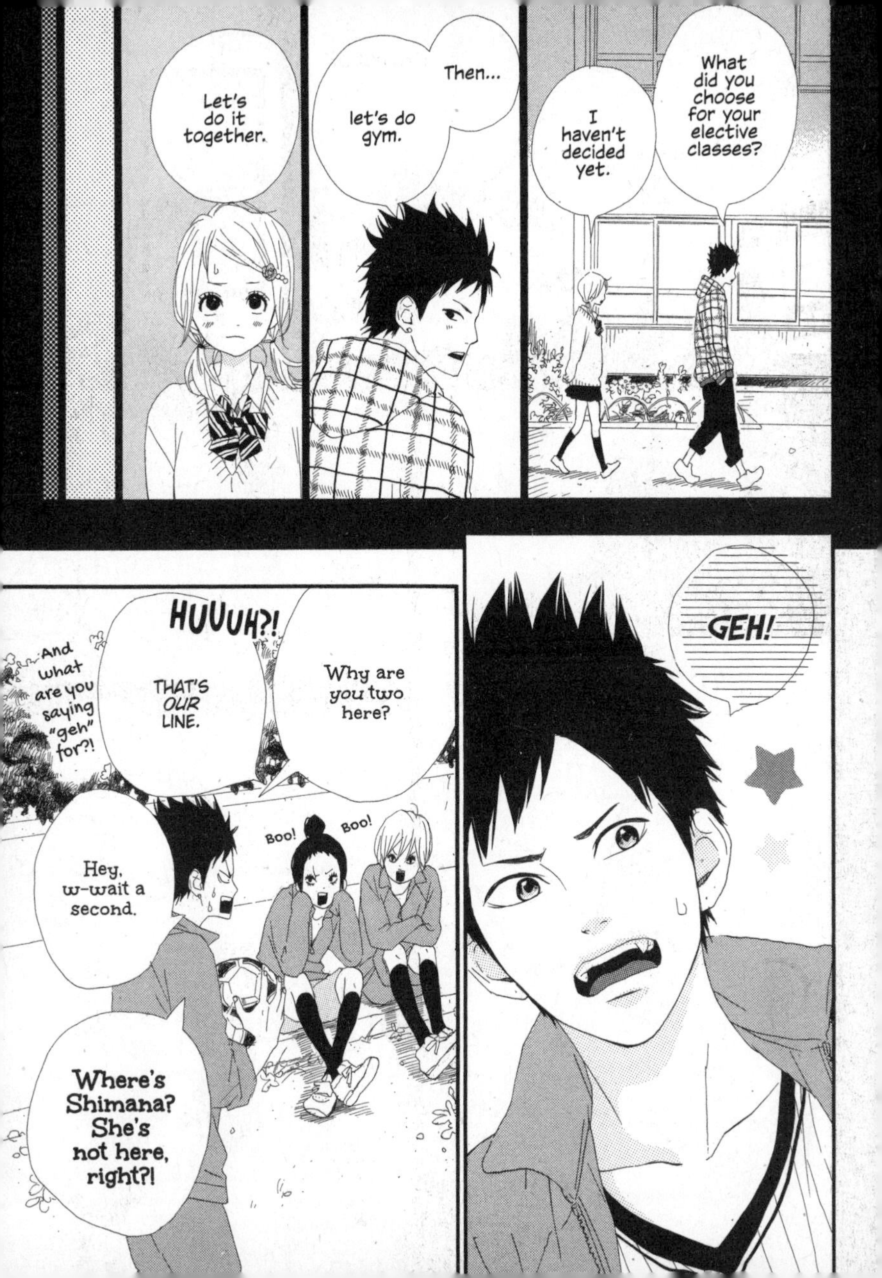

What did you choose for your elective classes?
I haven't decided yet.
Then...
let's do gym.
Let's do it together.
GEH!
Why are you two here?
HUUUH?!
THAT'S OUR LINE.
And what are you saying "geh" for?!
Boo!
Boo!
Hey, w-wait a second.
Where's Shimana? She's not here, right?!

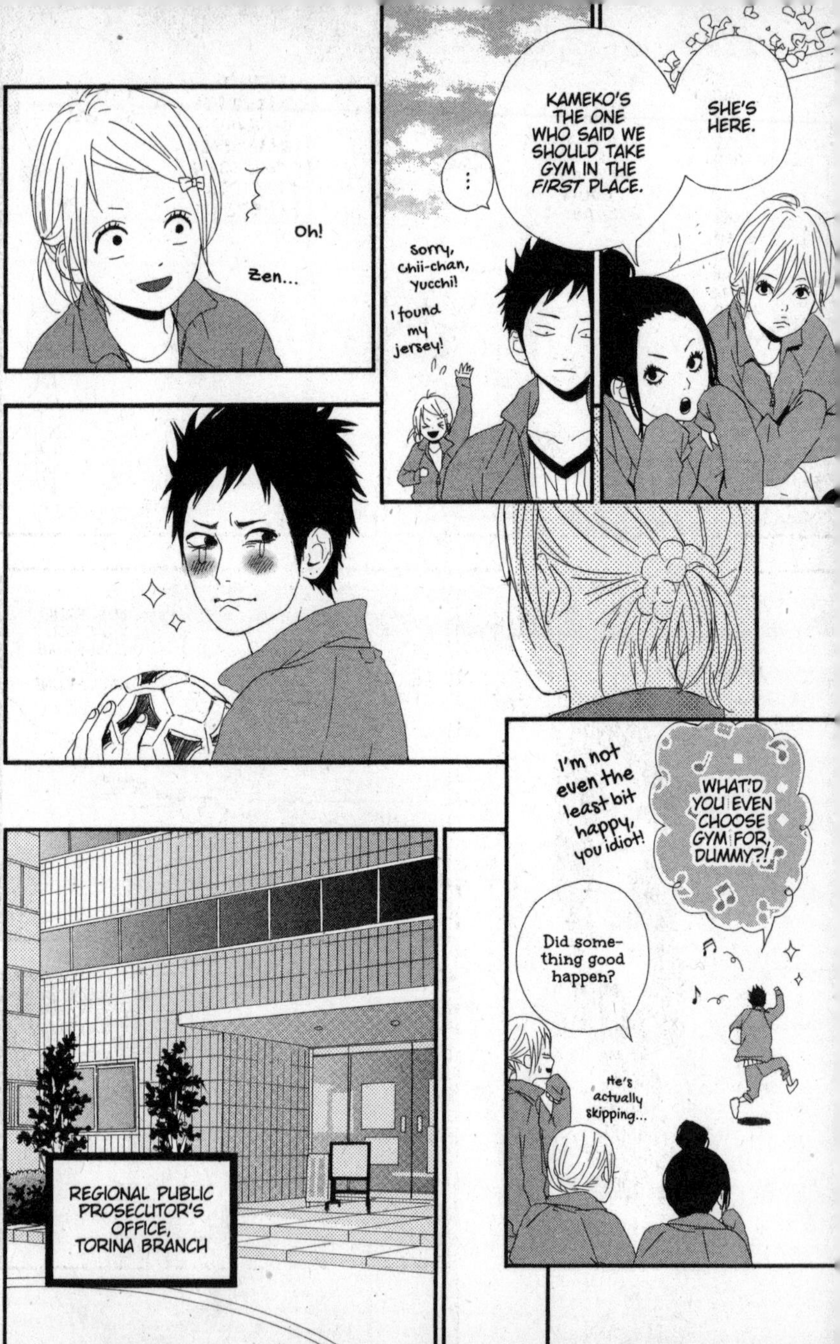
SHE'S HERE.
KAMEKO'S THE ONE WHO SAID WE SHOULD TAKE GYM IN THE *FIRST* PLACE.
...
Sorry, Chii-chan, Yucchi!
I found my jersey!
Oh!
Zen...
WHAT'D YOU EVEN CHOOSE GYM FOR, DUMMY?!
I'm not even the least bit happy, you idiot!
Did some-thing good happen?
He's actually skipping...
REGIONAL PUBLIC PROSECUTOR'S OFFICE, TORINA BRANCH

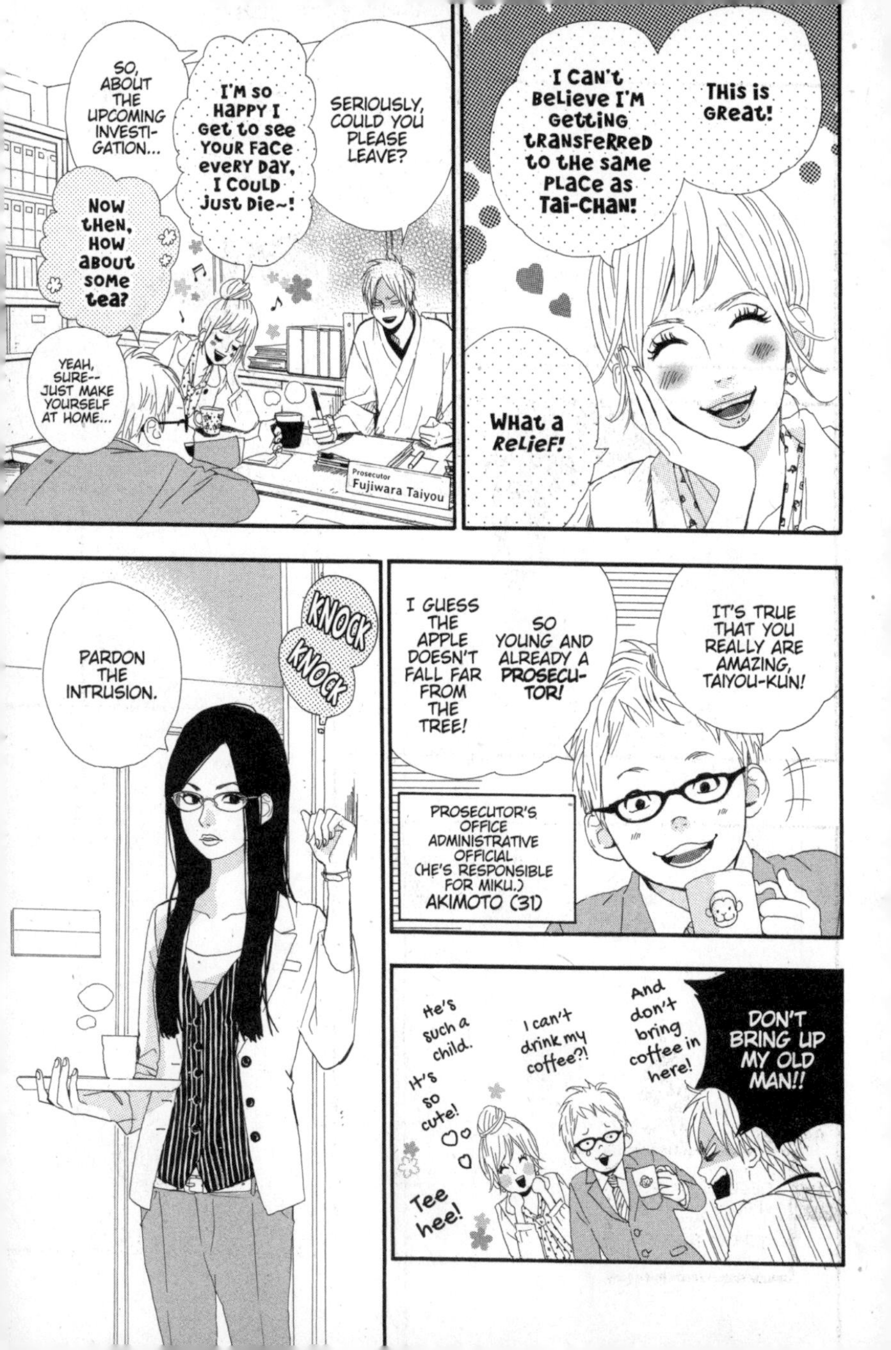
THIS IS GREAT!
I CAN'T BELIEVE I'M GETTING TRANSFERRED TO THE SAME PLACE AS TAI-CHAN!
WHAT A RELIEF!
SERIOUSLY, COULD YOU PLEASE LEAVE?
I'M SO HAPPY I GET TO SEE YOUR FACE EVERY DAY, I COULD JUST DIE~!
SO, ABOUT THE UPCOMING INVESTI-GATION...
NOW THEN, HOW ABOUT SOME TEA?
YEAH, SURE-- JUST MAKE YOURSELF AT HOME...
Prosecutor Fujiwara Taiyou
IT'S TRUE THAT YOU REALLY ARE AMAZING, TAIYOU-KUN!
SO YOUNG AND ALREADY A PROSECU-TOR!
I GUESS THE APPLE DOESN'T FALL FAR FROM THE TREE!
PROSECUTOR'S OFFICE ADMINISTRATIVE OFFICIAL (HE'S RESPONSIBLE FOR MIKU.) AKIMOTO (31)
DON'T BRING UP MY OLD MAN!!
And don't bring coffee in here!
I can't drink my coffee?!
He's such a child.
It's so cute!
Tee hee!
KNOCK
KNOCK
PARDON THE INTRUSION.

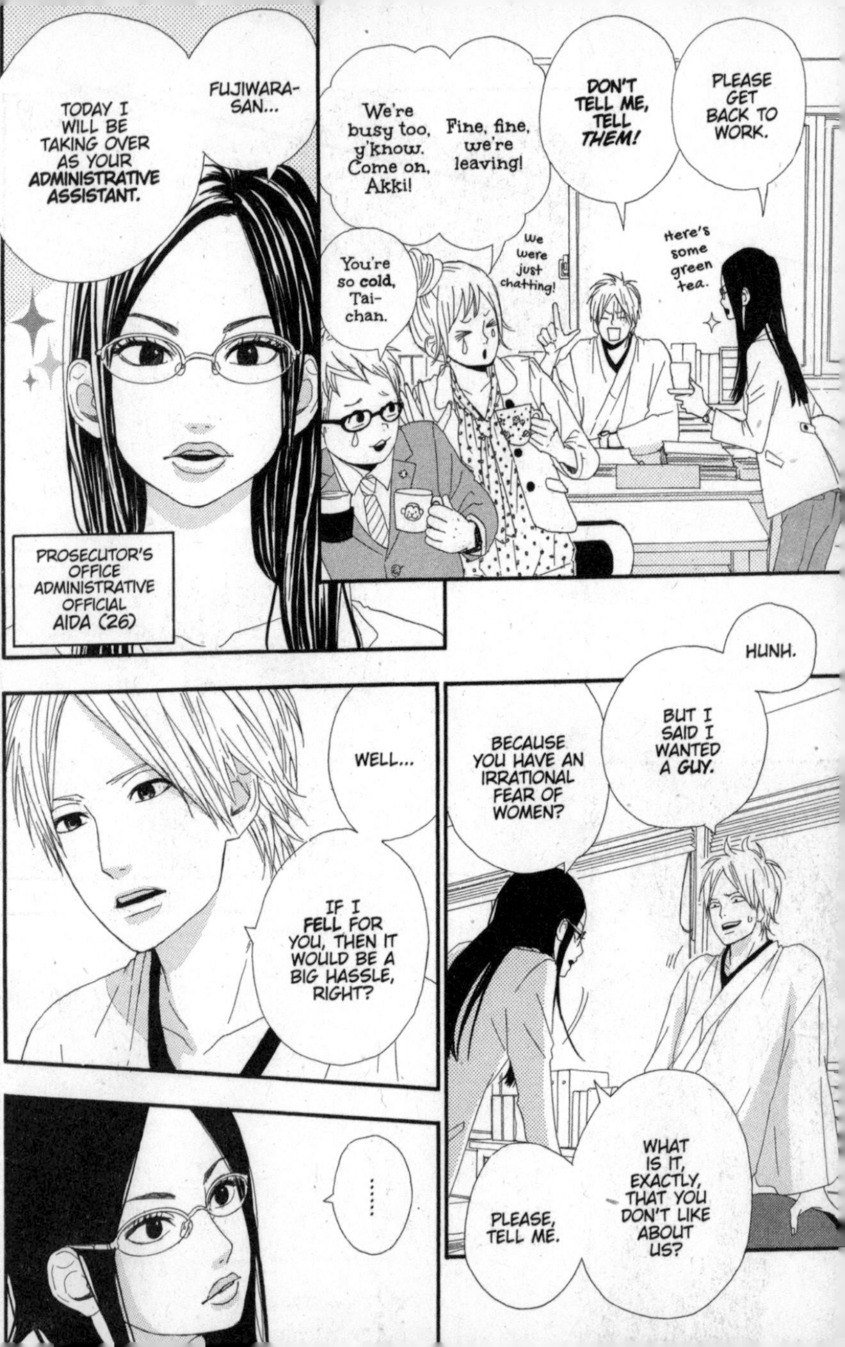
PLEASE GET BACK TO WORK.
DON'T TELL ME, TELL THEM!
Here's some green tea.
We were just chatting!
Fine, fine, we're leaving!
We're busy too, y'know. Come on, Akki!
You're so cold, Tai-chan.
FUJIWARA-SAN...
TODAY I WILL BE TAKING OVER AS YOUR ADMINISTRATIVE ASSISTANT.
PROSECUTOR'S OFFICE ADMINISTRATIVE OFFICIAL AIDA (26)
HUNH.
BUT I SAID I WANTED A GUY.
BECAUSE YOU HAVE AN IRRATIONAL FEAR OF WOMEN?
WHAT IS IT, EXACTLY, THAT YOU DON'T LIKE ABOUT US?
PLEASE, TELL ME.
WELL...
IF I FELL FOR YOU, THEN IT WOULD BE A BIG HASSLE, RIGHT?
......

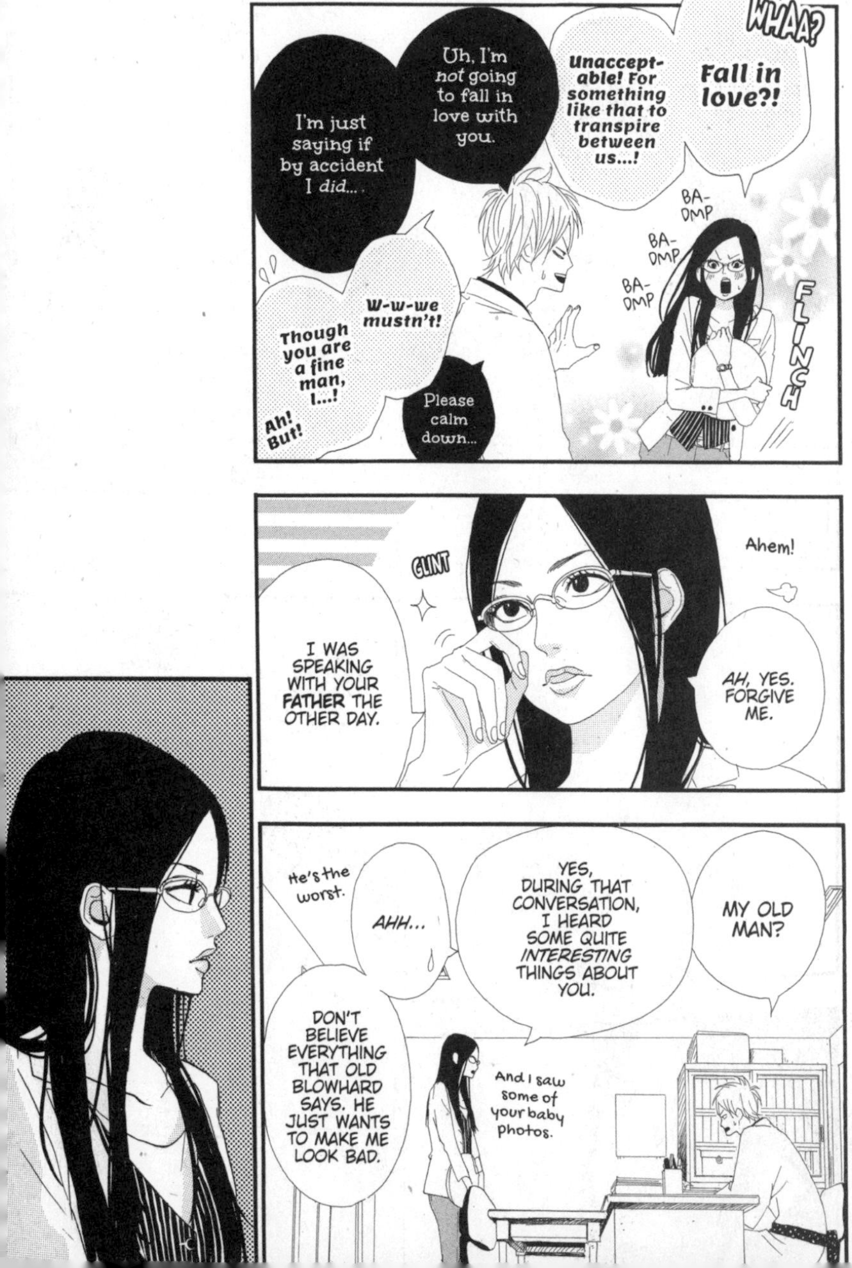
WHAA?
Fall in love?!
Unacceptable! For something like that to transpire between us...!
Uh, I'm not going to fall in love with you.
I'm just saying if by accident I did...
BA-DMP
BA-DMP
BA-DMP
FLINCH
W-w-we mustn't!
Though you are a fine man, I...!
Ah! But!
Please calm down...
Ahem!
AH, YES. FORGIVE ME.
GLINT
I WAS SPEAKING WITH YOUR FATHER THE OTHER DAY.
MY OLD MAN?
YES, DURING THAT CONVERSATION, I HEARD SOME QUITE INTERESTING THINGS ABOUT YOU.
AHH...
He's the worst.
And I saw some of your baby photos.
DON'T BELIEVE EVERYTHING THAT OLD BLOWHARD SAYS. HE JUST WANTS TO MAKE ME LOOK BAD.

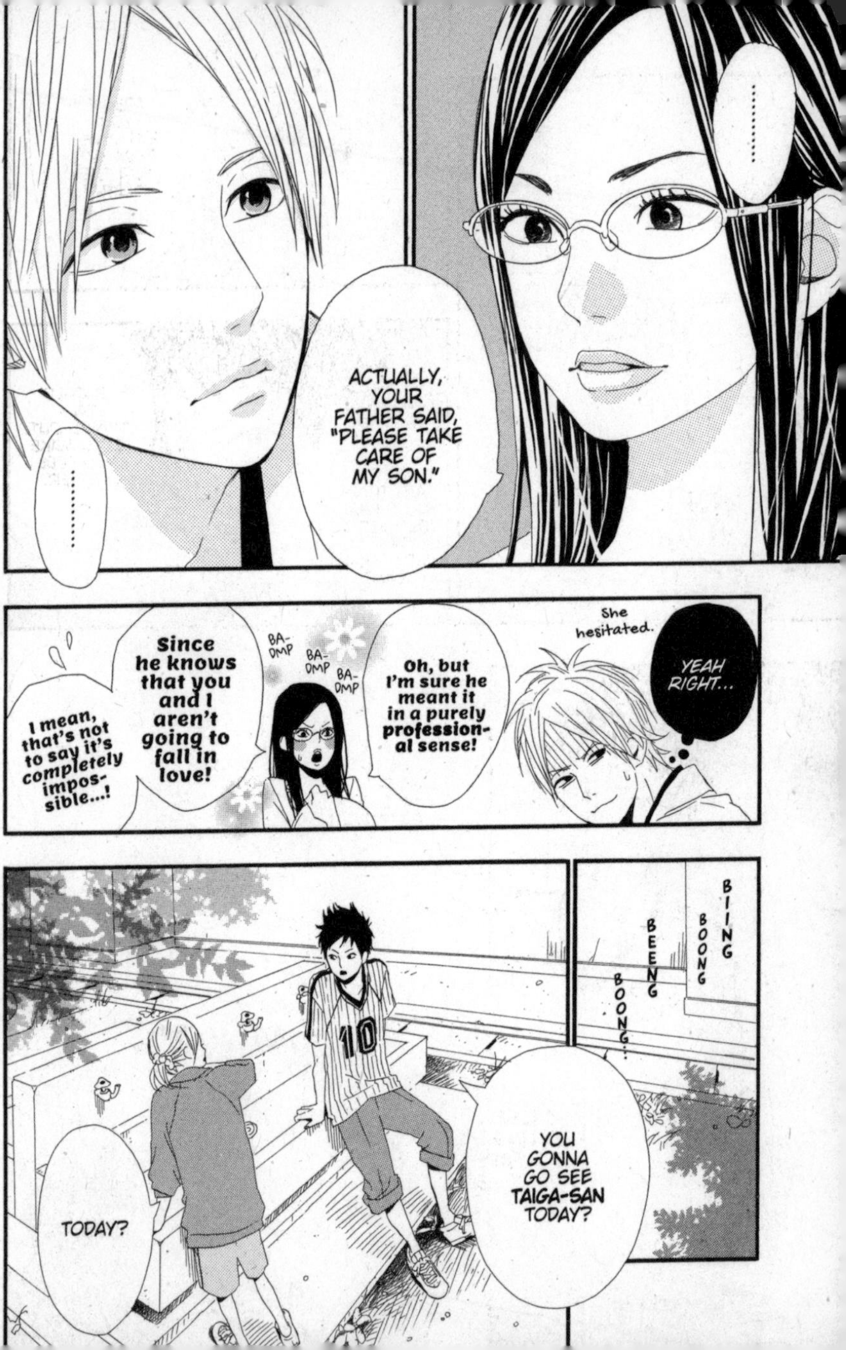

......
ACTUALLY, YOUR FATHER SAID, "PLEASE TAKE CARE OF MY SON."
......
She hesitated.
YEAH RIGHT...
Oh, but I'm sure he meant it in a purely profession-al sense!
BA-DMP BA-DMP BA-DMP
Since he knows that you and I aren't going to fall in love!
I mean, that's not to say it's completely impos-sible...!
BIING BOONG
BEENG BOONG...
YOU GONNA GO SEE TAIGA-SAN TODAY?
TODAY?

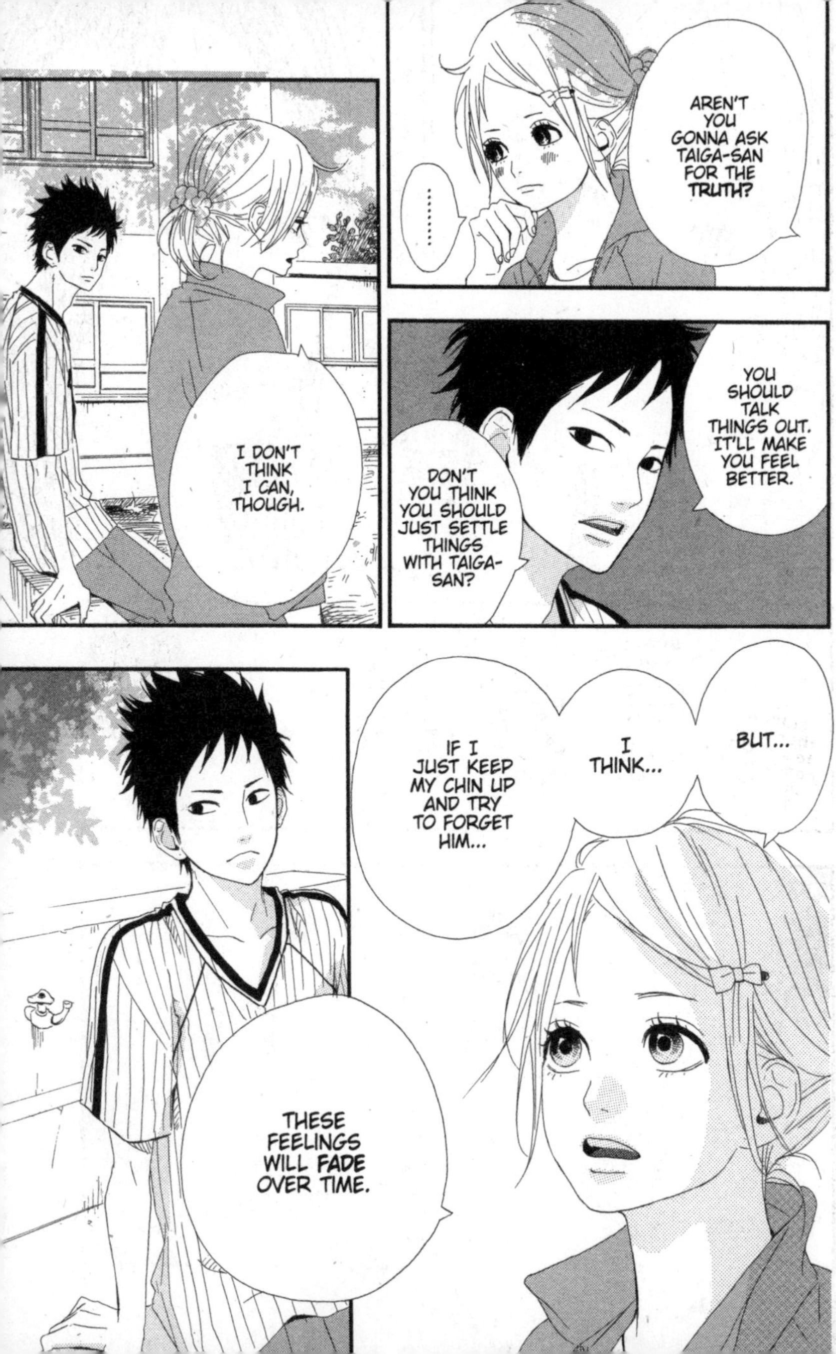
AREN'T YOU GONNA ASK TAIGA-SAN FOR THE TRUTH?
......
YOU SHOULD TALK THINGS OUT. IT'LL MAKE YOU FEEL BETTER.
DON'T YOU THINK YOU SHOULD JUST SETTLE THINGS WITH TAIGA-SAN?
I DON'T THINK I CAN, THOUGH.
BUT...
I THINK...
IF I JUST KEEP MY CHIN UP AND TRY TO FORGET HIM...
THESE FEELINGS WILL FADE OVER TIME.

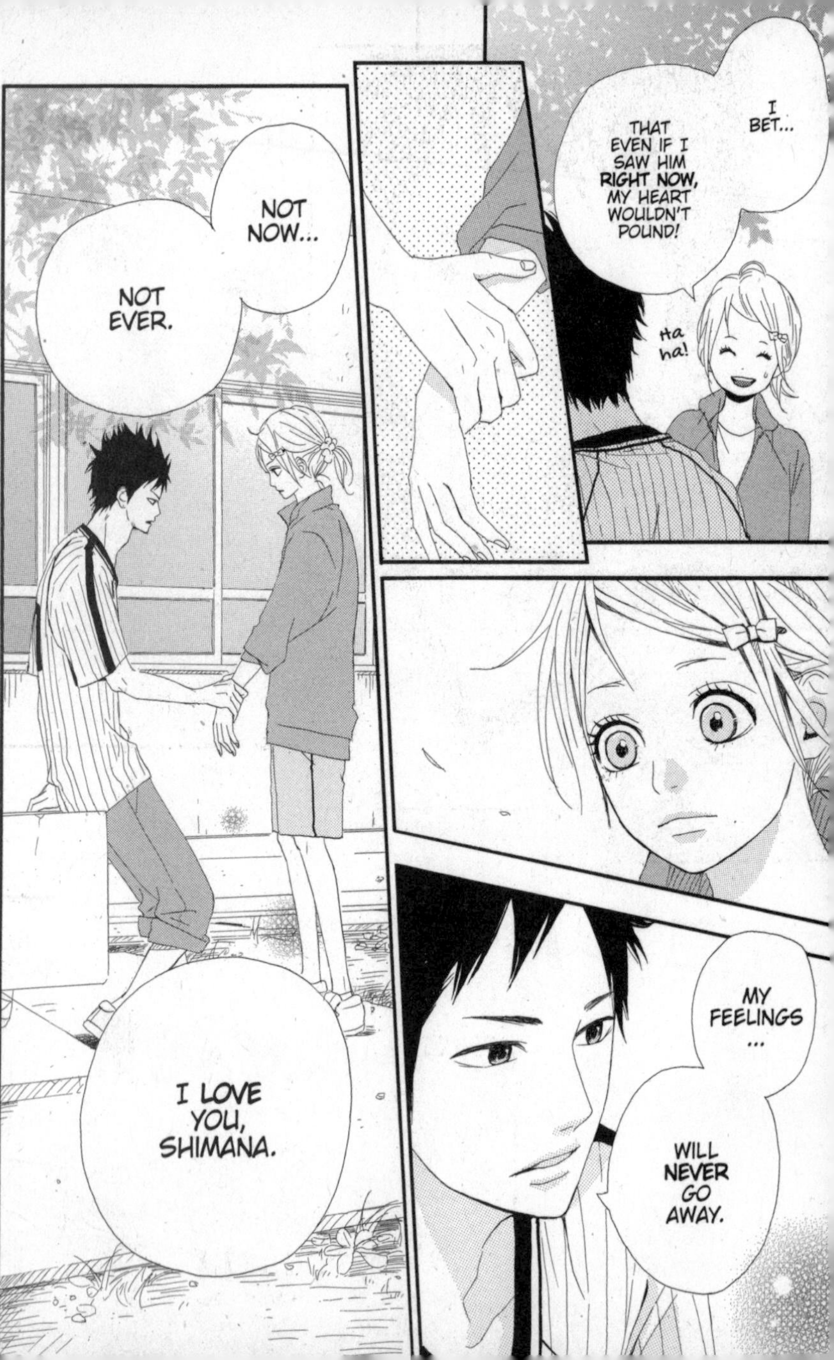
I BET... THAT EVEN IF I SAW HIM RIGHT NOW, MY HEART WOULDN'T POUND!
Ha ha!
MY FEELINGS ...
WILL NEVER GO AWAY.
NOT NOW...
NOT EVER.
I LOVE YOU, SHIMANA.

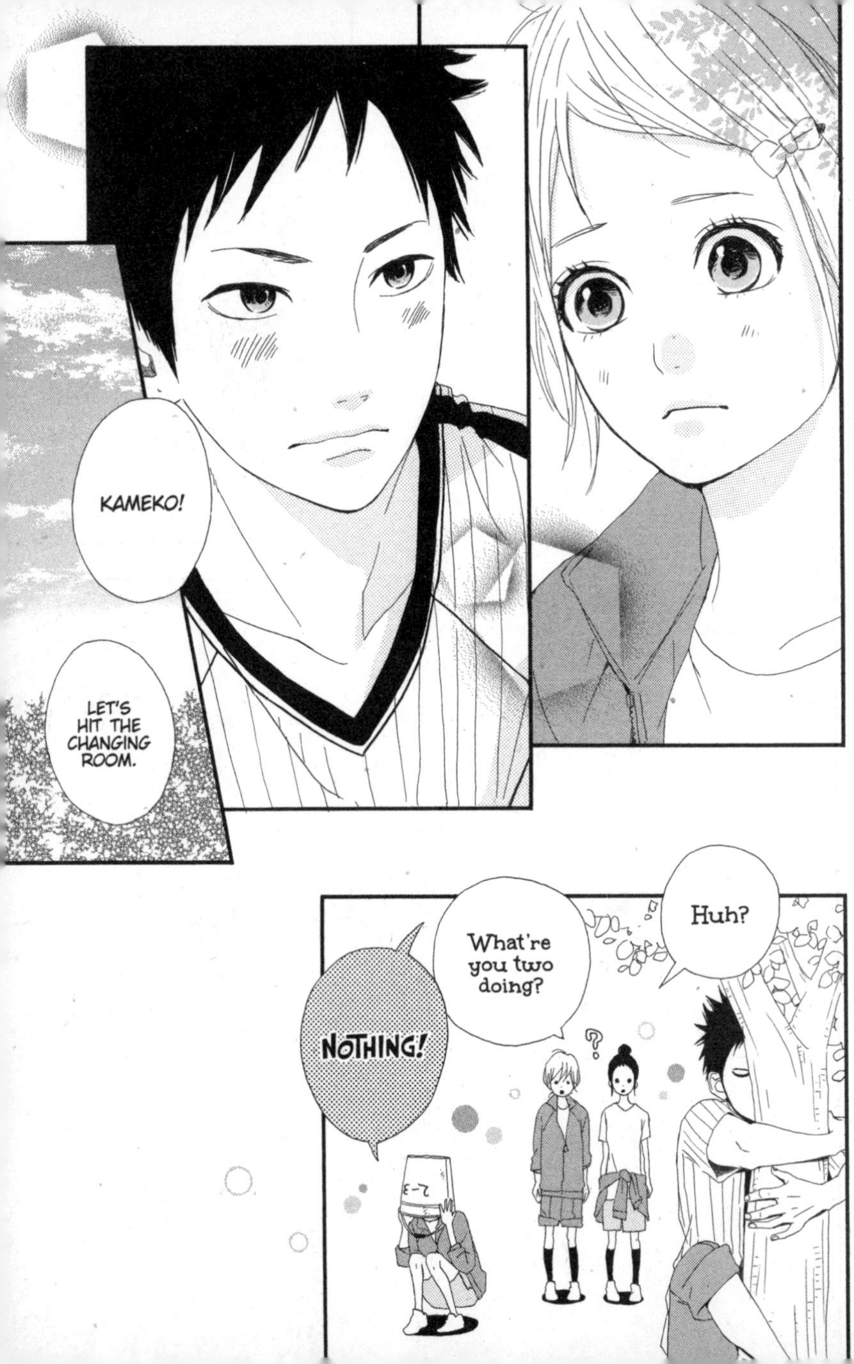
KAMEKO!
LET'S HIT THE CHANGING ROOM.
Huh?
What're you two doing?
NOTHING!

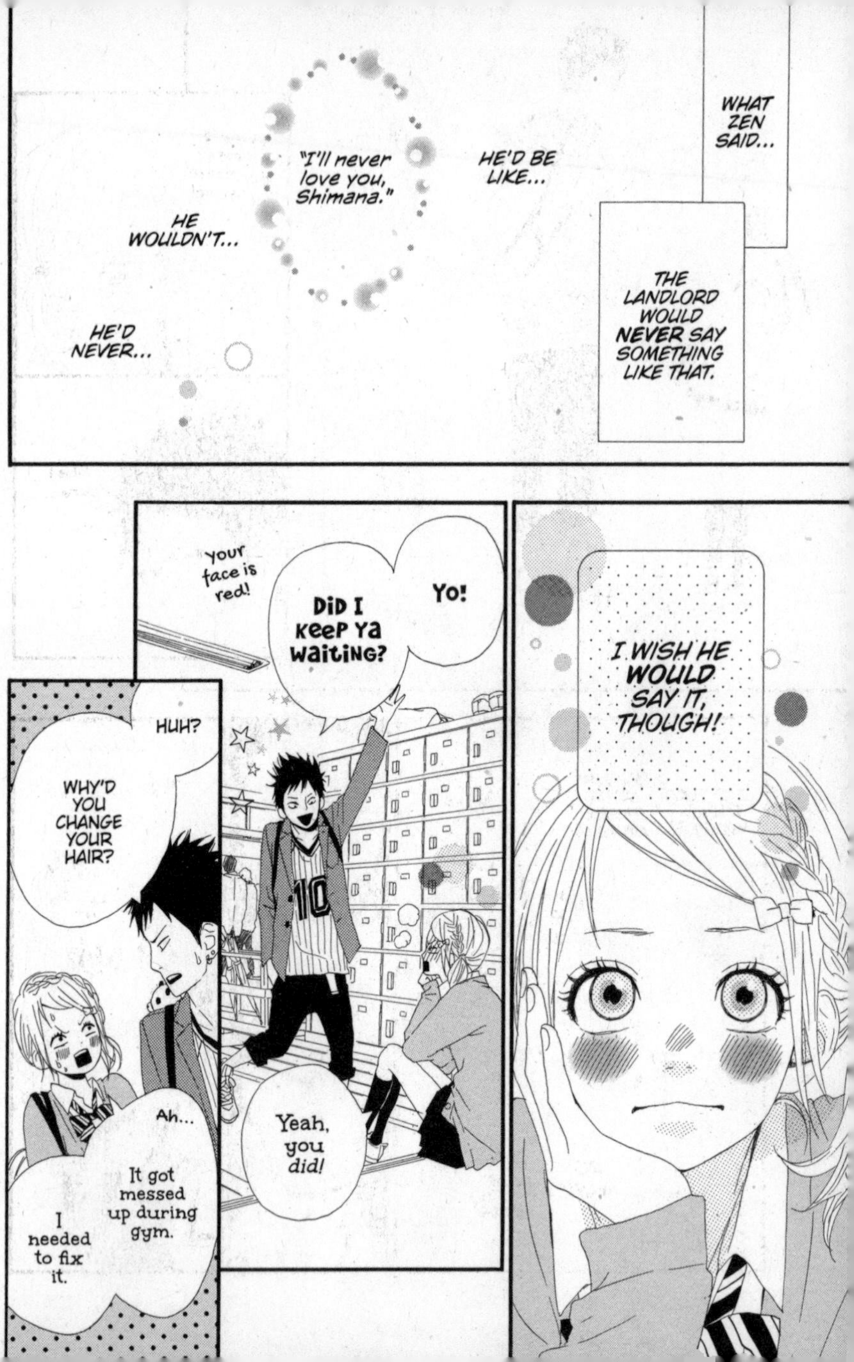

WHAT ZEN SAID...
THE LANDLORD WOULD NEVER SAY SOMETHING LIKE THAT.
HE'D BE LIKE...
"I'll never love you, Shimana."
HE WOULDN'T...
HE'D NEVER...
I WISH HE WOULD SAY IT, THOUGH!
Yo!
DID I KEEP YA WAITING?
your face is red!
Yeah, you did!
HUH?
WHY'D YOU CHANGE YOUR HAIR?
Ah...
It got messed up during gym.
I needed to fix it.

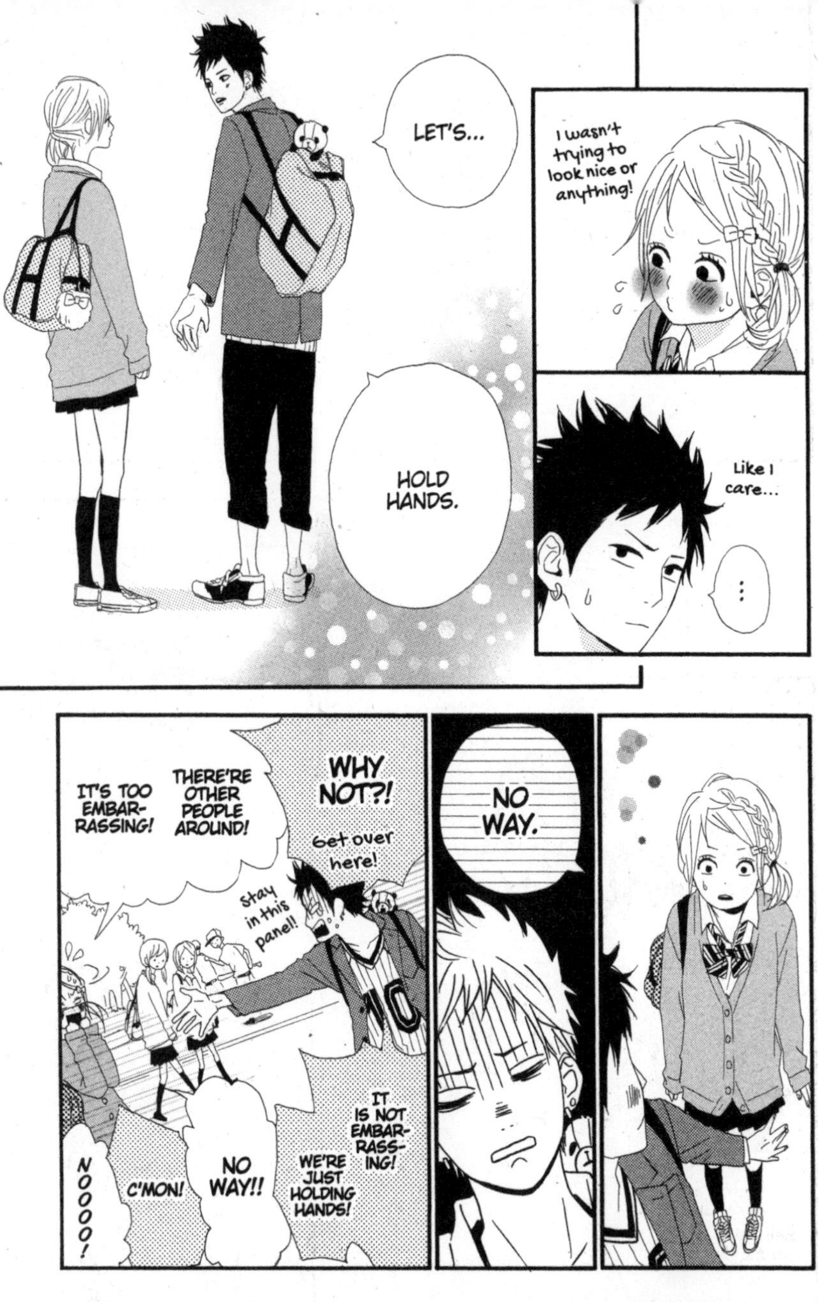
I wasn't trying to look nice or anything!
Like I care...
...
LET'S...
HOLD HANDS.
NO WAY.
WHY NOT?!
Get over here!
Stay in this panel!
THERE'RE OTHER PEOPLE AROUND!
IT'S TOO EMBARRASSING!
IT IS NOT EMBARRASSING!
WE'RE JUST HOLDING HANDS!
NO WAY!!
C'MON!
NOOOOO!

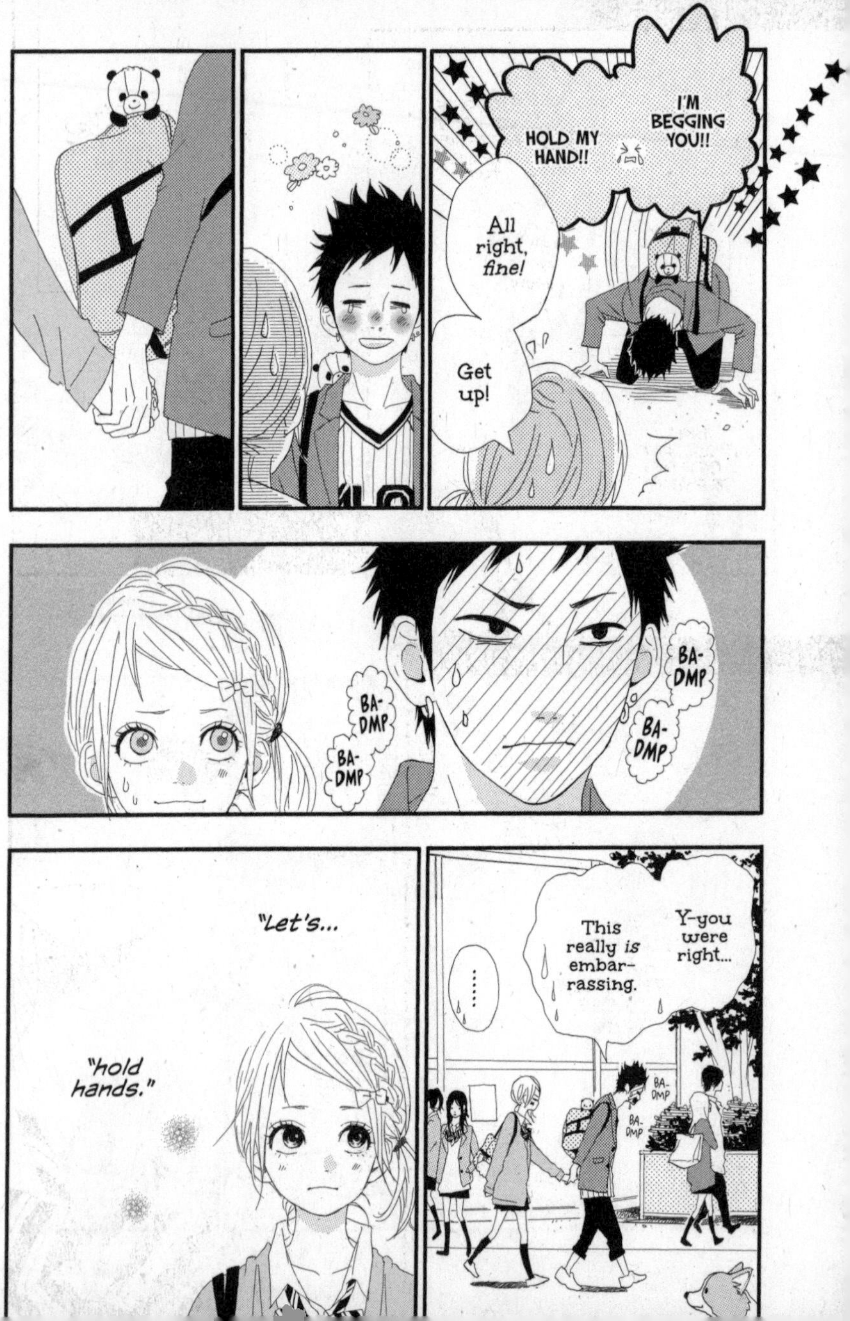
I'M BEGGING YOU!!
HOLD MY HAND!!
All right, fine!
Get up!
BA-DMP
BA-DMP
BA-DMP
BA-DMP
Y-you were right...
This really is embarrassing.
......
BA-DMP
BA-DMP
"Let's...
"hold hands."

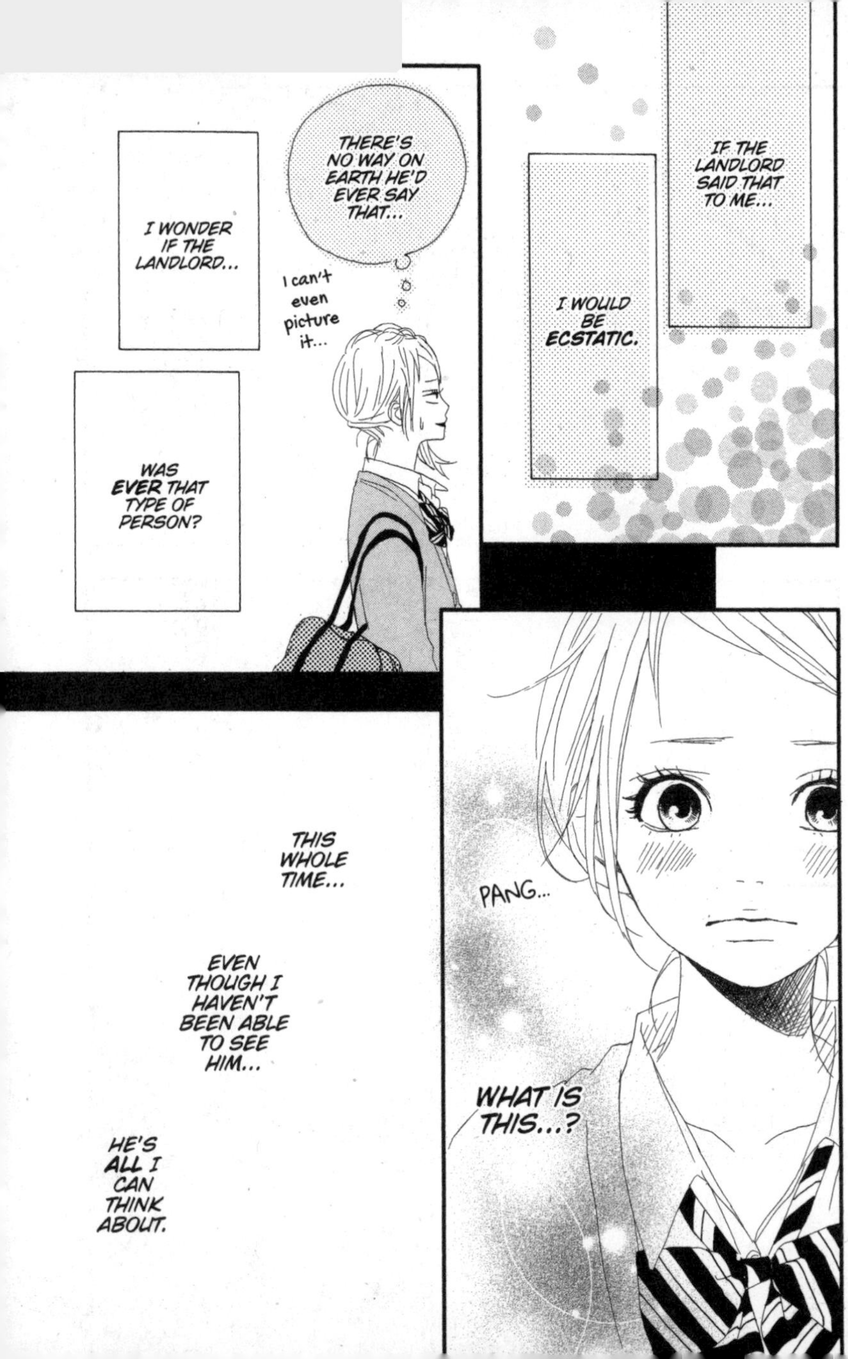
IF THE LANDLORD SAID THAT TO ME...
I WOULD BE ECSTATIC.
THERE'S NO WAY ON EARTH HE'D EVER SAY THAT...
I can't even picture it...
I WONDER IF THE LANDLORD...
WAS EVER THAT TYPE OF PERSON?
PANG...
WHAT IS THIS...?
THIS WHOLE TIME...
EVEN THOUGH I HAVEN'T BEEN ABLE TO SEE HIM...
HE'S ALL I CAN THINK ABOUT.

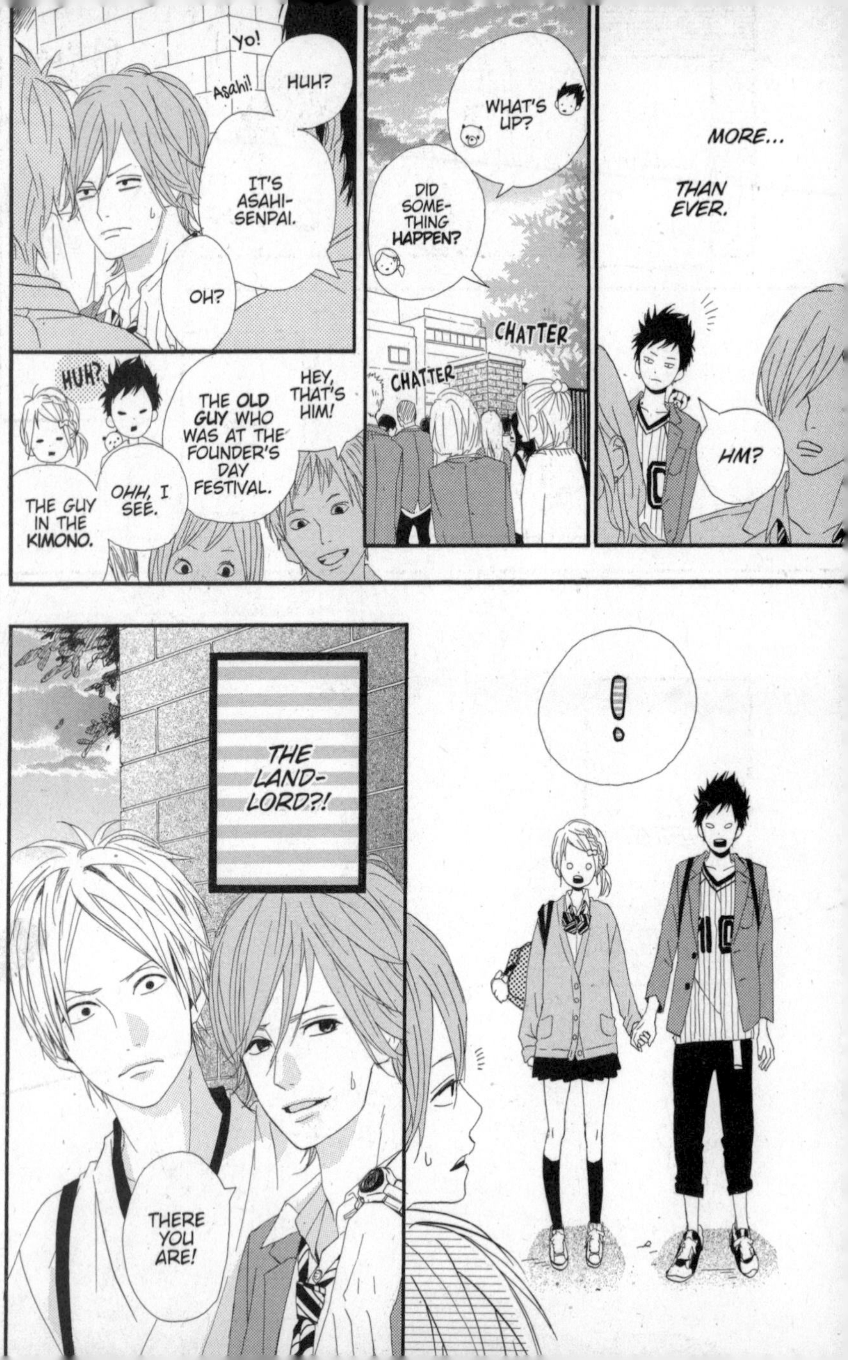
MORE...
THAN EVER.
HM?
WHAT'S UP?
DID SOMETHING HAPPEN?
CHATTER
CHATTER
Yo!
Asahi!
HUH?
IT'S ASAHI-SENPAI.
OH?
HEY, THAT'S HIM!
THE OLD GUY WHO WAS AT THE FOUNDER'S DAY FESTIVAL.
HUH?
OHH, I SEE.
THE GUY IN THE KIMONO.
!
THE LAND-LORD?!
THERE YOU ARE!

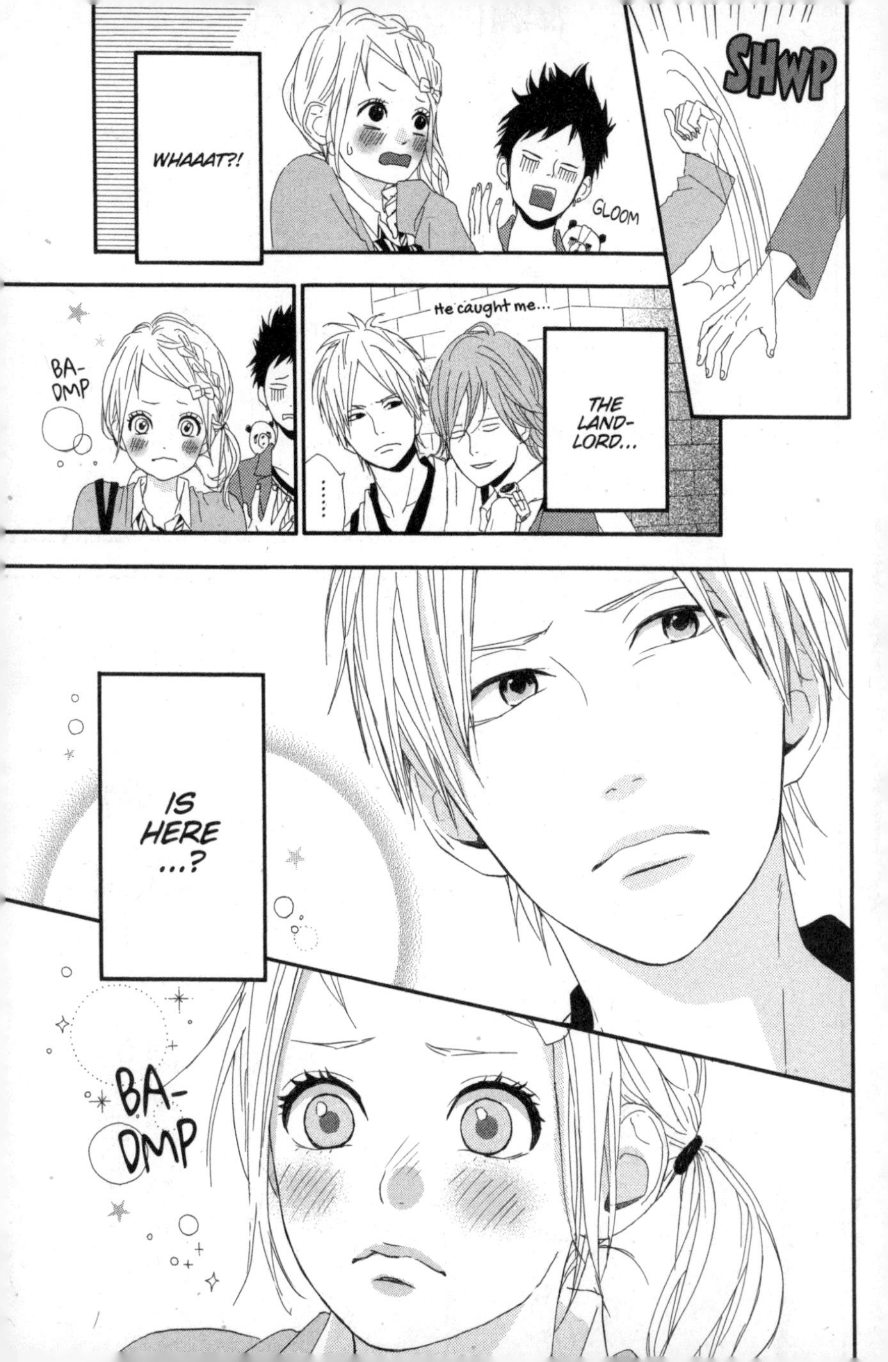
SHWP
WHAAAT?!
GLOOM
He caught me...
THE LAND-LORD...
......
BA-DMP
IS HERE ...?
BA-DMP

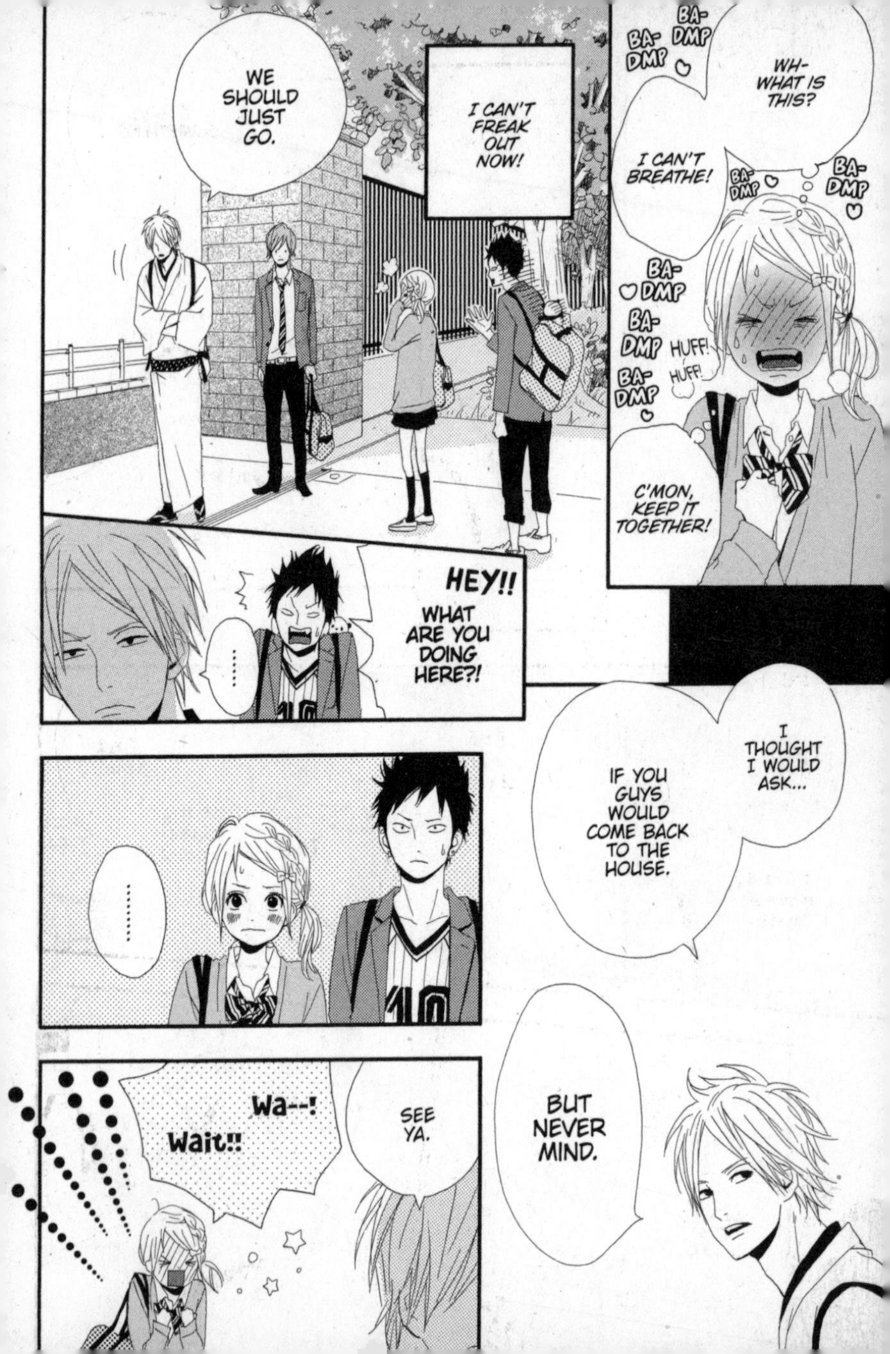
BA-DMP
BA-DMP
WH- WHAT IS THIS?
I CAN'T BREATHE!
BA-DMP
BA-DMP
BA-DMP
BA-DMP
BA-DMP
HUFF! HUFF!
C'MON, KEEP IT TOGETHER!
I CAN'T FREAK OUT NOW!
WE SHOULD JUST GO.
HEY!! WHAT ARE YOU DOING HERE?!
......
I THOUGHT I WOULD ASK...
IF YOU GUYS WOULD COME BACK TO THE HOUSE.
......
BUT NEVER MIND.
SEE YA.
Wa--! Wait!!

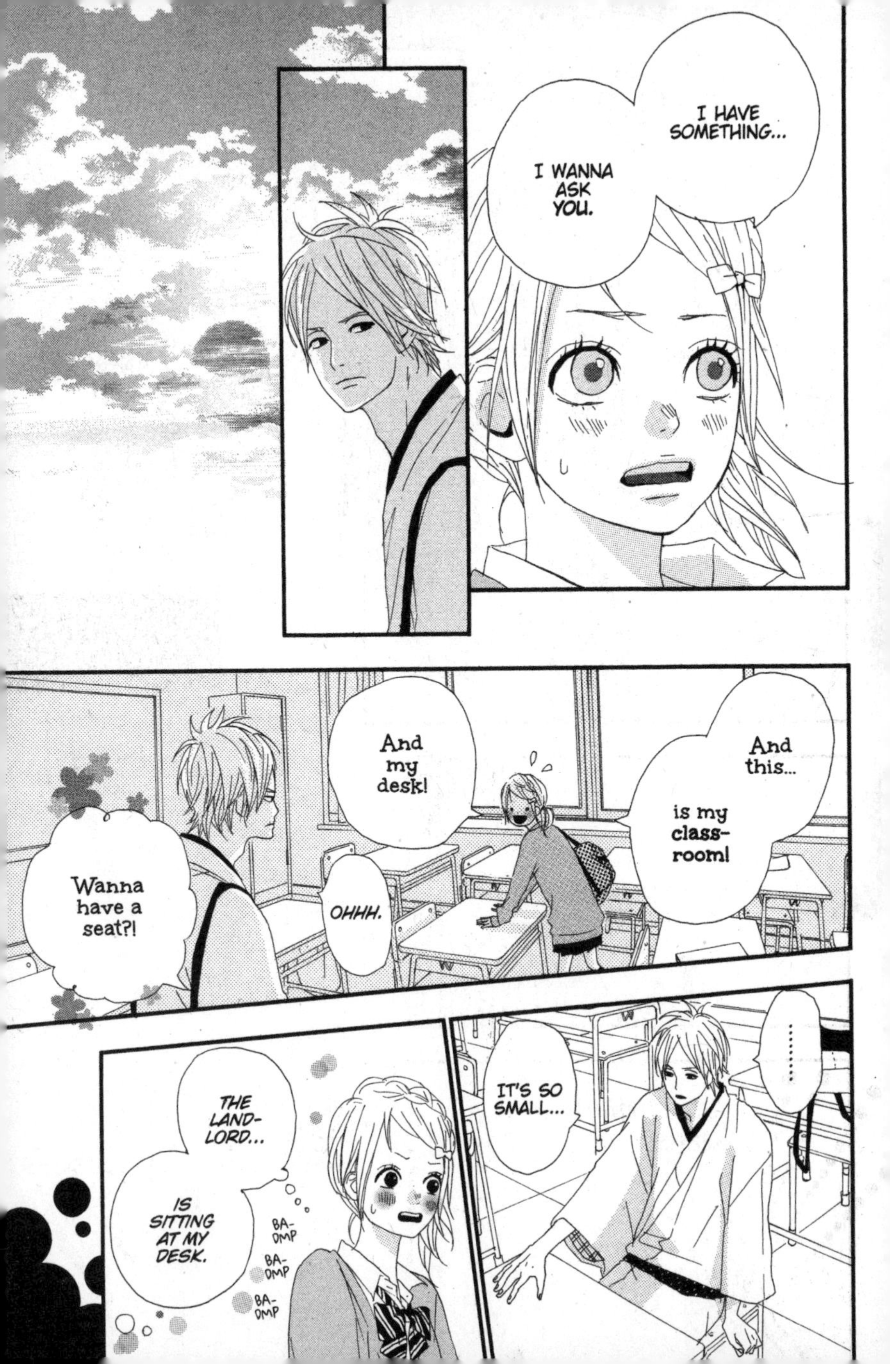
I HAVE SOMETHING...
I WANNA ASK YOU.
And this...
is my class-room!
And my desk!
OHHH.
Wanna have a seat?!
......
IT'S SO SMALL...
THE LAND-LORD...
IS SITTING AT MY DESK.
BA-DMP
BA-DMP
BA-DMP

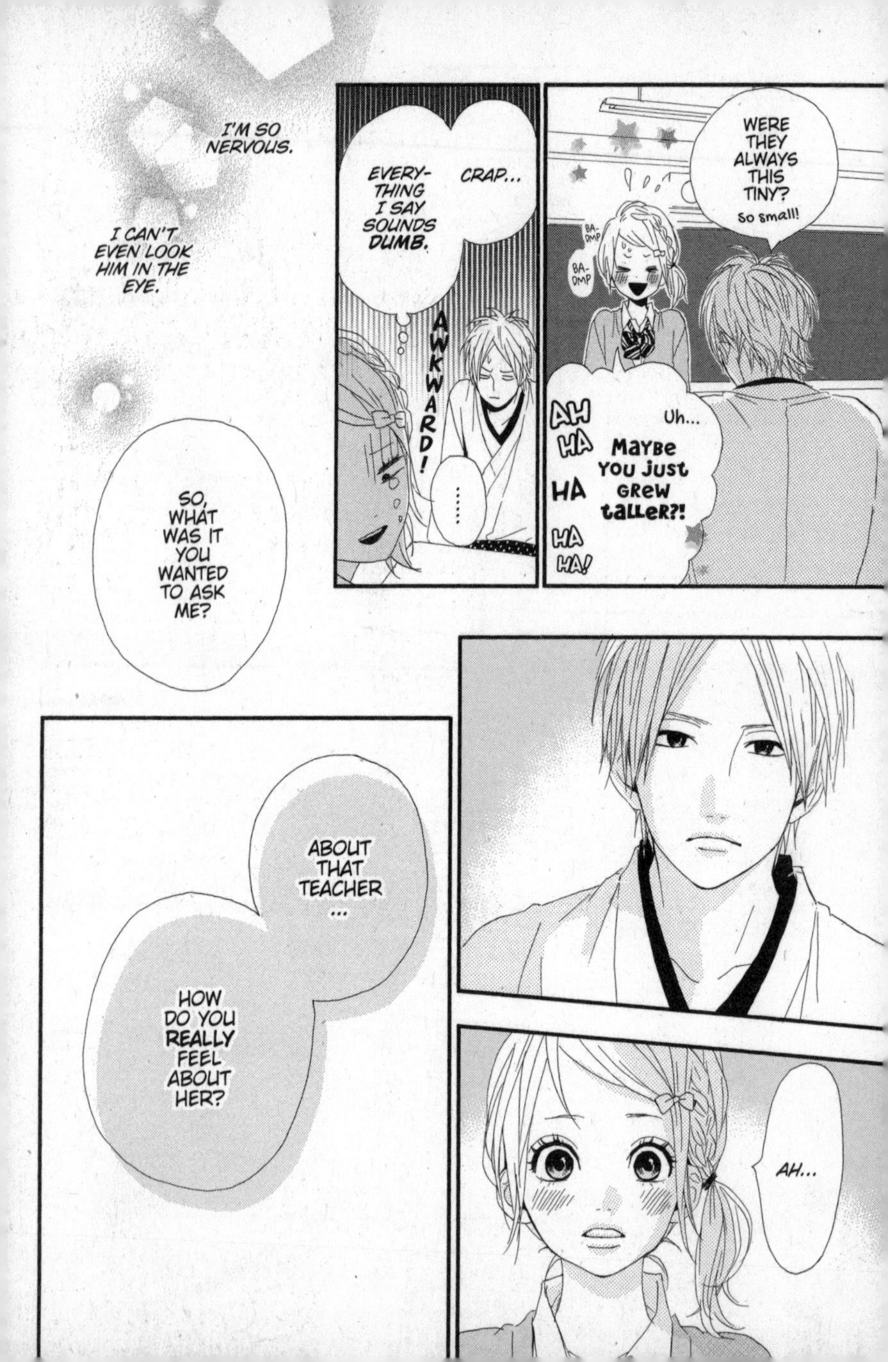
WERE THEY ALWAYS THIS TINY?
So small!
BA-DMP
BA-DMP
Uh...
Maybe you just grew taller?!
AH HA HA HA HA HA!
CRAP...
EVERYTHING I SAY SOUNDS DUMB.
AWKWARD!
......
I'M SO NERVOUS.
I CAN'T EVEN LOOK HIM IN THE EYE.
SO, WHAT WAS IT YOU WANTED TO ASK ME?
AH...
ABOUT THAT TEACHER...
HOW DO YOU REALLY FEEL ABOUT HER?

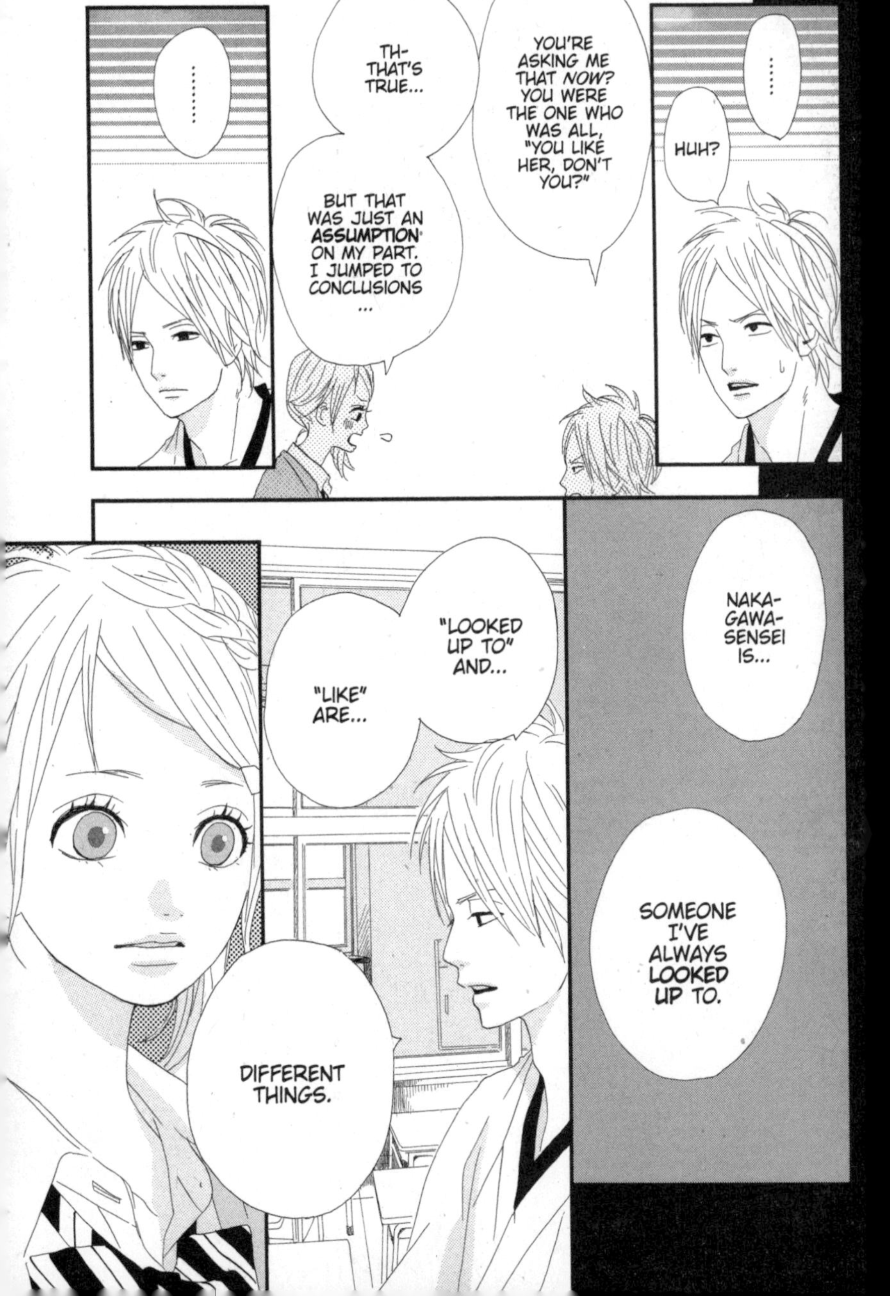
......
HUH?
YOU'RE ASKING ME THAT *NOW*? YOU WERE THE ONE WHO WAS ALL, "YOU LIKE HER, DON'T YOU?"
TH- THAT'S TRUE...
BUT THAT WAS JUST AN **ASSUMPTION** ON MY PART. I JUMPED TO CONCLUSIONS ...
....
NAKA-GAWA-SENSEI IS...
SOMEONE I'VE ALWAYS **LOOKED UP TO.**
"LOOKED UP TO" AND...
"LIKE" ARE...
DIFFERENT THINGS.

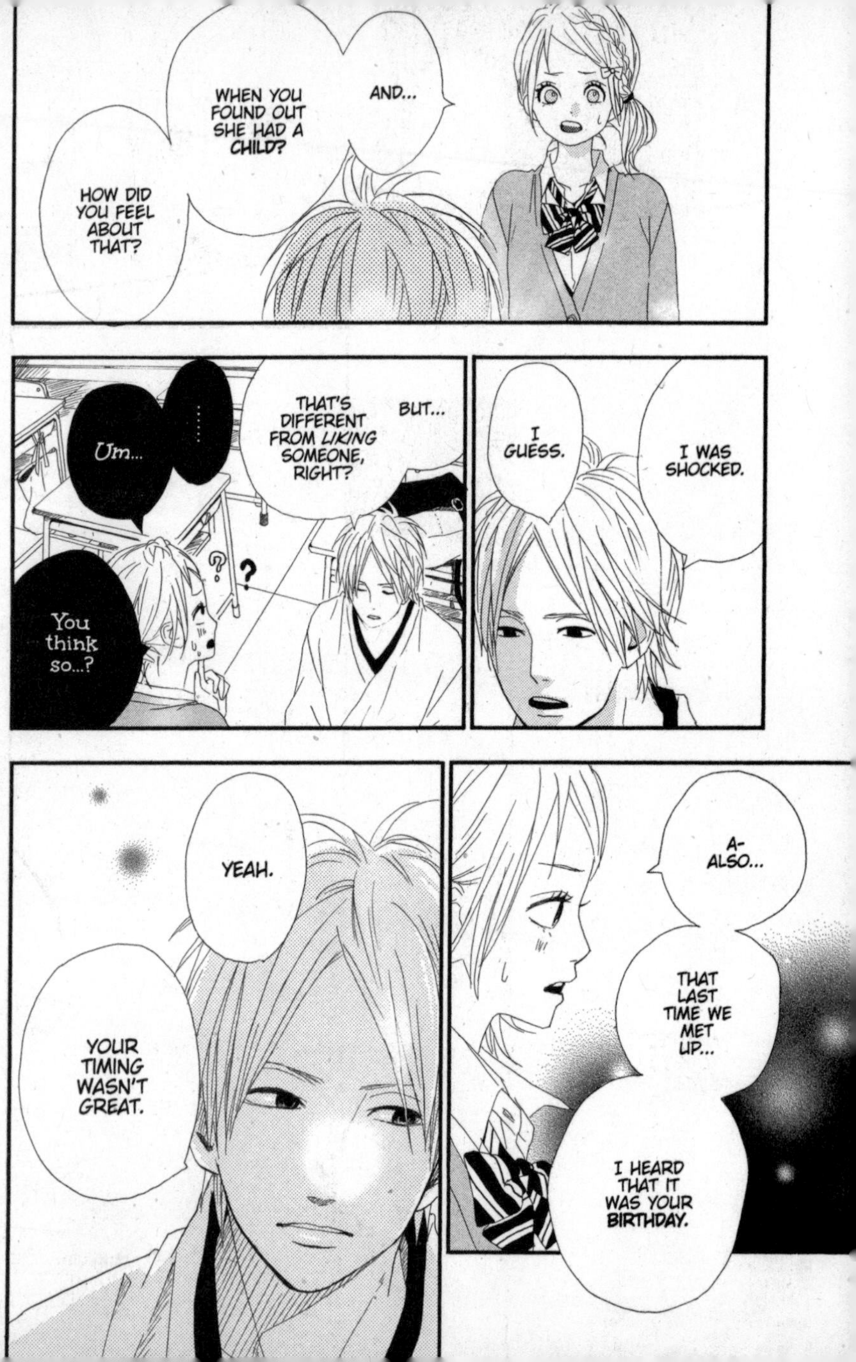
AND...
WHEN YOU FOUND OUT SHE HAD A CHILD?
HOW DID YOU FEEL ABOUT THAT?
I WAS SHOCKED.
I GUESS.
BUT...
THAT'S DIFFERENT FROM *LIKING* SOMEONE, RIGHT?
......
Um...
You think so...?
A- ALSO...
THAT LAST TIME WE MET UP...
I HEARD THAT IT WAS YOUR BIRTHDAY.
YEAH.
YOUR TIMING WASN'T GREAT.

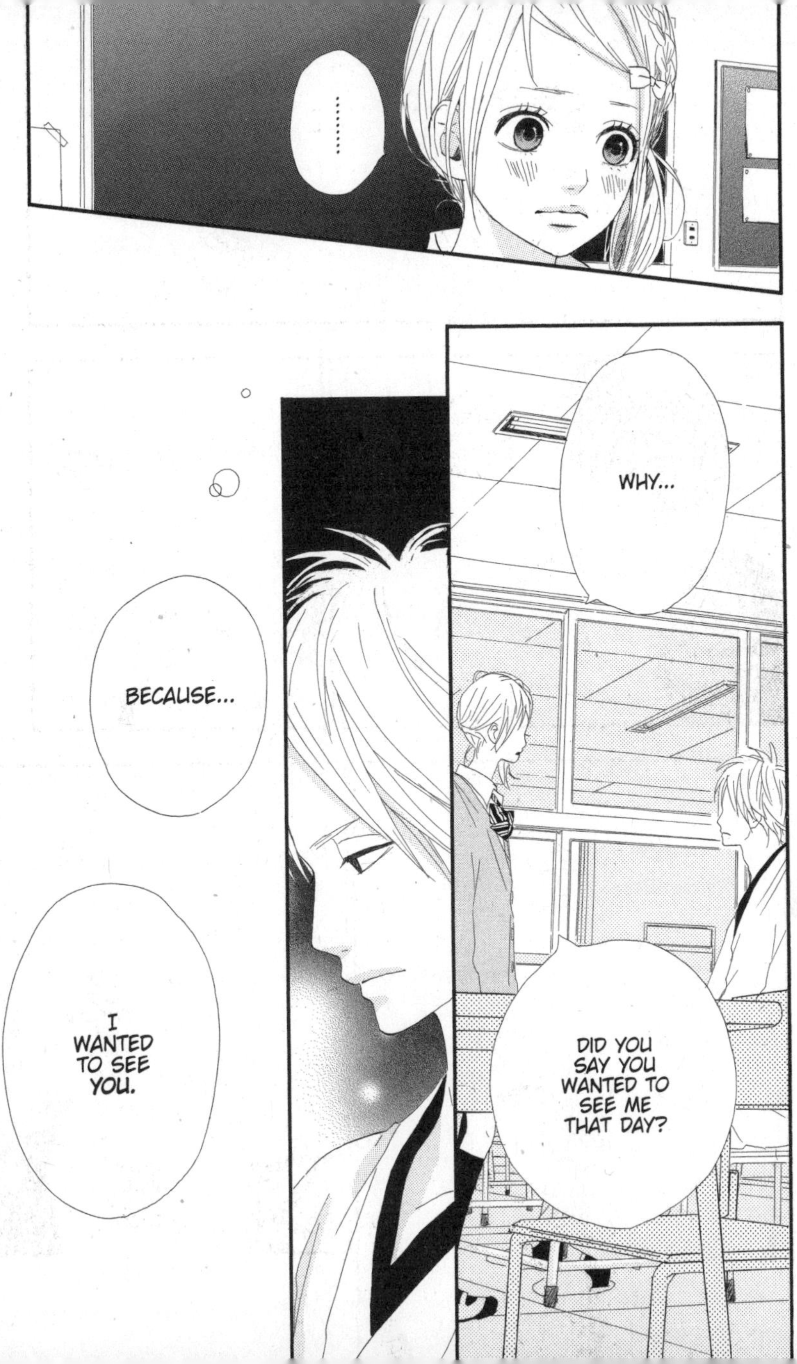
......
WHY...
DID YOU SAY YOU WANTED TO SEE ME THAT DAY?
BECAUSE...
I WANTED TO SEE YOU.

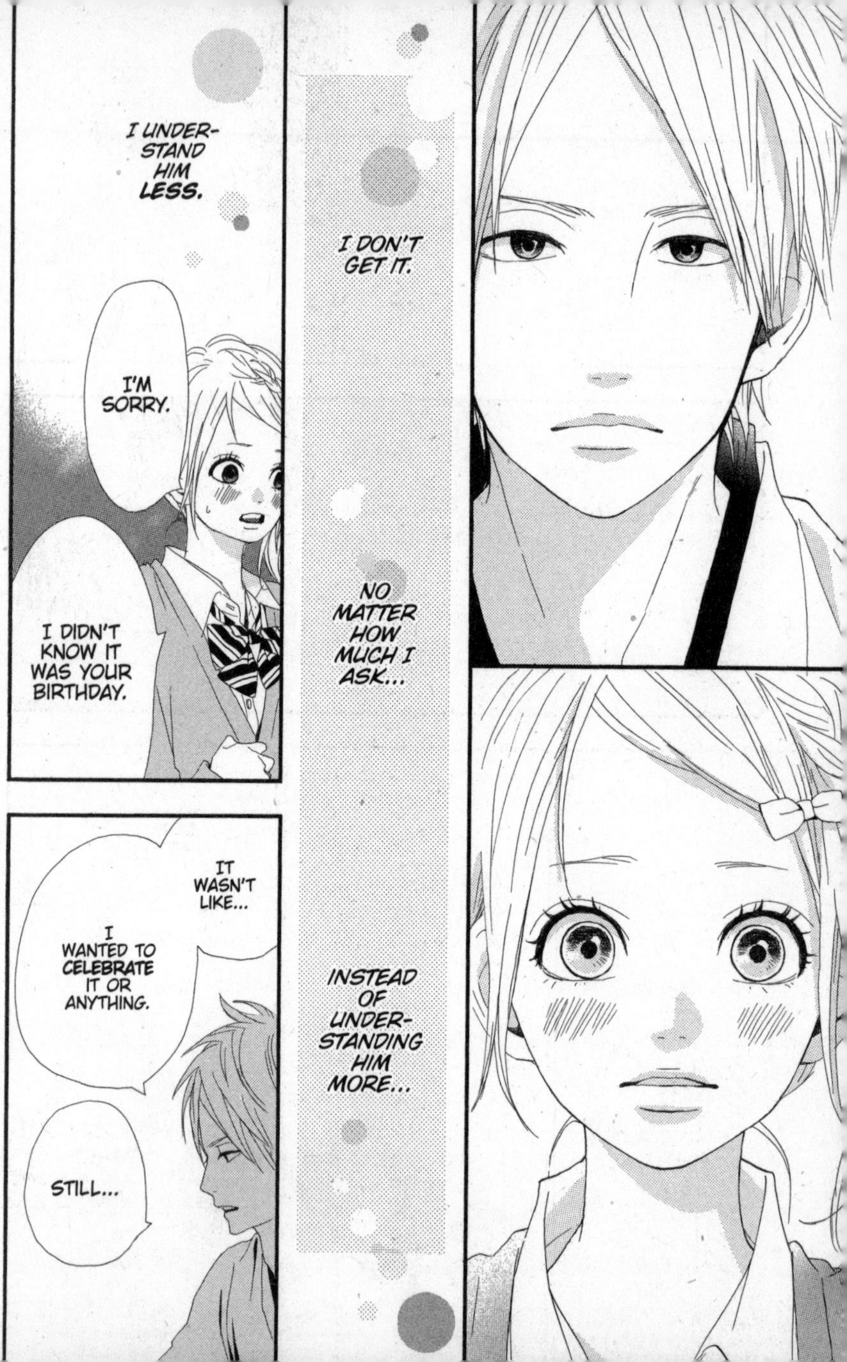
I DON'T GET IT.
NO MATTER HOW MUCH I ASK...
INSTEAD OF UNDER-STANDING HIM MORE...
I UNDER-STAND HIM LESS.
I'M SORRY.
I DIDN'T KNOW IT WAS YOUR BIRTHDAY.
IT WASN'T LIKE...
I WANTED TO CELEBRATE IT OR ANYTHING.
STILL...

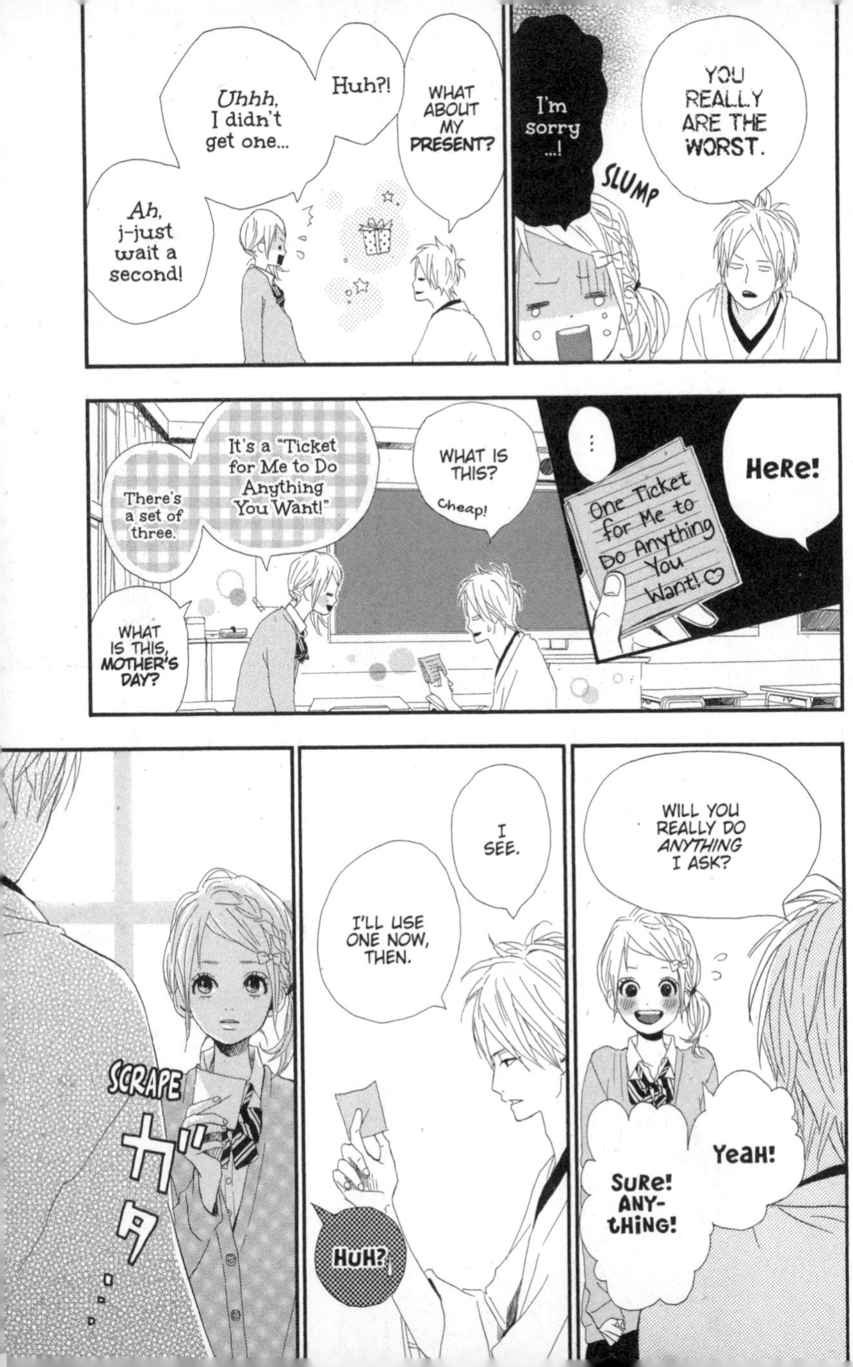
YOU REALLY ARE THE WORST.
I'm sorry ...!
SLUMP
WHAT ABOUT MY PRESENT?
Huh?!
Uhhh, I didn't get one...
Ah, j-just wait a second!
Here!
...
One Ticket for Me to Do Anything You Want! ♡
WHAT IS THIS?
Cheap!
It's a "Ticket for Me to Do Anything You Want!"
There's a set of three.
WHAT IS THIS, MOTHER'S DAY?
WILL YOU REALLY DO ANYTHING I ASK?
Yeah!
Sure! ANY-THING!
I SEE.
I'LL USE ONE NOW, THEN.
HUH?!
SCRAPE
ガタ...

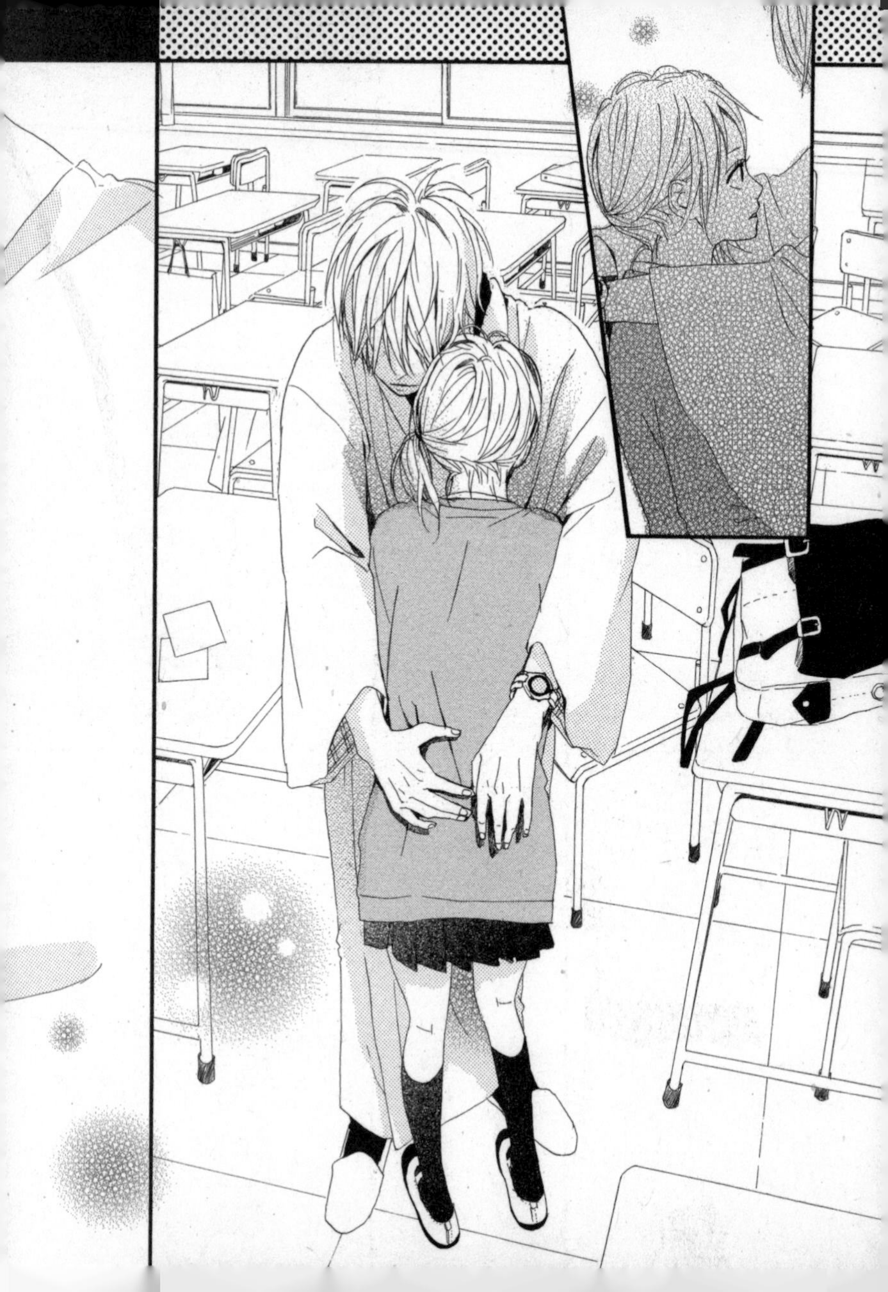

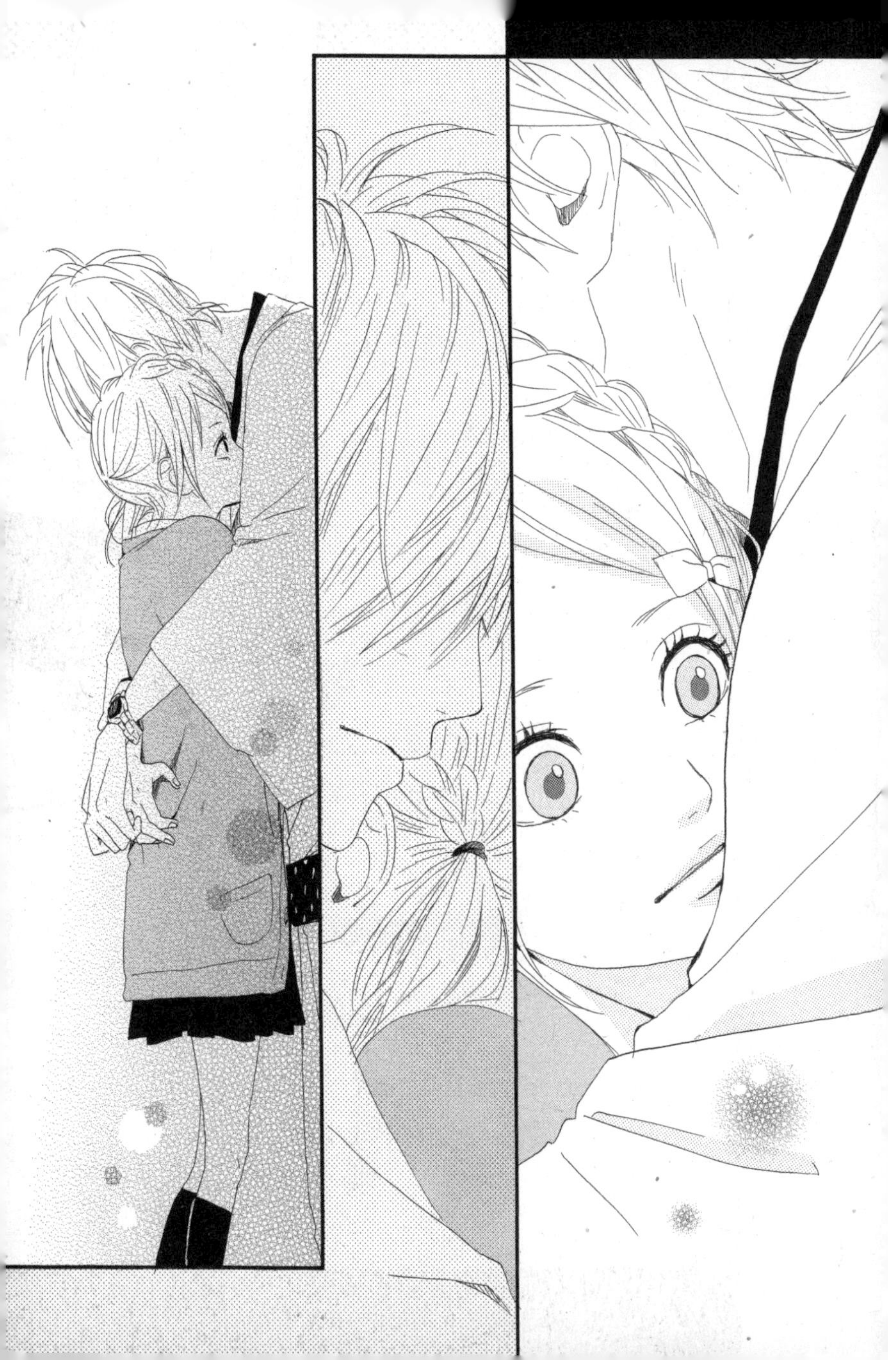

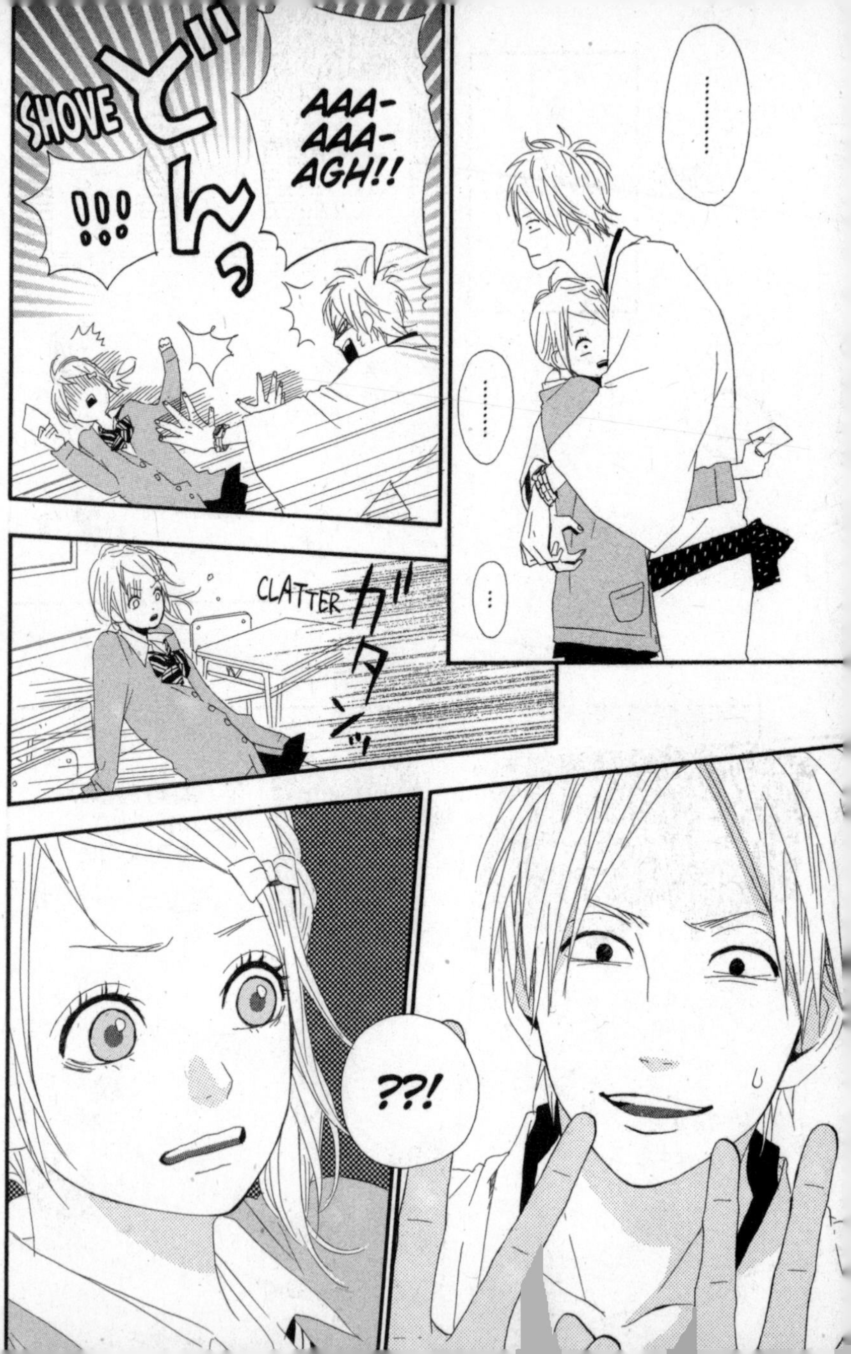
……
……
…
AAA-AAA-AGH!!
SHOVE
どんっ
!!!
CLATTER
ガタンッ
??!

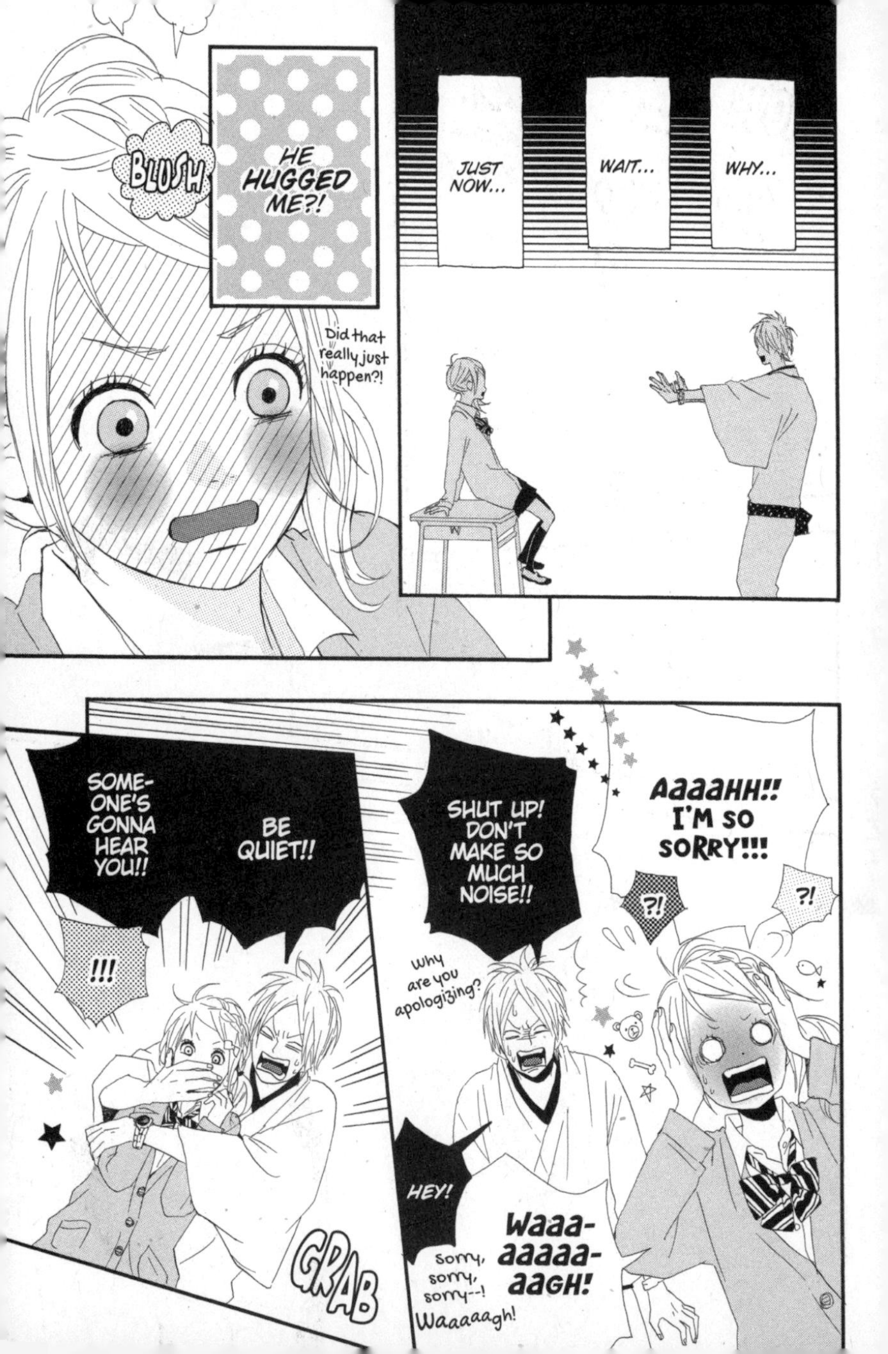

WHY...
WAIT...
JUST NOW...
BLUSH
HE HUGGED ME?!
Did that really just happen?!
AAAAHH!! I'M SO SORRY!!!
?!
?!
SHUT UP! DON'T MAKE SO MUCH NOISE!!
Why are you apologizing?
HEY!
Waaa-aaaaa-aagh!
sorry, sorry, sorry--!
Waaaaagh!
BE QUIET!!
SOME-ONE'S GONNA HEAR YOU!!
!!!
GRAB

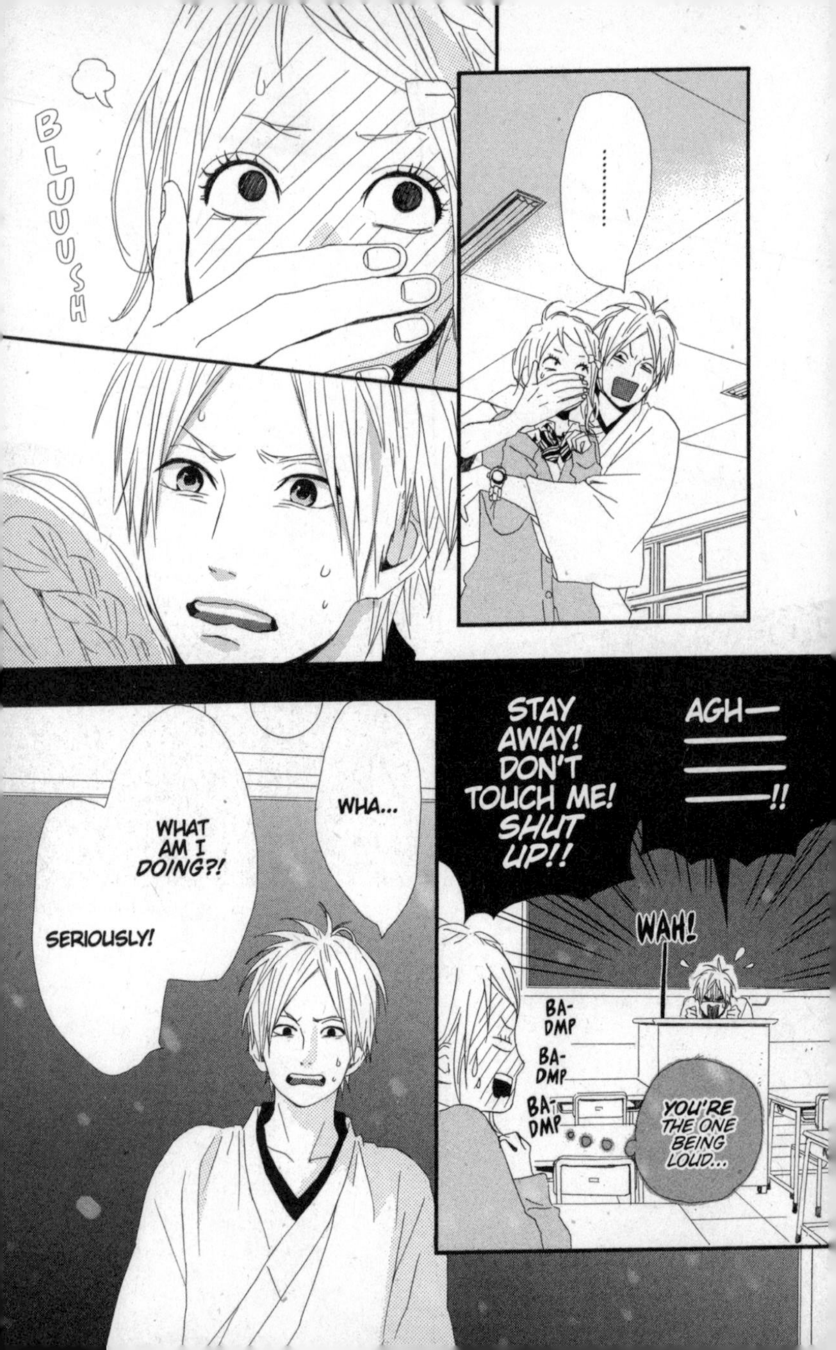
......
BLUUUSH
AGH————!!
STAY AWAY! DON'T TOUCH ME! SHUT UP!!
WAH!
BA-DMP
BA-DMP
BA-DMP
YOU'RE THE ONE BEING LOUD...
WHA...
WHAT AM I DOING?!
SERIOUSLY!

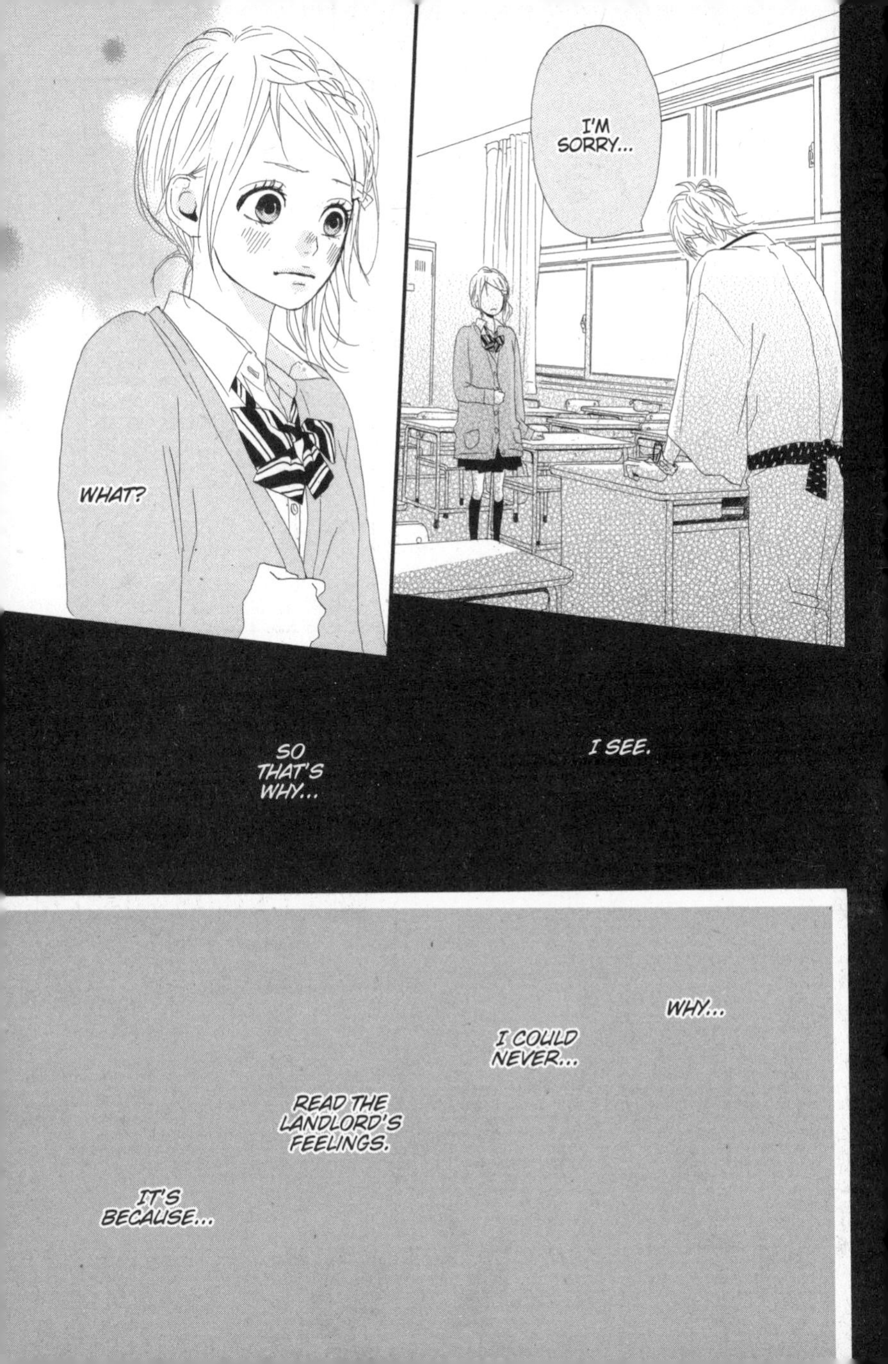
I'M SORRY...
WHAT?
I SEE.
SO THAT'S WHY...
WHY...
I COULD NEVER...
READ THE LANDLORD'S FEELINGS.
IT'S BECAUSE...

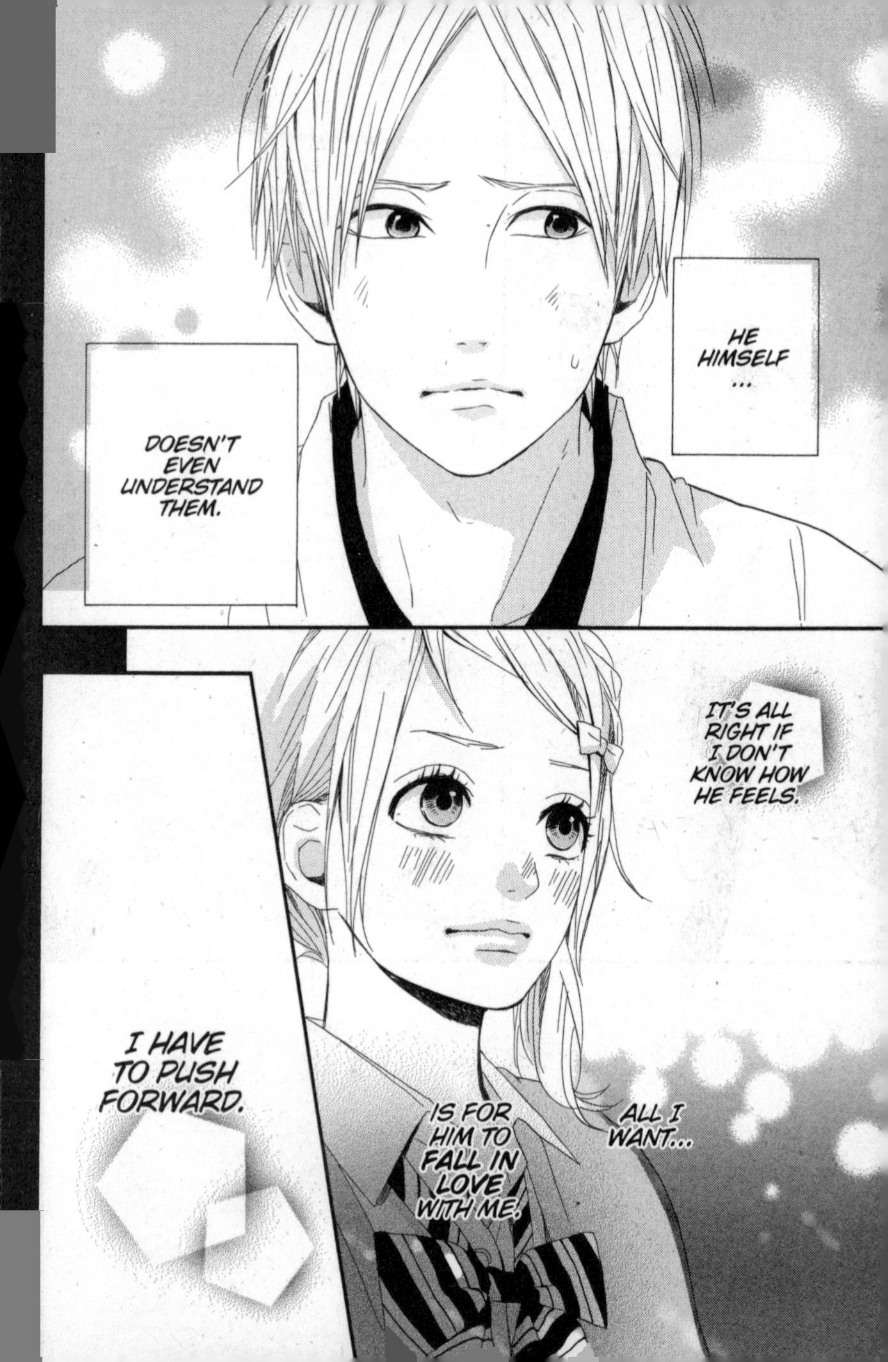
HE HIMSELF ...
DOESN'T EVEN UNDERSTAND THEM.
IT'S ALL RIGHT IF I DON'T KNOW HOW HE FEELS.
ALL I WANT...
IS FOR HIM TO FALL IN LOVE WITH ME.
I HAVE TO PUSH FORWARD.

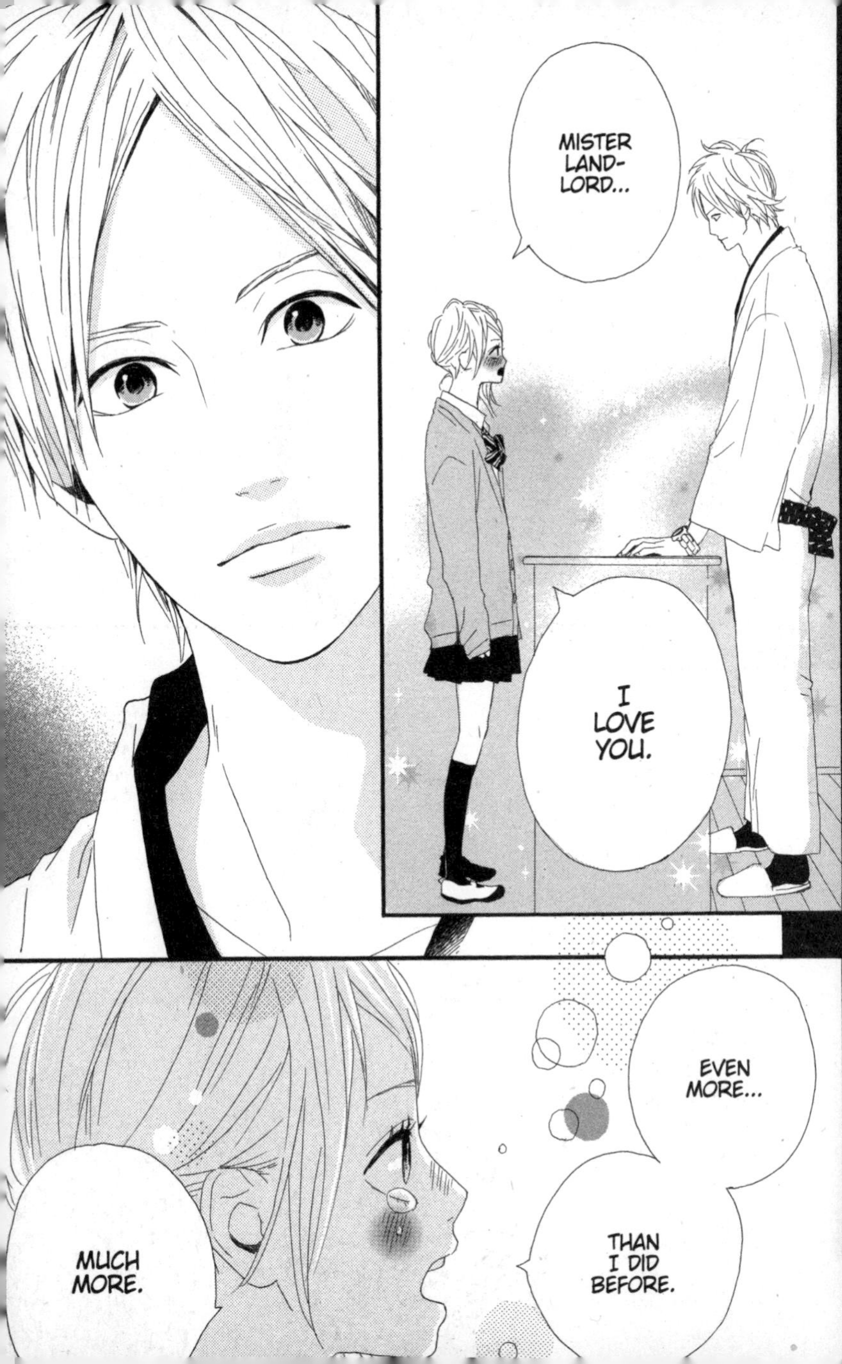
MISTER LAND-LORD...
I LOVE YOU.
EVEN MORE...
THAN I DID BEFORE.
MUCH MORE.

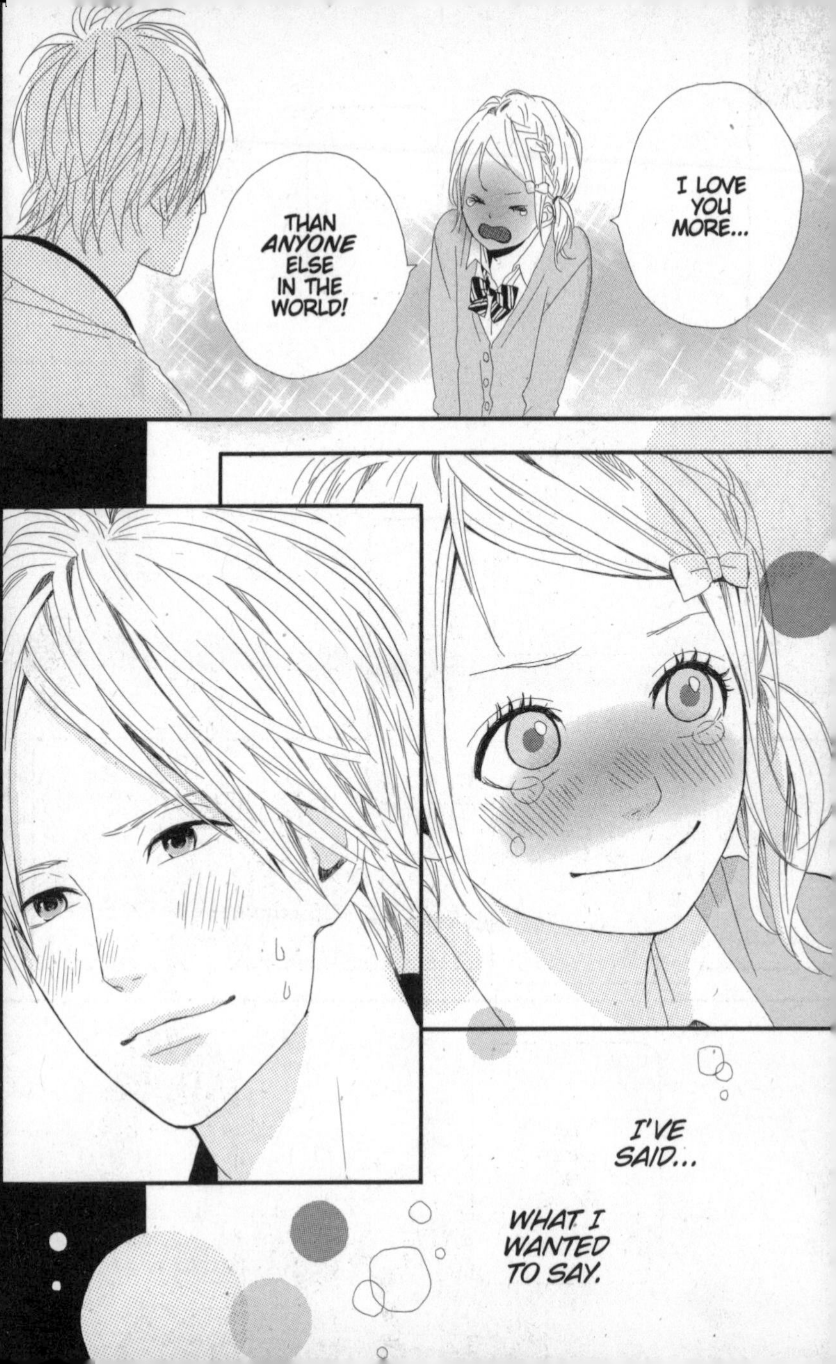
I LOVE YOU MORE...
THAN ANYONE ELSE IN THE WORLD!
I'VE SAID...
WHAT I WANTED TO SAY.

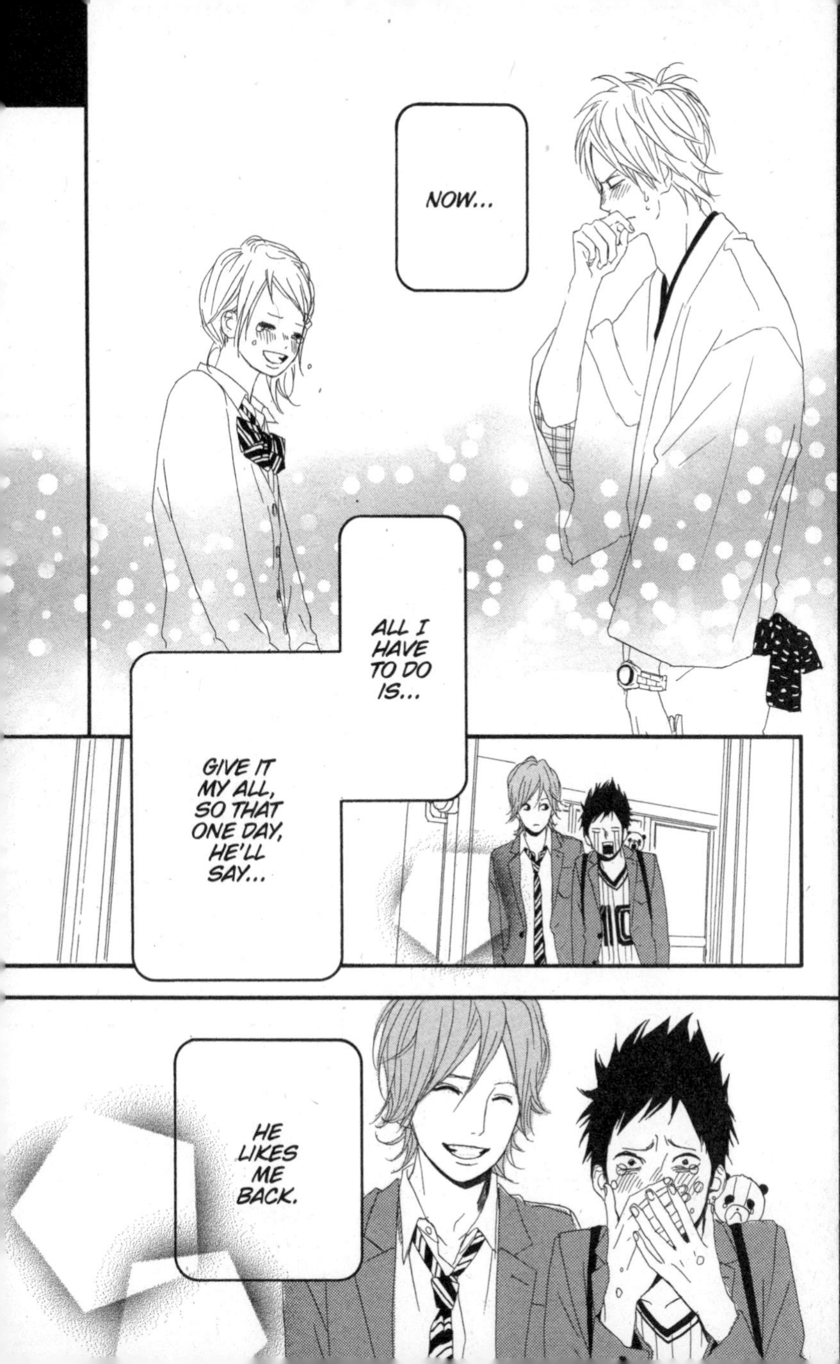
NOW...
ALL I HAVE TO DO IS...
GIVE IT MY ALL, SO THAT ONE DAY, HE'LL SAY...
HE LIKES ME BACK.

Just playing!!

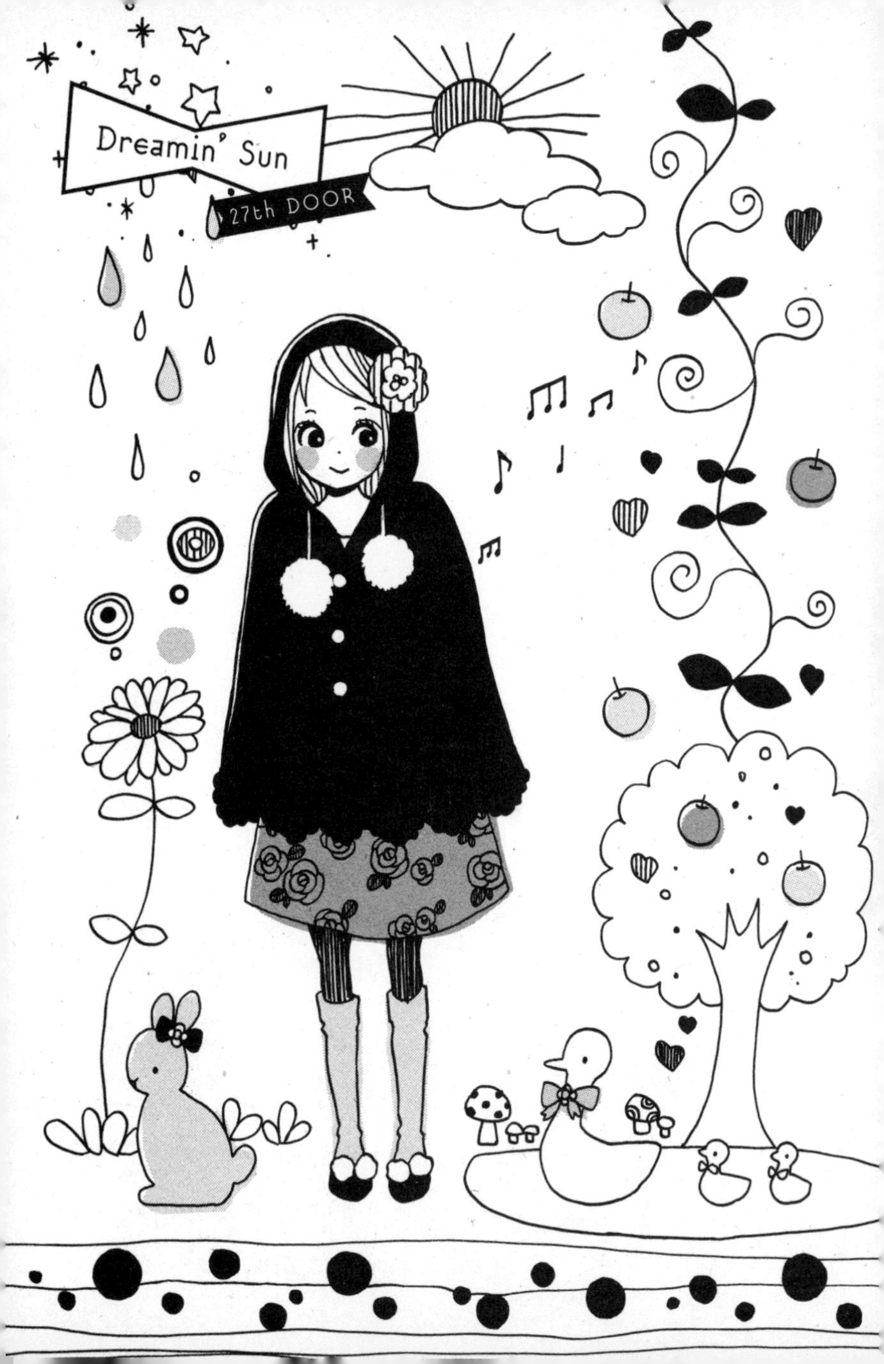
Dreamin' Sun
27th DOOR

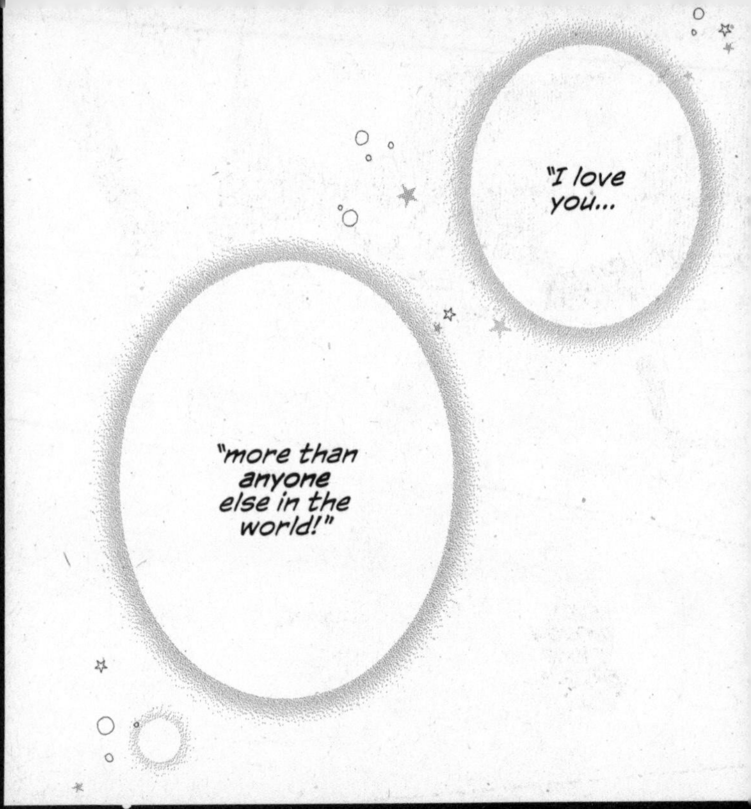
"I love you...
"more than anyone else in the world!"

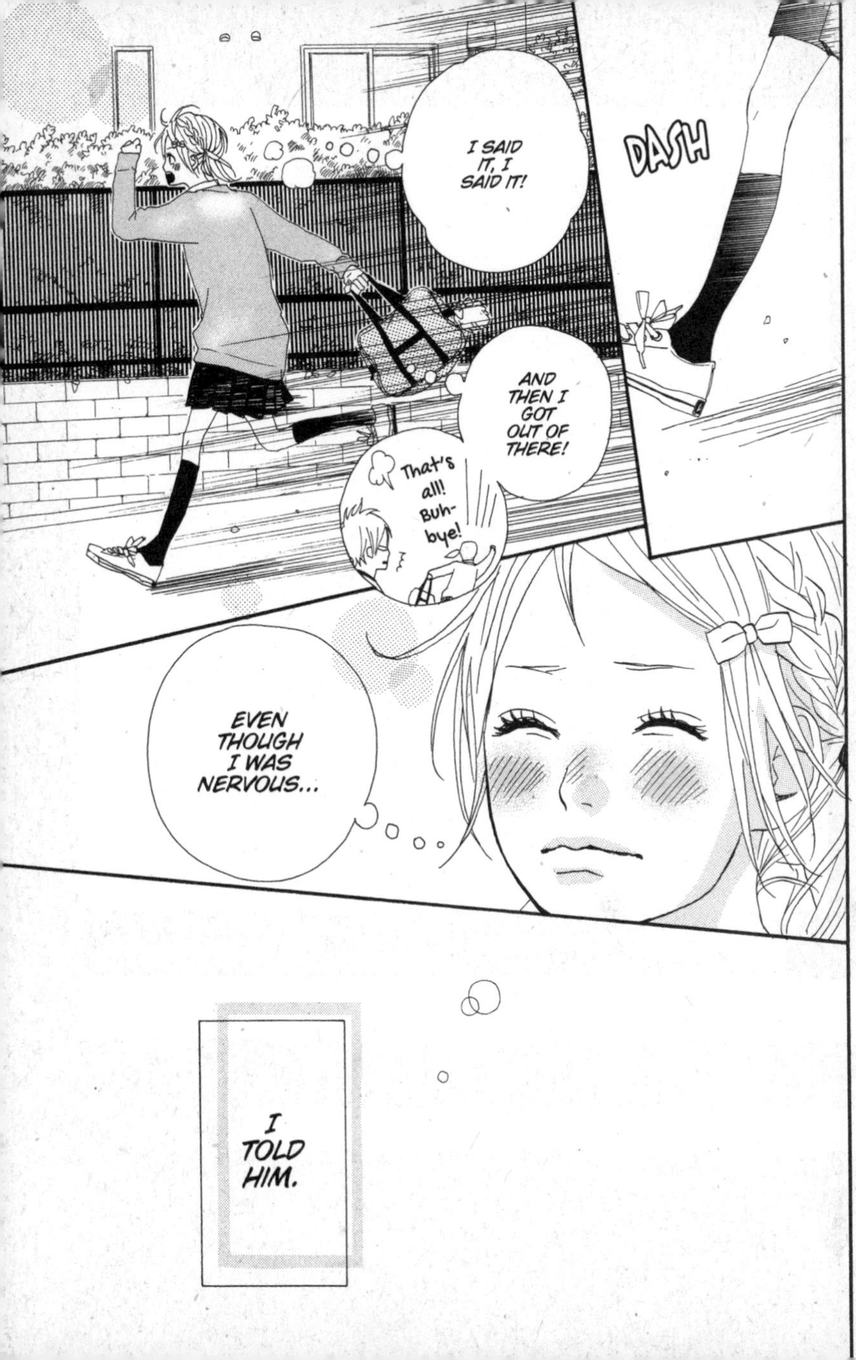
DASH
I SAID IT, I SAID IT!
AND THEN I GOT OUT OF THERE!
That's all! Buh-bye!
EVEN THOUGH I WAS NERVOUS...
I TOLD HIM.

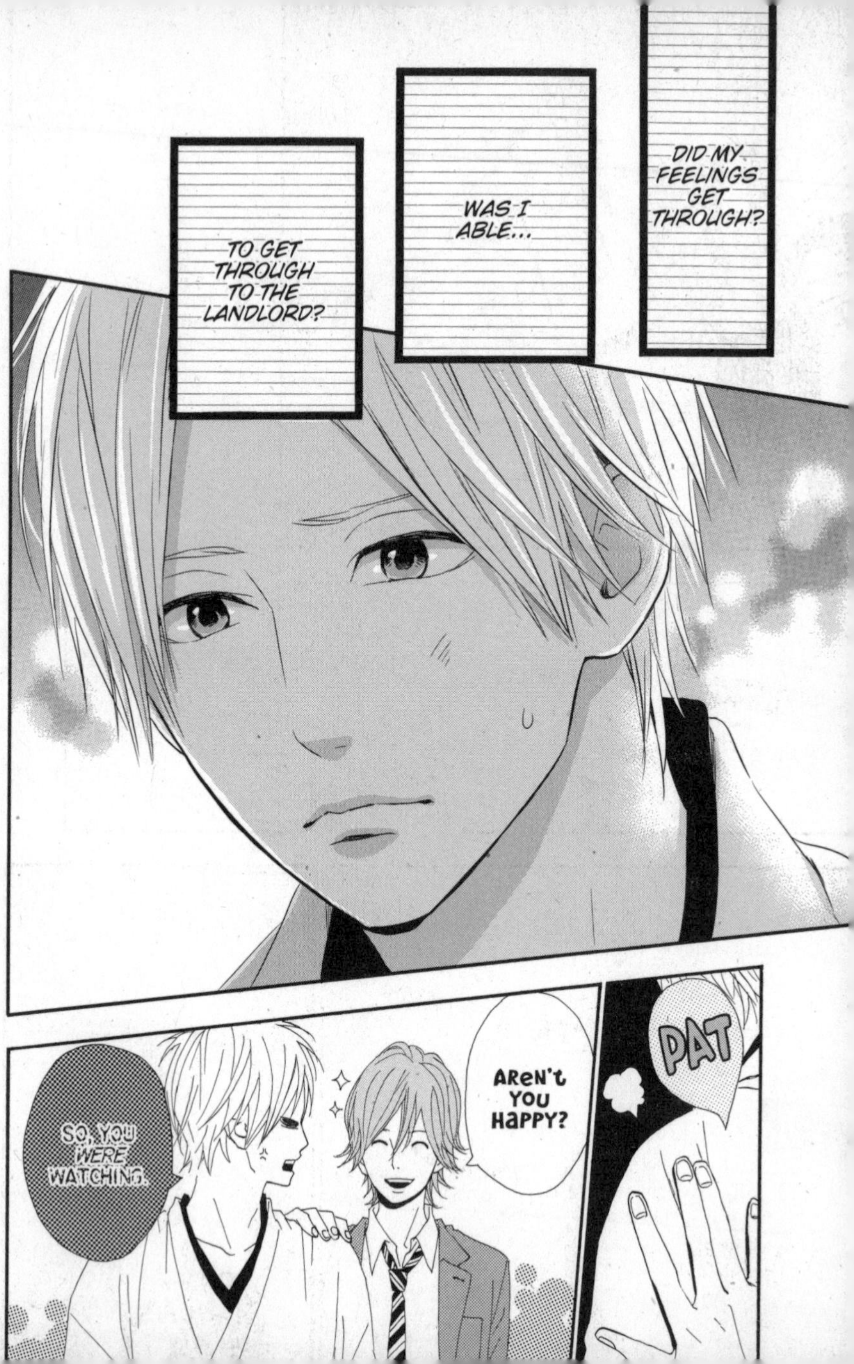
DID MY FEELINGS GET THROUGH?
WAS I ABLE...
TO GET THROUGH TO THE LANDLORD?
PAT
AREN'T YOU HAPPY?
SO, YOU WERE WATCHING.

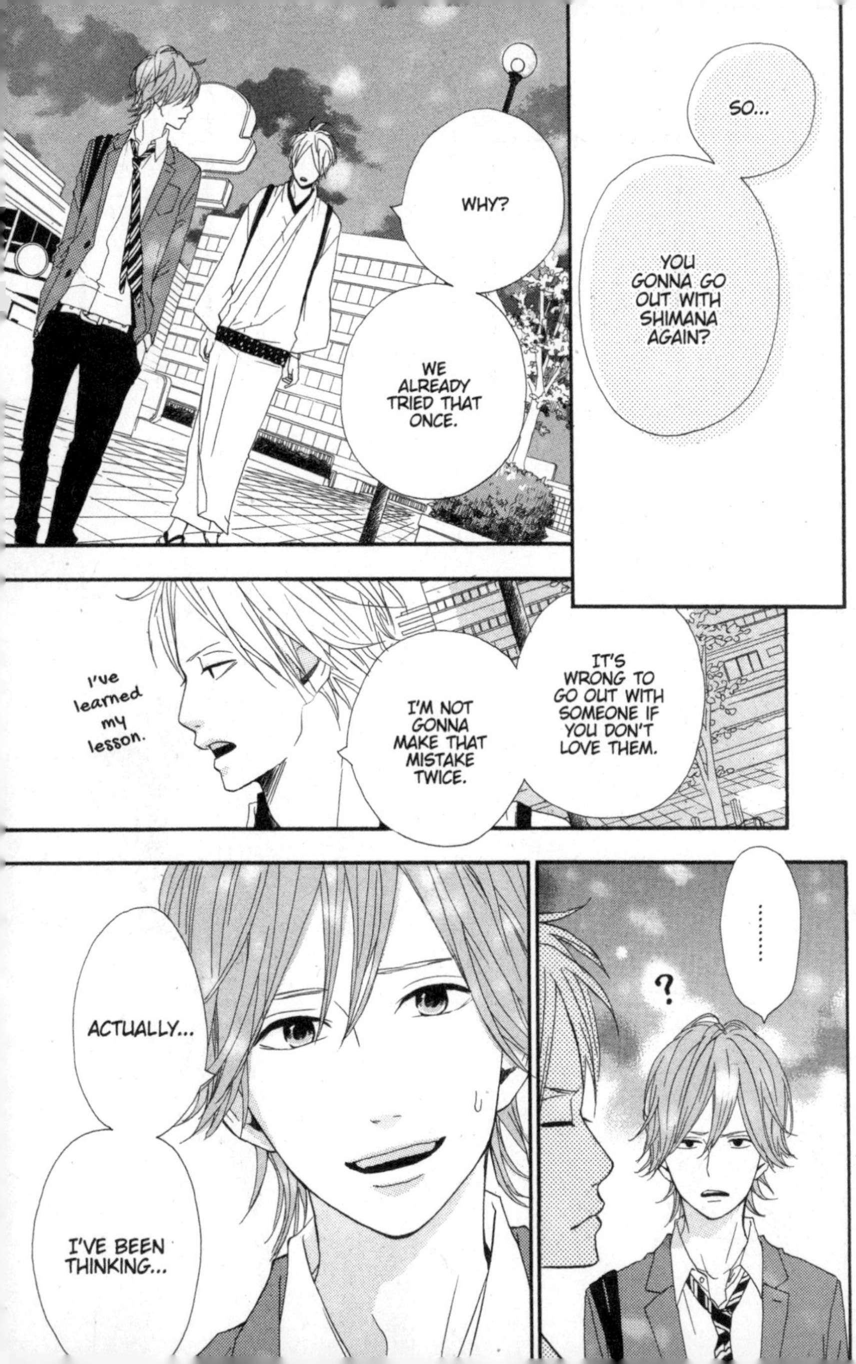
SO...
YOU GONNA GO OUT WITH SHIMANA AGAIN?
WHY?
WE ALREADY TRIED THAT ONCE.
IT'S WRONG TO GO OUT WITH SOMEONE IF YOU DON'T LOVE THEM.
I'M NOT GONNA MAKE THAT MISTAKE TWICE.
I've learned my lesson.
......
?
ACTUALLY...
I'VE BEEN THINKING...

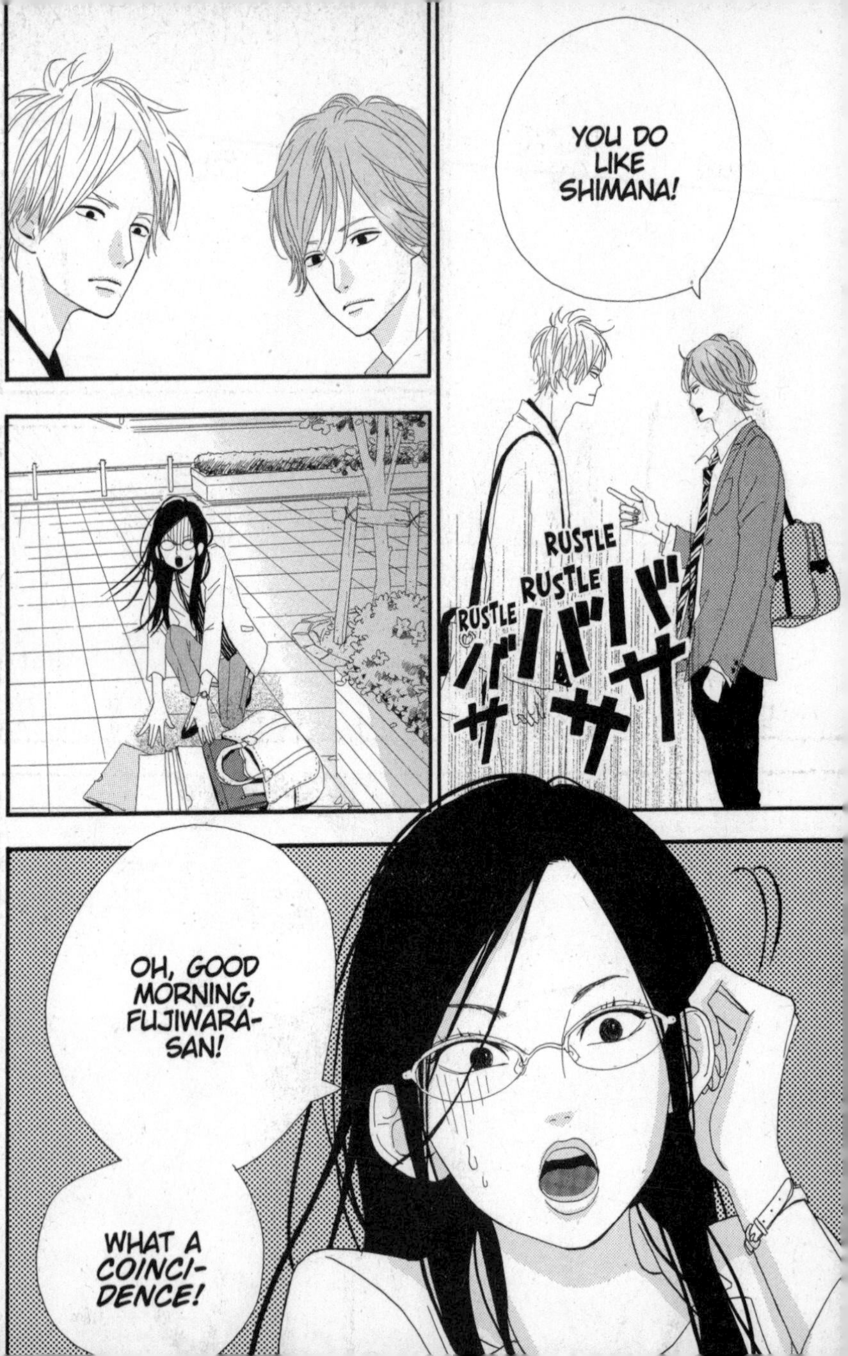
YOU DO LIKE SHIMANA!
RUSTLE
RUSTLE
RUSTLE
OH, GOOD MORNING, FUJIWARA-SAN!
WHAT A COINCI-DENCE!

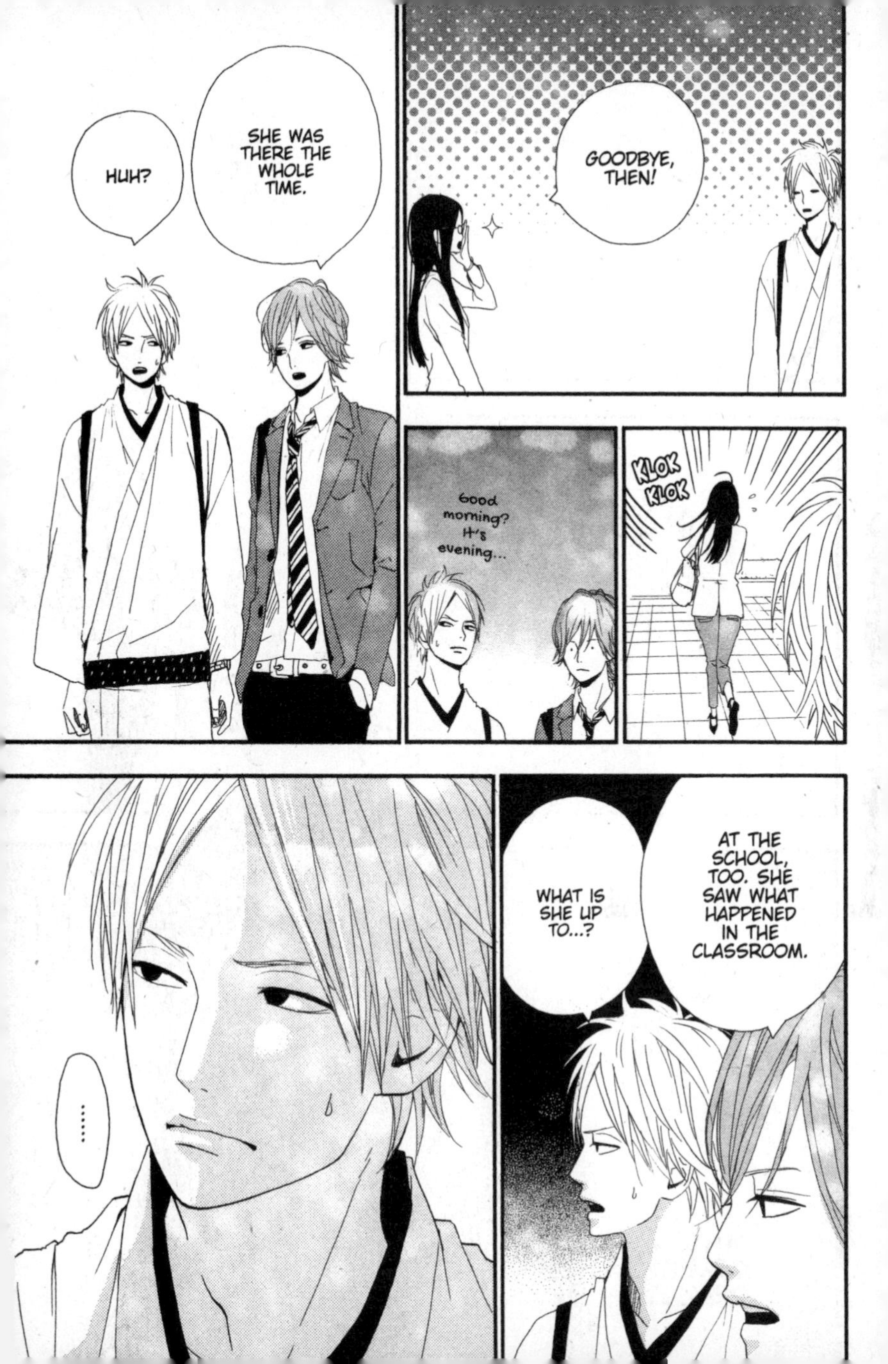
GOODBYE, THEN!
KLOK KLOK
Good morning? It's evening...
SHE WAS THERE THE WHOLE TIME.
HUH?
AT THE SCHOOL, TOO. SHE SAW WHAT HAPPENED IN THE CLASSROOM.
WHAT IS SHE UP TO...?
......

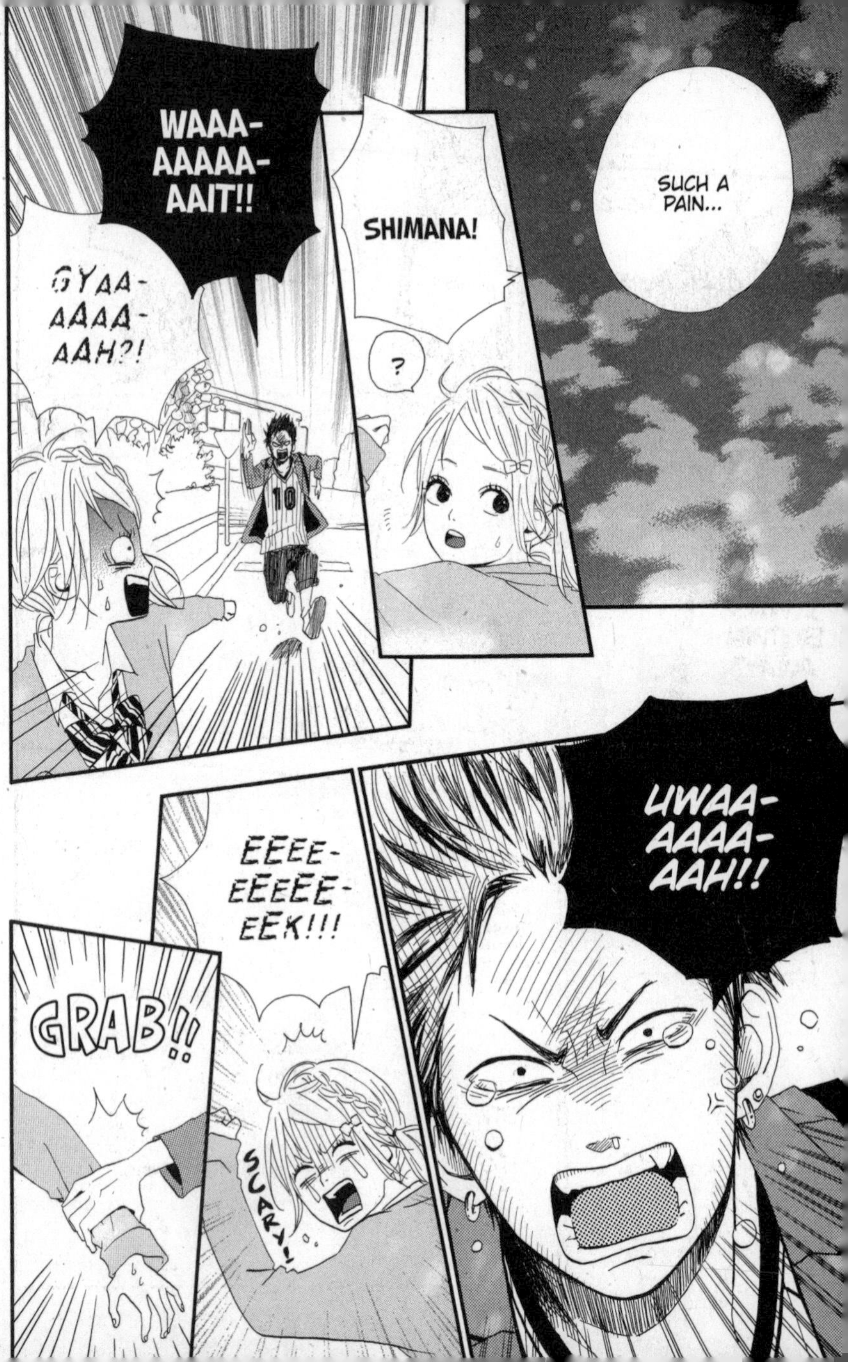
SUCH A PAIN...
SHIMANA!
?
WAAA-AAAAA-AAIT!!
GYAA-AAAA-AAH?!
UWAA-AAAA-AAH!!
EEEE-EEEEE-EEK!!!
SCARY!
GRAB!!

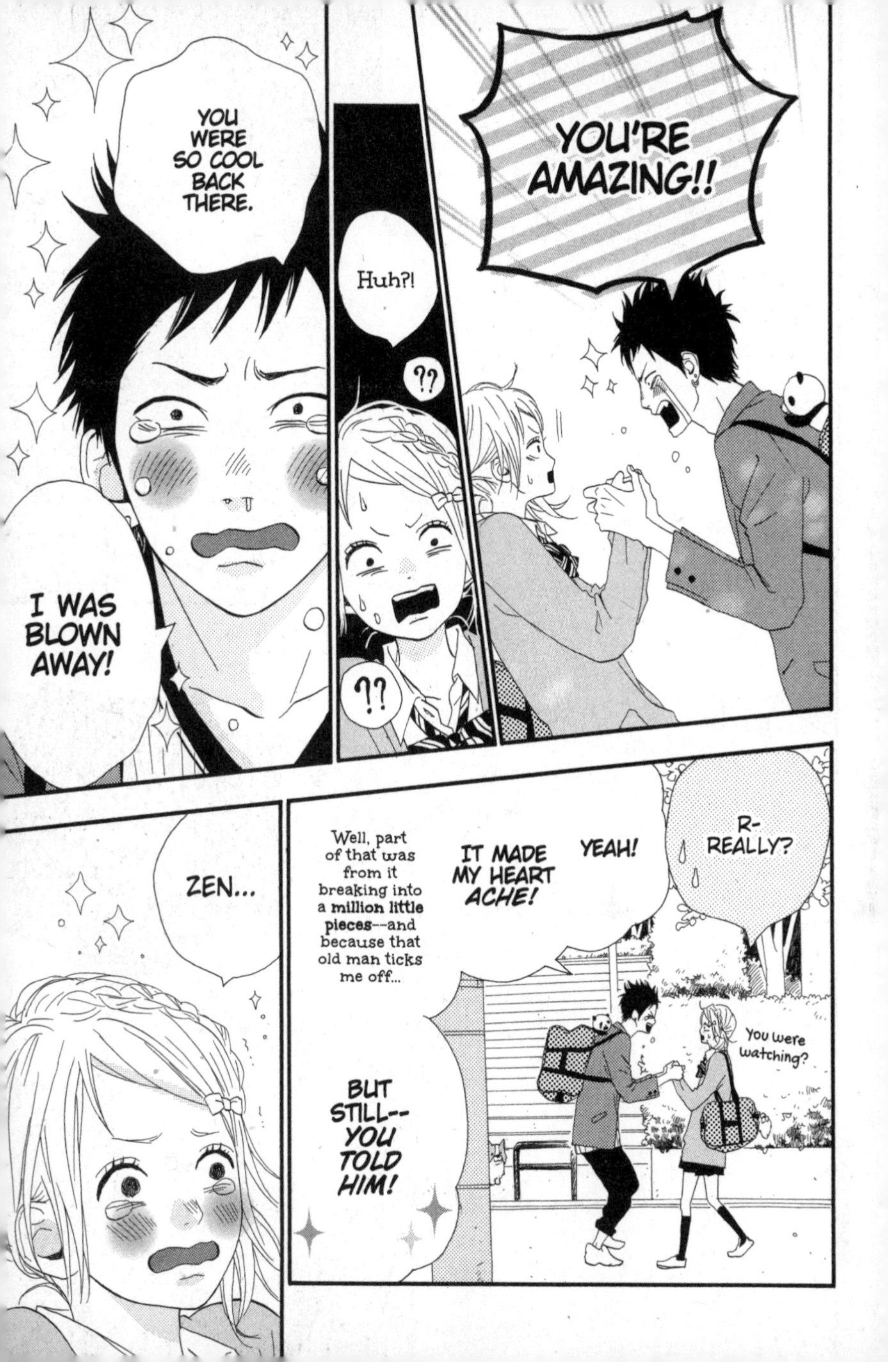
YOU'RE AMAZING!!
Huh?!
??
??
YOU WERE SO COOL BACK THERE.
I WAS BLOWN AWAY!
R-REALLY?
You were watching?
YEAH!
IT MADE MY HEART ACHE!
Well, part of that was from it breaking into a **million little pieces**--and because that old man ticks me off...
BUT STILL--YOU TOLD HIM!
ZEN...

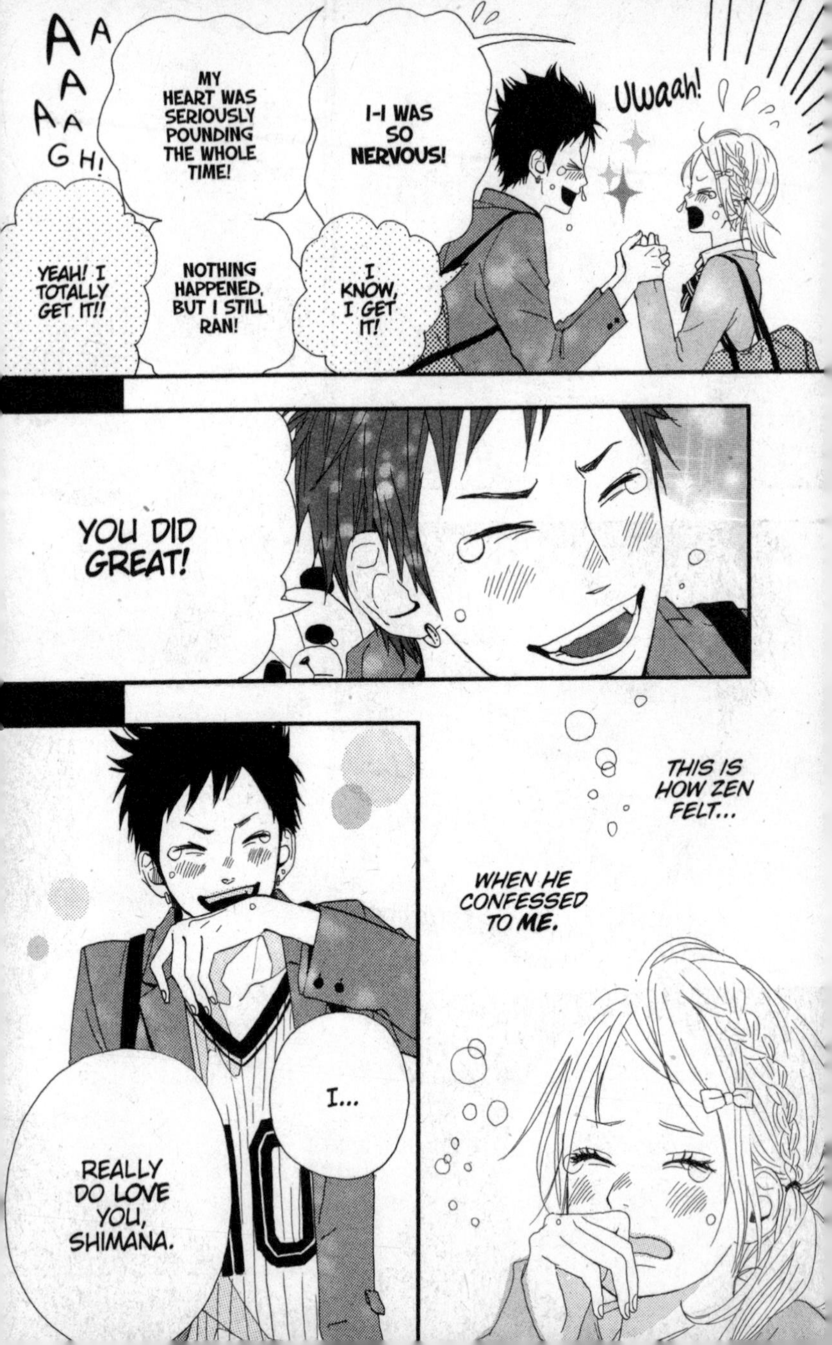
UWAAH!
I-I WAS SO NERVOUS!
MY HEART WAS SERIOUSLY POUNDING THE WHOLE TIME!
AAAAAGH!
I KNOW, I GET IT!
NOTHING HAPPENED, BUT I STILL RAN!
YEAH! I TOTALLY GET IT!!
YOU DID GREAT!
THIS IS HOW ZEN FELT...
WHEN HE CONFESSED TO ME.
I...
REALLY DO LOVE YOU, SHIMANA.

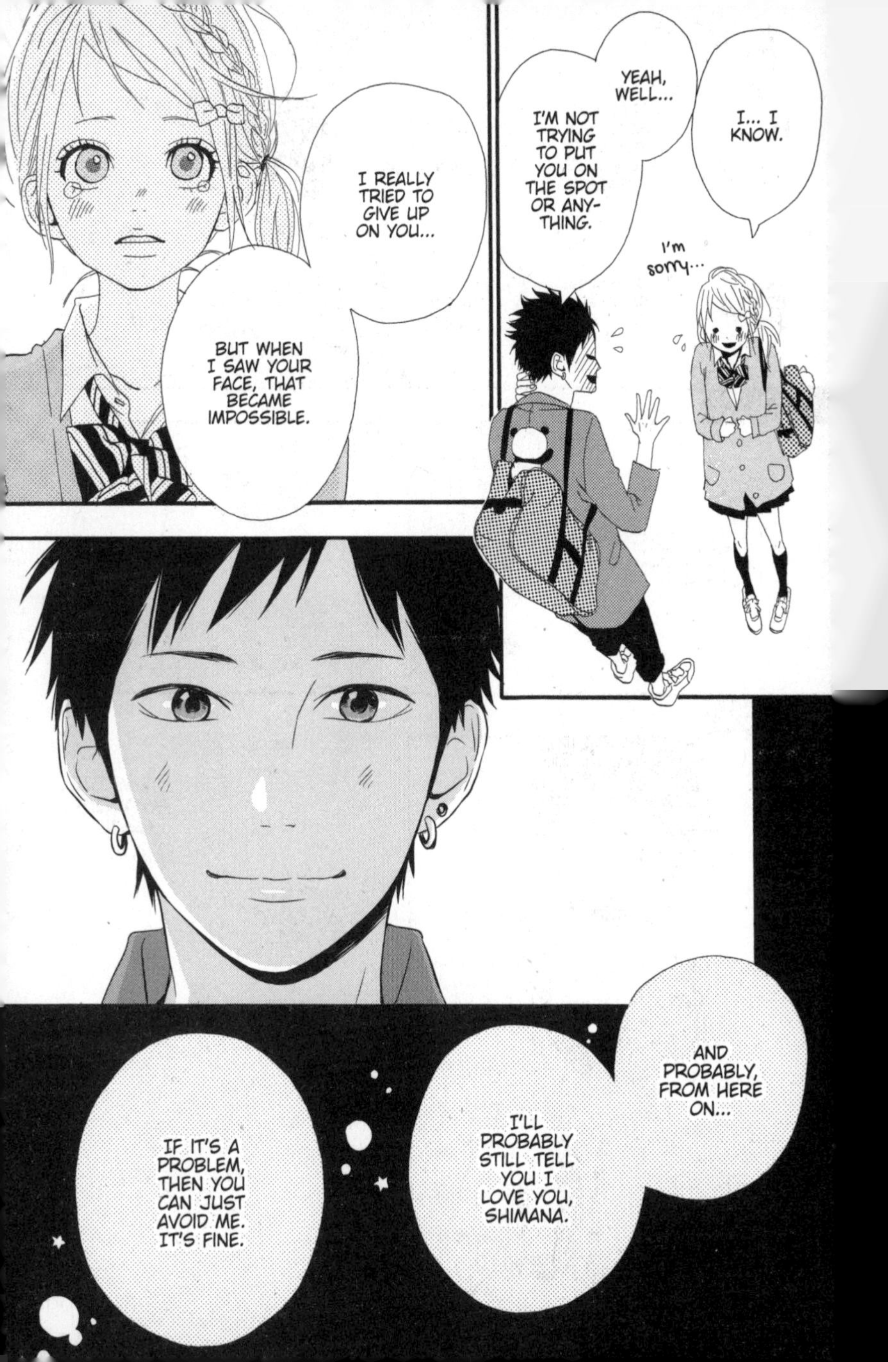
I... I KNOW.
YEAH, WELL...
I'M NOT TRYING TO PUT YOU ON THE SPOT OR ANY-THING.
I'm sorry...
I REALLY TRIED TO GIVE UP ON YOU...
BUT WHEN I SAW YOUR FACE, THAT BECAME IMPOSSIBLE.
AND PROBABLY, FROM HERE ON...
I'LL PROBABLY STILL TELL YOU I LOVE YOU, SHIMANA.
IF IT'S A PROBLEM, THEN YOU CAN JUST AVOID ME. IT'S FINE.

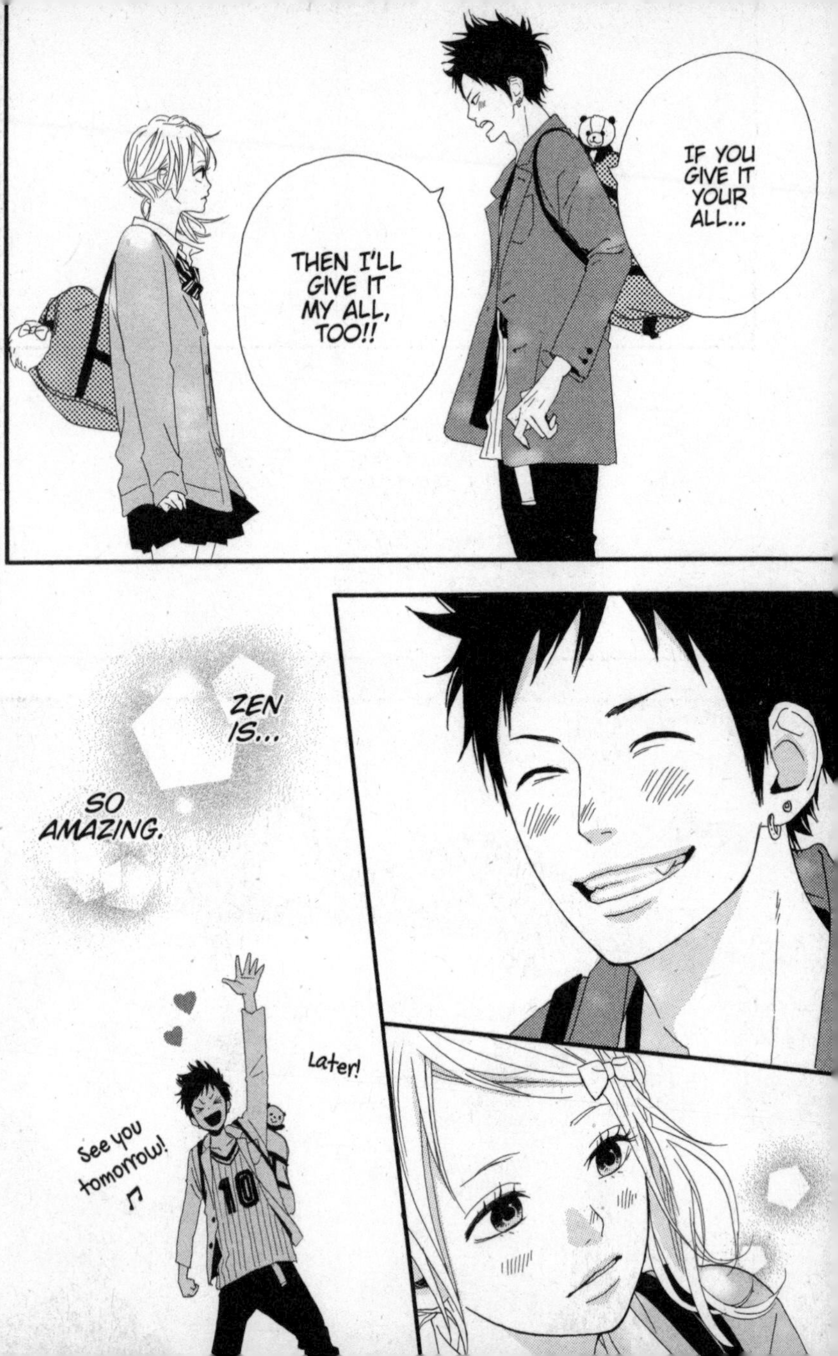
IF YOU GIVE IT YOUR ALL...
THEN I'LL GIVE IT MY ALL, TOO!!
ZEN IS...
SO AMAZING.
Later!
See you tomorrow! ♫

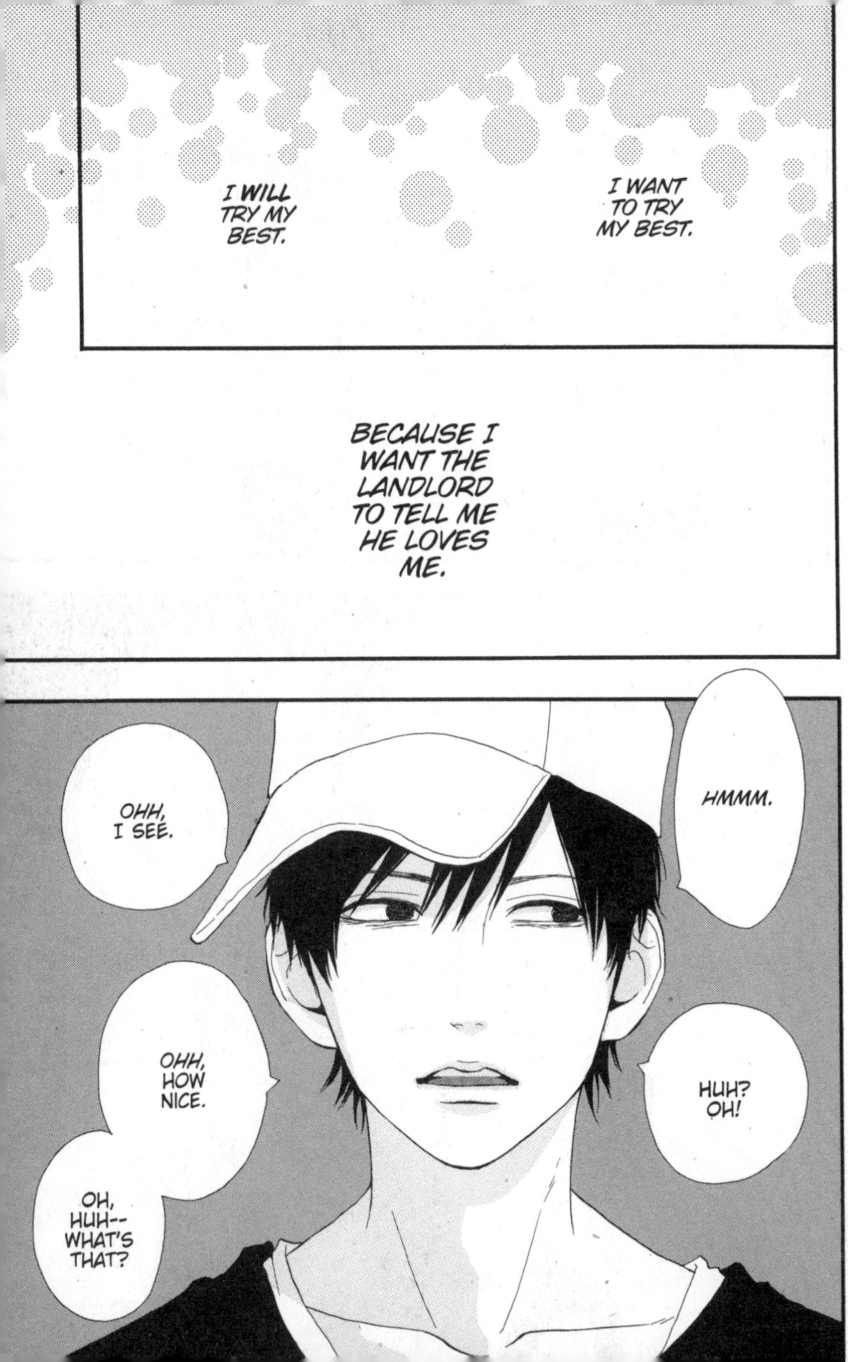
I WANT TO TRY MY BEST.
I WILL TRY MY BEST.
BECAUSE I WANT THE LANDLORD TO TELL ME HE LOVES ME.
HMMM.
OHH, I SEE.
HUH? OH!
OHH, HOW NICE.
OH, HUH-- WHAT'S THAT?

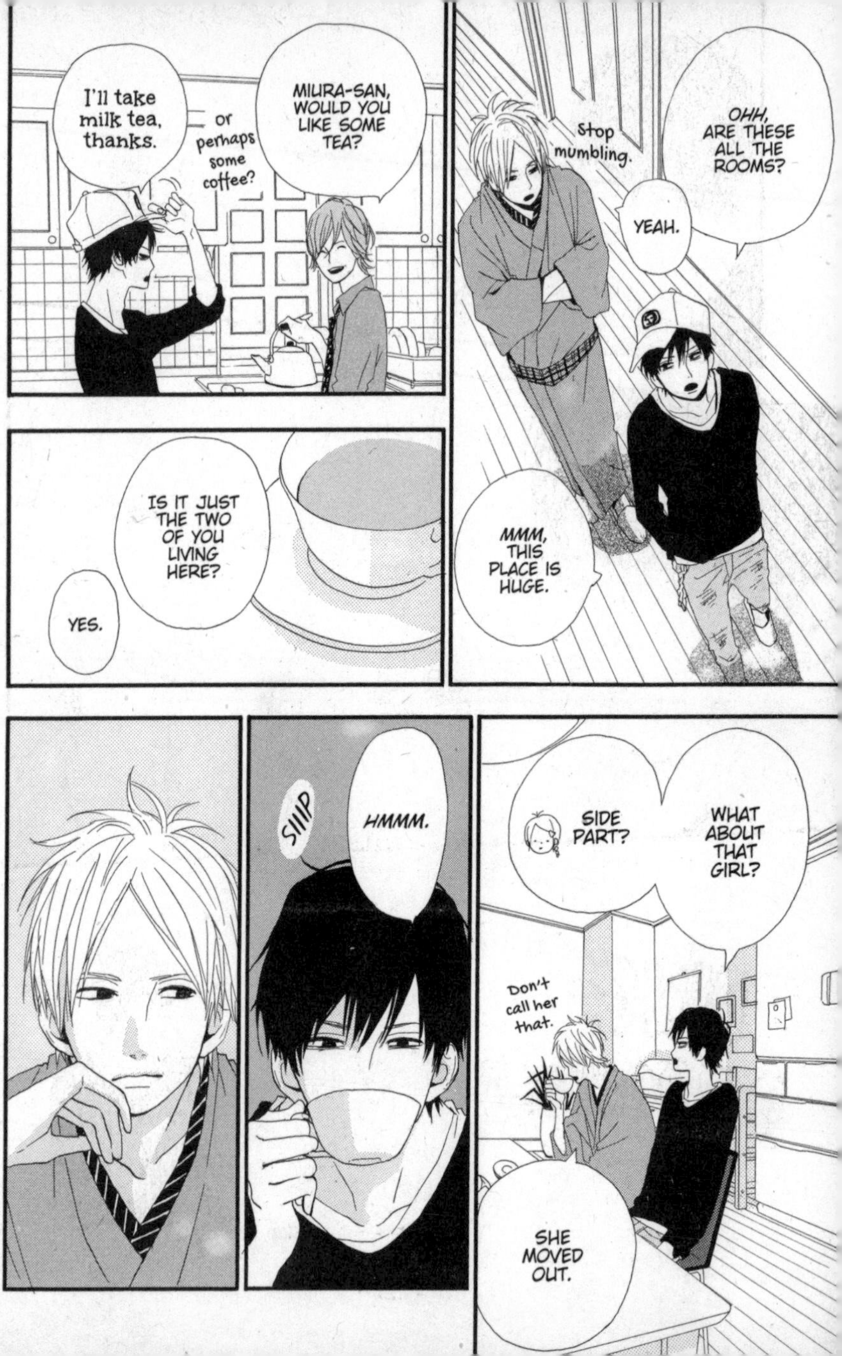
OHH, ARE THESE ALL THE ROOMS?
YEAH.
Stop mumbling.
MMM, THIS PLACE IS HUGE.
MIURA-SAN, WOULD YOU LIKE SOME TEA?
or perhaps some coffee?
I'll take milk tea, thanks.
IS IT JUST THE TWO OF YOU LIVING HERE?
YES.
WHAT ABOUT THAT GIRL?
SIDE PART?
Don't call her that.
SHE MOVED OUT.
HMMM.
SIIIP

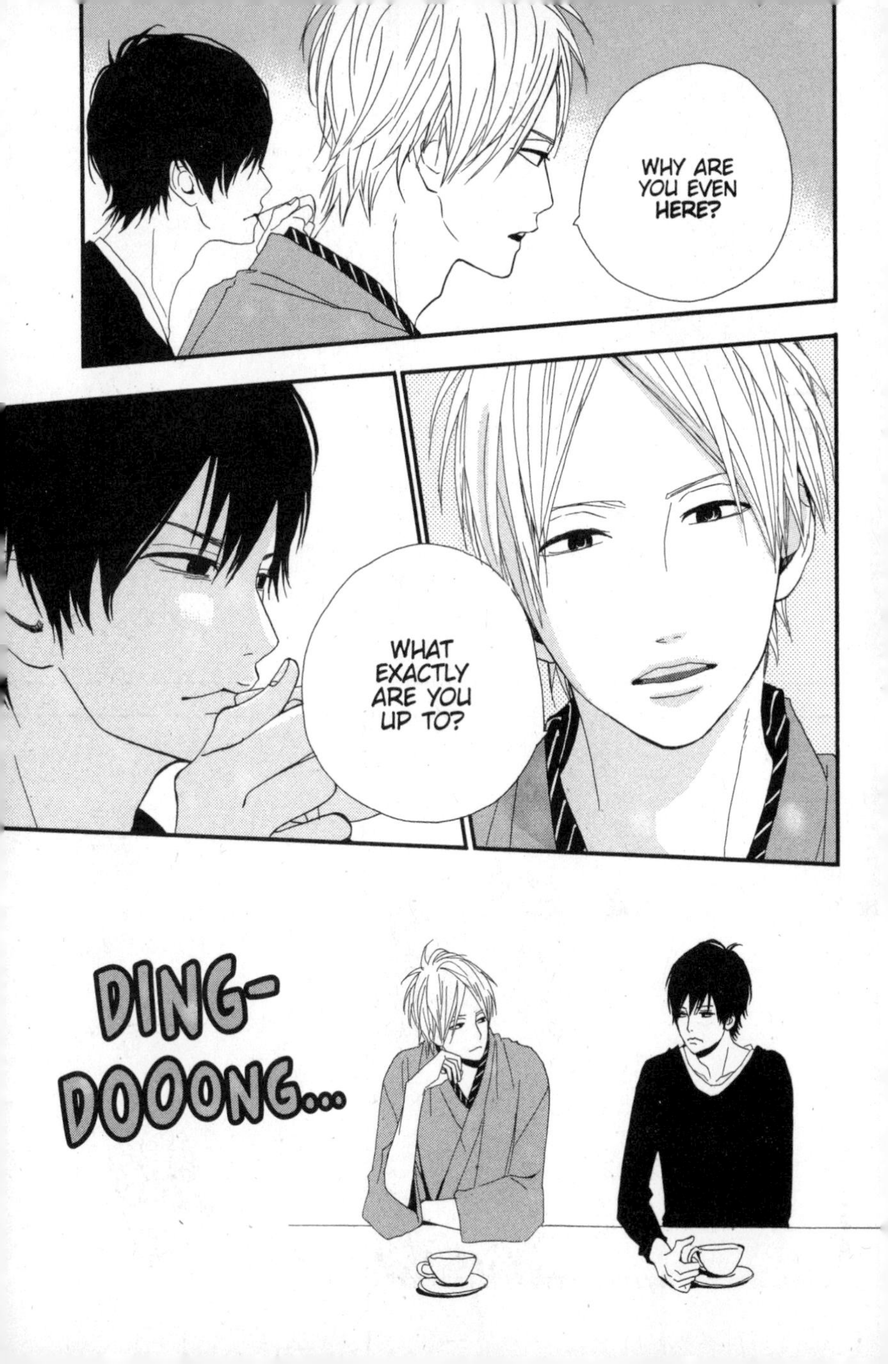
WHY ARE YOU EVEN HERE?
WHAT EXACTLY ARE YOU UP TO?
DING-DOOONG...

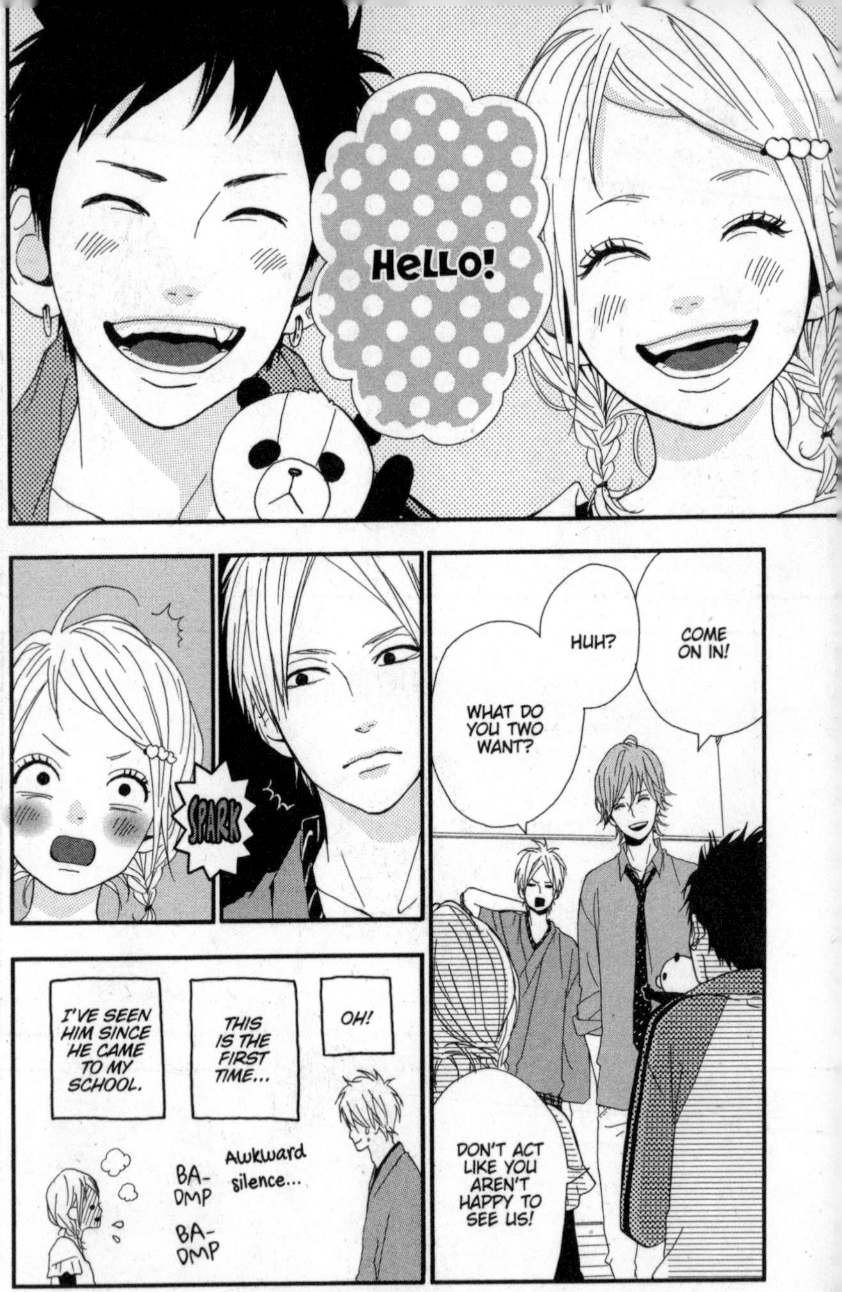
Hello!
COME ON IN!
HUH?
WHAT DO YOU TWO WANT?
DON'T ACT LIKE YOU AREN'T HAPPY TO SEE US!
SPARK
OH!
THIS IS THE FIRST TIME...
I'VE SEEN HIM SINCE HE CAME TO MY SCHOOL.
Awkward silence...
BA-DMP
BA-DMP

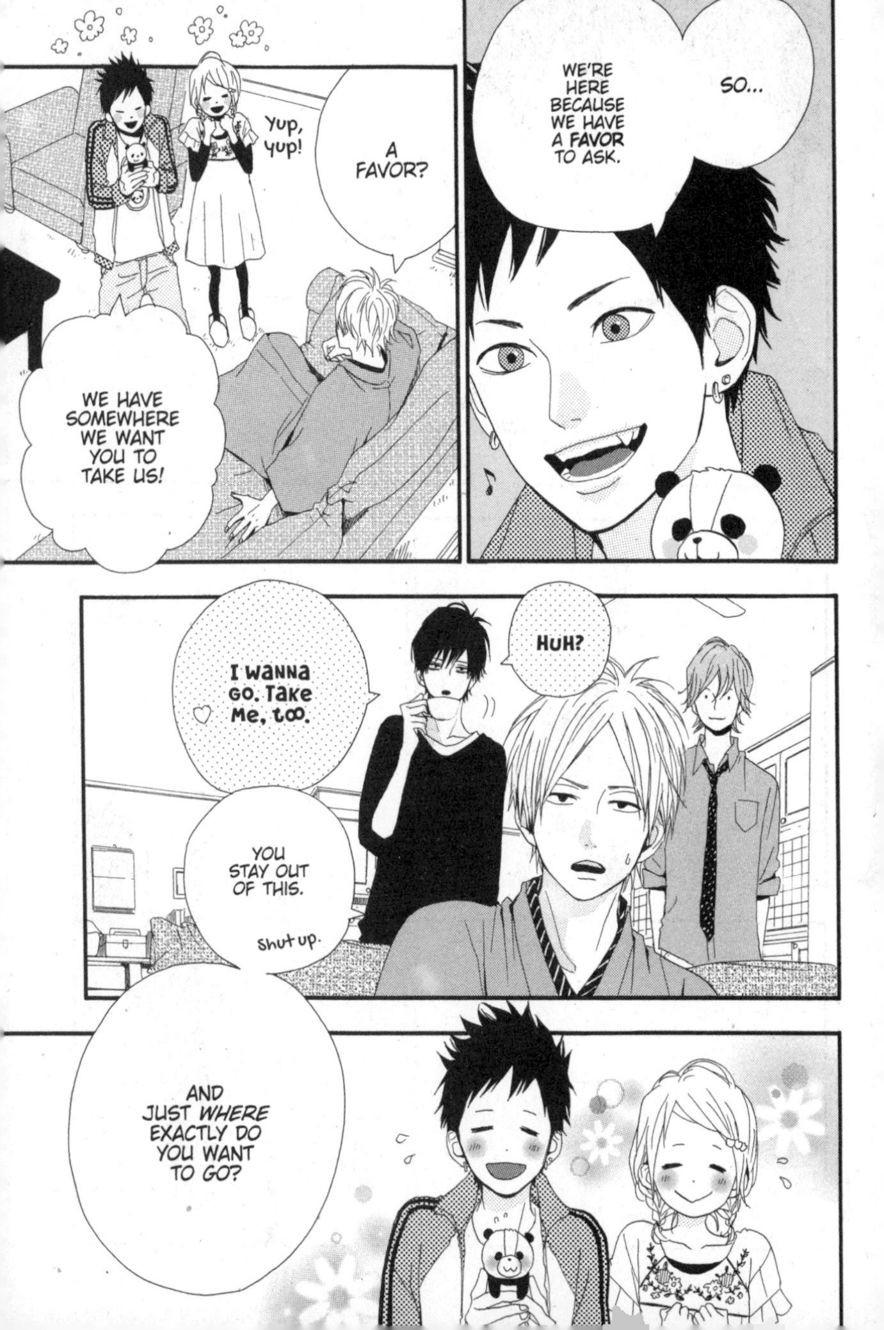
SO...
WE'RE HERE BECAUSE WE HAVE A FAVOR TO ASK.
A FAVOR?
Yup, yup!
WE HAVE SOMEWHERE WE WANT YOU TO TAKE US!
HUH?
I wanna go. Take me, too.
YOU STAY OUT OF THIS.
Shut up.
AND JUST WHERE EXACTLY DO YOU WANT TO GO?

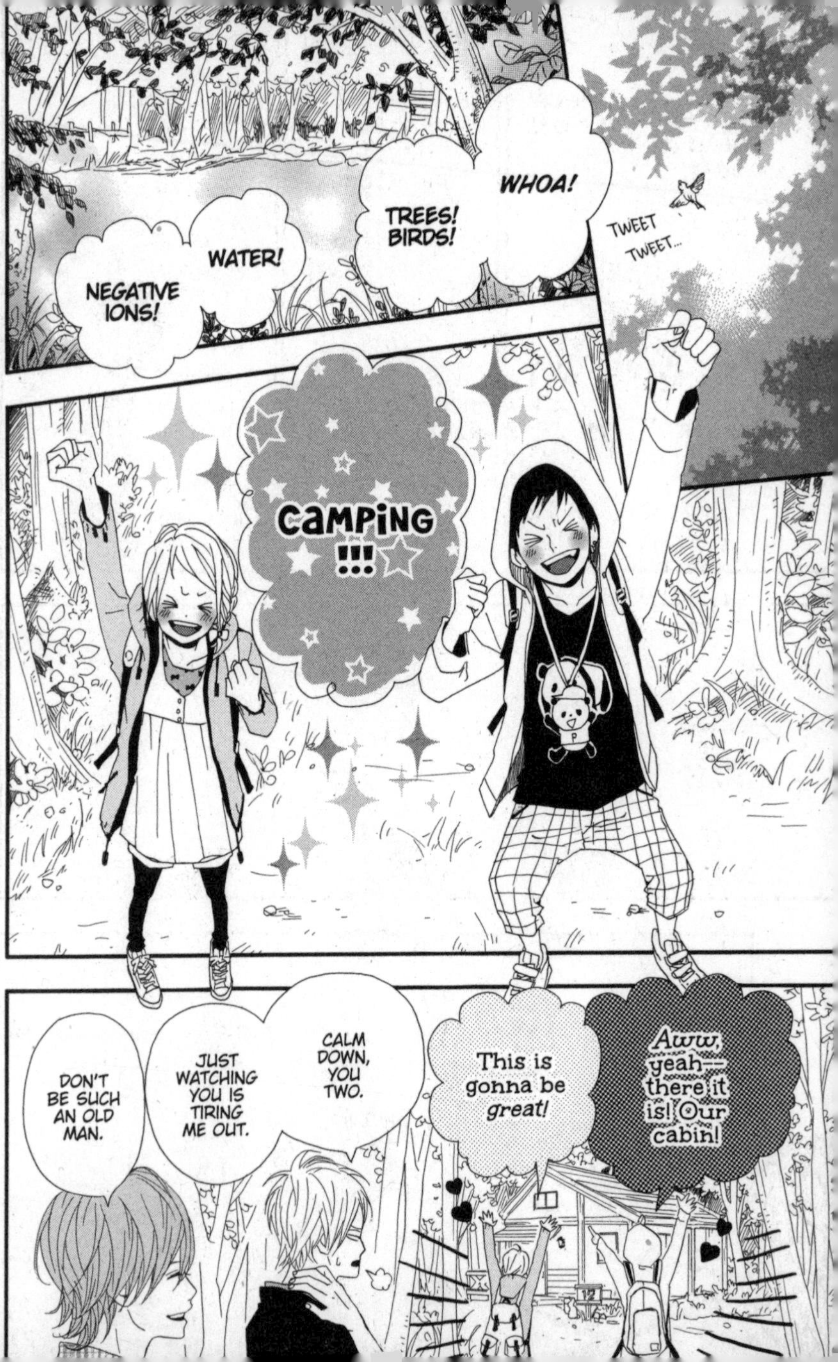
TWEET TWEET...
WHOA!
TREES! BIRDS!
WATER!
NEGATIVE IONS!
CAMPING !!!
Aww, yeah— there it is! Our cabin!
This is gonna be *great!*
CALM DOWN, YOU TWO.
JUST WATCHING YOU IS TIRING ME OUT.
DON'T BE SUCH AN OLD MAN.

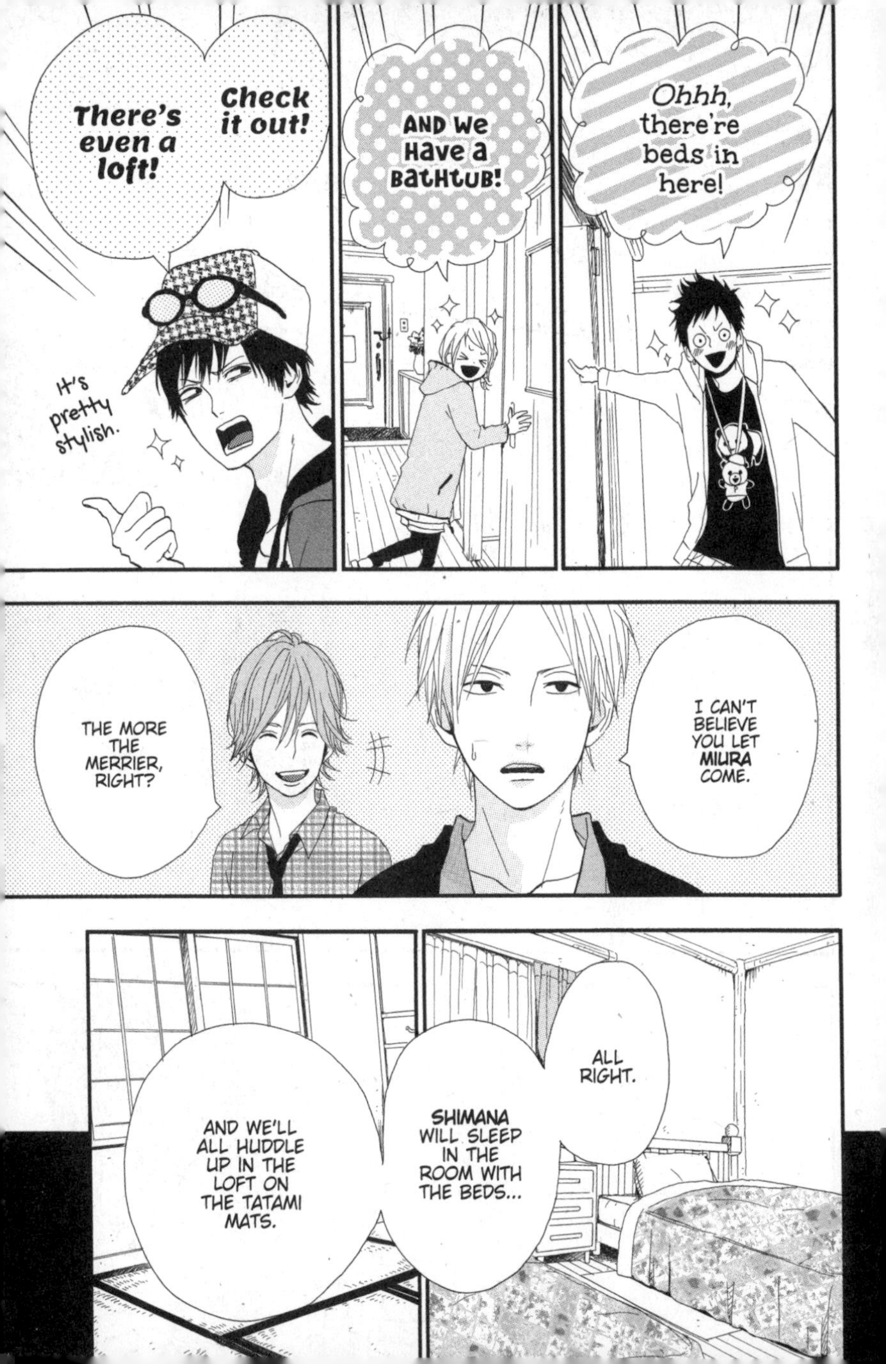
Ohhh, there're beds in here!
AND WE HAVE A BATHTUB!
Check it out!
There's even a loft!
It's pretty stylish.
I CAN'T BELIEVE YOU LET MIURA COME.
THE MORE THE MERRIER, RIGHT?
ALL RIGHT.
SHIMANA WILL SLEEP IN THE ROOM WITH THE BEDS...
AND WE'LL ALL HUDDLE UP IN THE LOFT ON THE TATAMI MATS.

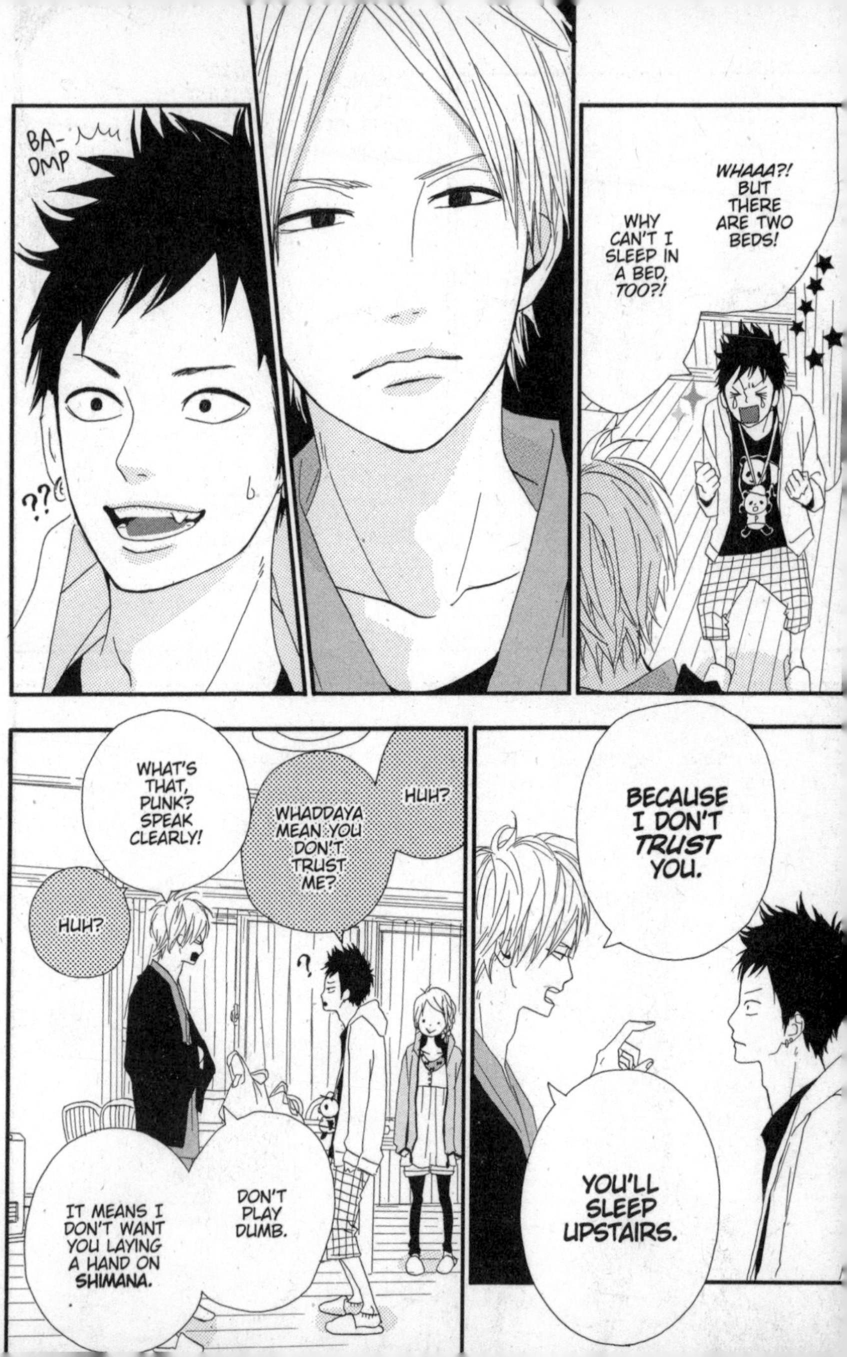
WHAAA?! BUT THERE ARE TWO BEDS!
WHY CAN'T I SLEEP IN A BED, *TOO?!*
BA-DMP
BECAUSE I DON'T *TRUST* YOU.
YOU'LL SLEEP UPSTAIRS.
HUH?
WHADDAYA MEAN YOU DON'T TRUST ME?
WHAT'S THAT, PUNK? SPEAK CLEARLY!
HUH?
DON'T PLAY DUMB.
IT MEANS I DON'T WANT YOU LAYING A HAND ON **SHIMANA.**

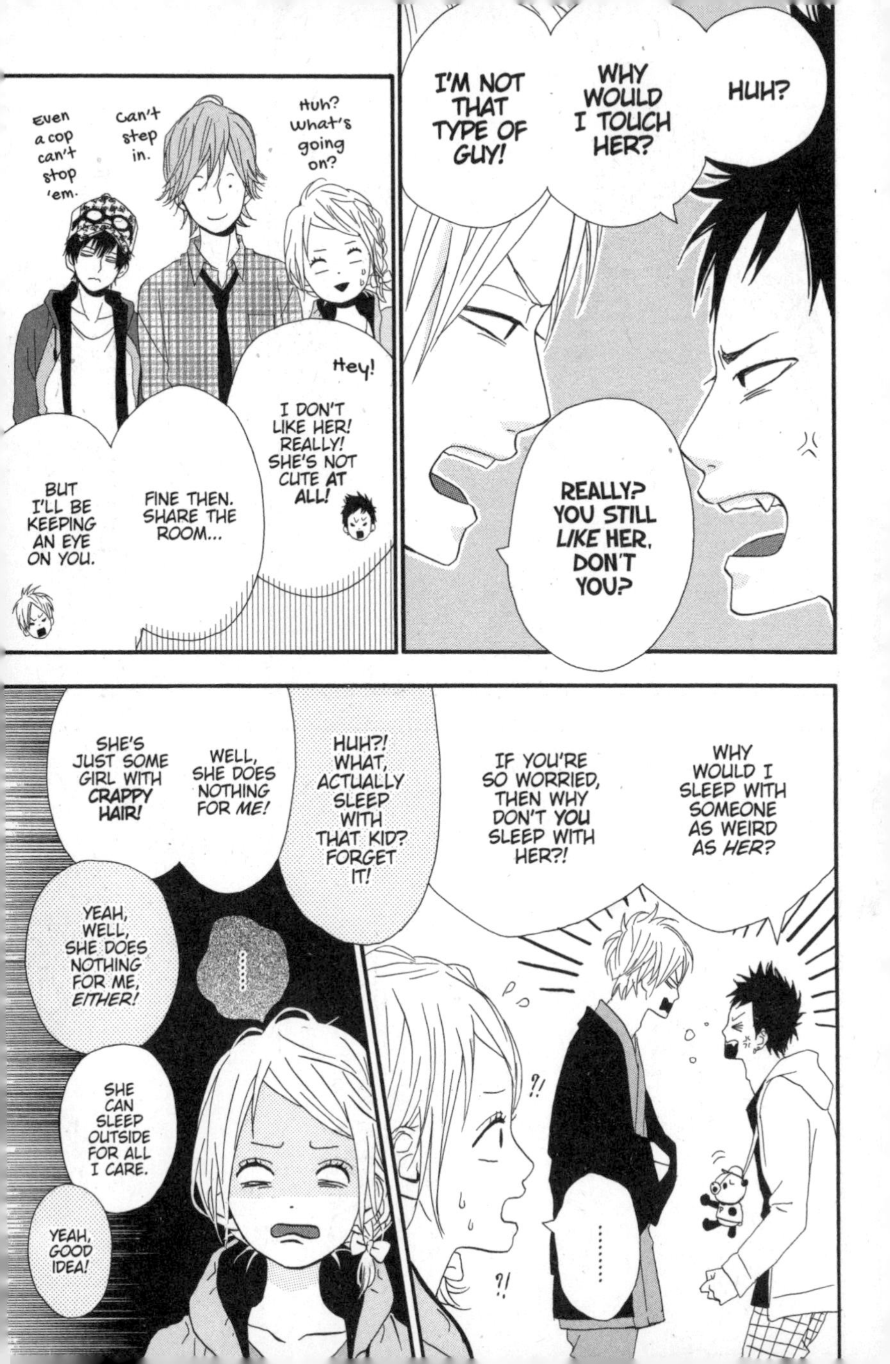
HUH?
WHY WOULD I TOUCH HER?
I'M NOT THAT TYPE OF GUY!
REALLY? YOU STILL LIKE HER, DON'T YOU?
Huh? What's going on?
Can't step in.
Even a cop can't stop 'em.
Hey!
I DON'T LIKE HER! REALLY! SHE'S NOT CUTE AT ALL!
FINE THEN. SHARE THE ROOM...
BUT I'LL BE KEEPING AN EYE ON YOU.
WHY WOULD I SLEEP WITH SOMEONE AS WEIRD AS HER?
IF YOU'RE SO WORRIED, THEN WHY DON'T YOU SLEEP WITH HER?!
?!
?!
......
HUH?! WHAT, ACTUALLY SLEEP WITH THAT KID? FORGET IT!
WELL, SHE DOES NOTHING FOR ME!
SHE'S JUST SOME GIRL WITH CRAPPY HAIR!
......
YEAH, WELL, SHE DOES NOTHING FOR ME, EITHER!
SHE CAN SLEEP OUTSIDE FOR ALL I CARE.
YEAH, GOOD IDEA!

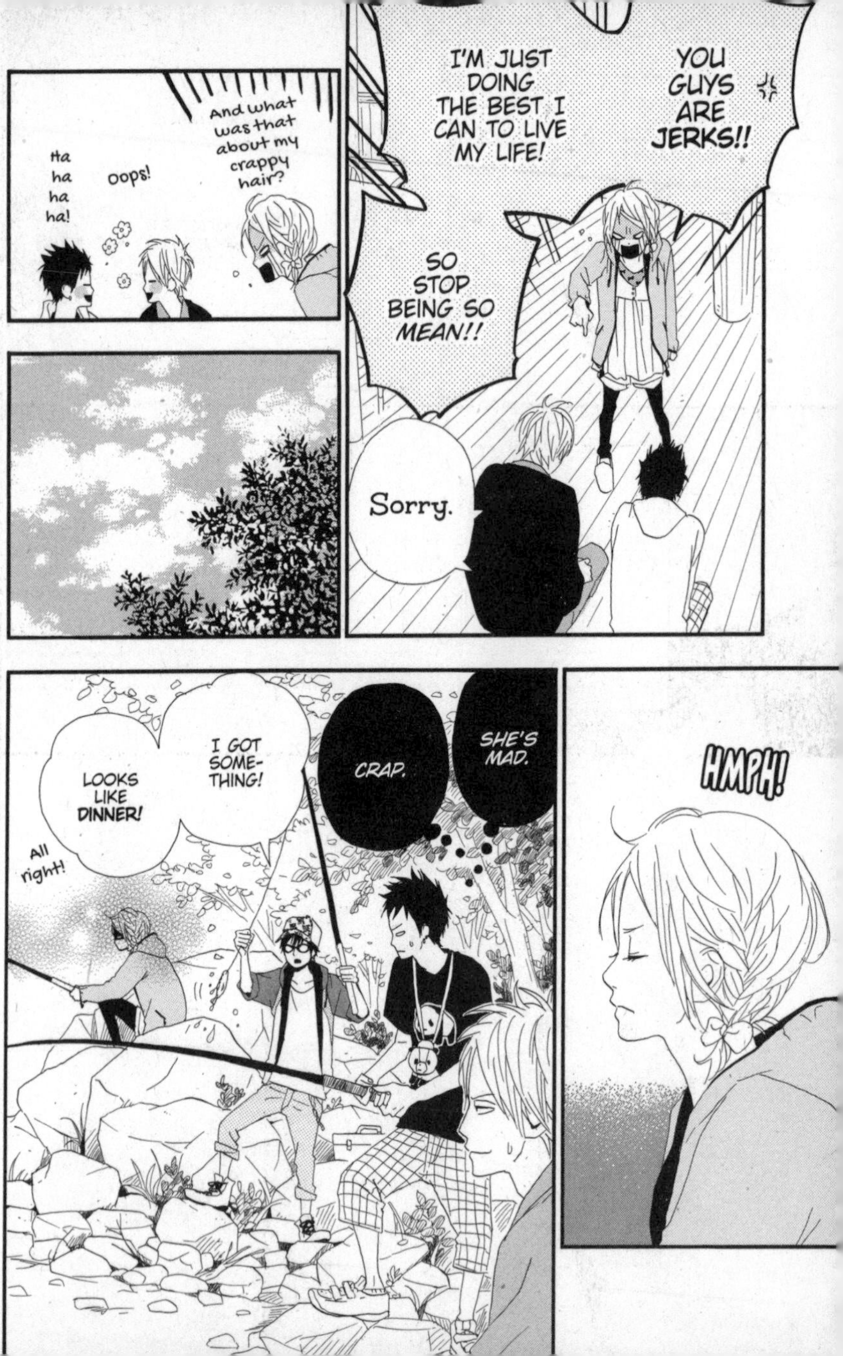
YOU GUYS ARE JERKS!!
I'M JUST DOING THE BEST I CAN TO LIVE MY LIFE!
SO STOP BEING SO MEAN!!
Sorry.
And what was that about my crappy hair?
Oops!
Ha ha ha ha!
HMPH!
SHE'S MAD.
CRAP.
I GOT SOME-THING!
LOOKS LIKE DINNER!
All right!

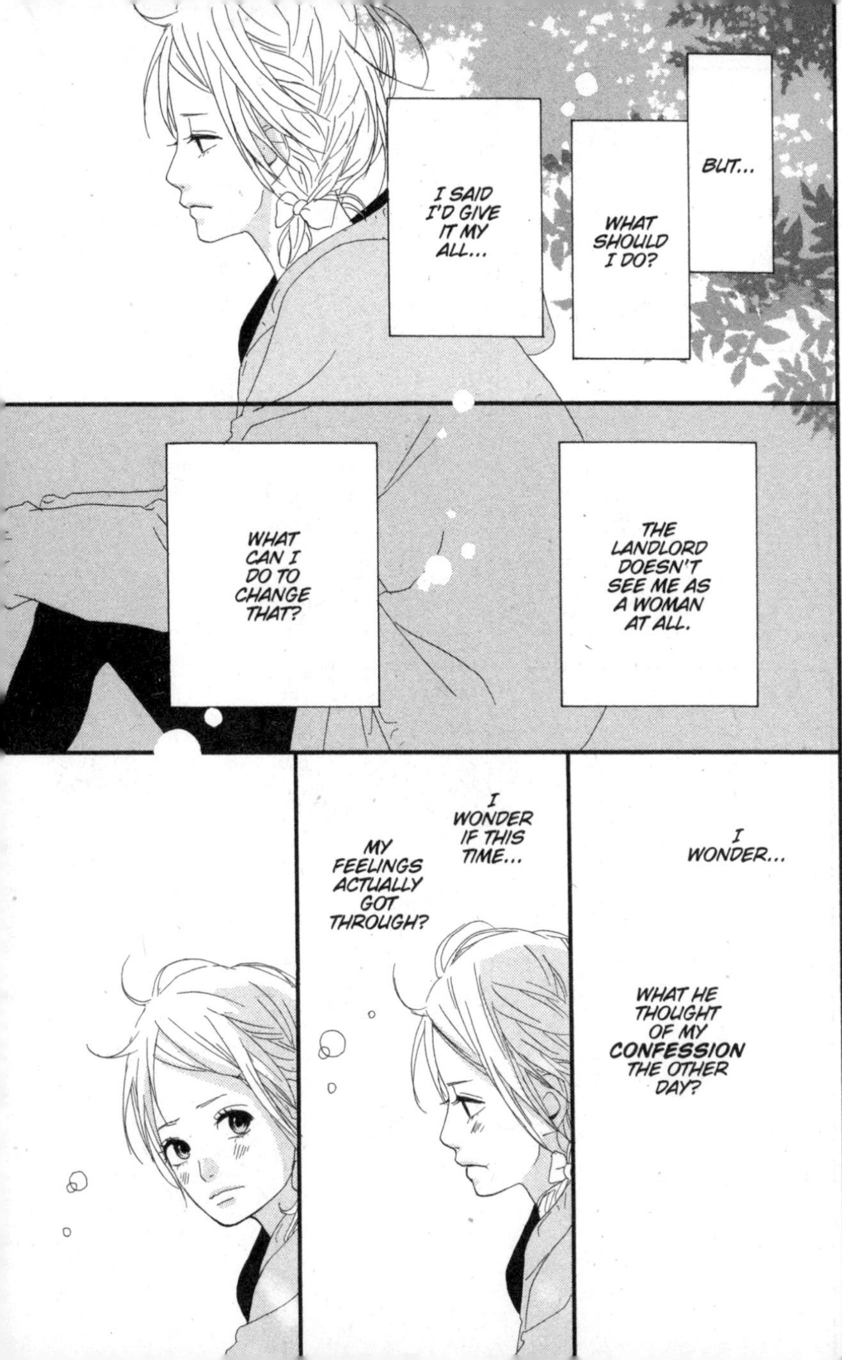
BUT...
WHAT SHOULD I DO?
I SAID I'D GIVE IT MY ALL...
THE LANDLORD DOESN'T SEE ME AS A WOMAN AT ALL.
WHAT CAN I DO TO CHANGE THAT?
I WONDER...
WHAT HE THOUGHT OF MY CONFESSION THE OTHER DAY?
I WONDER IF THIS TIME...
MY FEELINGS ACTUALLY GOT THROUGH?

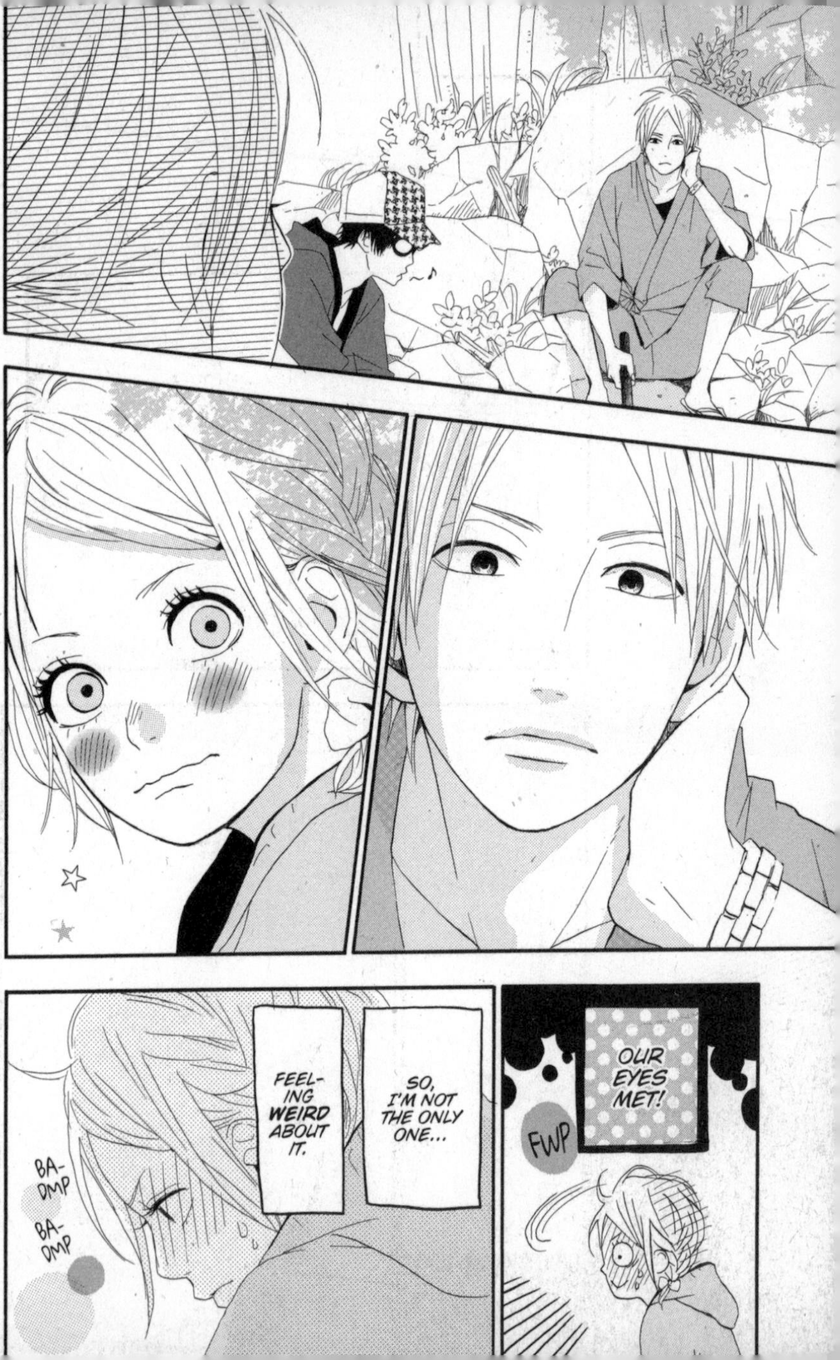
OUR EYES MET!
FWP
SO, I'M NOT THE ONLY ONE...
FEELING WEIRD ABOUT IT.
BA-DMP
BA-DMP

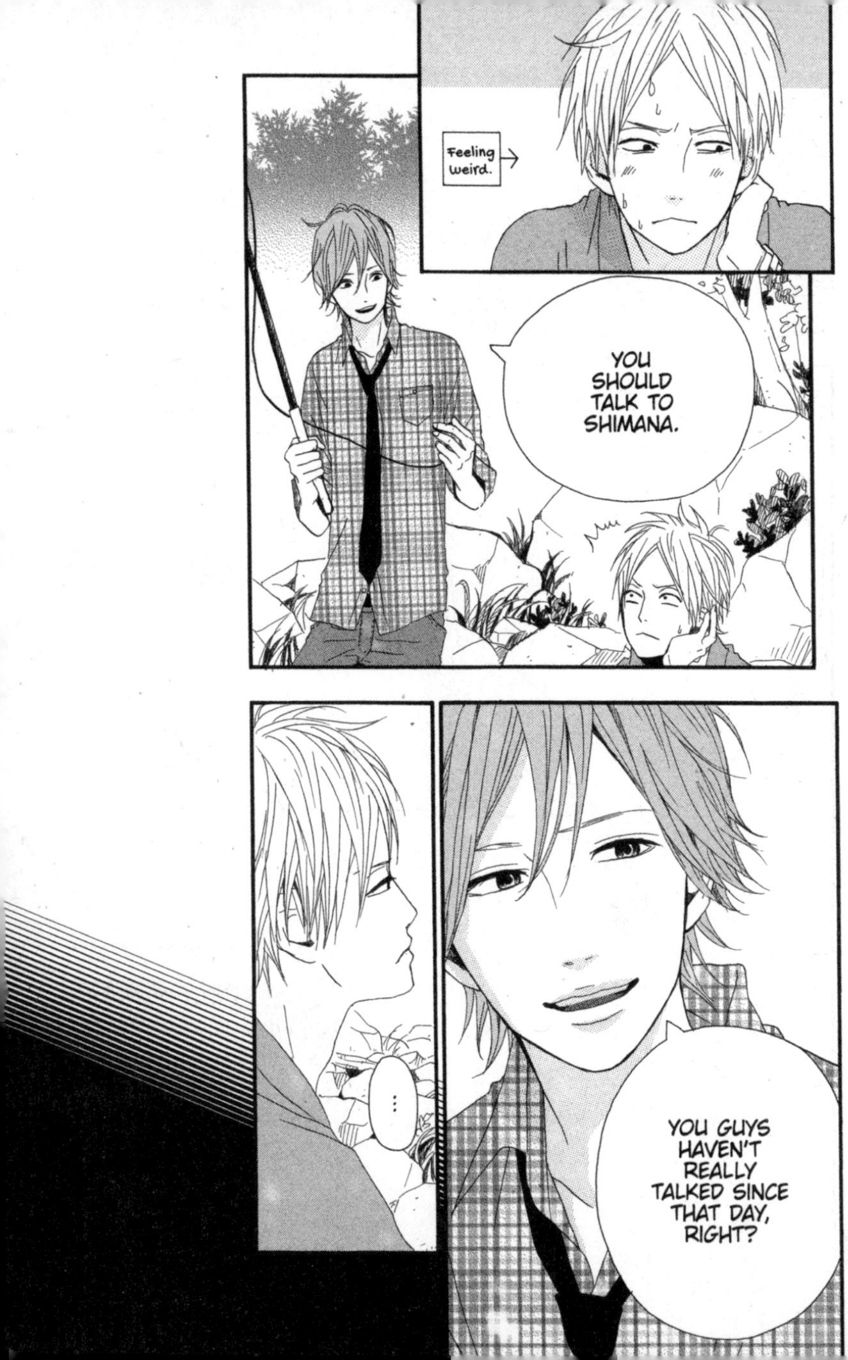
Feeling weird.
YOU SHOULD TALK TO SHIMANA.
YOU GUYS HAVEN'T REALLY TALKED SINCE THAT DAY, RIGHT?
...

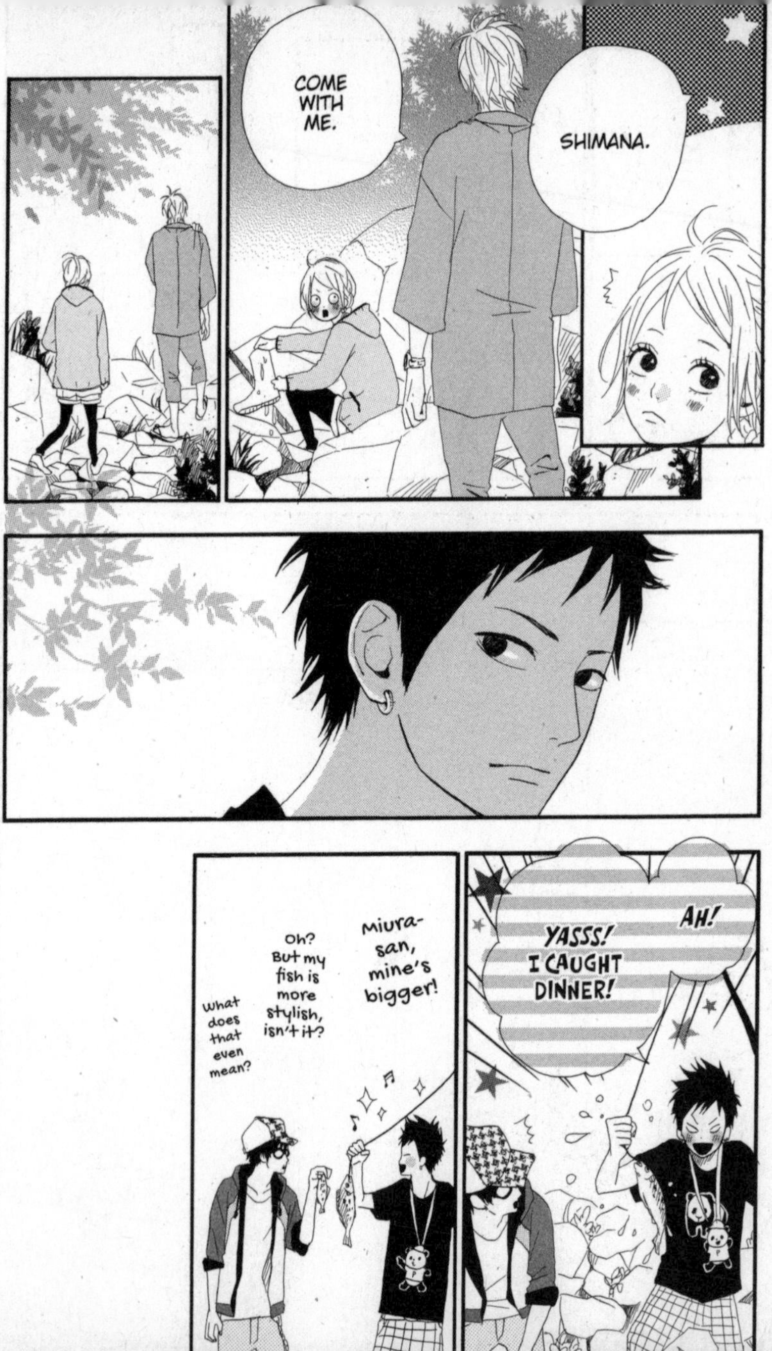

SHIMANA.
COME WITH ME.
AH!
YASSS! I CAUGHT DINNER!
Miura-san, mine's bigger!
Oh? But my fish is more stylish, isn't it?
What does that even mean?

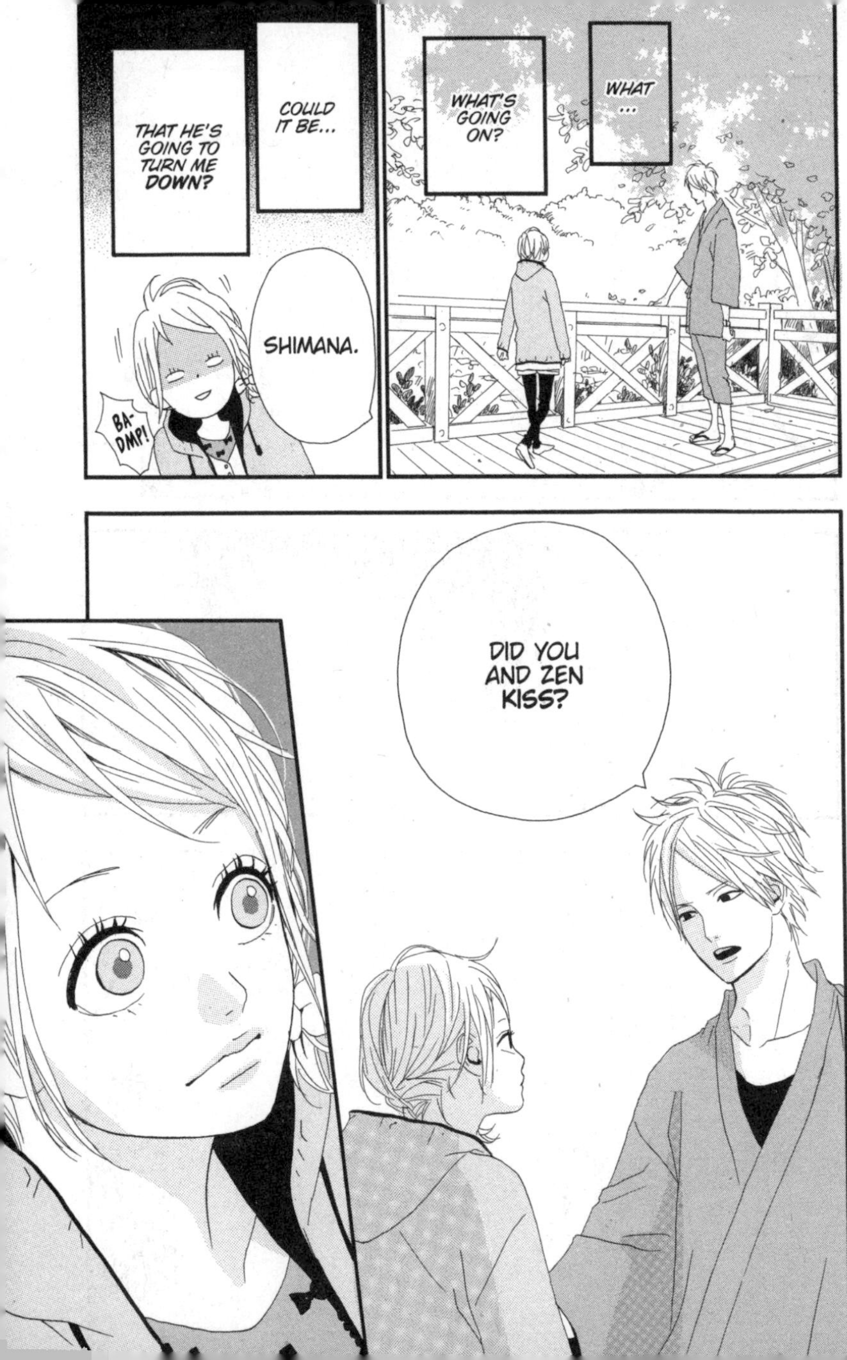
WHAT ...
WHAT'S GOING ON?
COULD IT BE...
THAT HE'S GOING TO TURN ME DOWN?
SHIMANA.
BA-DMP!
DID YOU AND ZEN KISS?

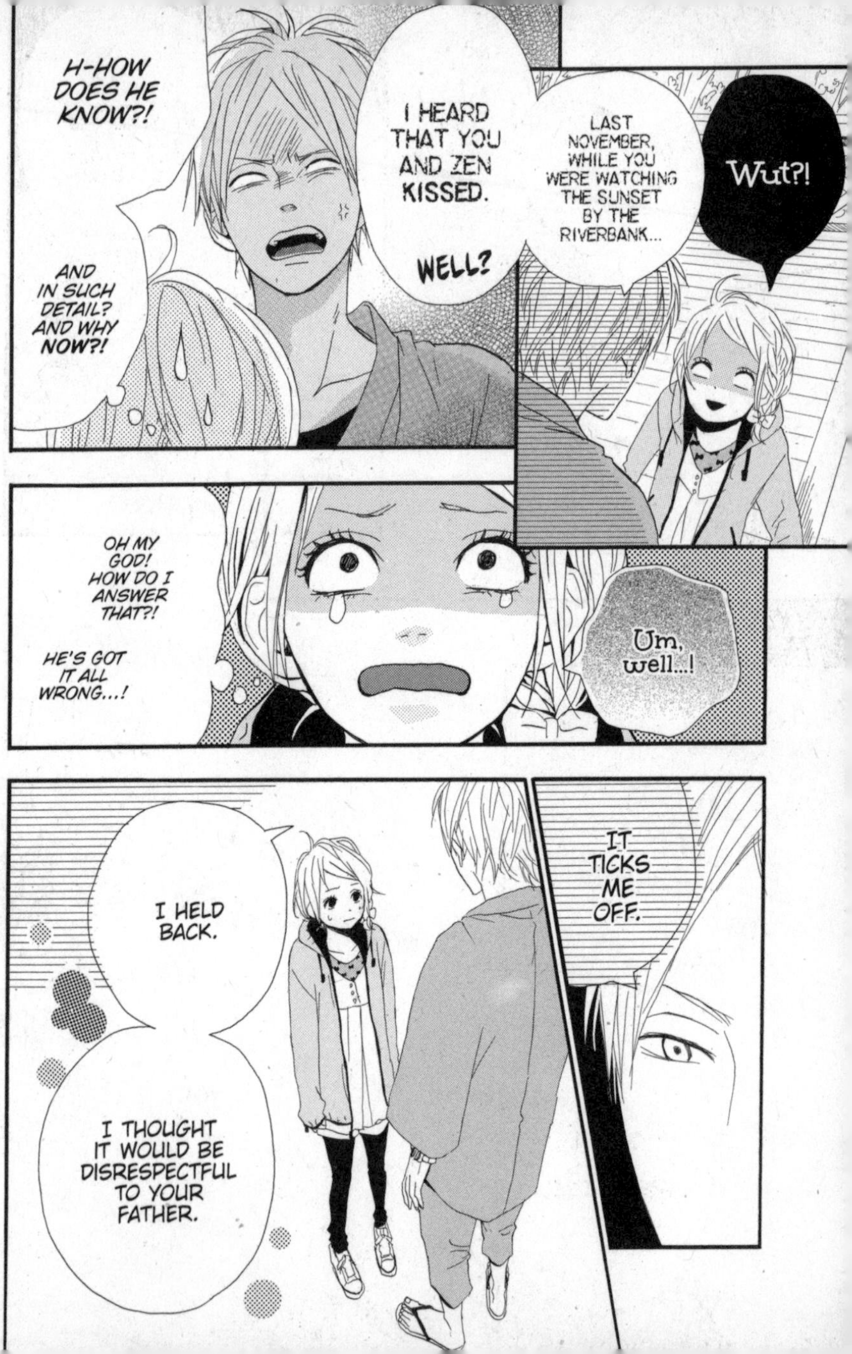

I HEARD THAT YOU AND ZEN KISSED.
LAST NOVEMBER, WHILE YOU WERE WATCHING THE SUNSET BY THE RIVERBANK...
WELL?
Wut?!
H-HOW DOES HE KNOW?!
AND IN SUCH DETAIL? AND WHY NOW?!
Um, well...!
OH MY GOD! HOW DO I ANSWER THAT?!
HE'S GOT IT ALL WRONG...!
IT TICKS ME OFF.
I HELD BACK.
I THOUGHT IT WOULD BE DISRESPECTFUL TO YOUR FATHER.

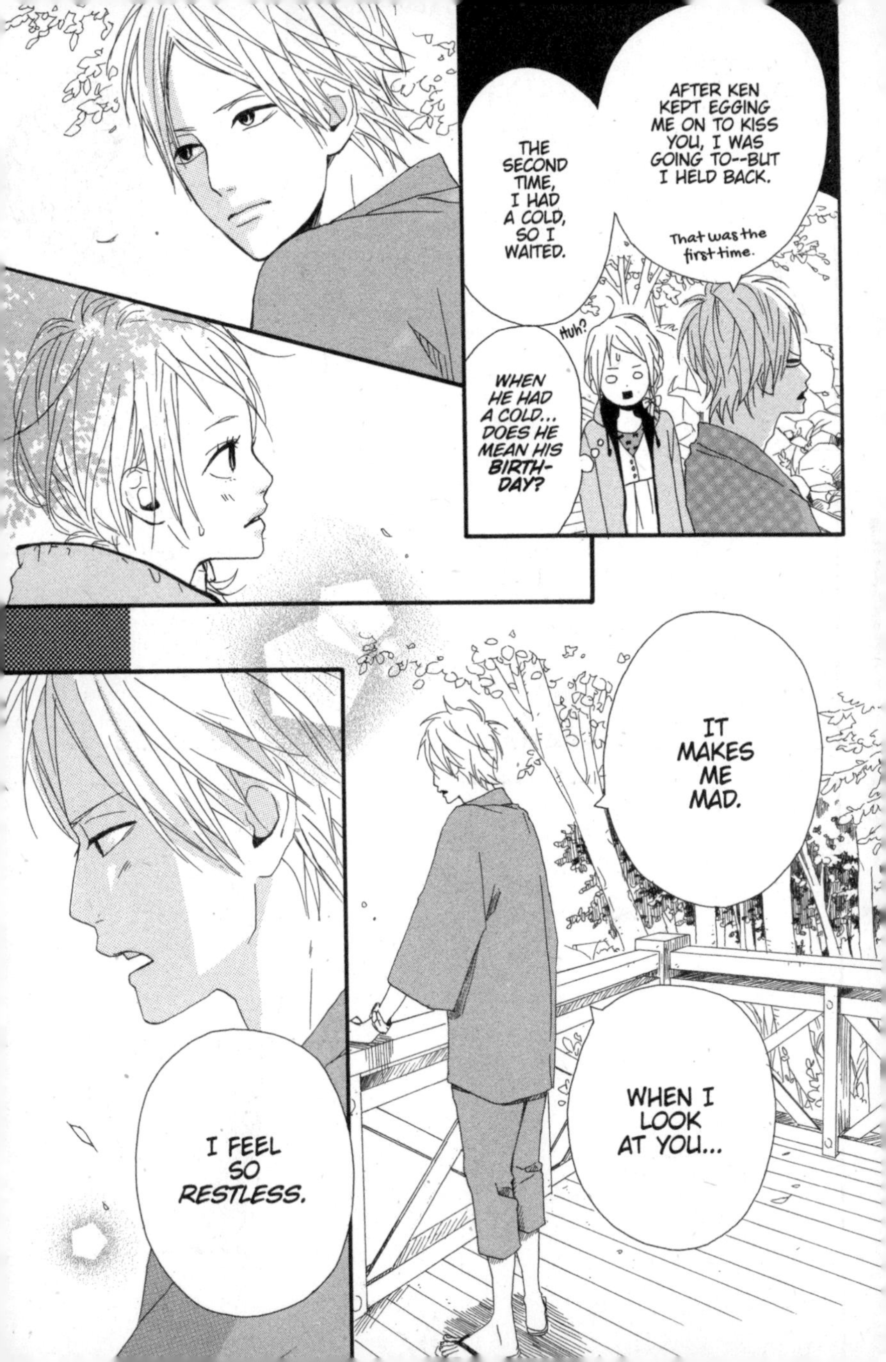
AFTER KEN KEPT EGGING ME ON TO KISS YOU, I WAS GOING TO--BUT I HELD BACK.
That was the first time.
THE SECOND TIME, I HAD A COLD, SO I WAITED.
Huh?
WHEN HE HAD A COLD... DOES HE MEAN HIS BIRTHDAY?
IT MAKES ME MAD.
WHEN I LOOK AT YOU...
I FEEL SO RESTLESS.

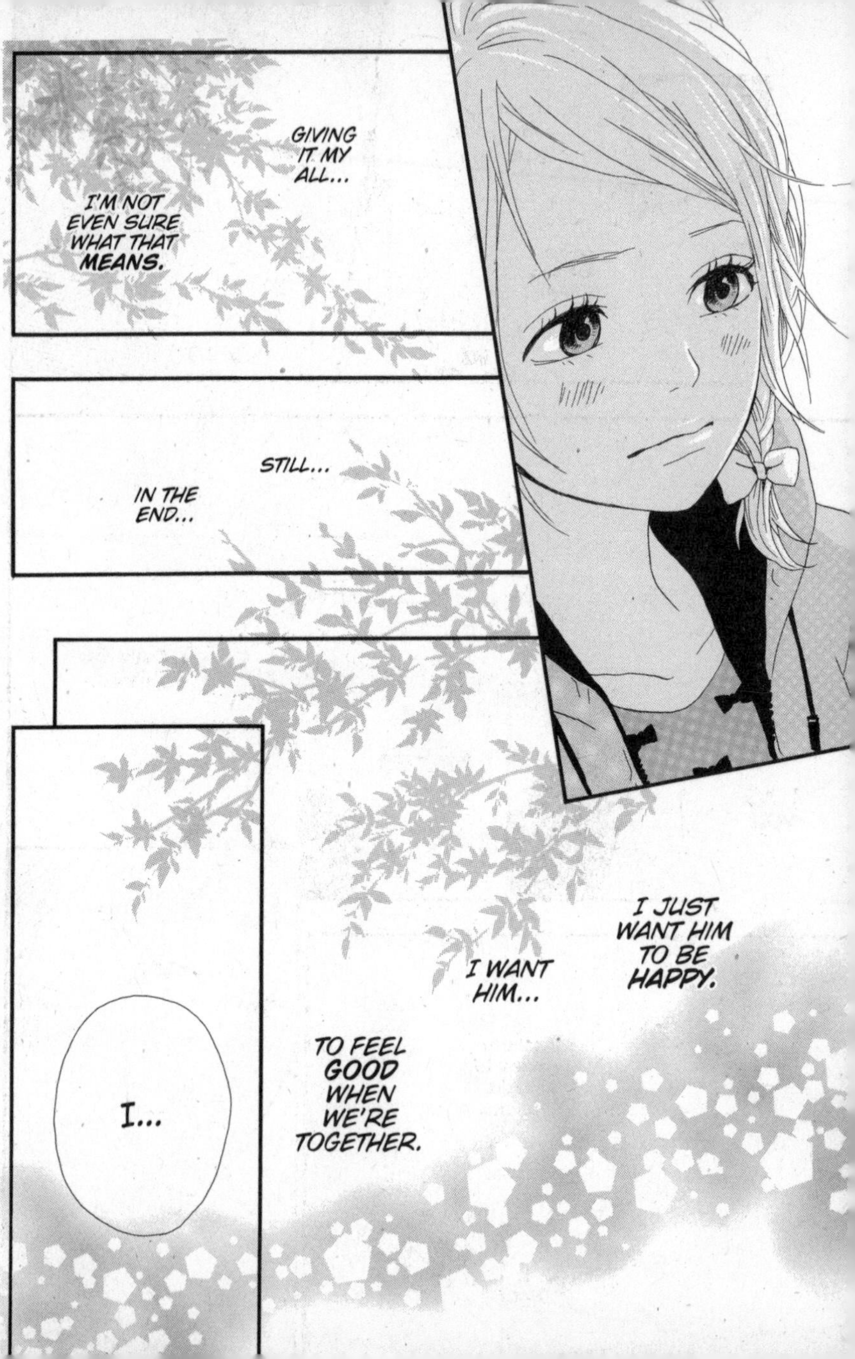
GIVING IT MY ALL...
I'M NOT EVEN SURE WHAT THAT MEANS.
STILL...
IN THE END...
I JUST WANT HIM TO BE HAPPY.
I WANT HIM...
TO FEEL GOOD WHEN WE'RE TOGETHER.
I...

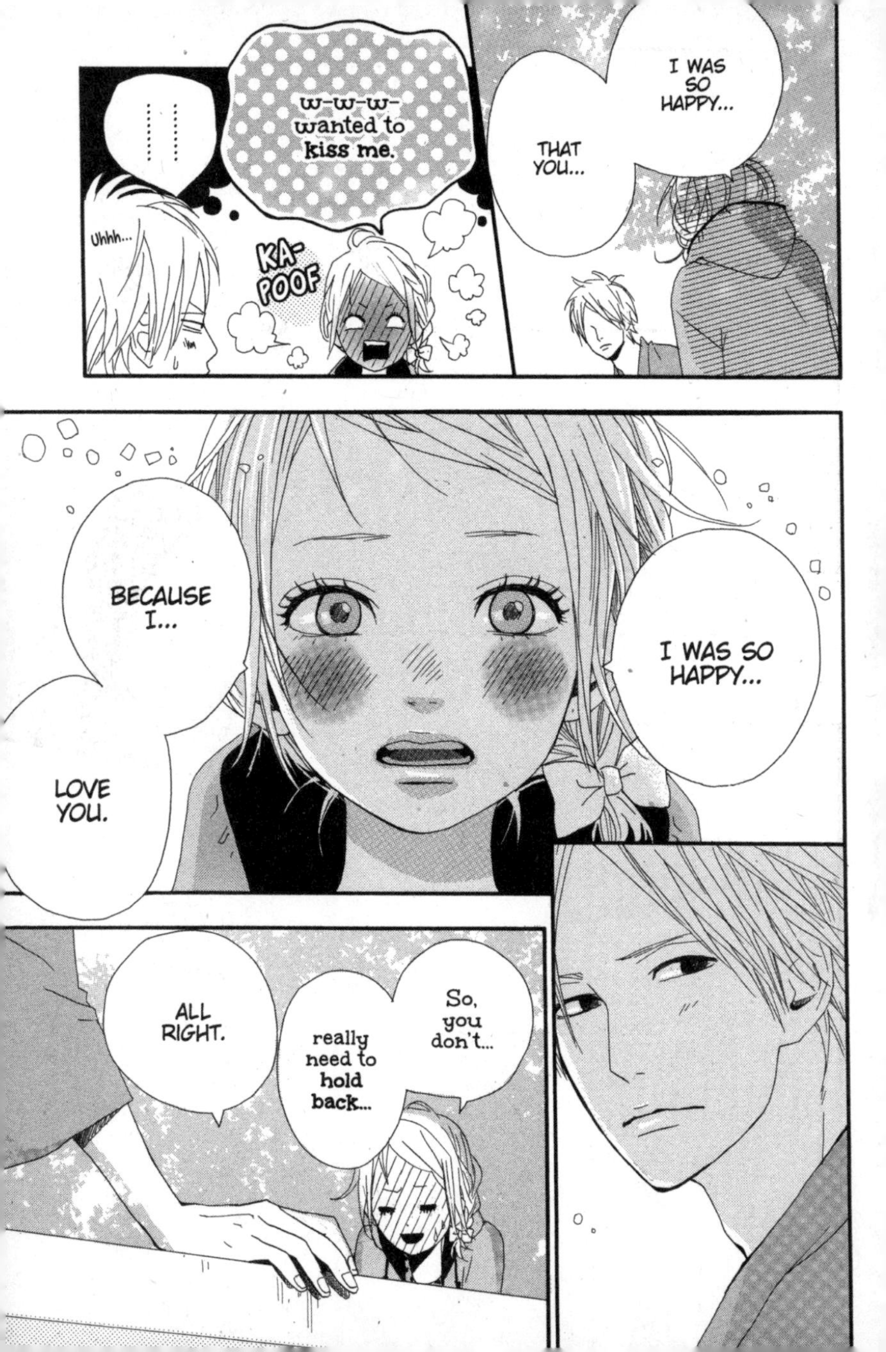
I WAS SO HAPPY...
THAT YOU...
w-w-w-wanted to kiss me.
......
KA-POOF
Uhhh...
I WAS SO HAPPY...
BECAUSE I...
LOVE YOU.
So, you don't...
really need to hold back...
ALL RIGHT.

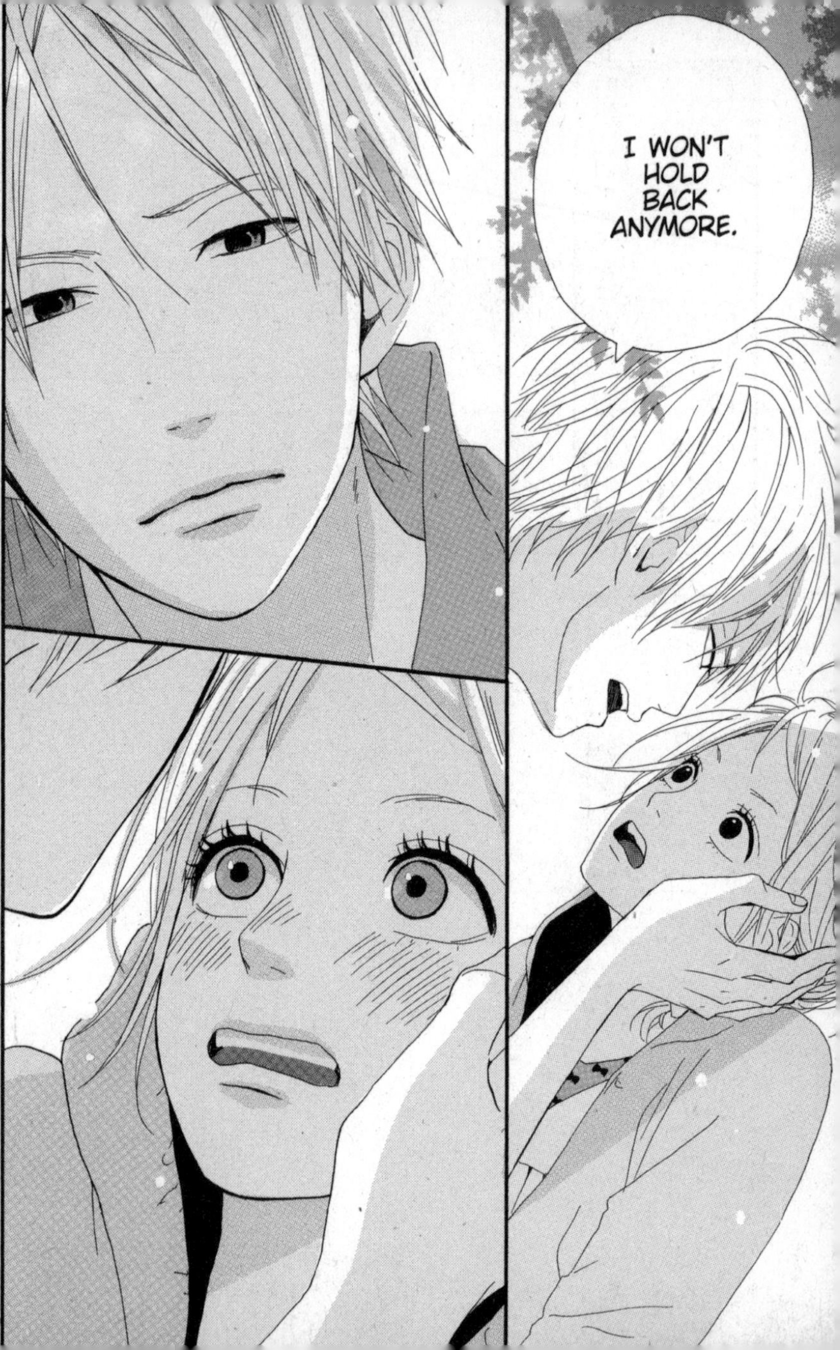
I WON'T HOLD BACK ANYMORE.

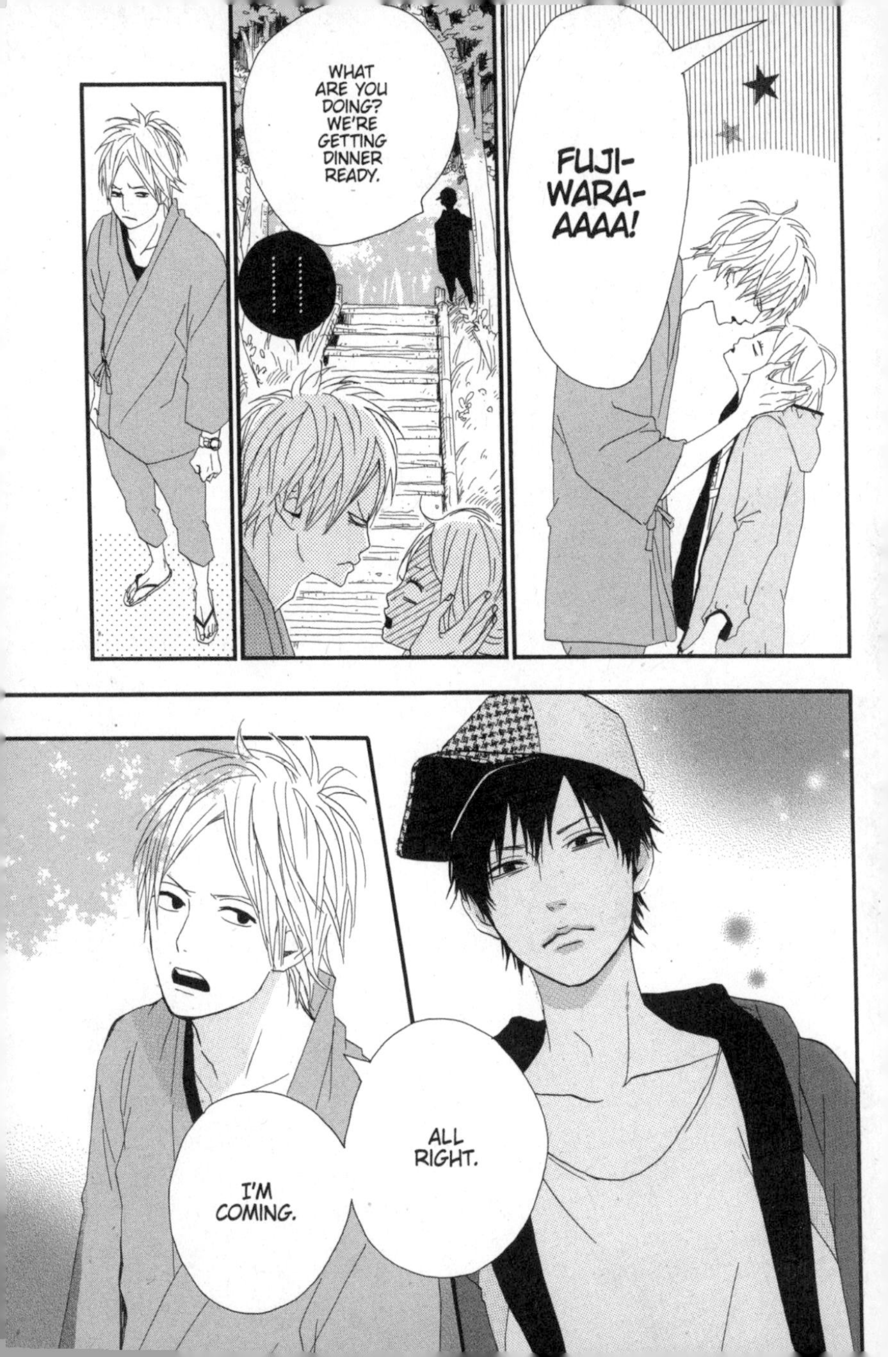
FUJI-WARA-AAAA!
WHAT ARE YOU DOING? WE'RE GETTING DINNER READY.
...
ALL RIGHT.
I'M COMING.

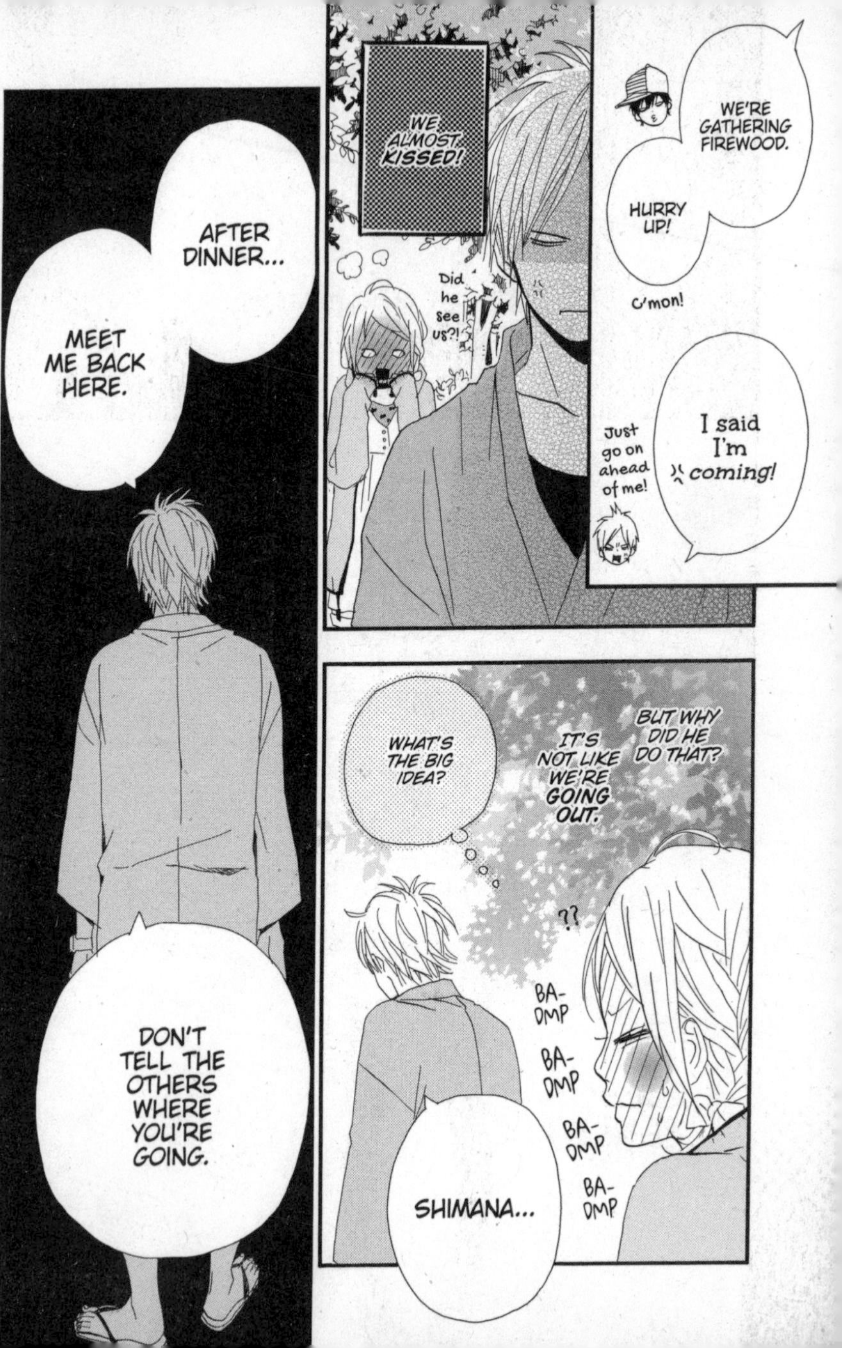
WE'RE GATHERING FIREWOOD.
HURRY UP!
C'mon!
I said I'm coming!
Just go on ahead of me!
WE ALMOST KISSED!
Did he see us?!
BUT WHY DID HE DO THAT?
IT'S NOT LIKE WE'RE GOING OUT.
WHAT'S THE BIG IDEA?
??
BA-DMP
BA-DMP
BA-DMP
BA-DMP
SHIMANA...
AFTER DINNER...
MEET ME BACK HERE.
DON'T TELL THE OTHERS WHERE YOU'RE GOING.

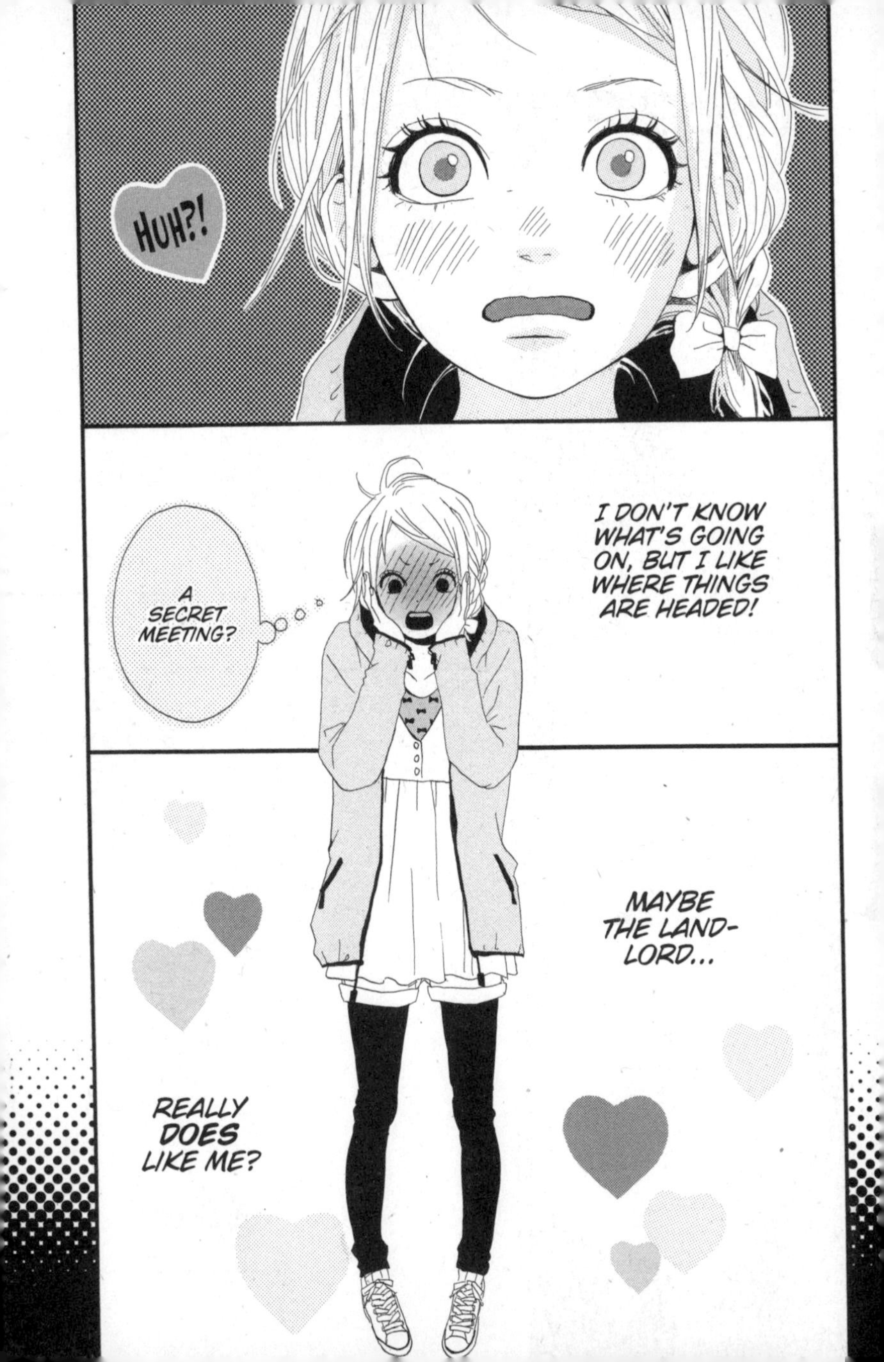
HUH?!
I DON'T KNOW WHAT'S GOING ON, BUT I LIKE WHERE THINGS ARE HEADED!
A SECRET MEETING?
MAYBE THE LAND-LORD...
REALLY DOES LIKE ME?

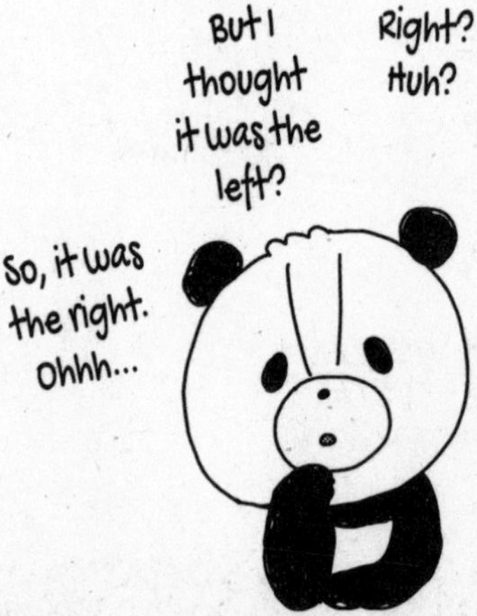
Right? Huh?
But I thought it was the left?
So, it was the right. Ohhh...

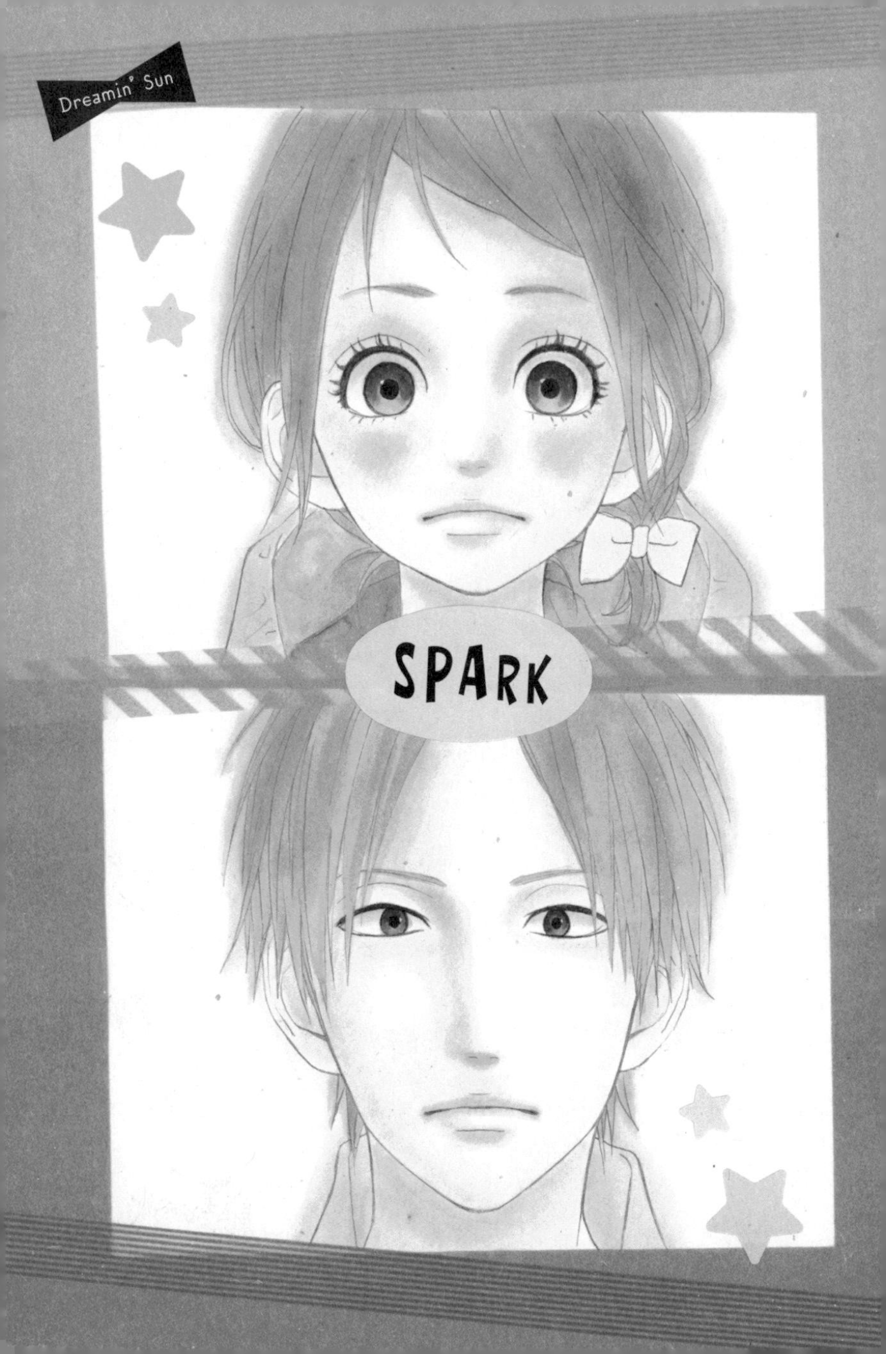
Dreamin' Sun
SPARK

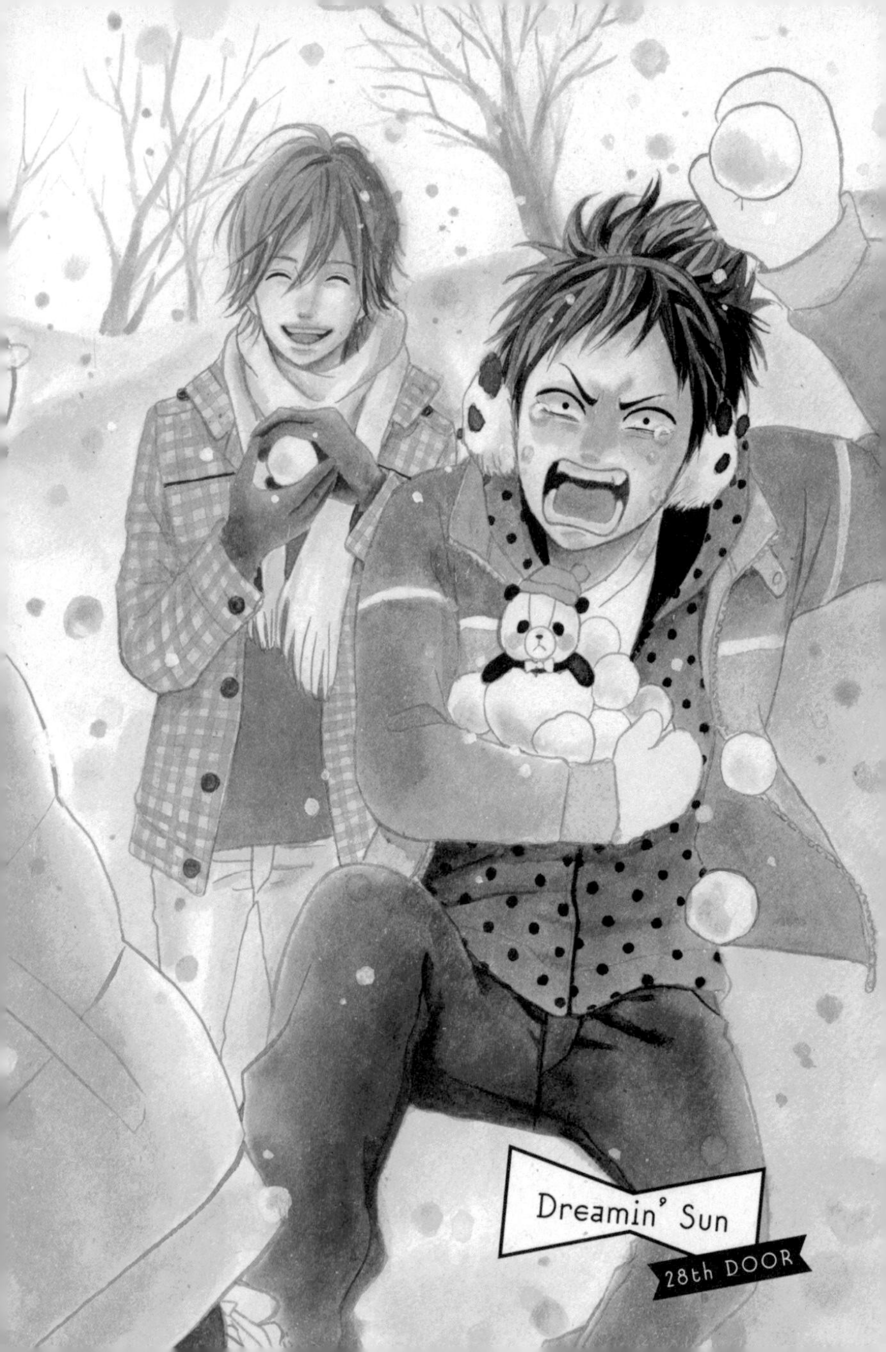
Dreamin' Sun
28th DOOR

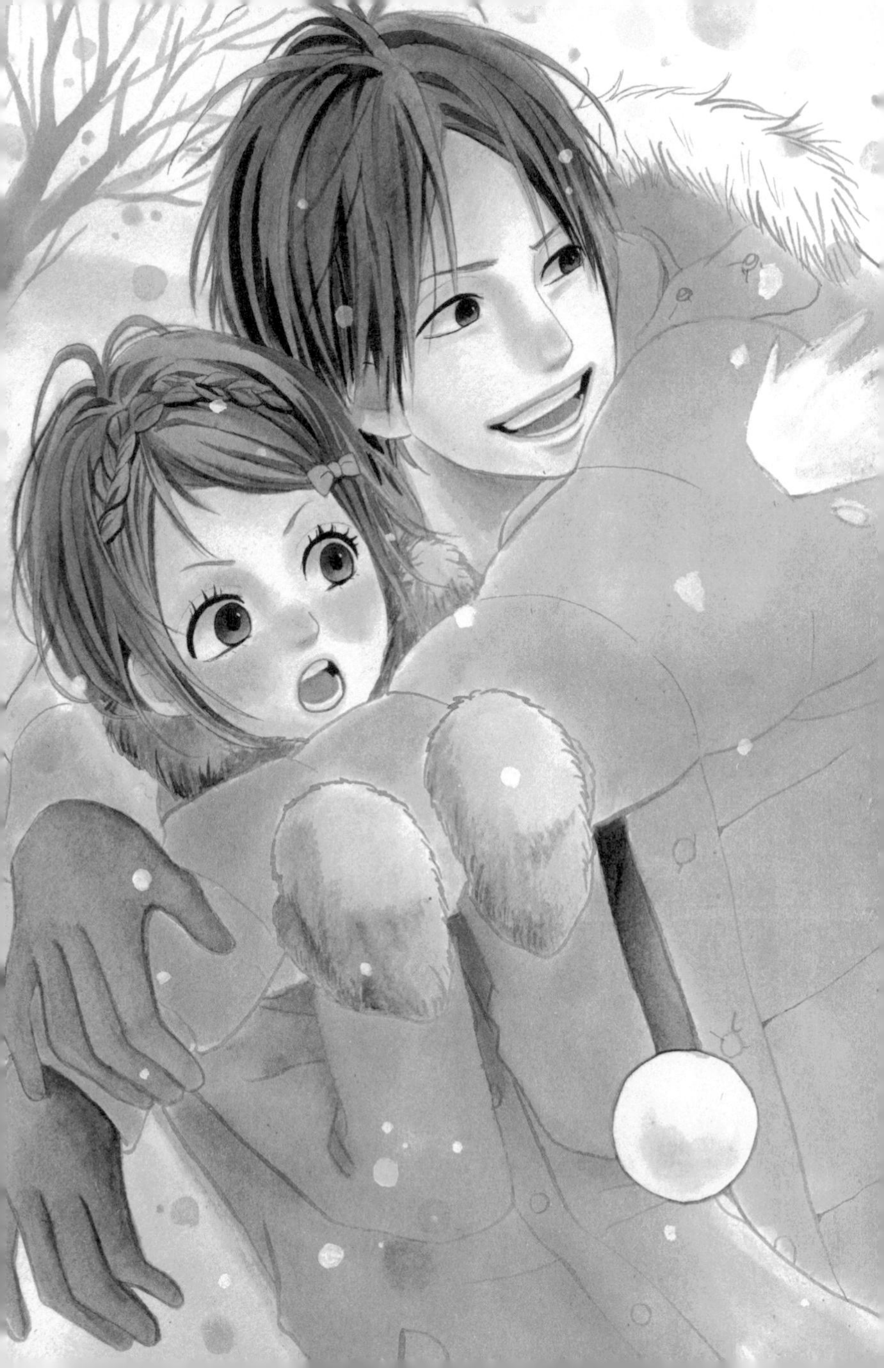

Dreamin'
Sun

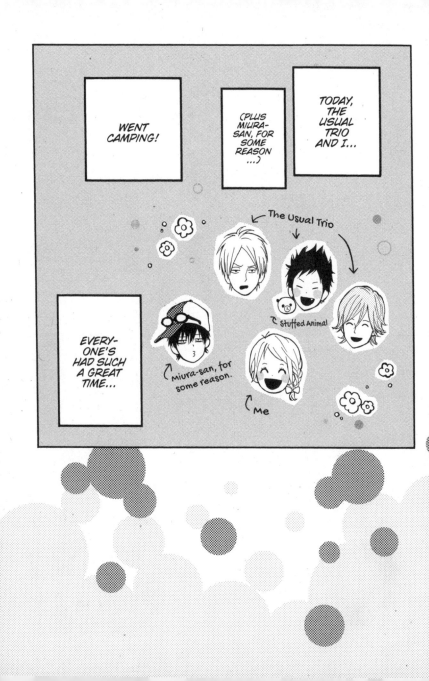

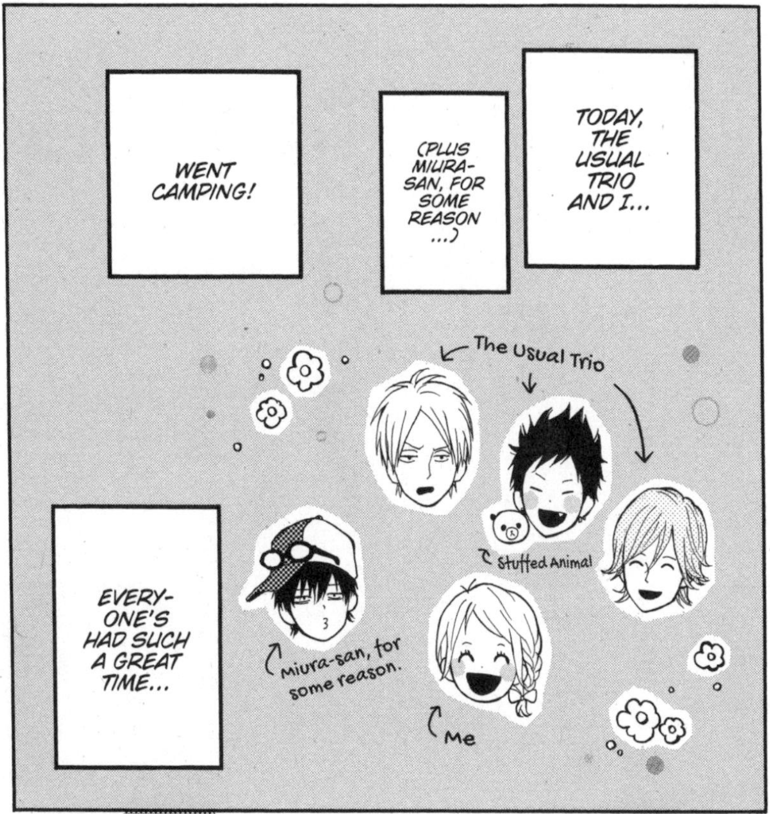
TODAY, THE USUAL TRIO AND I...
(PLUS MIURA-SAN, FOR SOME REASON...)
WENT CAMPING!
The Usual Trio
Stuffed Animal
Miura-san, for some reason.
Me
EVERYONE'S HAD SUCH A GREAT TIME...

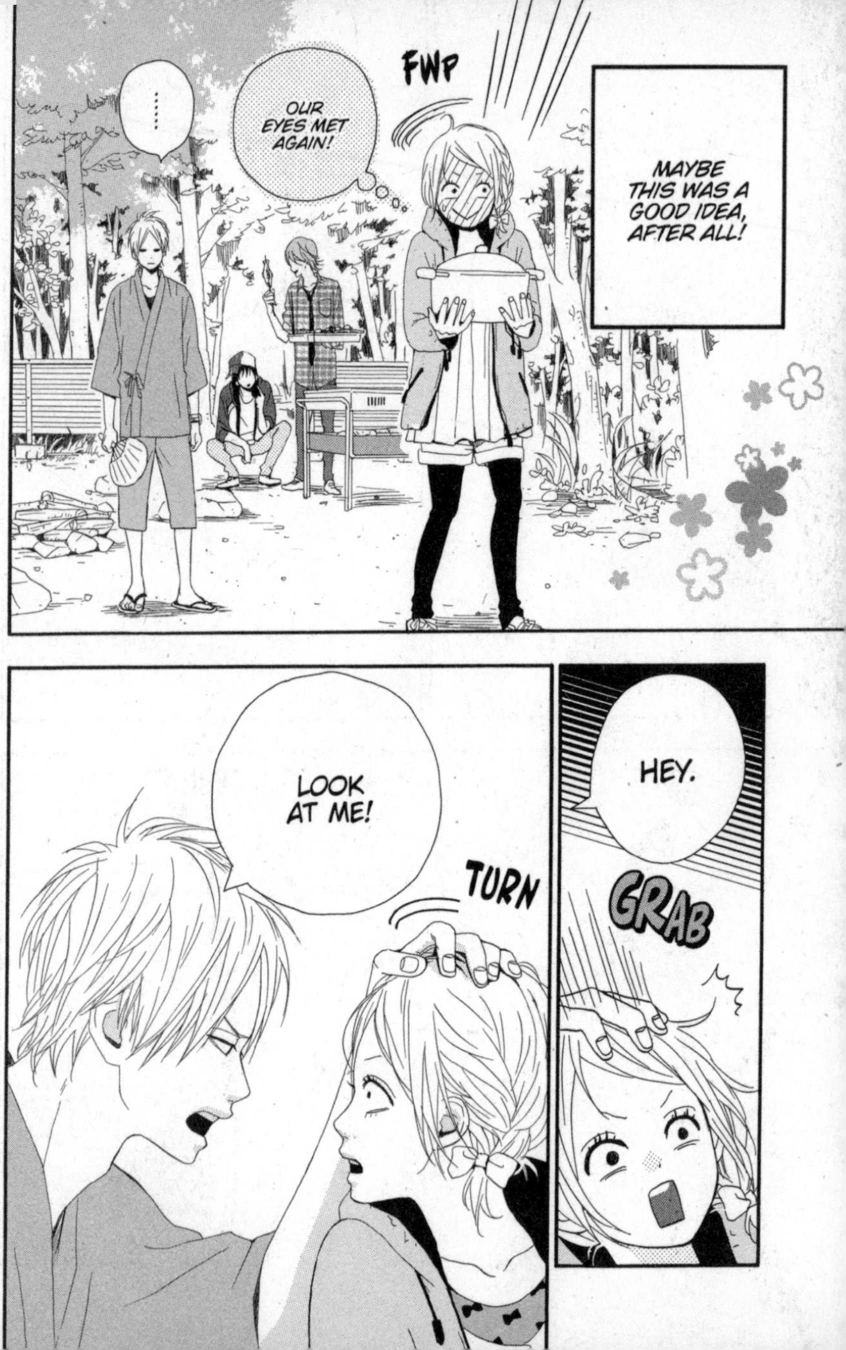
MAYBE THIS WAS A GOOD IDEA, AFTER ALL!
FWP
OUR EYES MET AGAIN!
......
HEY.
GRAB
TURN
LOOK AT ME!

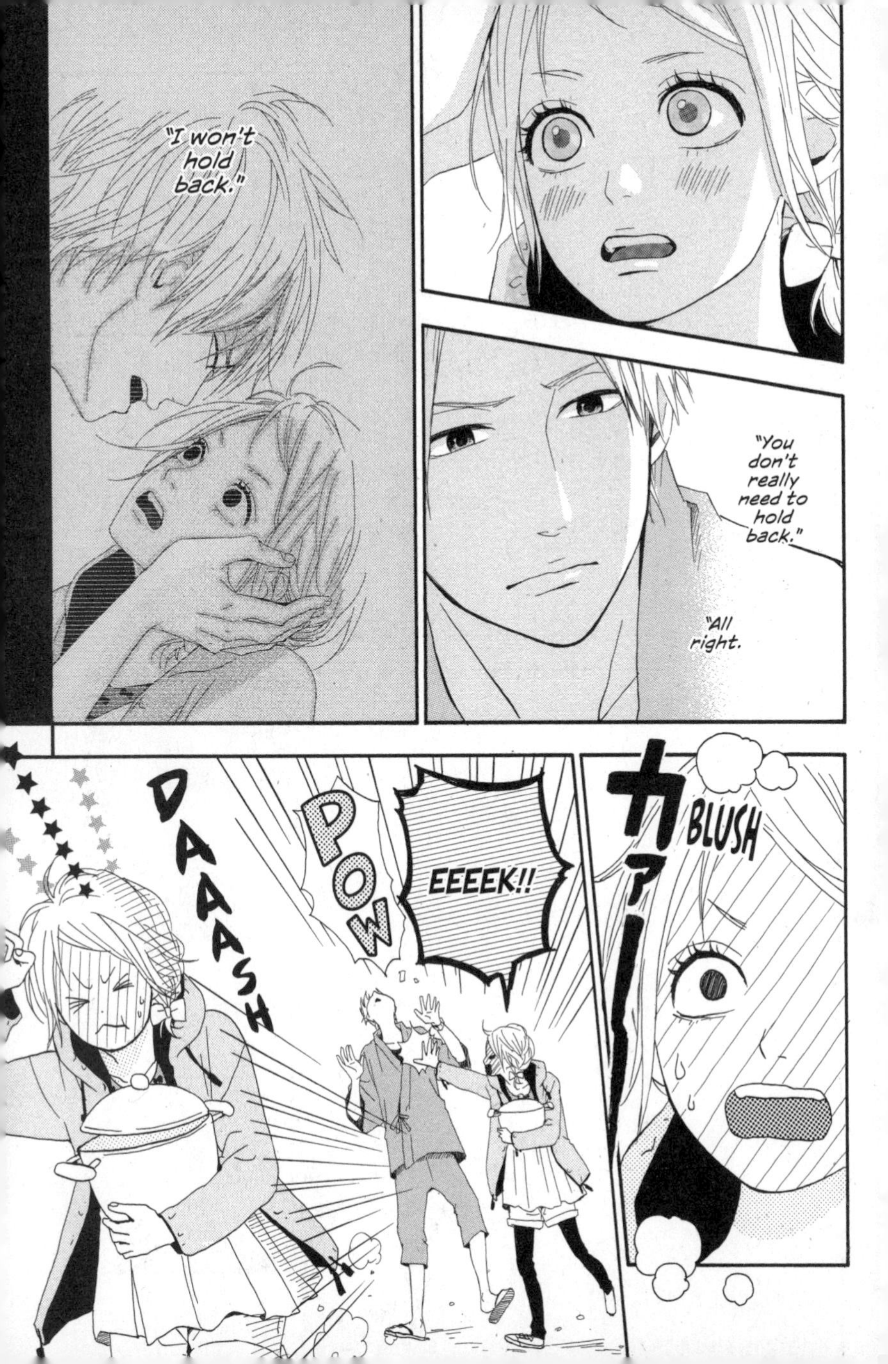
"You don't really need to hold back."
"All right.
"I won't hold back."
カァー
BLUSH
EEEEK!!
POW
DAAASH

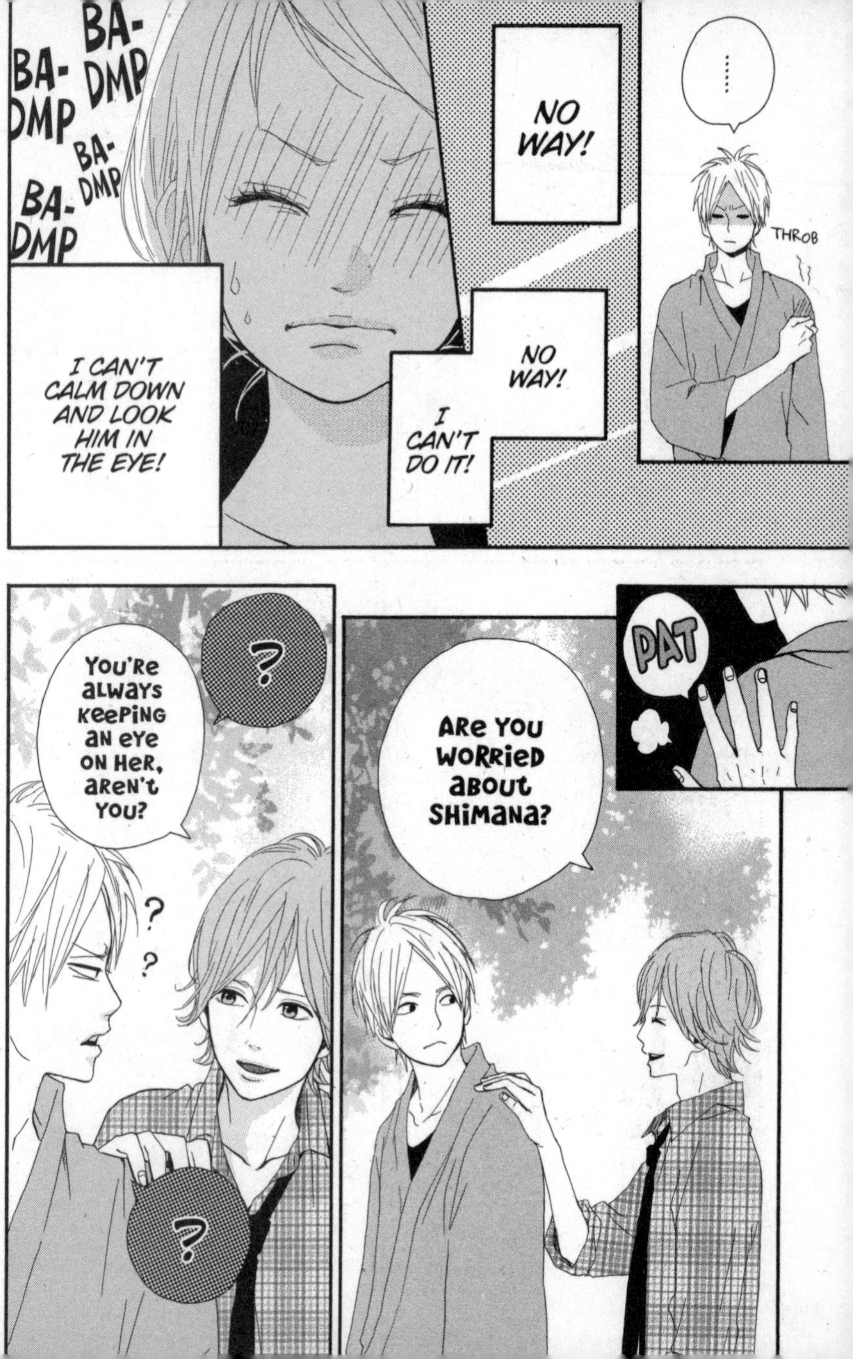
......
THROB
NO WAY!
NO WAY!
I CAN'T DO IT!
BA-DMP
BA-DMP
BA-DMP
BA-DMP
I CAN'T CALM DOWN AND LOOK HIM IN THE EYE!
PAT
Are you worried about Shimana?
?
You're always keeping an eye on her, aren't you?
? ?
?

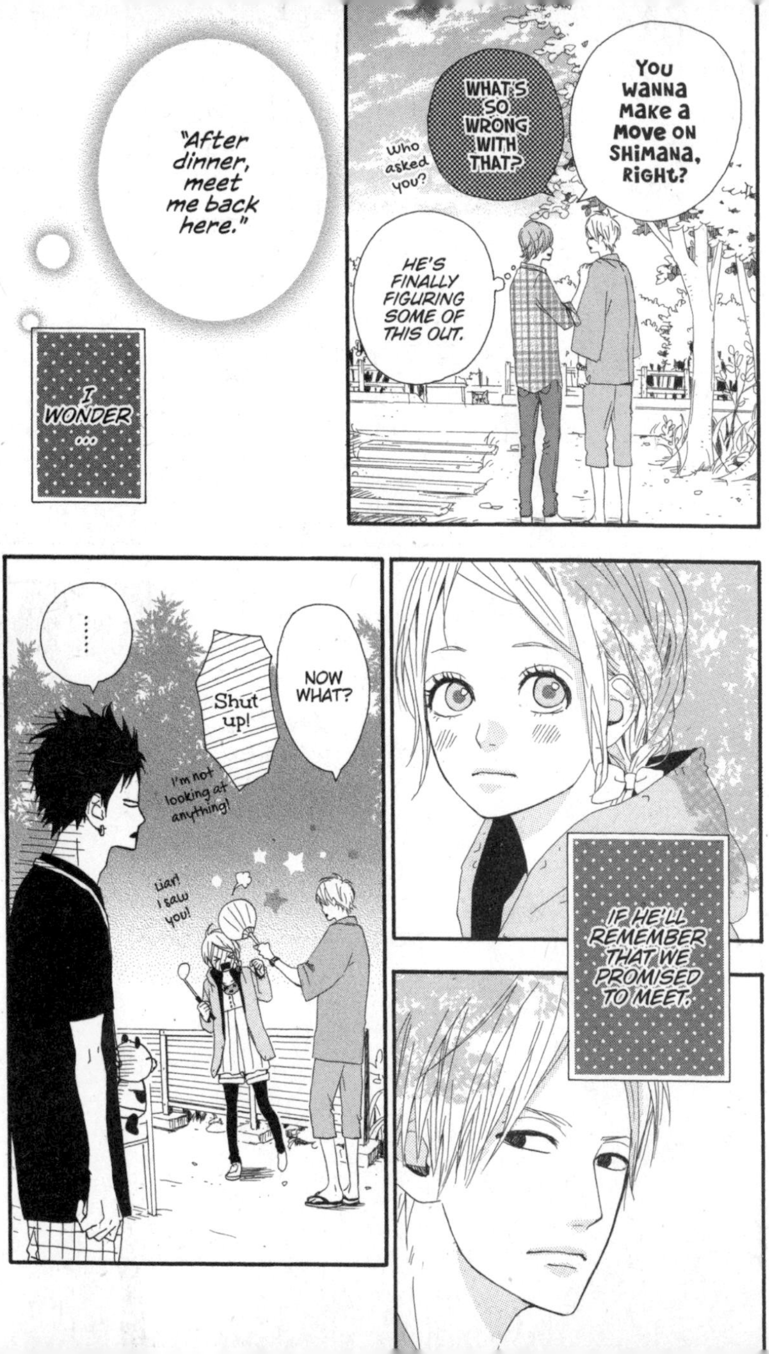
You wanna make a move on SHIMANA, right?
WHAT'S SO WRONG WITH THAT?
Who asked you?
HE'S FINALLY FIGURING SOME OF THIS OUT.
"After dinner, meet me back here."
I WONDER...
IF HE'LL REMEMBER THAT WE PROMISED TO MEET.
NOW WHAT?
Shut up!
I'm not looking at anything!
Liar! I saw you!
......

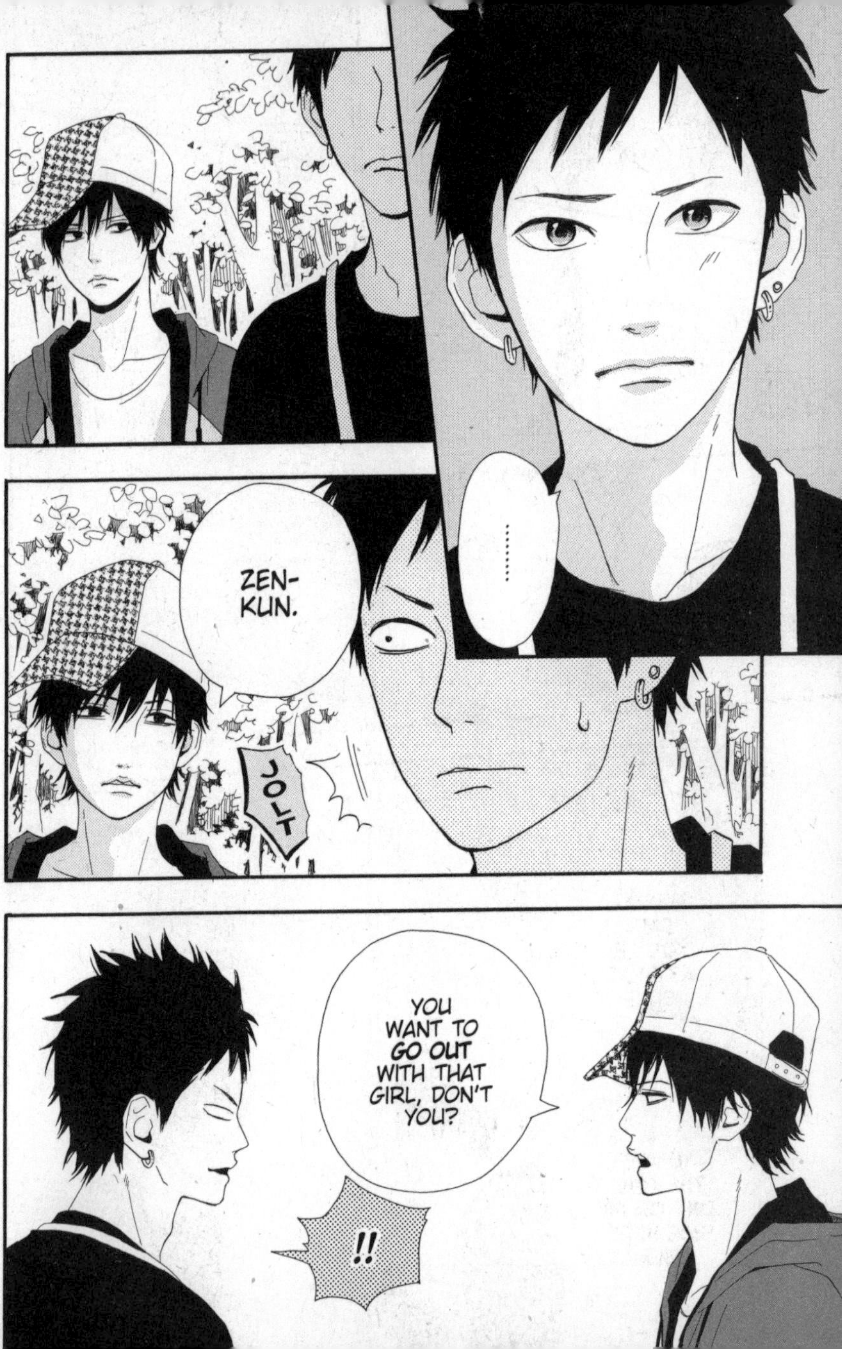
......
ZEN-KUN.
JOLT
YOU WANT TO GO OUT WITH THAT GIRL, DON'T YOU?
!!

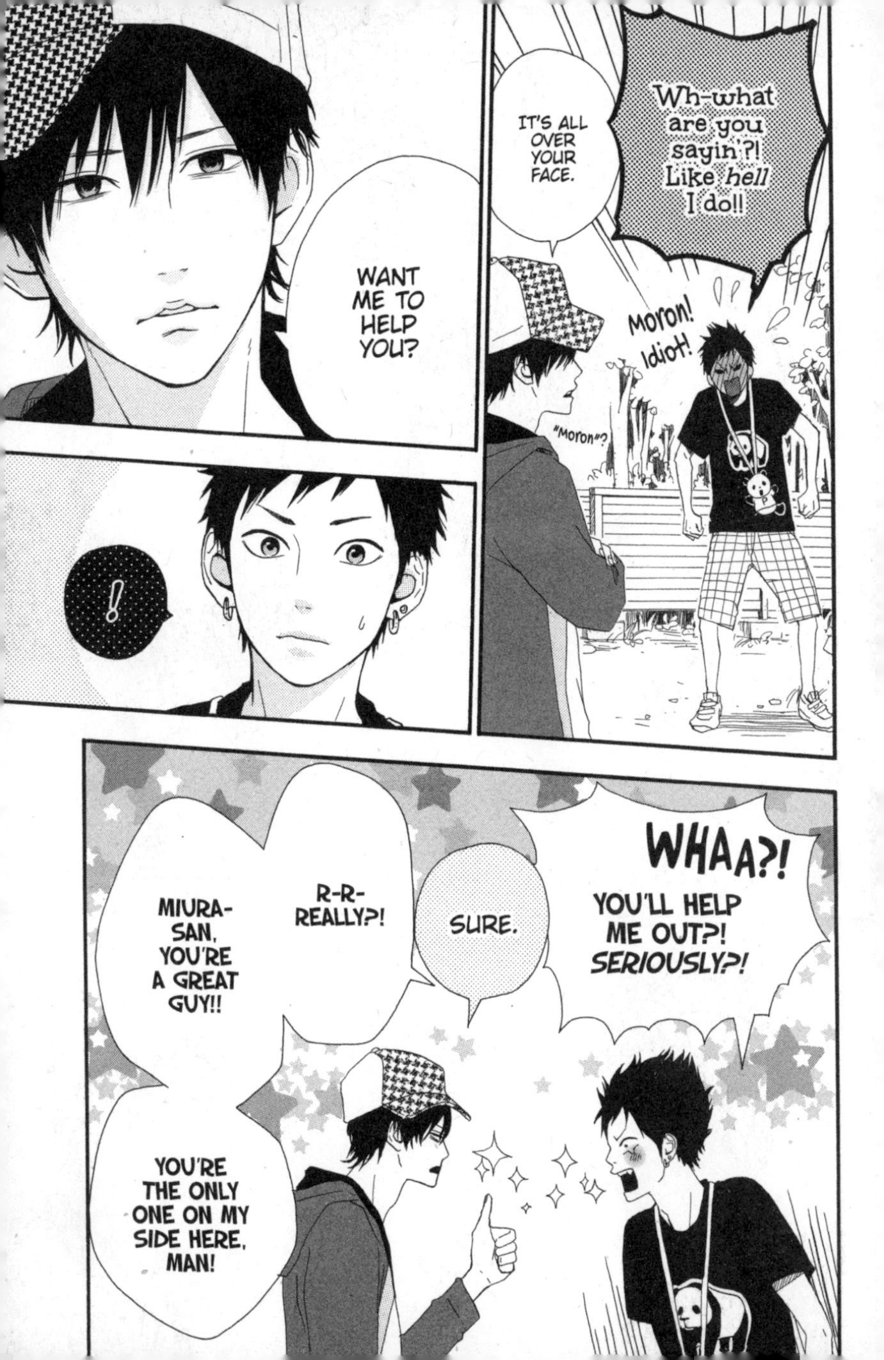

Wh-what are you sayin'?! Like *hell* I do!!
IT'S ALL OVER YOUR FACE.
Moron! Idiot!
"Moron"?
WANT ME TO HELP YOU?
!
WHAA?!
YOU'LL HELP ME OUT?! *SERIOUSLY?!*
SURE.
R-R-REALLY?!
MIURA-SAN, YOU'RE A GREAT GUY!!
YOU'RE THE ONLY ONE ON MY SIDE HERE, MAN!

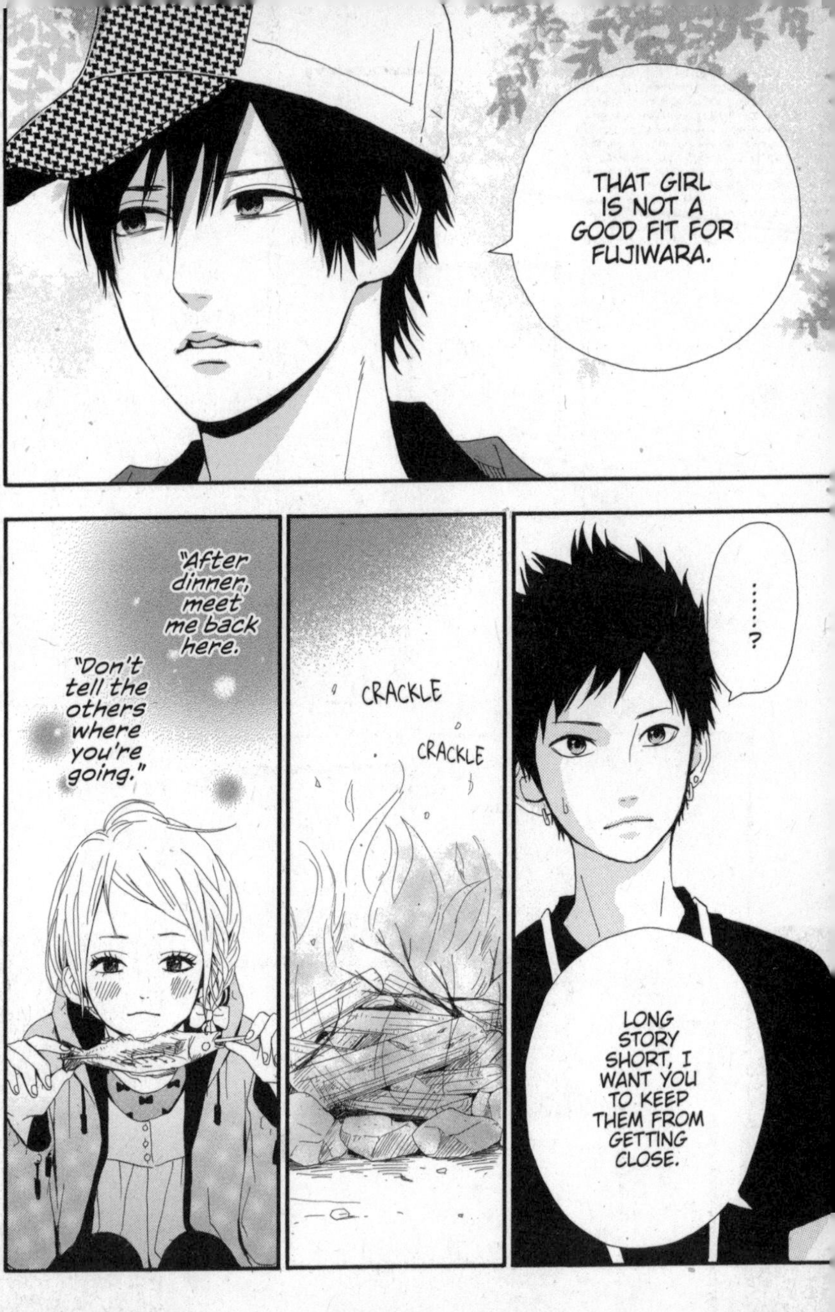
THAT GIRL IS NOT A GOOD FIT FOR FUJIWARA.
.....?
LONG STORY SHORT, I WANT YOU TO KEEP THEM FROM GETTING CLOSE.
CRACKLE
CRACKLE
"After dinner, meet me back here.
"Don't tell the others where you're going."

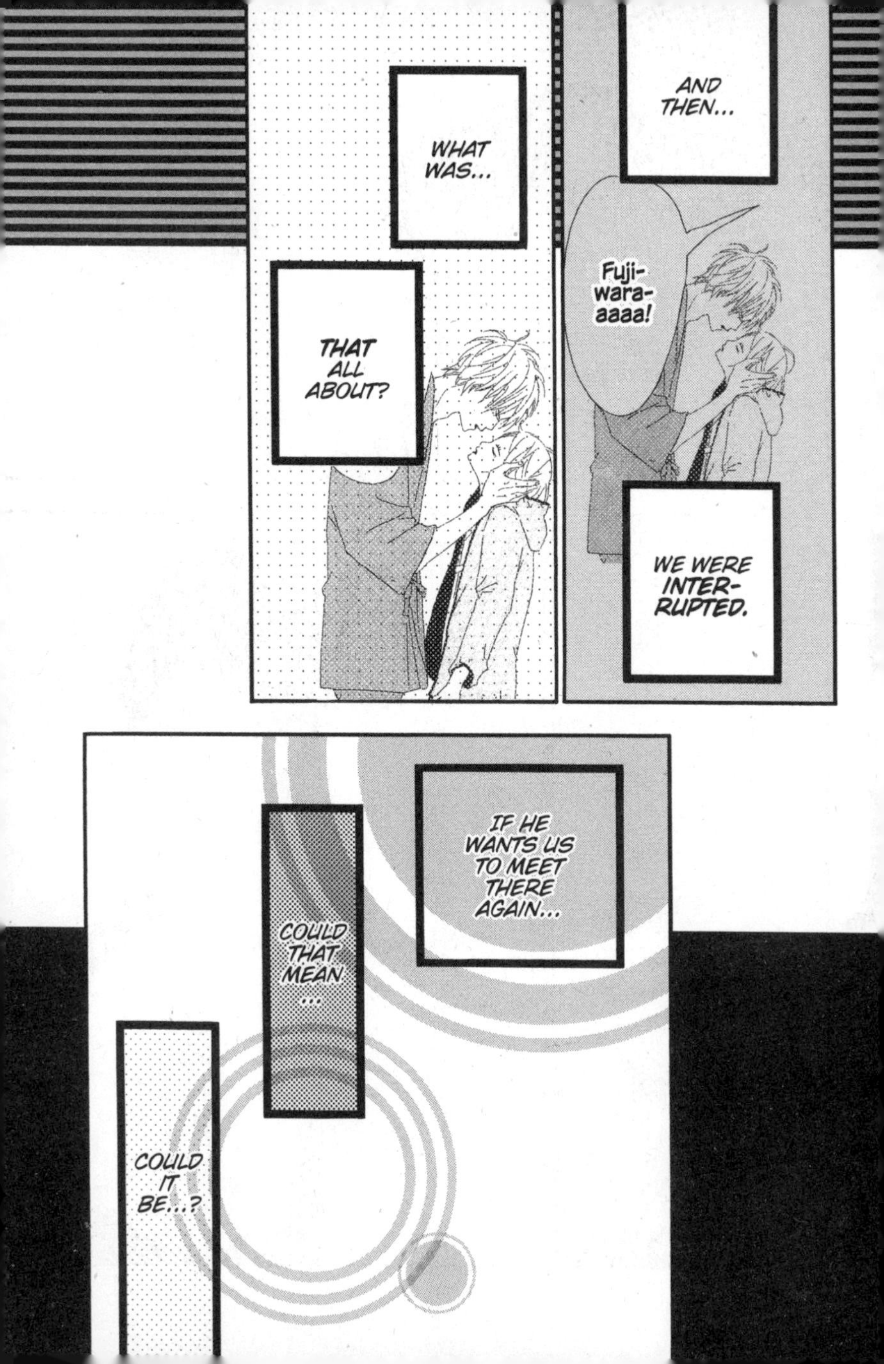
AND THEN...
Fuji-wara-aaaa!
WE WERE INTER-RUPTED.
WHAT WAS...
THAT ALL ABOUT?
IF HE WANTS US TO MEET THERE AGAIN...
COULD THAT MEAN...
COULD IT BE...?

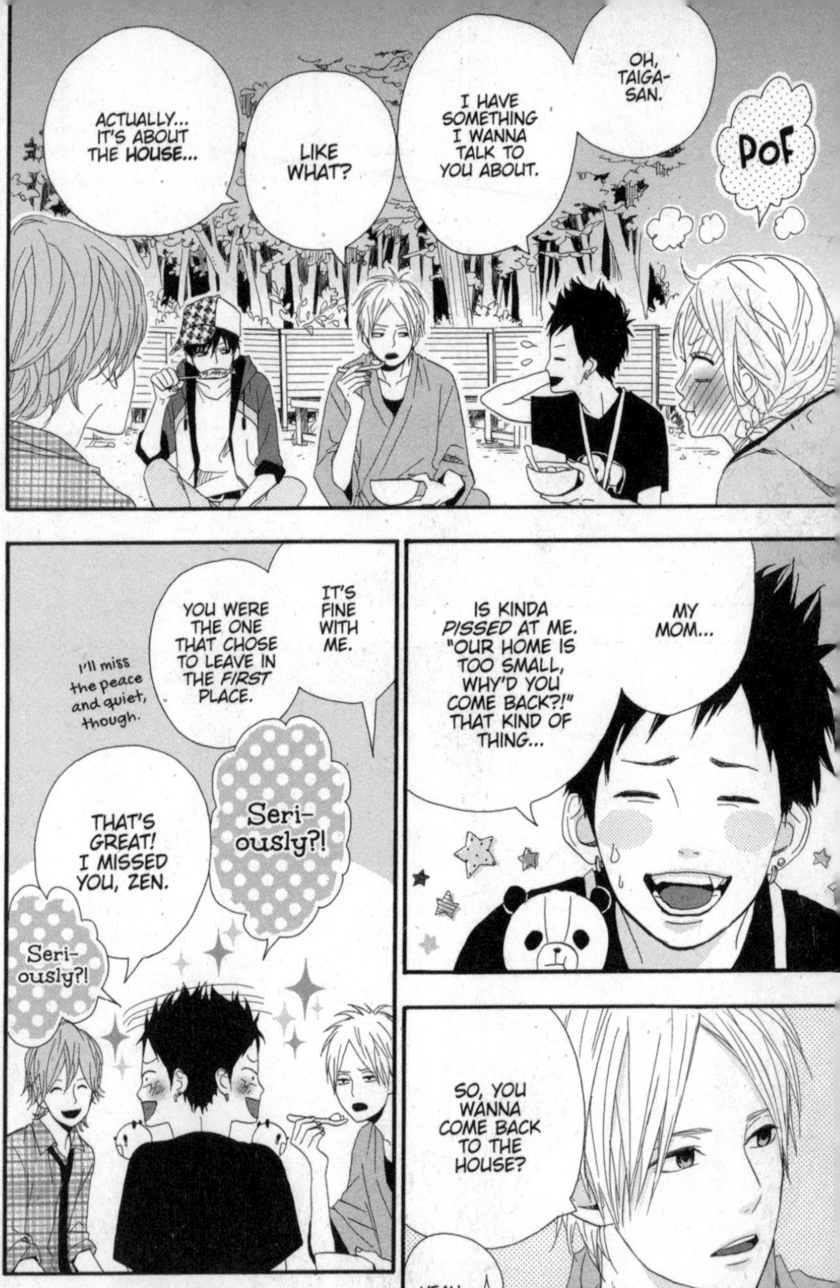
POF
OH, TAIGA-SAN.
I HAVE SOMETHING I WANNA TALK TO YOU ABOUT.
LIKE WHAT?
ACTUALLY... IT'S ABOUT THE HOUSE...
MY MOM...
IS KINDA *PISSED* AT ME. "OUR HOME IS TOO SMALL, WHY'D YOU COME BACK?!" THAT KIND OF THING...
SO, YOU WANNA COME BACK TO THE HOUSE?
YEAH...
IT'S FINE WITH ME.
YOU WERE THE ONE THAT CHOSE TO LEAVE IN THE *FIRST* PLACE.
I'll miss the peace and quiet, though.
Seri-ously?!
THAT'S GREAT! I MISSED YOU, ZEN.
Seri-ously?!

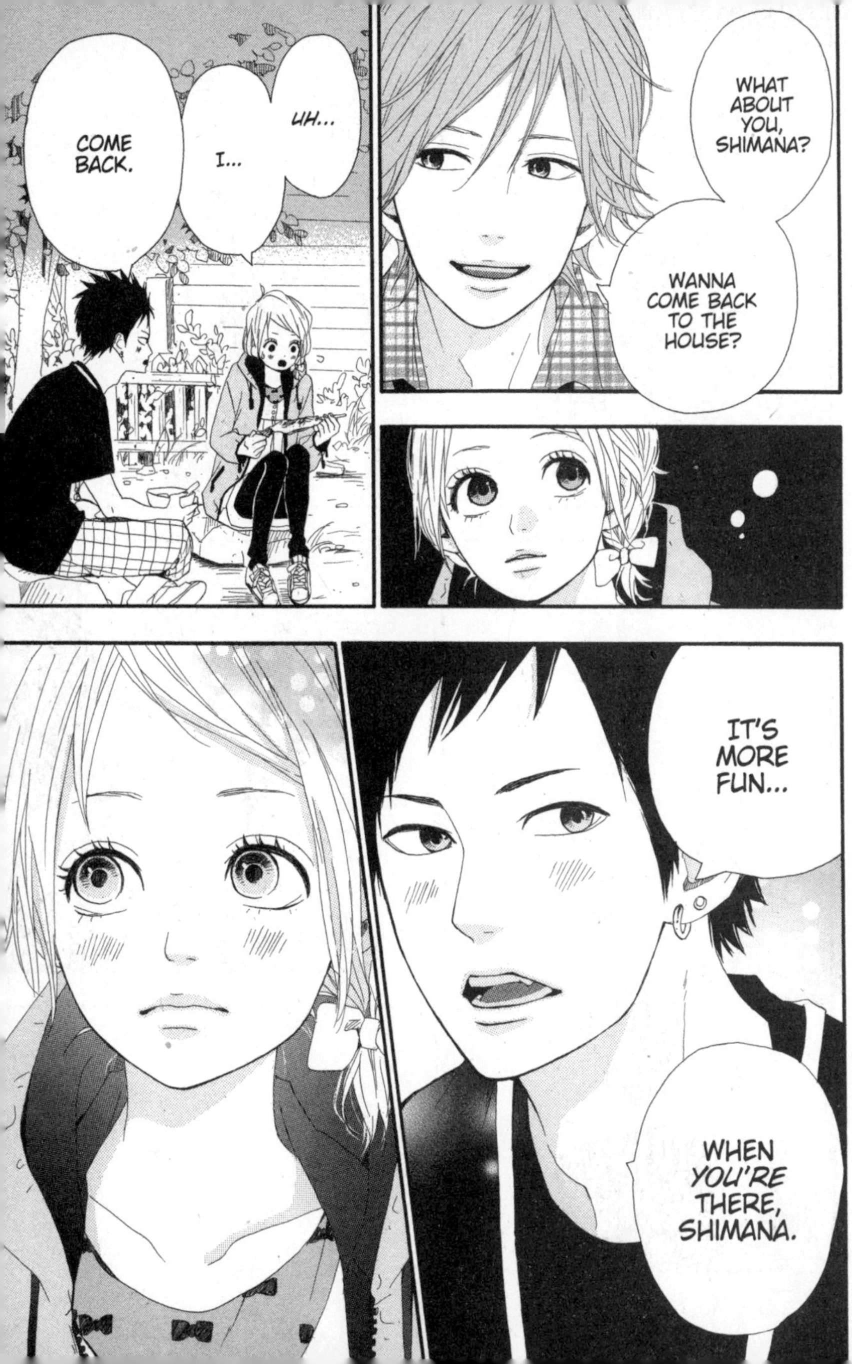
WHAT ABOUT YOU, SHIMANA?
WANNA COME BACK TO THE HOUSE?
UH...
I...
COME BACK.
IT'S MORE FUN...
WHEN *YOU'RE* THERE, SHIMANA.

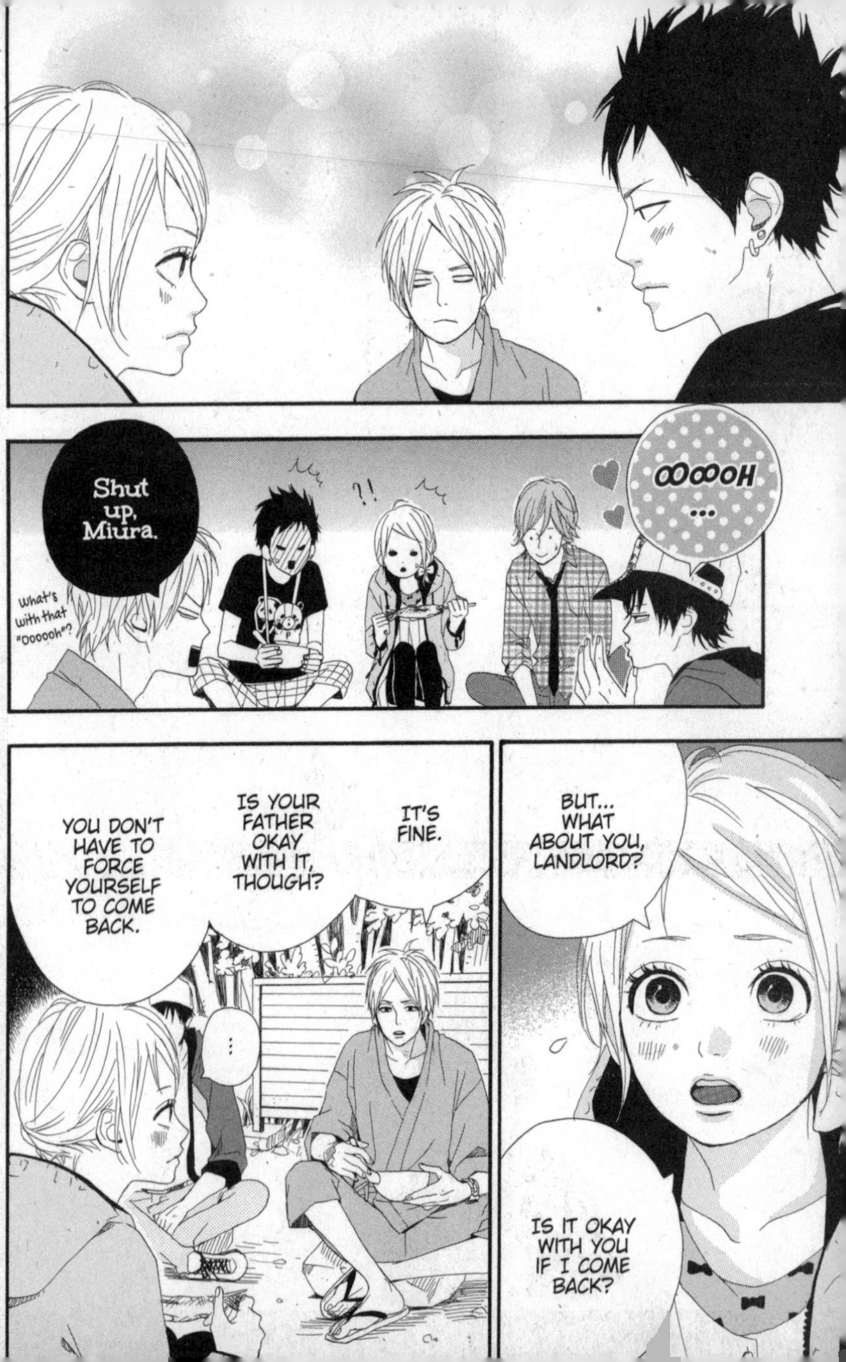
OOOOOH
...
Shut up, Miura.
What's with that "Oooooh"?
BUT... WHAT ABOUT YOU, LANDLORD?
IS IT OKAY WITH YOU IF I COME BACK?
IT'S FINE.
IS YOUR FATHER OKAY WITH IT, THOUGH?
YOU DON'T HAVE TO FORCE YOURSELF TO COME BACK.
...

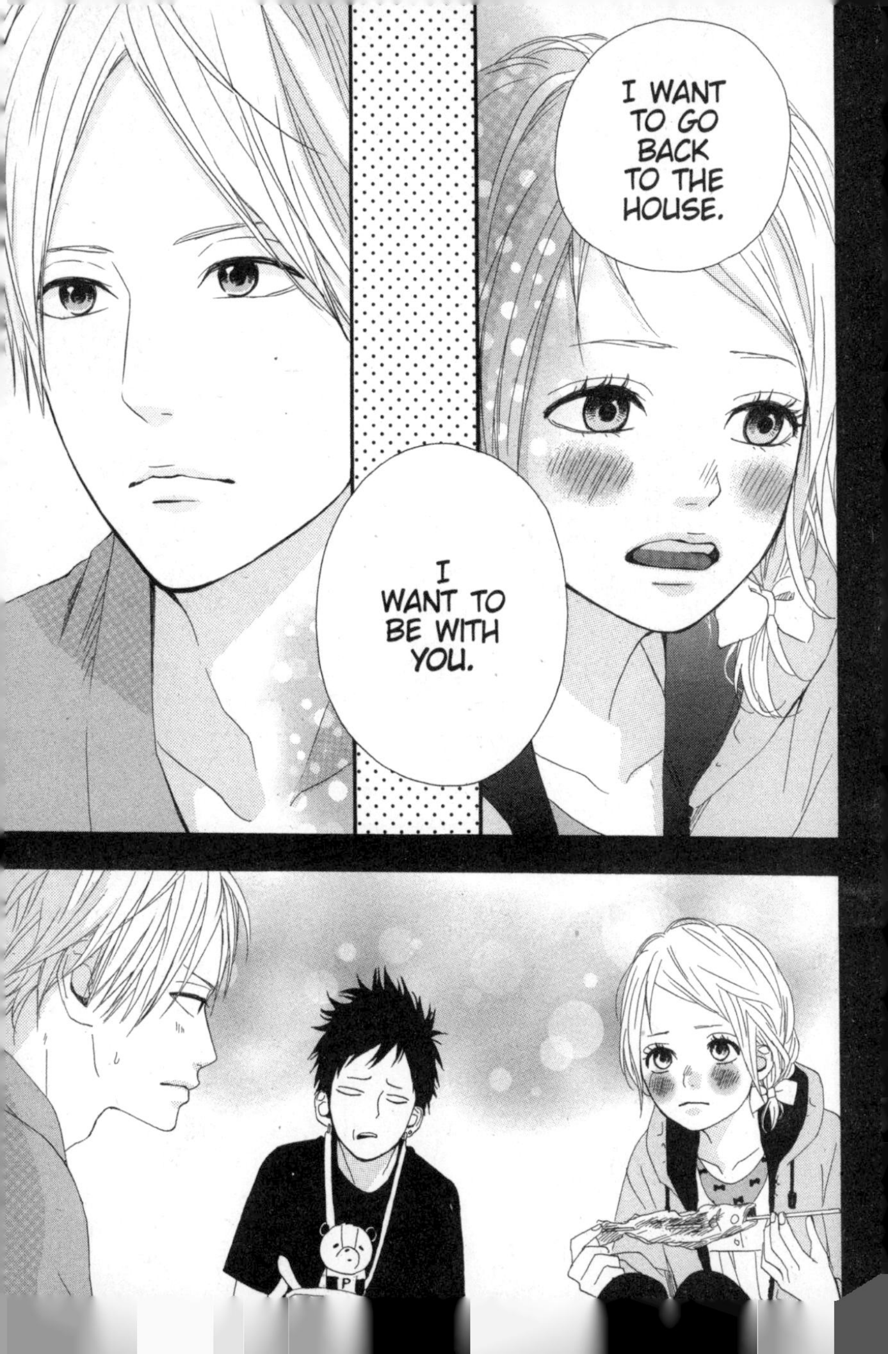
I WANT TO GO BACK TO THE HOUSE.
I WANT TO BE WITH YOU.

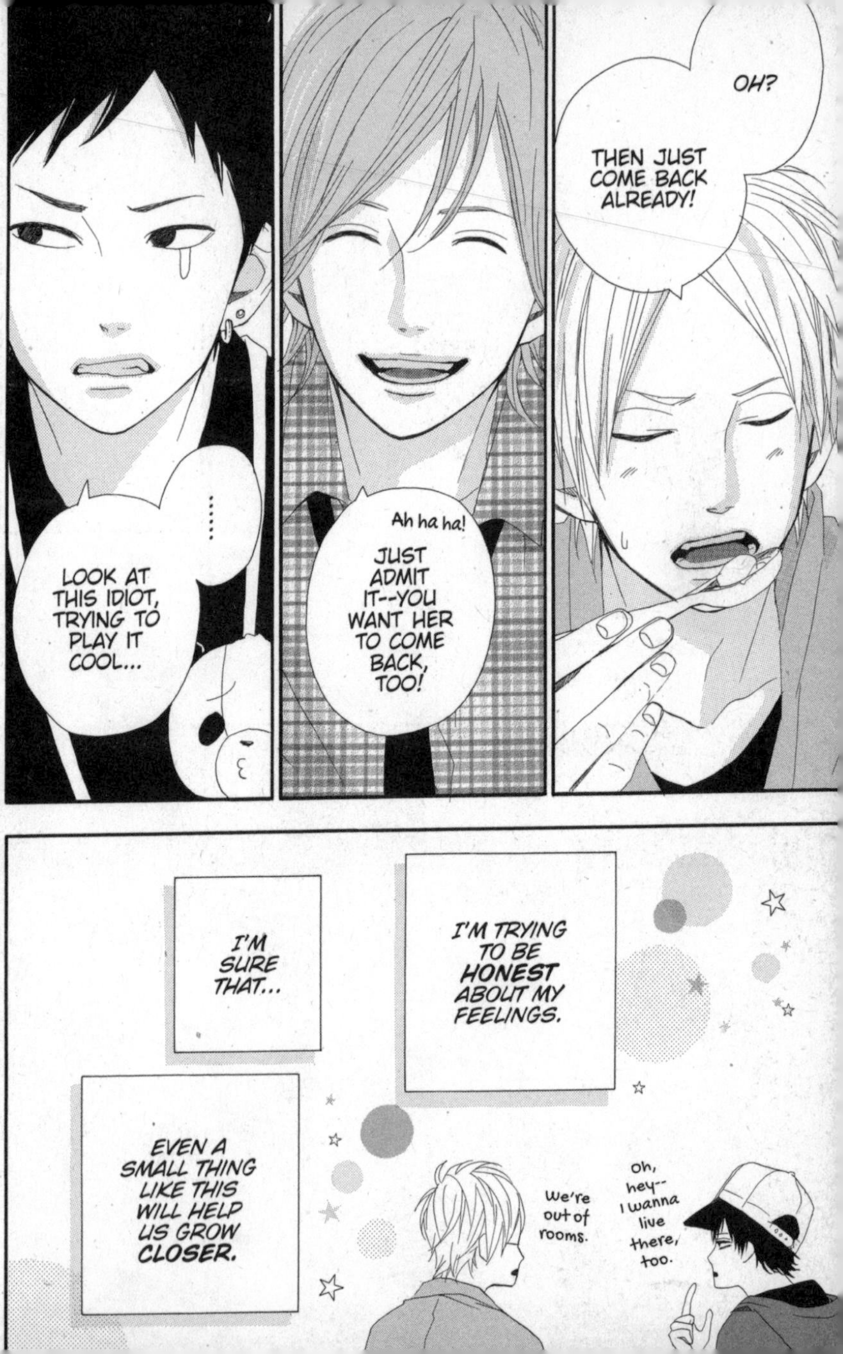
OH?
THEN JUST COME BACK ALREADY!
Ah ha ha!
JUST ADMIT IT--YOU WANT HER TO COME BACK, TOO!
......
LOOK AT THIS IDIOT, TRYING TO PLAY IT COOL...
I'M TRYING TO BE HONEST ABOUT MY FEELINGS.
I'M SURE THAT...
EVEN A SMALL THING LIKE THIS WILL HELP US GROW CLOSER.
Oh, hey-- I wanna live there, too.
We're out of rooms.

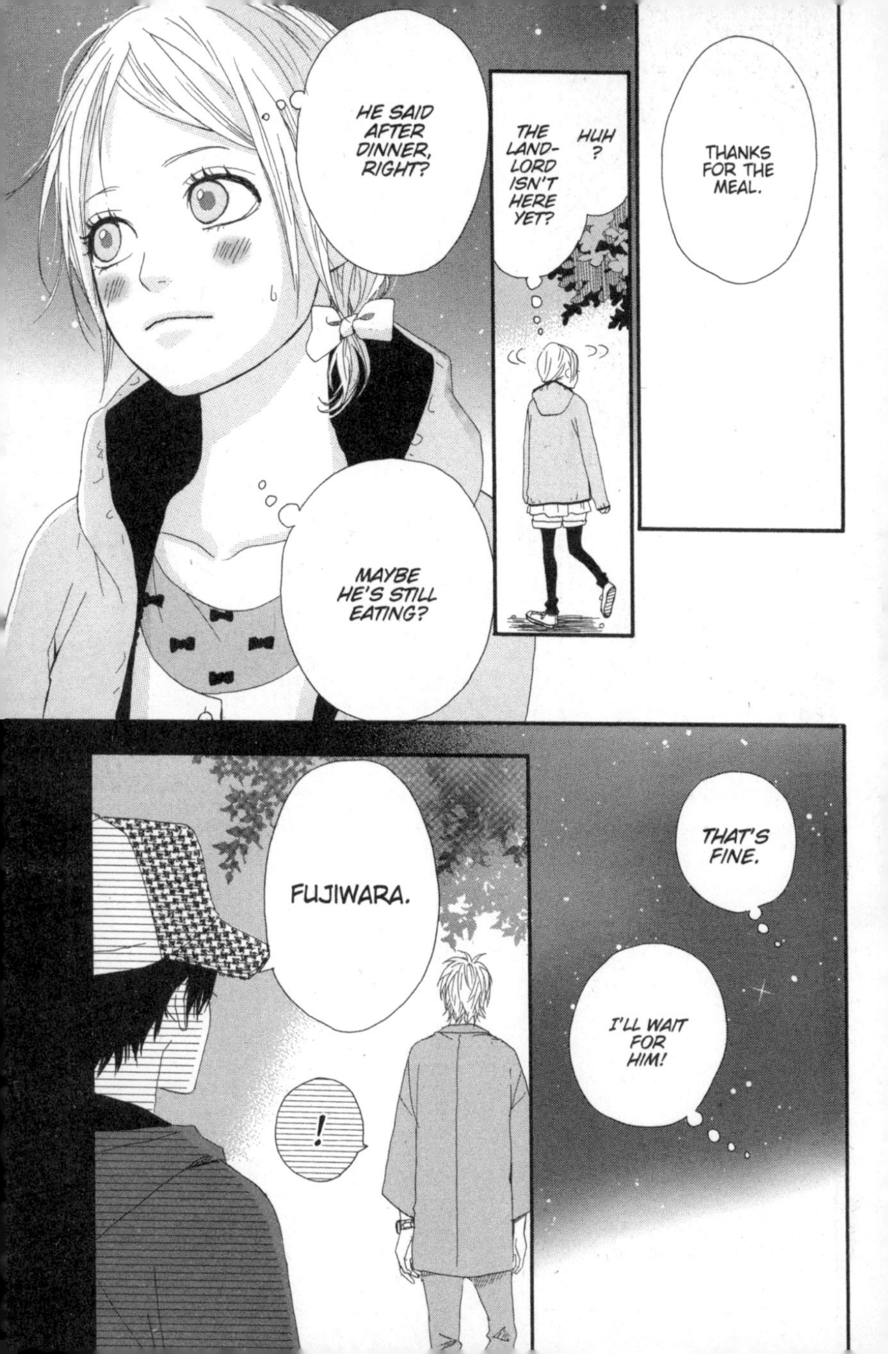
THANKS FOR THE MEAL.
HUH?
THE LAND-LORD ISN'T HERE YET?
HE SAID AFTER DINNER, RIGHT?
MAYBE HE'S STILL EATING?
THAT'S FINE.
I'LL WAIT FOR HIM!
FUJIWARA.
!

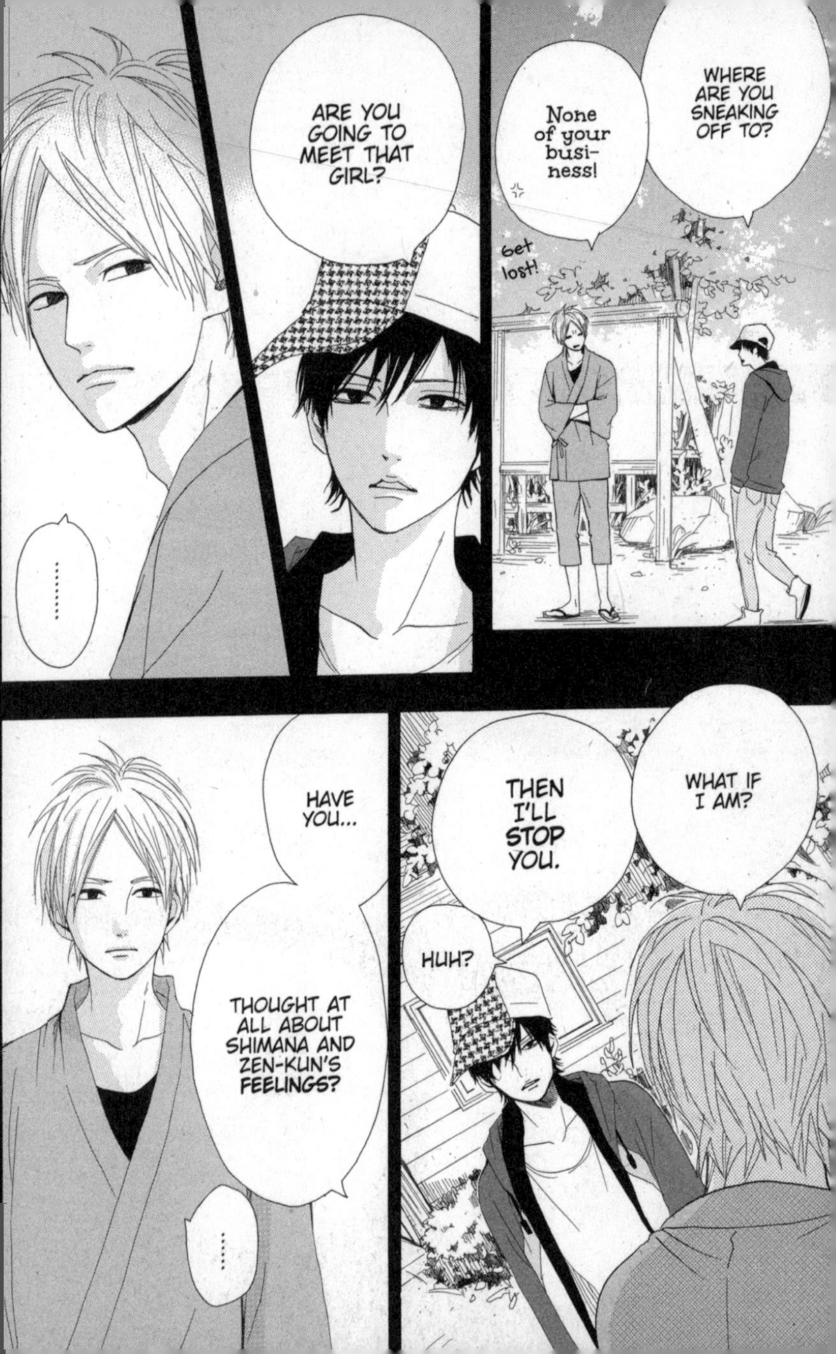
WHERE ARE YOU SNEAKING OFF TO?
None of your busi-ness!
Get lost!
ARE YOU GOING TO MEET THAT GIRL?
......
WHAT IF I AM?
THEN I'LL STOP YOU.
HUH?
HAVE YOU...
THOUGHT AT ALL ABOUT SHIMANA AND ZEN-KUN'S FEELINGS?
......

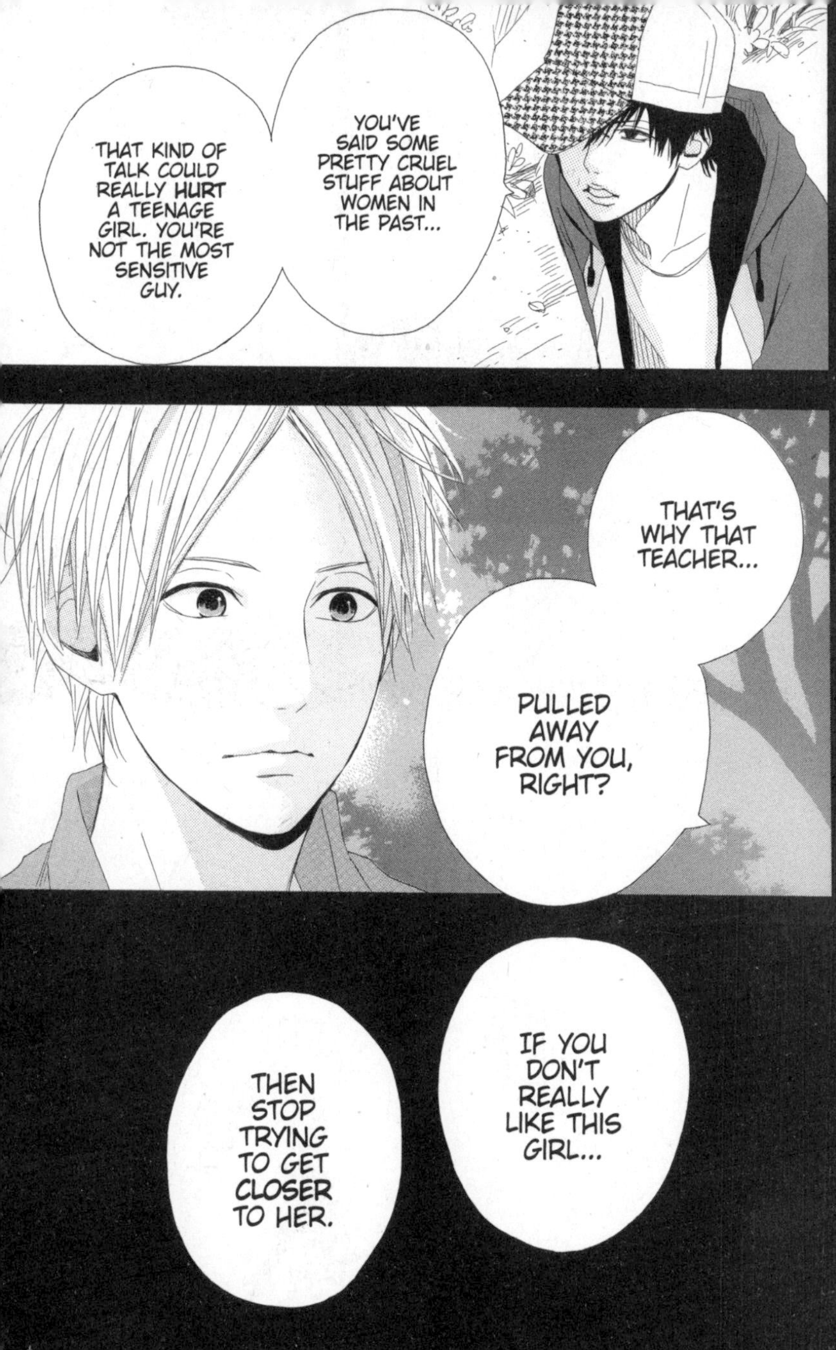
YOU'VE SAID SOME PRETTY CRUEL STUFF ABOUT WOMEN IN THE PAST...
THAT KIND OF TALK COULD REALLY **HURT** A TEENAGE GIRL. YOU'RE NOT THE MOST SENSITIVE GUY.
THAT'S WHY THAT TEACHER...
PULLED AWAY FROM YOU, RIGHT?
IF YOU DON'T REALLY LIKE THIS GIRL...
THEN STOP TRYING TO GET CLOSER TO HER.

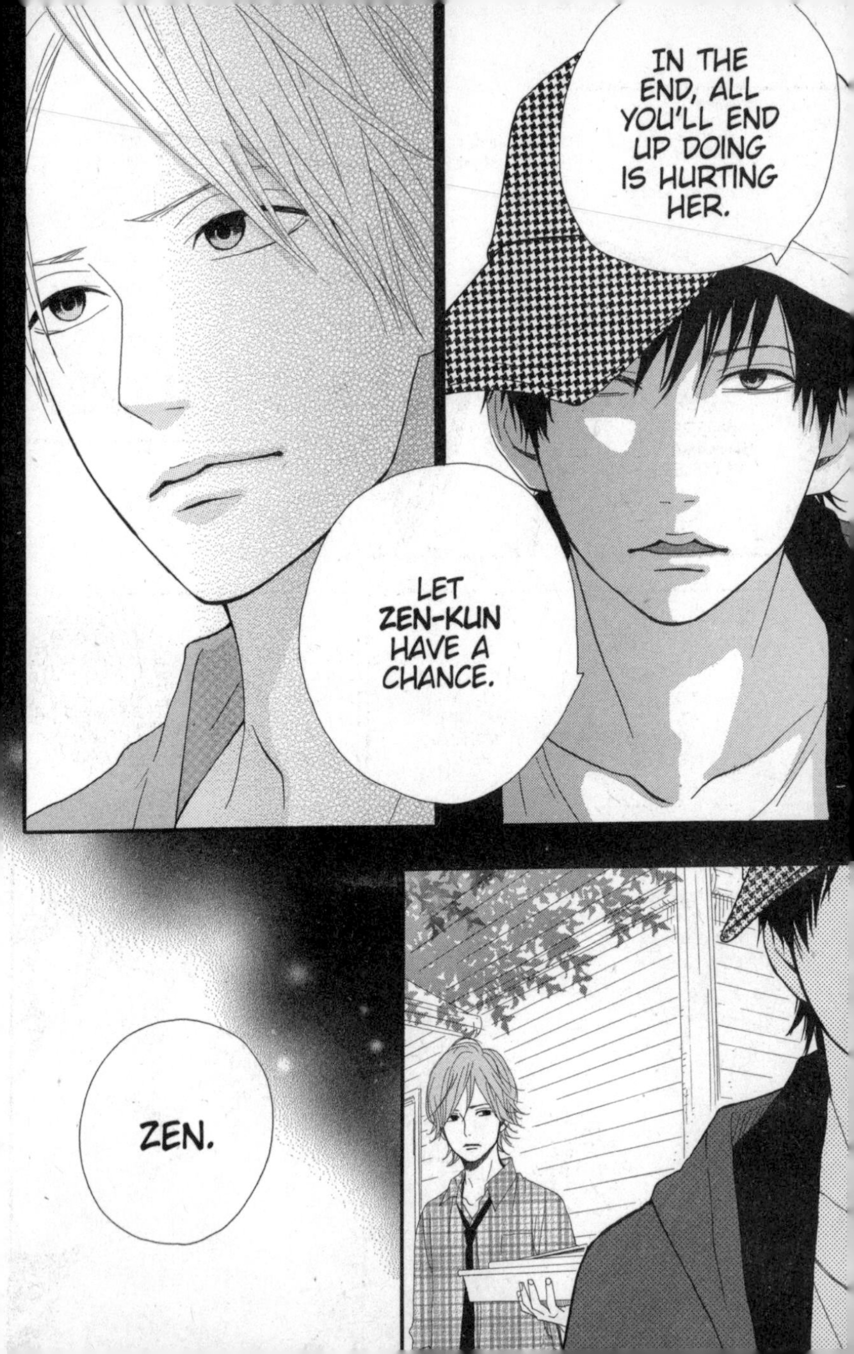
IN THE END, ALL YOU'LL END UP DOING IS HURTING HER.
LET ZEN-KUN HAVE A CHANCE.
ZEN.

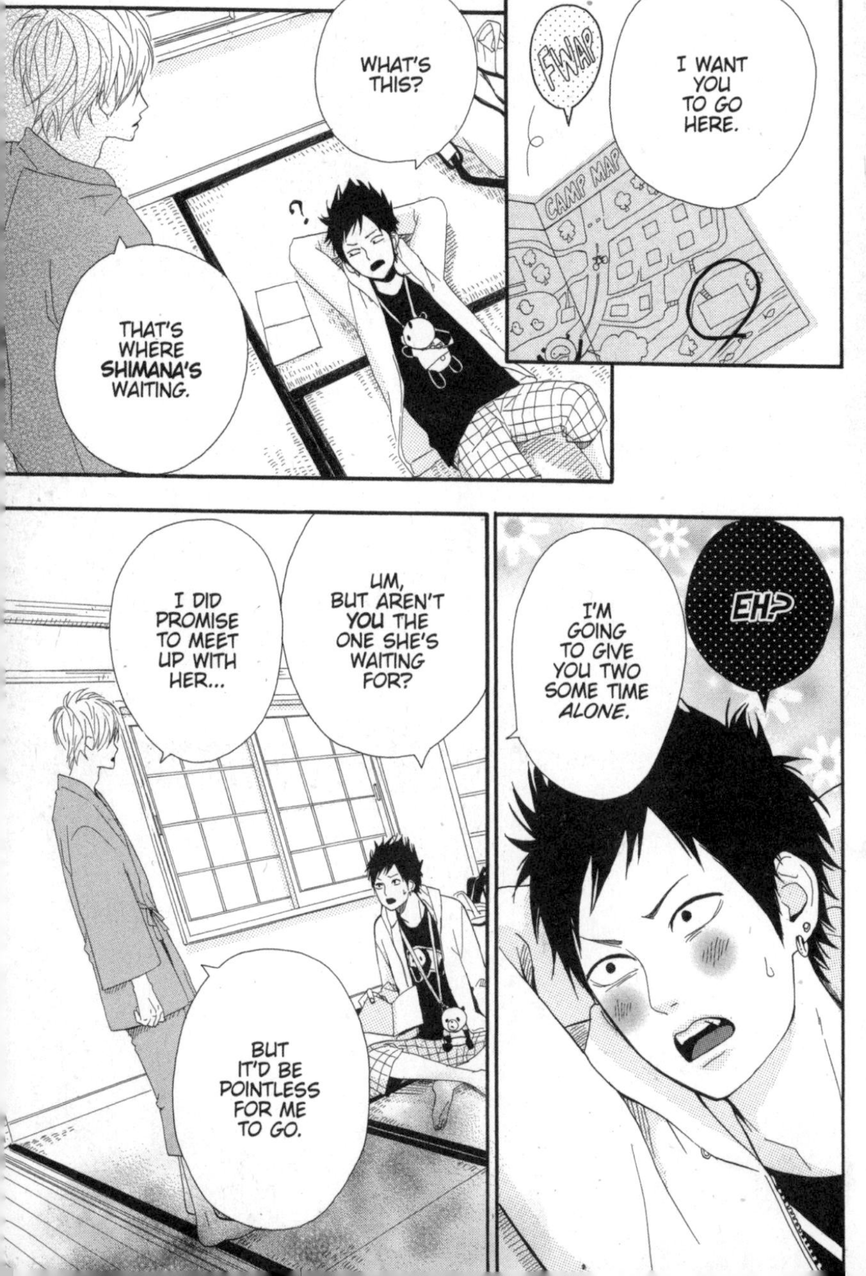
FWAP
I WANT YOU TO GO HERE.
CAMP MAP
WHAT'S THIS?
?
THAT'S WHERE SHIMANA'S WAITING.
I'M GOING TO GIVE YOU TWO SOME TIME ALONE.
EH?
UM, BUT AREN'T YOU THE ONE SHE'S WAITING FOR?
I DID PROMISE TO MEET UP WITH HER...
BUT IT'D BE POINTLESS FOR ME TO GO.

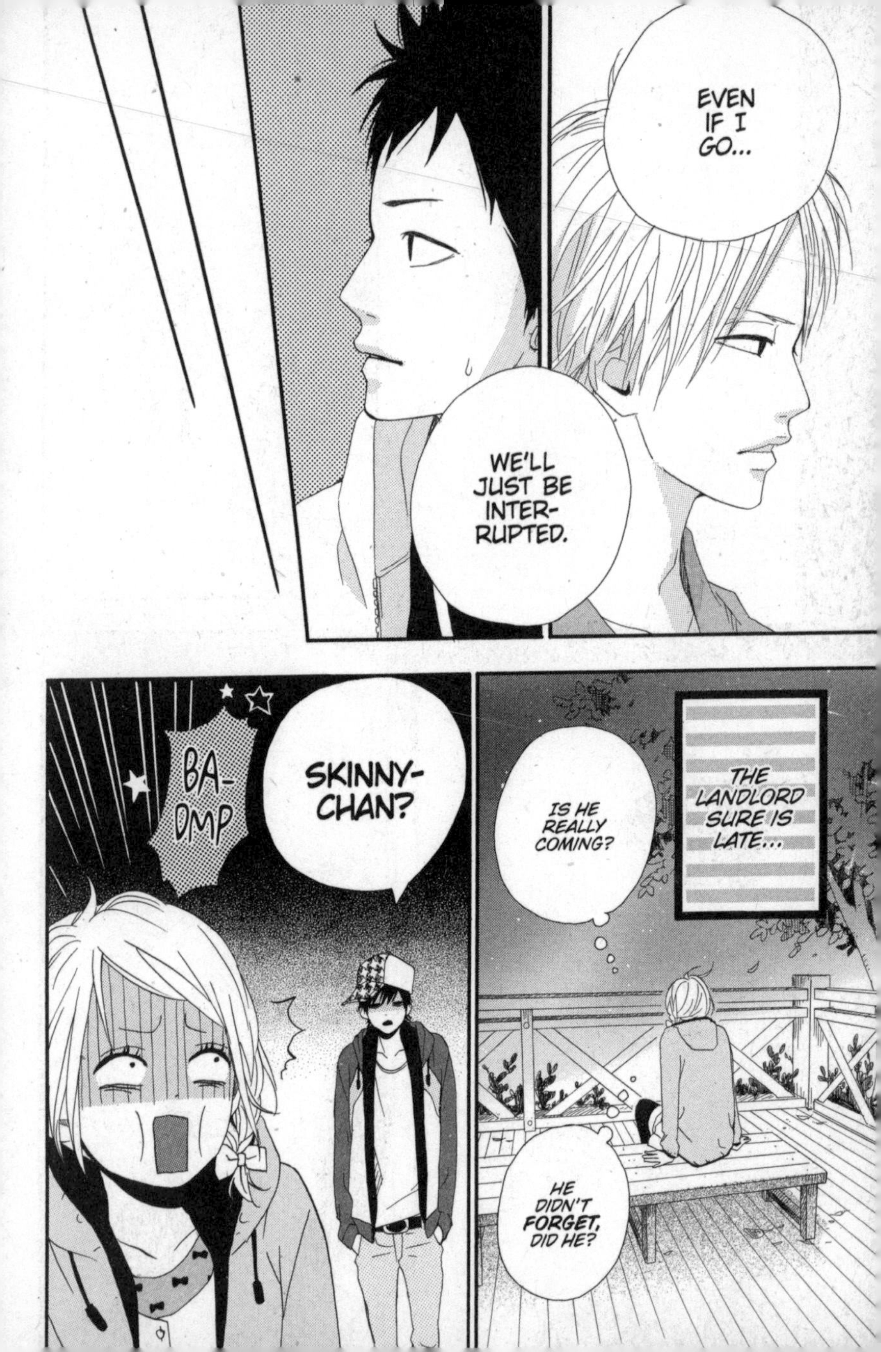
EVEN IF I GO...
WE'LL JUST BE INTER-RUPTED.
THE LANDLORD SURE IS LATE...
IS HE REALLY COMING?
HE DIDN'T FORGET, DID HE?
SKINNY-CHAN?
BA-DMP

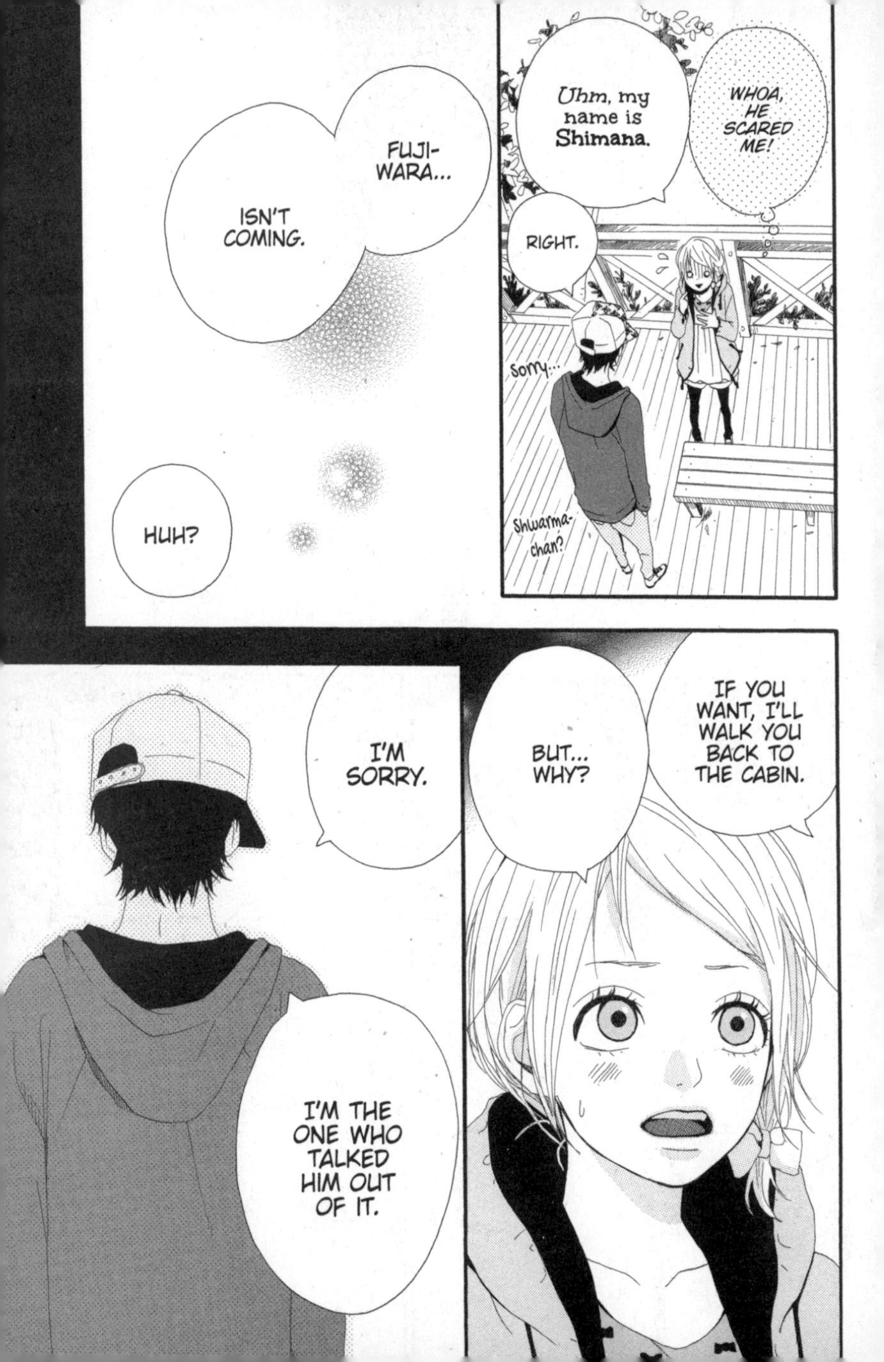
WHOA, HE SCARED ME!
Uhm, my name is Shimana.
RIGHT.
Sorry...
Shwarma-chan?
FUJI-WARA...
ISN'T COMING.
HUH?
IF YOU WANT, I'LL WALK YOU BACK TO THE CABIN.
BUT... WHY?
I'M SORRY.
I'M THE ONE WHO TALKED HIM OUT OF IT.

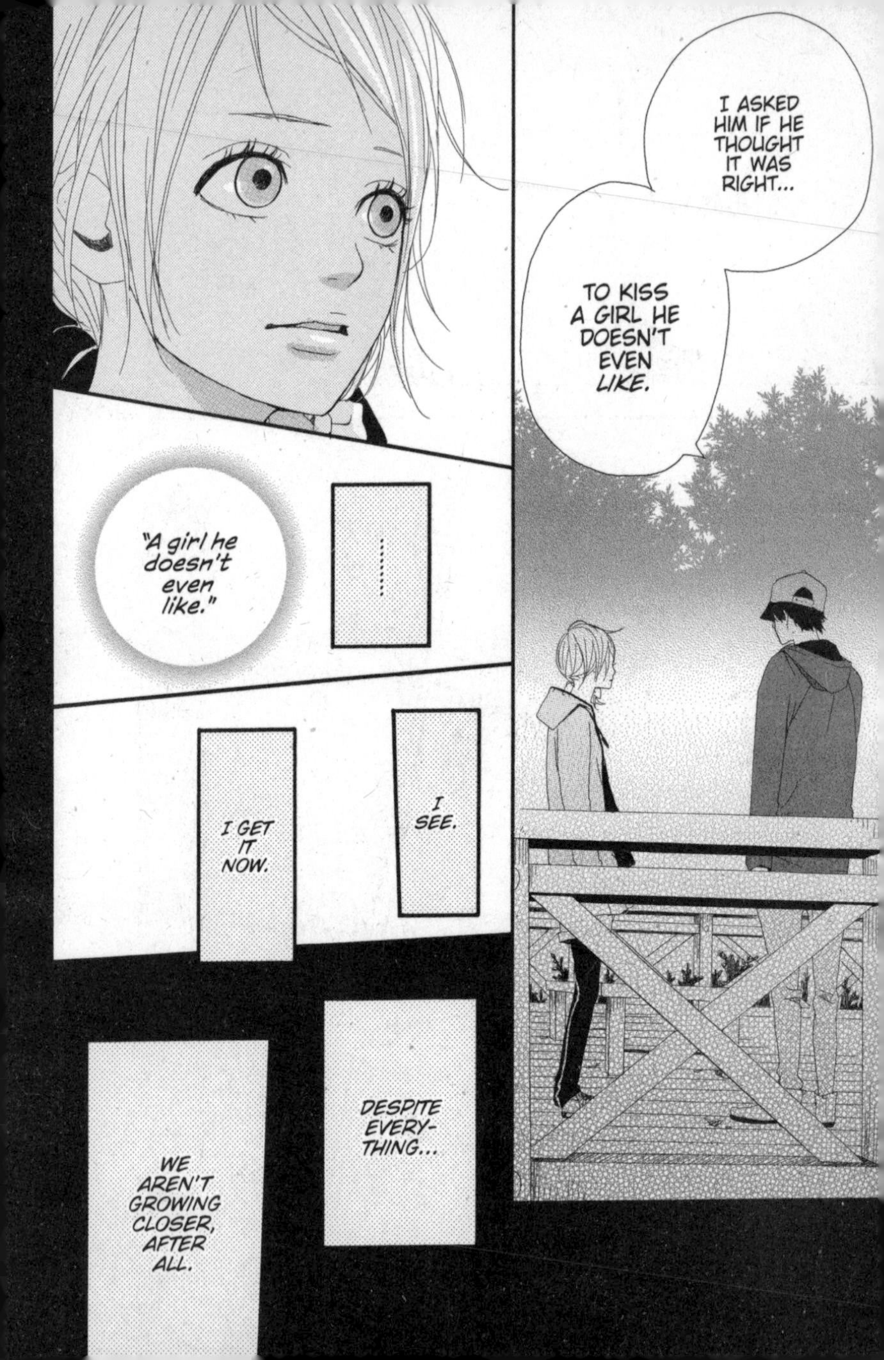
I ASKED HIM IF HE THOUGHT IT WAS RIGHT...
TO KISS A GIRL HE DOESN'T EVEN LIKE.
......
"A girl he doesn't even like."
I SEE.
I GET IT NOW.
DESPITE EVERY-THING...
WE AREN'T GROWING CLOSER, AFTER ALL.

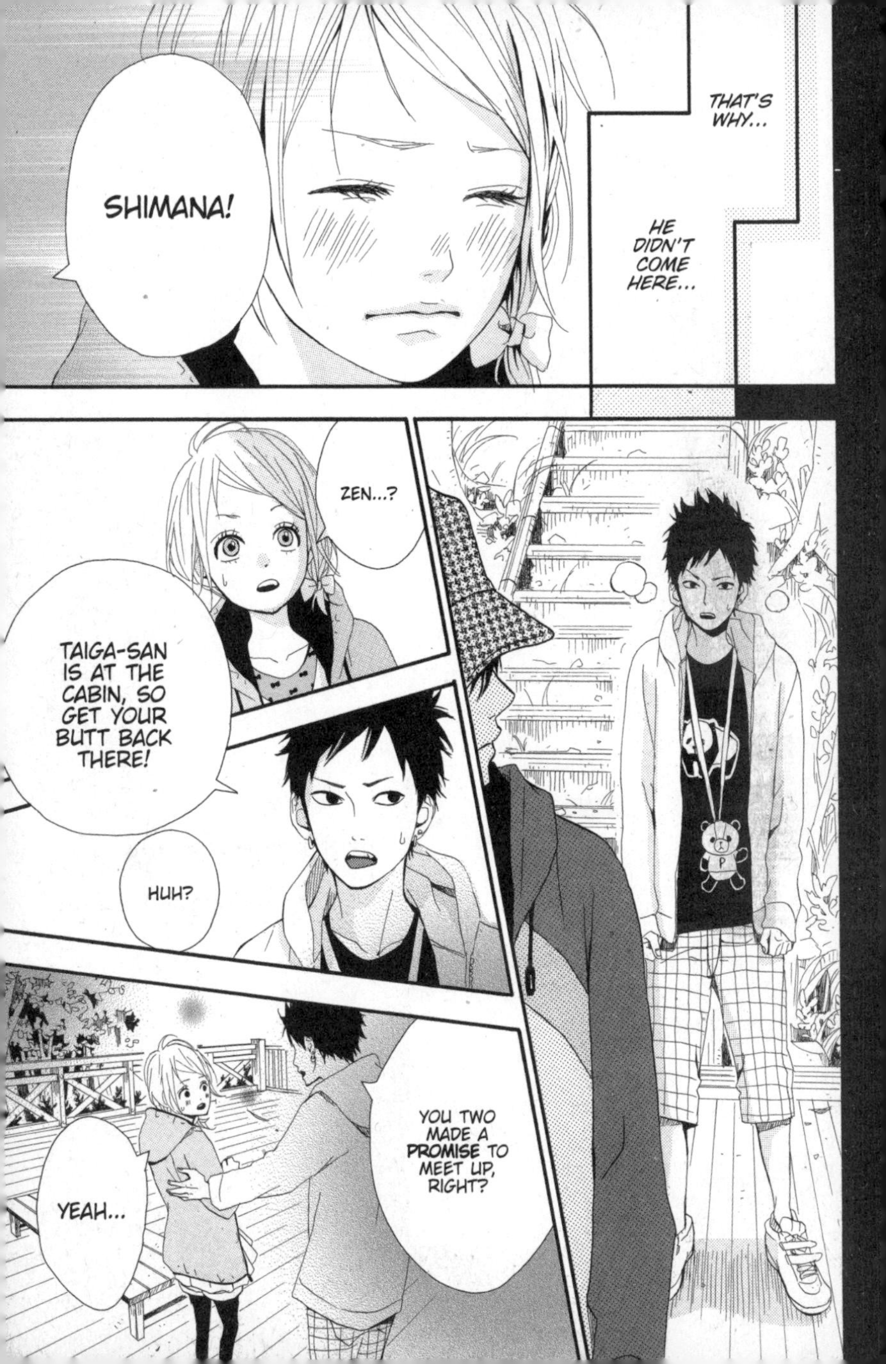
THAT'S WHY...
HE DIDN'T COME HERE...
SHIMANA!
ZEN...?
TAIGA-SAN IS AT THE CABIN, SO GET YOUR BUTT BACK THERE!
HUH?
YOU TWO MADE A **PROMISE** TO MEET UP, RIGHT?
YEAH...

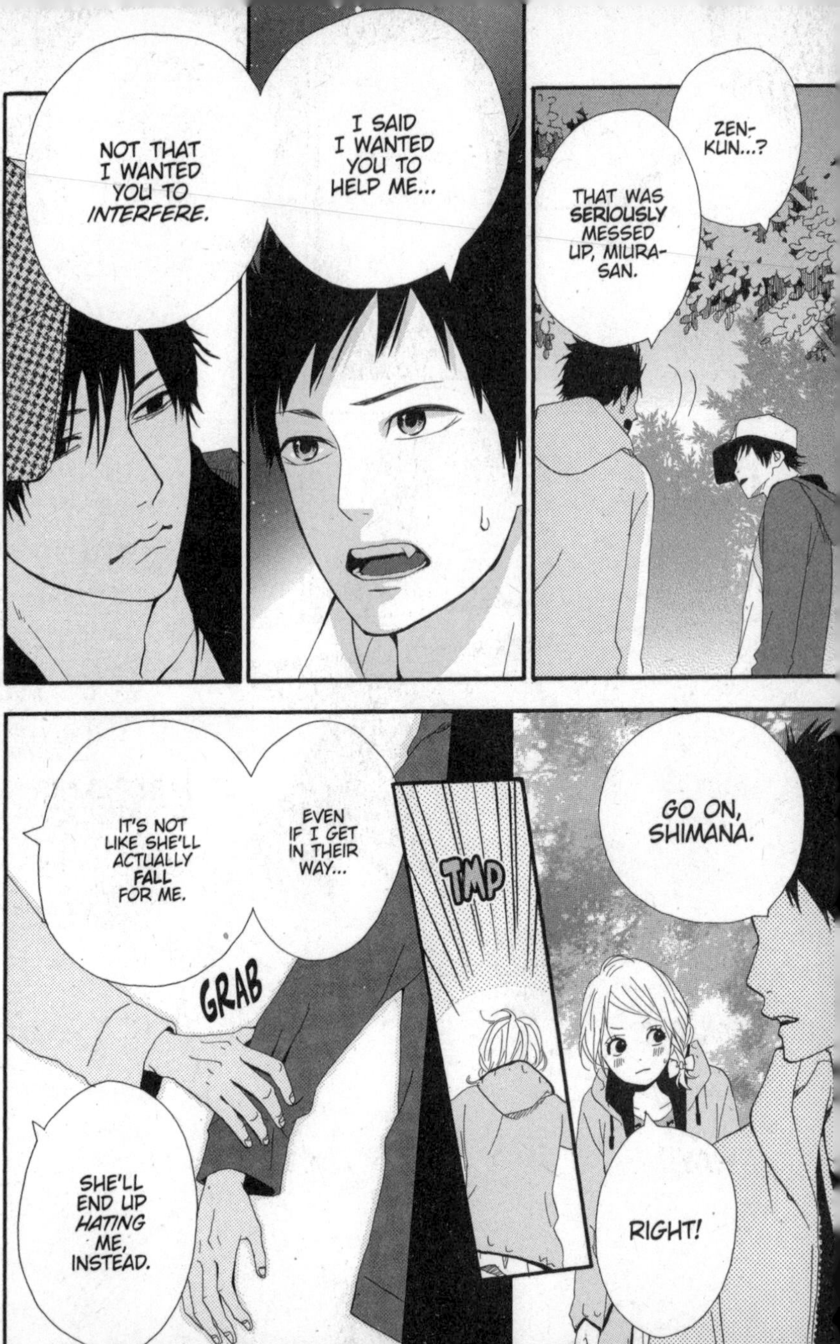
ZEN-KUN...?
THAT WAS SERIOUSLY MESSED UP, MIURA-SAN.
I SAID I WANTED YOU TO HELP ME...
NOT THAT I WANTED YOU TO *INTERFERE*.
GO ON, SHIMANA.
RIGHT!
TMP
EVEN IF I GET IN THEIR WAY...
IT'S NOT LIKE SHE'LL ACTUALLY FALL FOR ME.
GRAB
SHE'LL END UP *HATING* ME, INSTEAD.

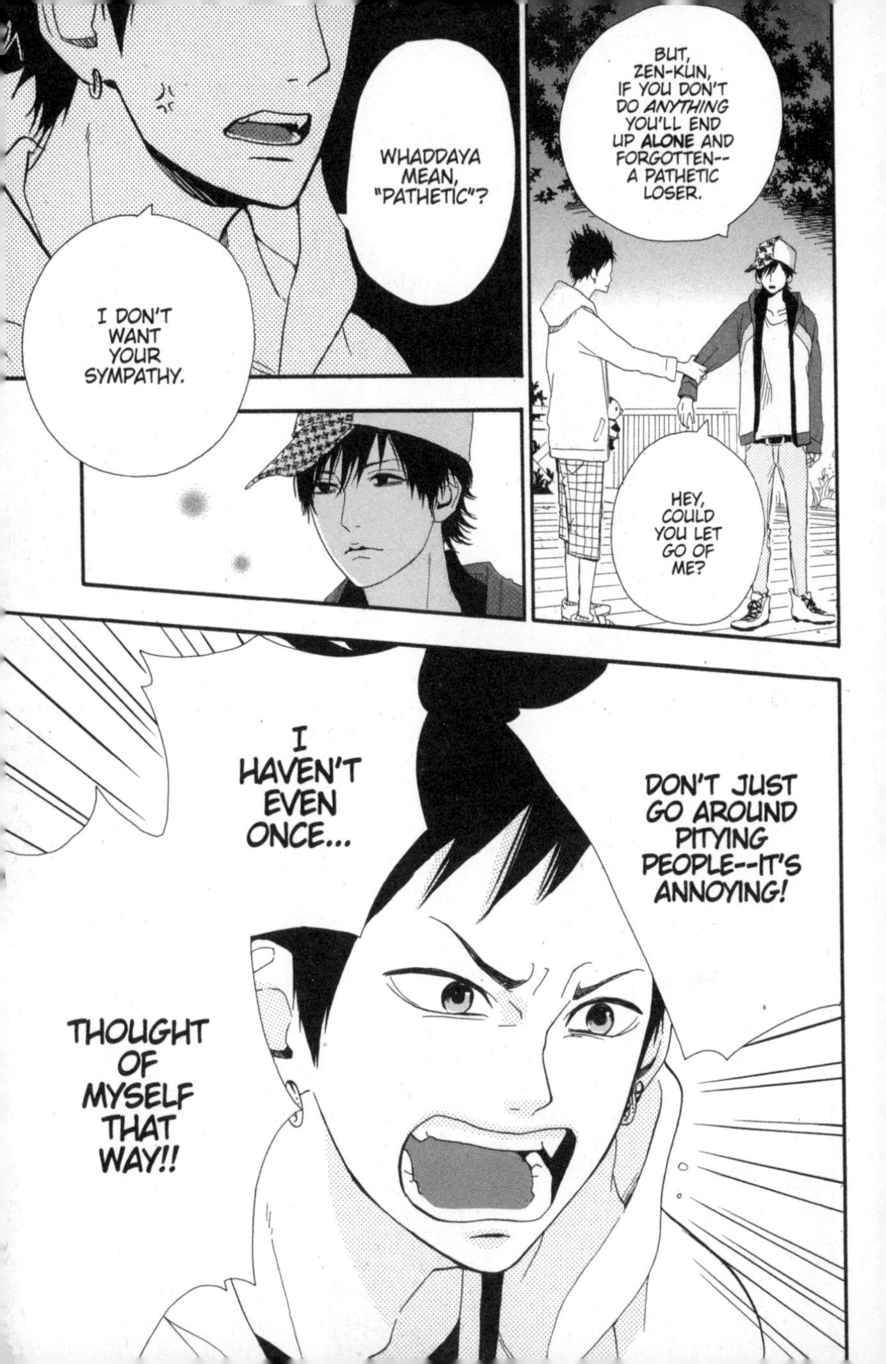

BUT, ZEN-KUN, IF YOU DON'T DO *ANYTHING* YOU'LL END UP **ALONE** AND FORGOTTEN--A PATHETIC LOSER.
HEY, COULD YOU LET GO OF ME?
WHADDAYA MEAN, "PATHETIC"?
I DON'T WANT YOUR SYMPATHY.
DON'T JUST GO AROUND PITYING PEOPLE--IT'S ANNOYING!
I HAVEN'T EVEN ONCE...
THOUGHT OF MYSELF THAT WAY!!

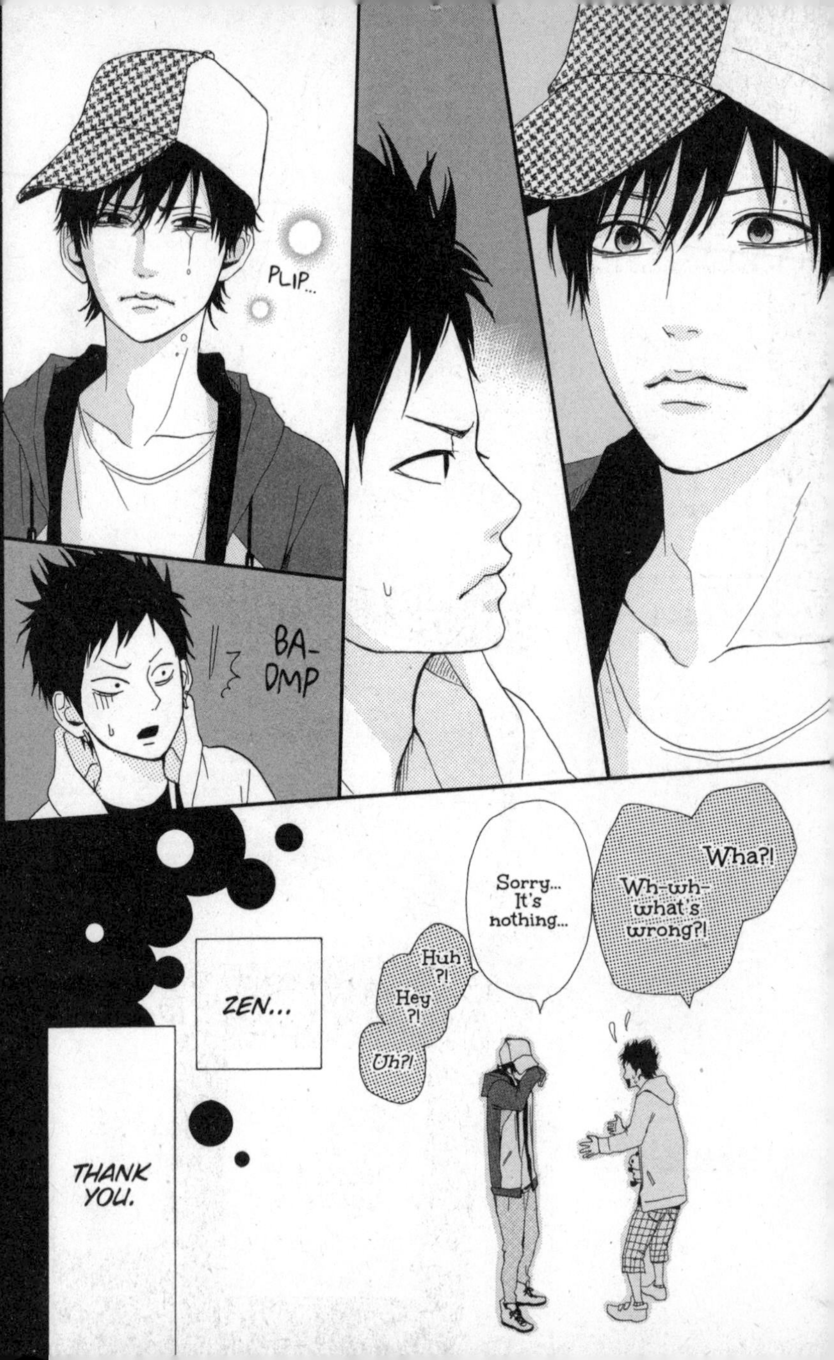
PLIP...
BA-DMP
Wha?!
Wh-wh-what's wrong?!
Sorry... It's nothing...
Huh?!
Hey?!
Uh?!
ZEN...
THANK YOU.

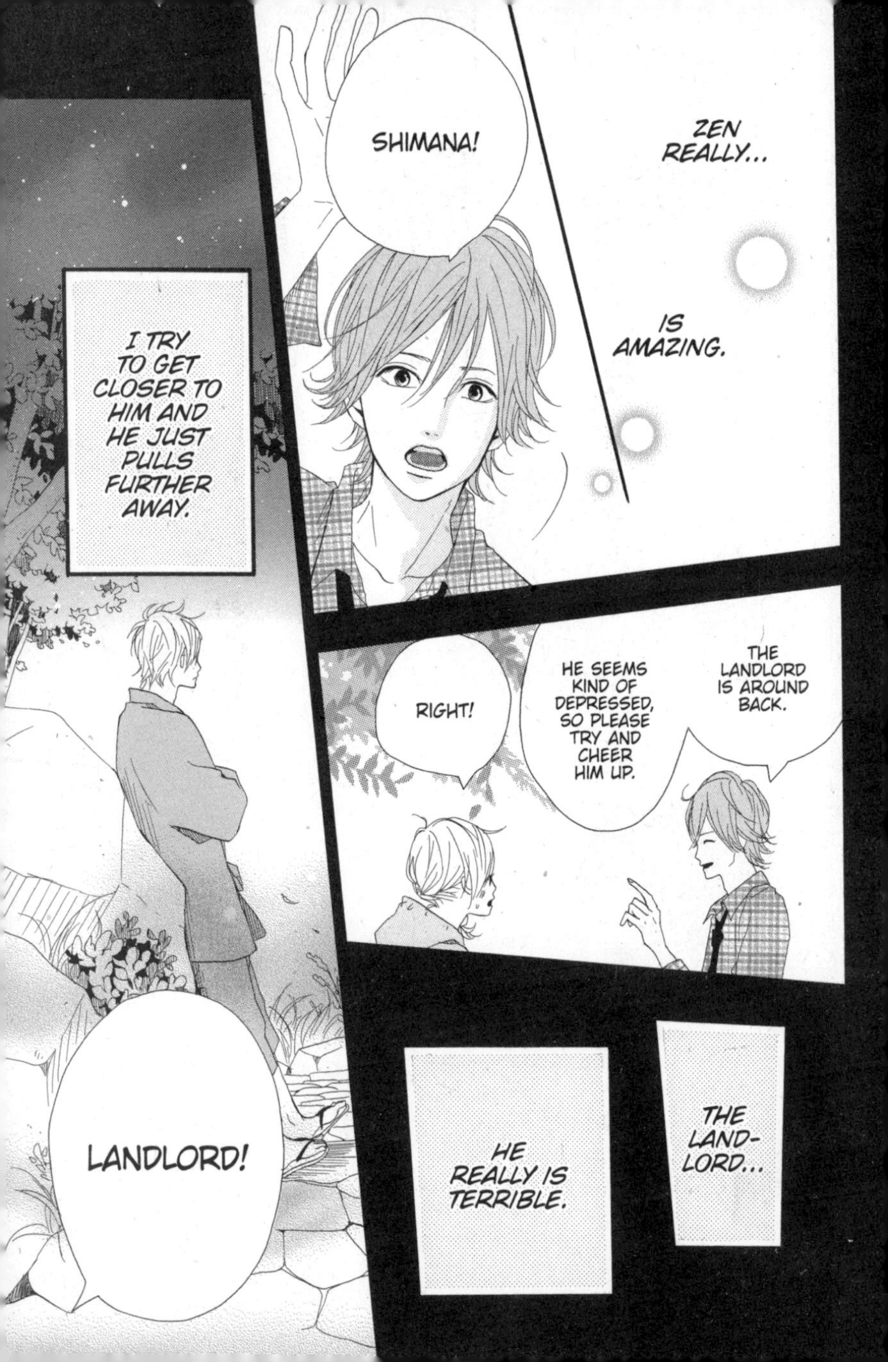
ZEN REALLY...
IS AMAZING.
SHIMANA!
THE LANDLORD IS AROUND BACK.
HE SEEMS KIND OF DEPRESSED, SO PLEASE TRY AND CHEER HIM UP.
RIGHT!
THE LANDLORD...
HE REALLY IS TERRIBLE.
I TRY TO GET CLOSER TO HIM AND HE JUST PULLS FURTHER AWAY.
LANDLORD!

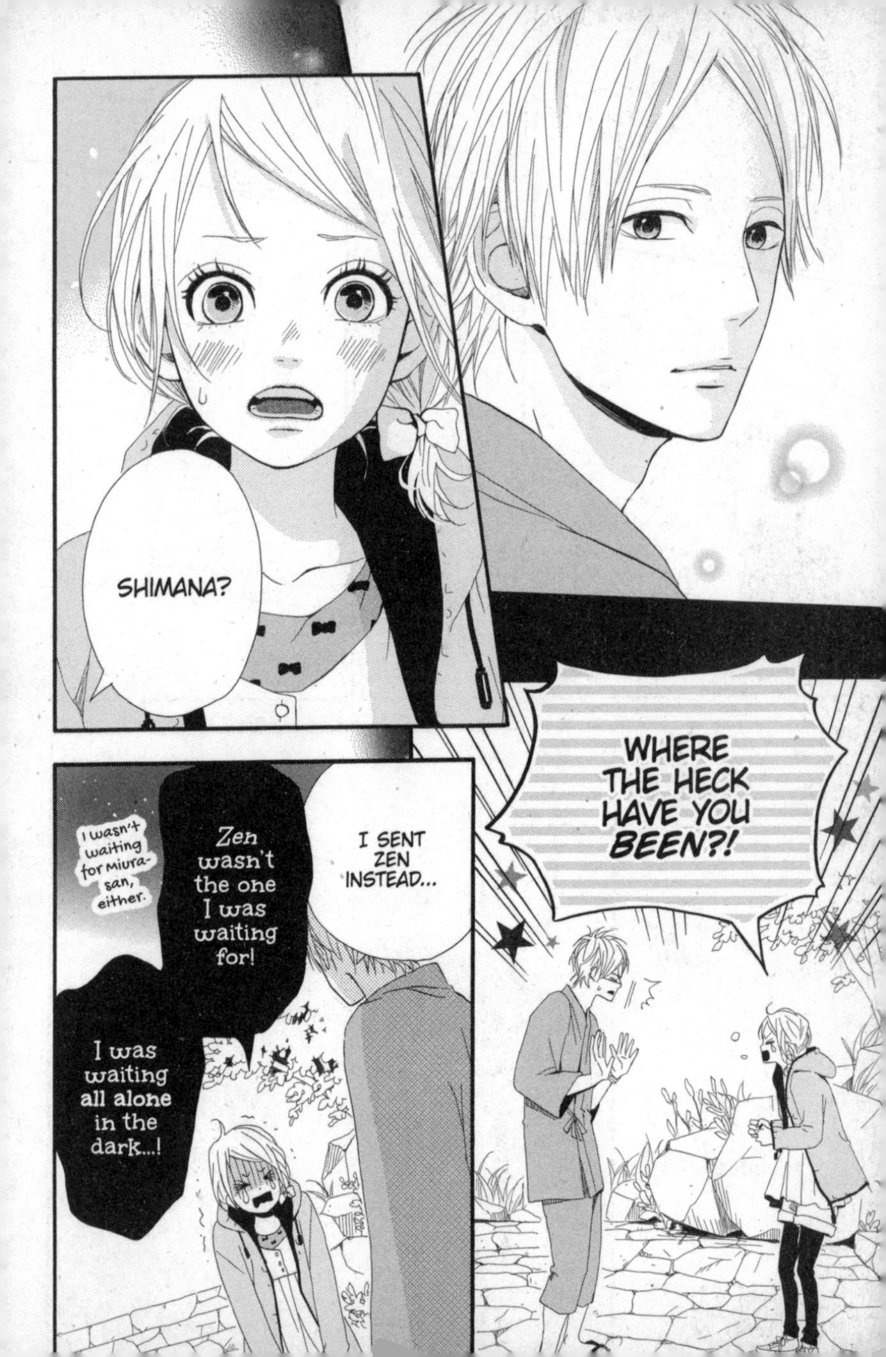
SHIMANA?
WHERE THE HECK HAVE YOU BEEN?!
I SENT ZEN INSTEAD...
Zen wasn't the one I was waiting for!
I wasn't waiting for Miura-san, either.
I was waiting all alone in the dark...!

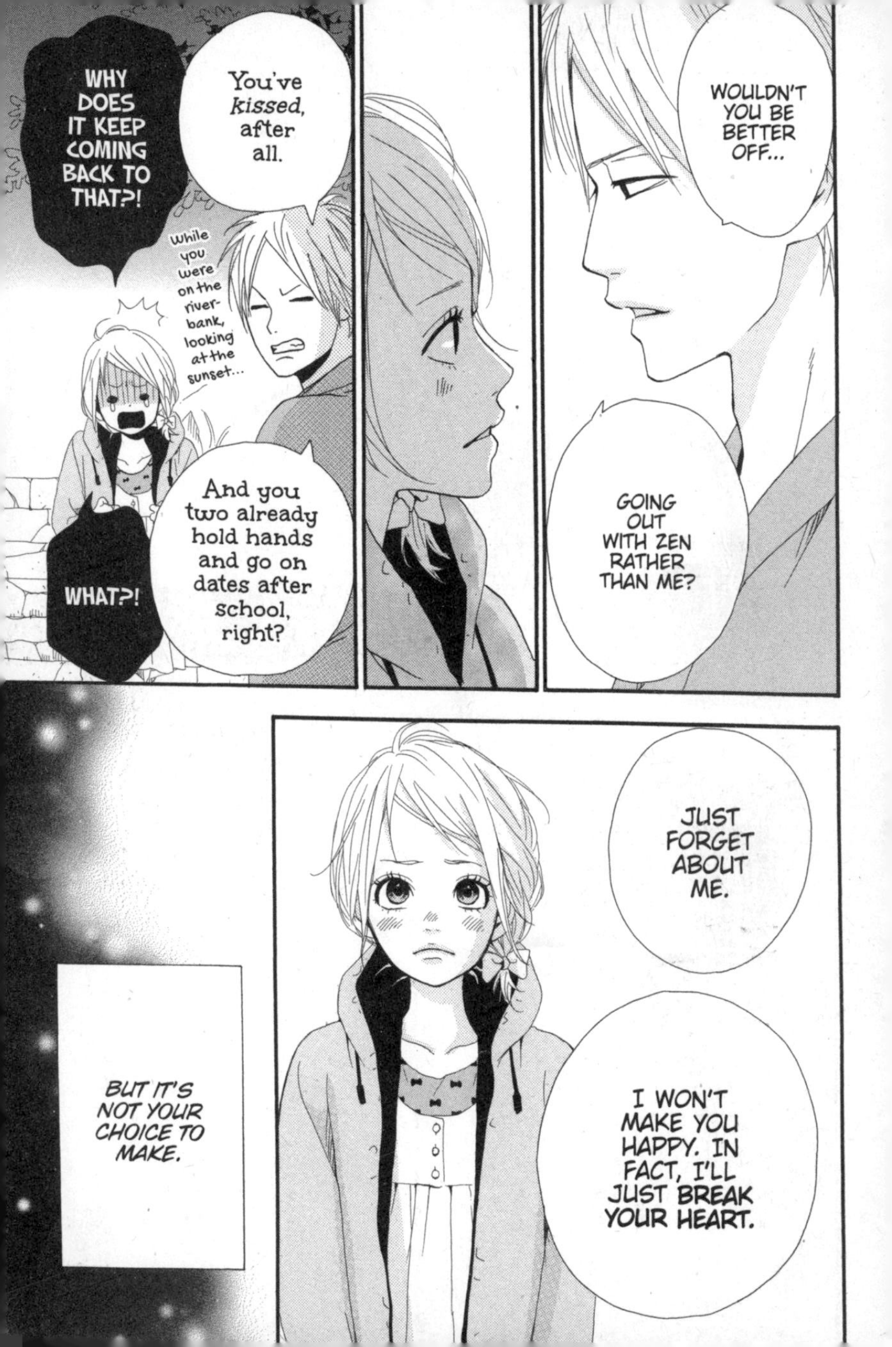

WOULDN'T YOU BE BETTER OFF...
GOING OUT WITH ZEN RATHER THAN ME?
You've *kissed*, after all.
WHY DOES IT KEEP COMING BACK TO THAT?!
While you were on the river-bank, looking at the sunset...
And you two already hold hands and go on dates after school, right?
WHAT?!
JUST FORGET ABOUT ME.
I WON'T MAKE YOU HAPPY. IN FACT, I'LL JUST BREAK YOUR HEART.
BUT IT'S NOT YOUR CHOICE TO MAKE.

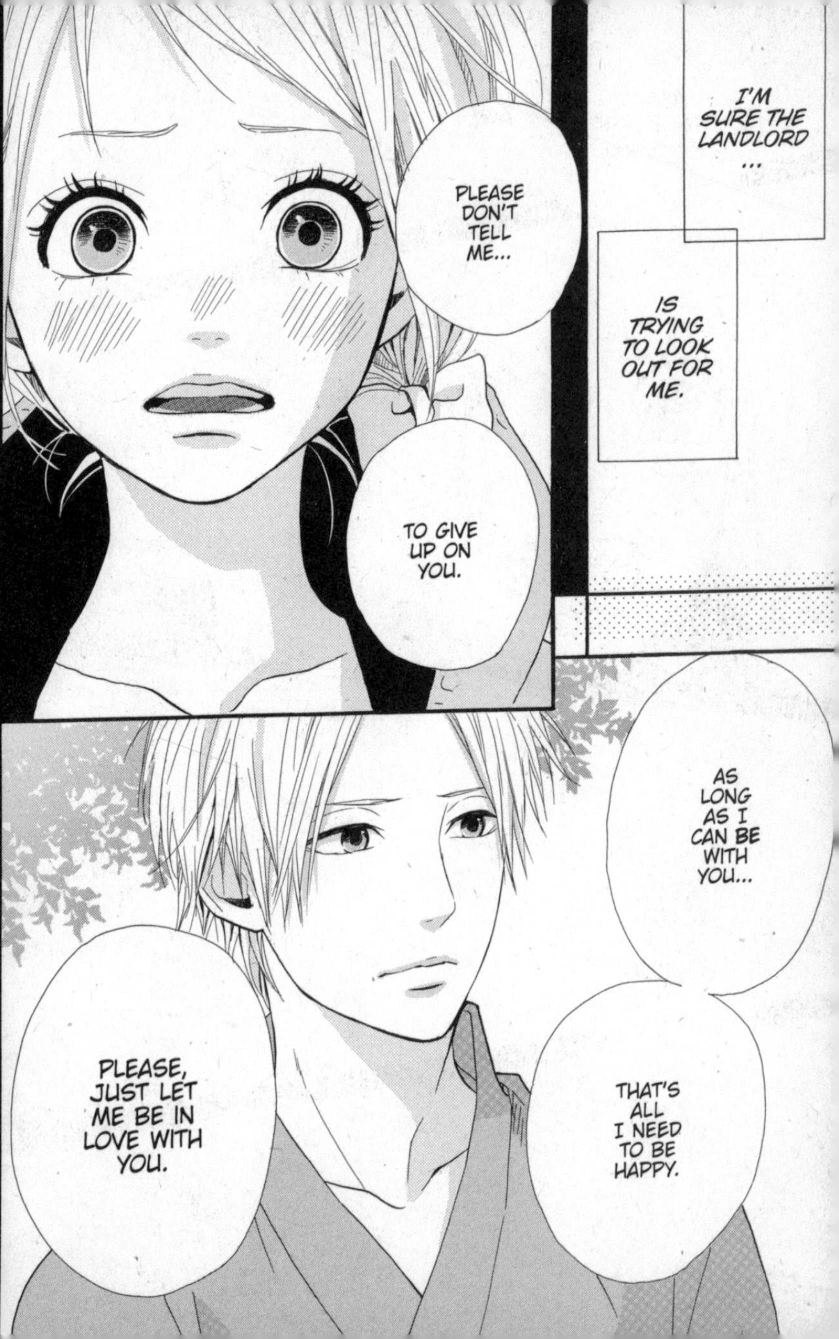
I'M SURE THE LANDLORD ...
IS TRYING TO LOOK OUT FOR ME.
PLEASE DON'T TELL ME...
TO GIVE UP ON YOU.
AS LONG AS I CAN BE WITH YOU...
THAT'S ALL I NEED TO BE HAPPY.
PLEASE, JUST LET ME BE IN LOVE WITH YOU.

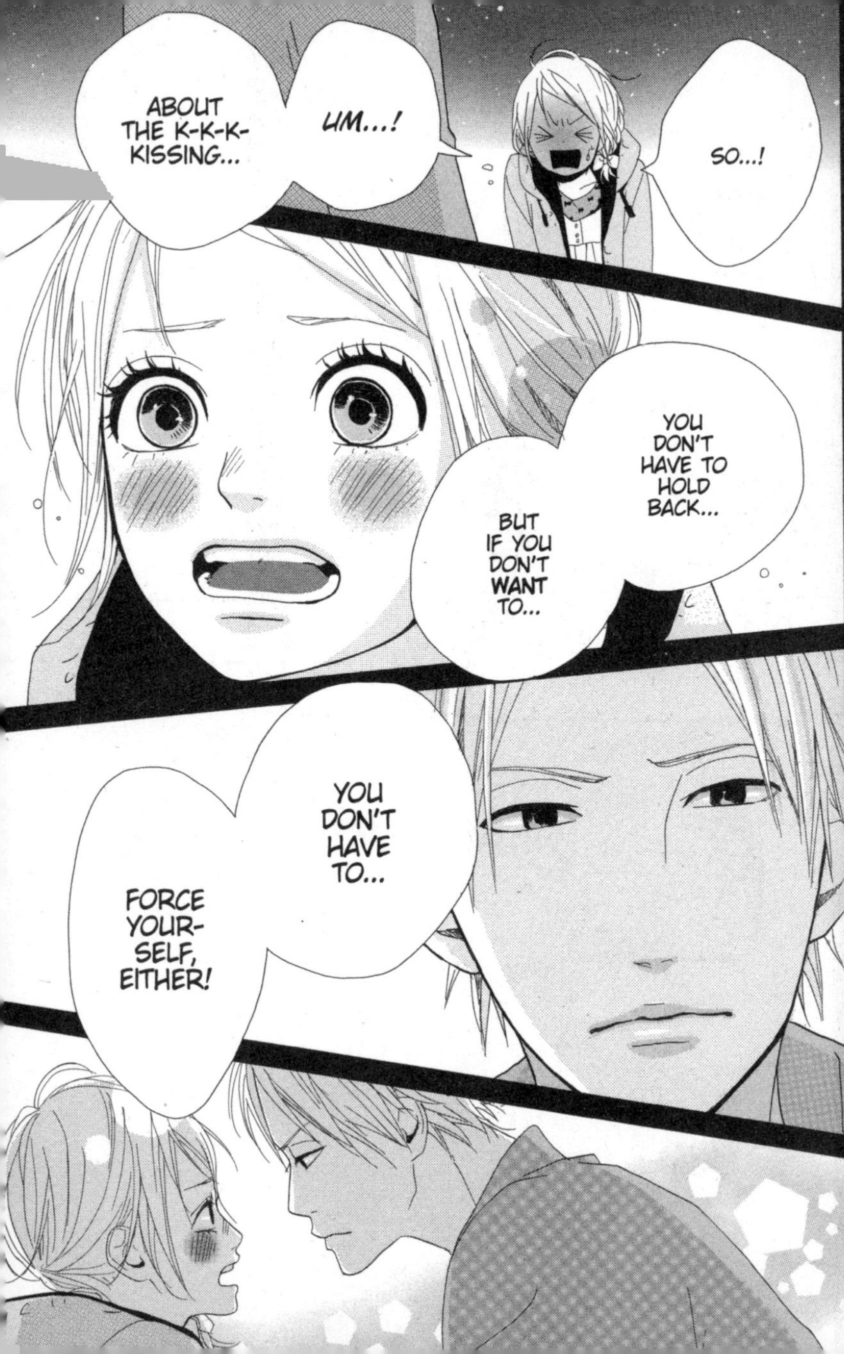
SO...!
UM...!
ABOUT THE K-K-K-KISSING...
YOU DON'T HAVE TO HOLD BACK...
BUT IF YOU DON'T WANT TO...
YOU DON'T HAVE TO...
FORCE YOUR-SELF, EITHER!

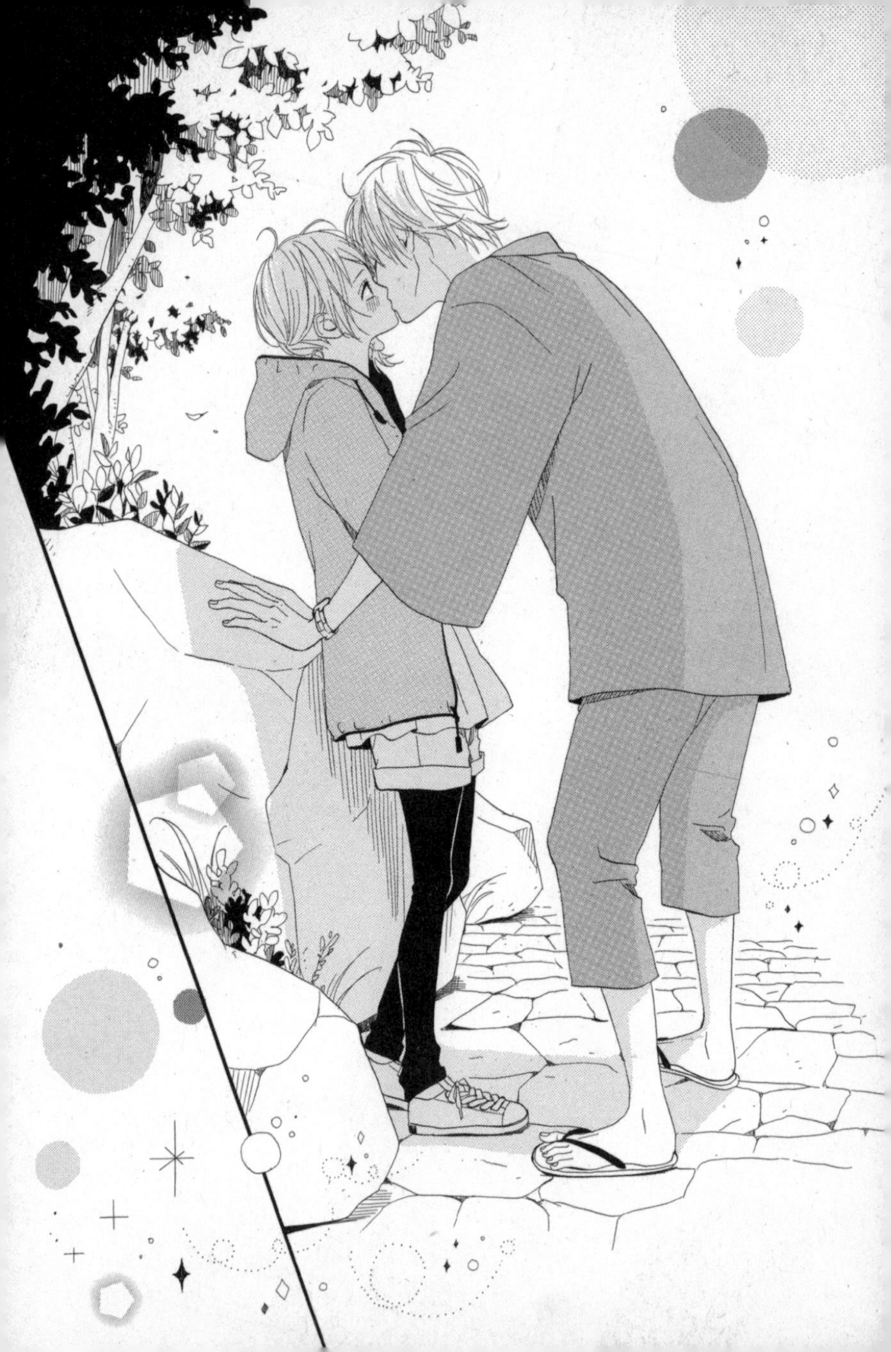

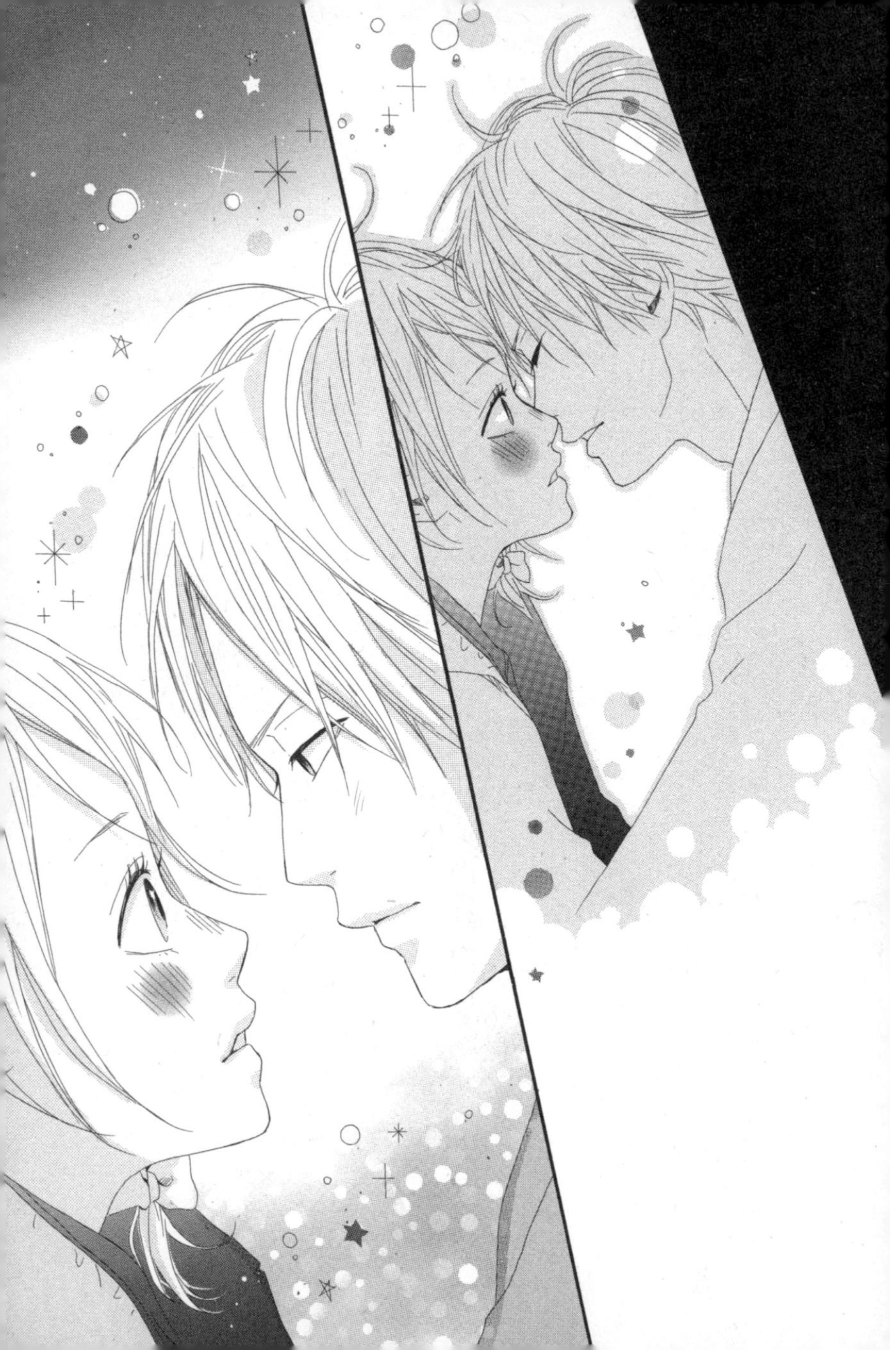

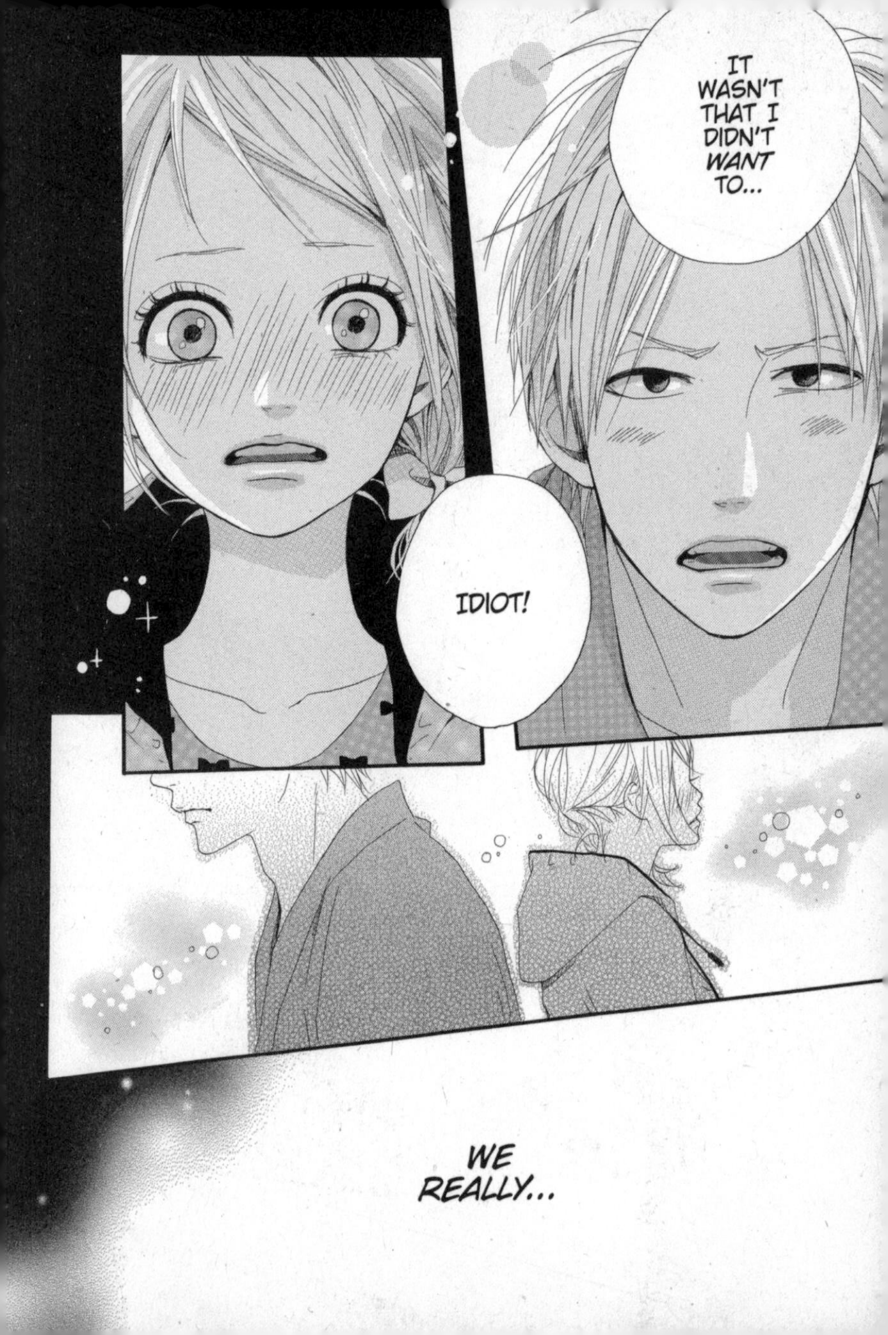
IT WASN'T THAT I DIDN'T WANT TO...
IDIOT!
WE REALLY...

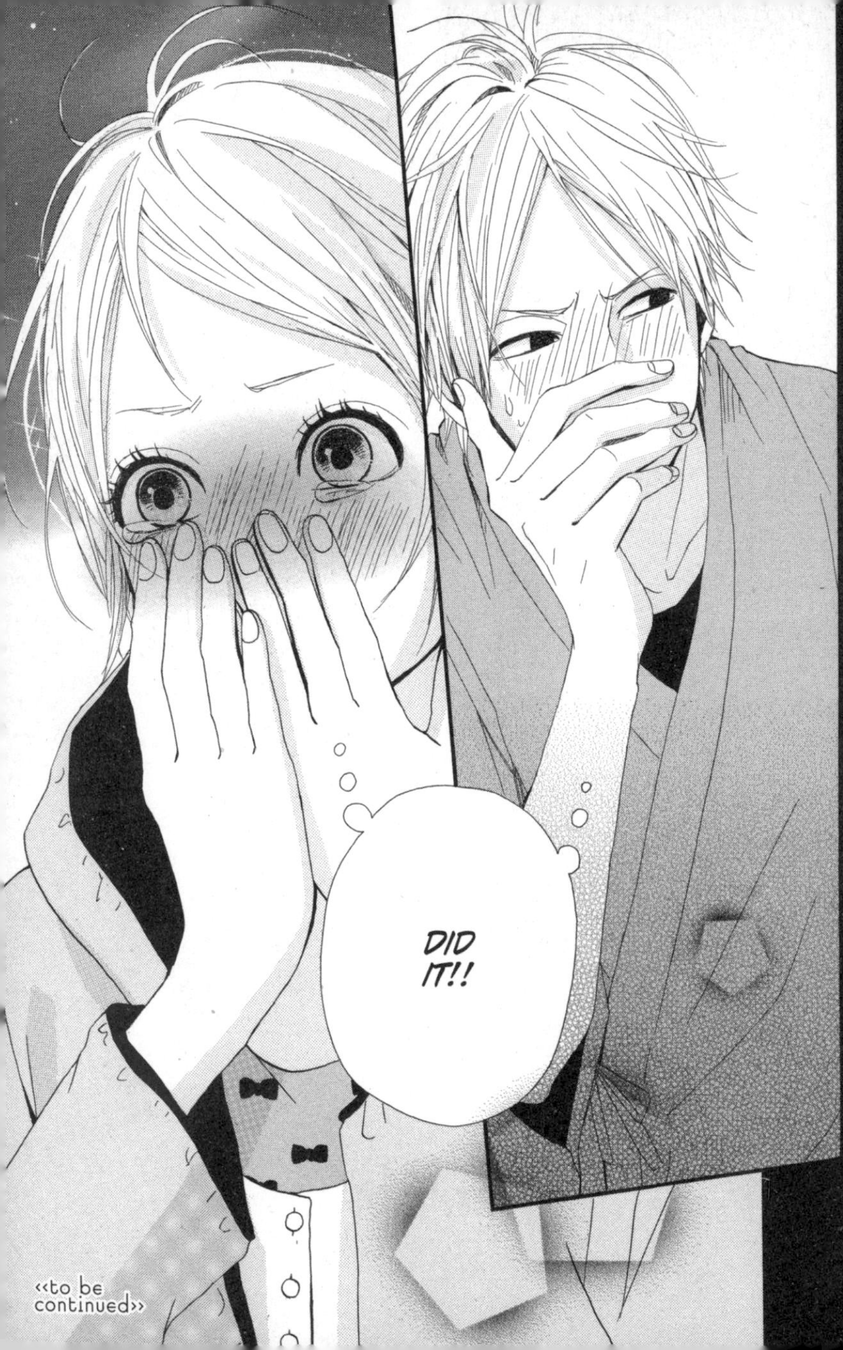
DID IT!!
‹‹to be continued››

THE FIND POKO GAME

Poko is hidden
throughout the manga!
Find him!

This time,
there are POKOS.

BONUS MANGA (The Day After the Landlord's Birthday)

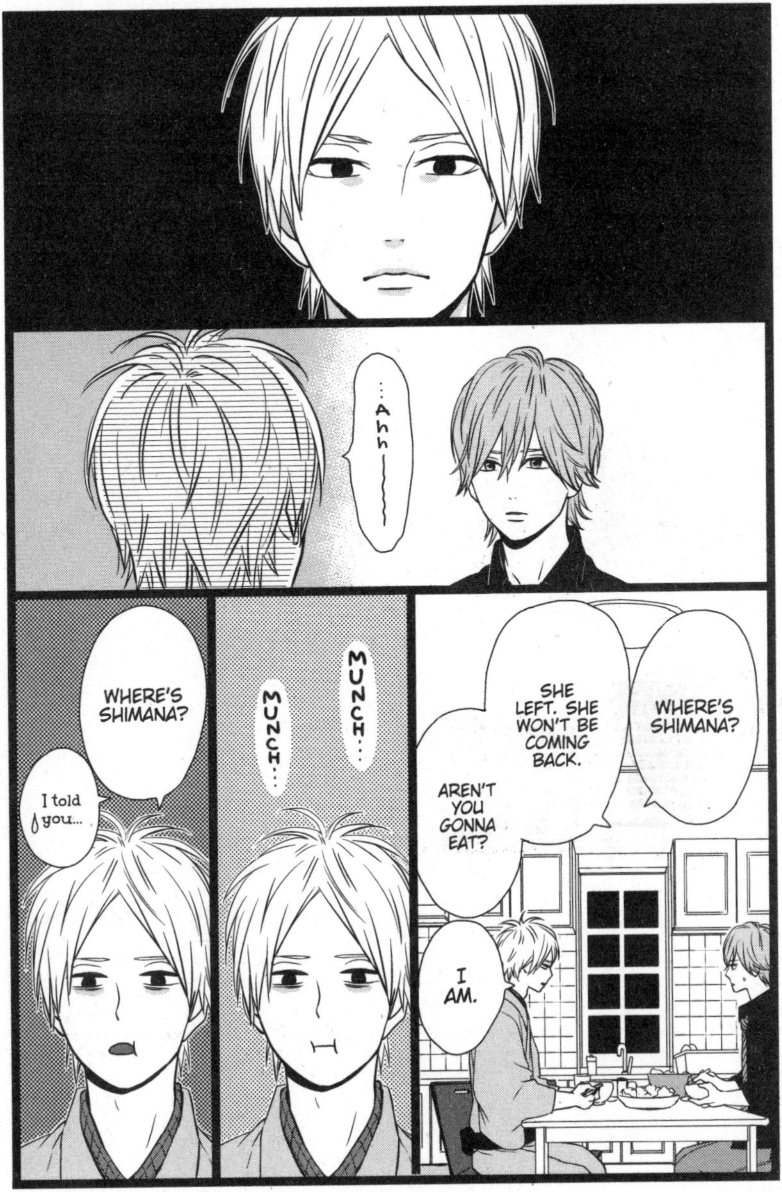
...Ahh~~~
WHERE'S SHIMANA?
SHE LEFT. SHE WON'T BE COMING BACK.
AREN'T YOU GONNA EAT?
I AM.
MUNCH...
MUNCH...
WHERE'S SHIMANA?
I told you...

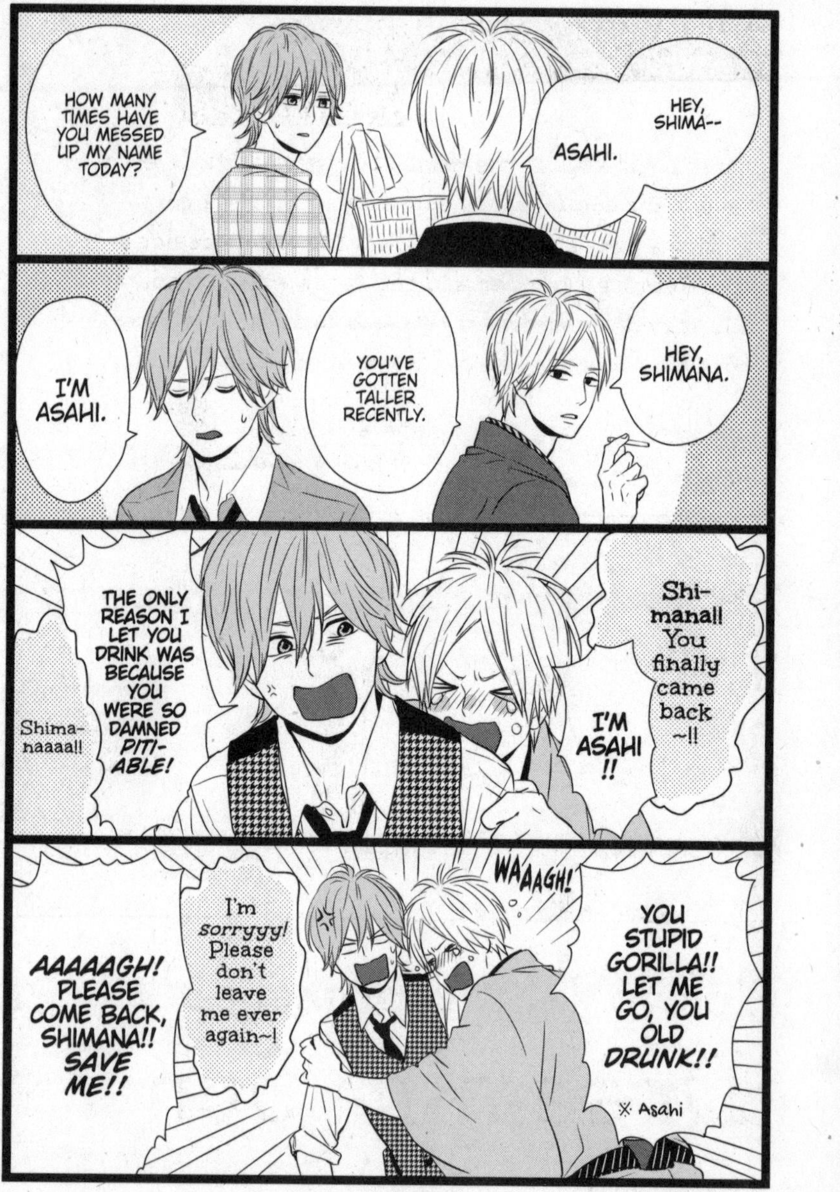
HEY, SHIMA--
ASAHI.
HOW MANY TIMES HAVE YOU MESSED UP MY NAME TODAY?
HEY, SHIMANA.
YOU'VE GOTTEN TALLER RECENTLY.
I'M ASAHI.
Shi-mana!! You finally came back~!!
I'M ASAHI!!
THE ONLY REASON I LET YOU DRINK WAS BECAUSE YOU WERE SO DAMNED PITI-ABLE!
Shima-naaaa!!
WAAAGH!
YOU STUPID GORILLA!! LET ME GO, YOU OLD DRUNK!!
※ Asahi
I'm sorryyy! Please don't leave me ever again~!
AAAAAGH! PLEASE COME BACK, SHIMANA!! SAVE ME!!

THE END

Next Volume Preview

"Is just wanting to be with you not enough?"

After their kiss at the campsite, Shimana falls even harder for the landlord and returns to the house. With the gang all back together, the group decides to celebrate both Zen and the landlord's birthdays. But when Miura brings a surprise guest to the party, Shimana's love for the landlord is put to the test...

Includes *Dreamin' Sun* chapters 29~32, plus side story ~monologue~ and a bonus manga!

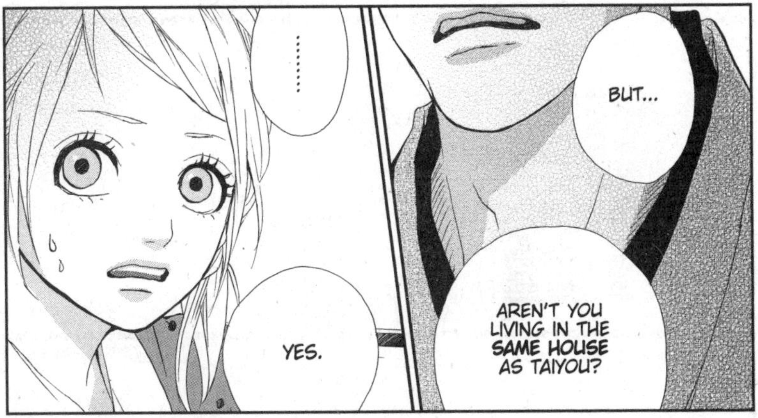
BUT...
AREN'T YOU LIVING IN THE SAME HOUSE AS TAIYOU?
......
YES.

Ichigo Takano presents

Dreamin' Sun 7

Coming Soon!

SEVEN SEAS ENTERTAINMENT PRESENTS

Dreamin' Sun

story and art by **ICHIGO TAKANO** **VOLUME 6**

TRANSLATION
Amber Tamosaitis

ADAPTATION
Shannon Fay

LETTERING AND RETOUCH
Lys Blakeslee

COVER DESIGN
Nicky Lim

PROOFREADER
Danielle King
Holly Kolodziejczak

EDITOR
Jenn Grunigen

PRODUCTION ASSISTANT
CK Russell

PRODUCTION MANAGER
Lissa Pattillo

EDITOR-IN-CHIEF
Adam Arnold

PUBLISHER
Jason DeAngelis

DREAMIN' SUN VOLUME 6

First published in Japan in 2015 by Futabasha Publishers Ltd., Tokyo.
English version published by Seven Seas Entertainment, LLC.
under license from Futabasha Publishers Ltd.

ISBN: 978-1-626927-20-9

Printed in Canada

First Printing: April 2018

10 9 8 7 6 5 4 3 2 1

FOLLOW US ONLINE: ***www.sevenseasentertainment.com***

READING DIRECTIONS

This book reads from ***right to left***, Japanese style. If this is your first time reading manga, you start reading from the top right panel on each page and take it from there. If you get lost, just follow the numbered diagram here. It may seem backwards at first, but you'll get the hang of it! Have fun!!

1
2
3
4
5
6
7
8
9

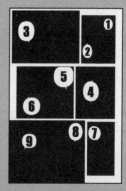

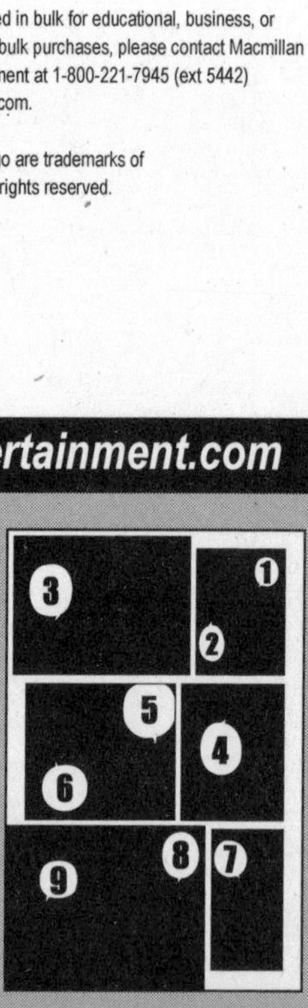